W9-BXD-827

NATIONAL
LEADERS OF
AMERICAN
CONSERVATION

NATIONAL LEADERS OF AMERICAN CONSERVATION

Edited by
RICHARD H. STROUD

Sponsored by
THE NATURAL RESOURCES COUNCIL
OF AMERICA

SMITHSONIAN INSTITUTION PRESS
WASHINGTON D.C. 1985

Library of Congress Cataloging in Publication Data
Main entry under title.
National leaders of American conservation.
  Bibliography: p.
  Includes index.
  1. Conservationists—United States—Biography. I. Stroud, Richard H. II. Natural Resources Council of America.
S926.A2N37 1985   333.7'1'0922   84–600245
ISBN 0–87474–867–4 (pbk)

The paper in this book meets the guidelines for permanence and durability of the Committee on Production Guidelines for Book Longevity of the Council on Library Resources.

Designer, Polly Sexton
Editor, SI Press, Jane McAllister

Cover: Thomas Cole (1801 England–1848 USA), *Falls at Catskill*, ca. 1828–29, lithograph. National Museum of American Art, Smithsonian Institution, Washington, D.C.

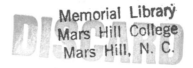

CONTENTS

7 Foreword
   Laurence R. Jahn

9 Preface
   Richard H. Stroud

11 Preface to First Edition
   Henry Clepper

13 Guidelines for Nomination of Individuals

15 Introduction

21 Biographical Sketches (arranged alphabetically)

422 APPENDIX.
   Member Organizations of the Natural Resources Council
   of America

424 Index of Individual Contributors to Second Edition

427 Index of Biographees

FOREWORD

T HE NATURAL RESOURCES COUNCIL OF AMERICA (NRCA) IS A PRI-
vate, nonprofit group of fifty-two national and regional conser-
vation/environmental organizations. Its primary purpose is to
serve as a forum for generating and exchanging information, as well as
for exploring different viewpoints on important current resource topics
and issues. NRCA is unique because it is the only organizational membership group that serves as a broad umbrella to bring together the many
conservation/environmental organizations.

Through an annual program of briefings on timely topics, members
are kept abreast of changes in resource programs. Among featured exchanges are briefings on proposed budgets for federal agencies having
responsibilities for maintaining and managing natural resources on a sustained basis in the best interests of citizens.

This book is a product of effective teamwork among NRCA member
organizations. It identifies national conservation leaders in the United
States. Most are active in NRCA; others are contributing in their own
ways to help advance sound management of the nation's resources.

With more than 230 million people in the United States in 1984,
and all of their activities having impact on the resource base, it is imperative that NRCA and other groups move forward to create awareness
and understanding of resource-management needs, programs, and sound
practices. With understanding and citizen support, appropriate factually
based management programs can be designed, continued, and carried
out successfully.

What is actually accomplished in the wise use of resources in future
years will depend to a considerable extent on the currently active individuals whose names are included in this volume. NRCA invites you to get
to know the conservation leaders and help provide firm support for meeting the numerous pending challenges to resource management.

LAURENCE R. JAHN, *Chairman*
Natural Resources Council of America

PREFACE

REPARATION OF THIS SECOND EDITION OF *National Leaders of American Conservation* followed closely the principles and criteria set forth by then-editor Henry Clepper in his introduction to the first edition, included verbatim in this edition, published in 1971. The decision by the Natural Resources Council of America (NRCA) to prepare an updated and extended second edition of that work reflected an awareness that the expiration of the 1970s had begun to render the first edition obsolete.

By 1980 it was evident to the executive committee of the NRCA that many of the biographees in the original volume were passing from their former leadership roles on the active conservation scene, either through retirement or death. It was equally evident that many new leaders were beginning to emerge onto the scene, either as successors to former leaders or as occupants of new roles in an expanding horizon of conservation/environmental interests. In consequence, the NRCA—now expanded correspondingly to include fifty-two member organizations—decided to prepare this second edition. In so doing, it reaffirmed the criteria for making nominations that were applied to the first edition and which appear on page 13. A key criterion used in screening nominated candidates is that each individual must have achieved recognition or been active at the national level in the United States. Outstanding achievements largely or only at the local or regional levels, while of tremendous importance, would not qualify an individual for inclusion in this volume. Only national leaders are included.

Serving as my colleagues on the editorial committee were Laurence R. Jahn (chairman), vice-president of the Wildlife Management Institute; Louis S. Clapper, executive secretary of the NRCA; Henry Clepper, retired editorial consultant to the NRCA; Paul C. Pritchard, president of the National Parks and Conservation Association; and James R. Lyons, director for resource policy of the Society of American Foresters. Richard E. McCabe, director of publications of the Wildlife Management Institute, coordinated production of the book with the Smithsonian Institu-

9

tion Press. Many otherwise difficult problems were speedily resolved through the competent and dedicated assistance of Margaret Pyles, who performed far beyond the requirements of her part-time secretarial duties as part of NRCA's staff.

Readers who are familiar with the first edition and who may become inspired to peruse the present volume will discover that the "face" of conservation is undergoing significant change. It will be evident that an older generation of leaders—in majority, pragmatic resource specialists—is in the process of transferring the reins of the conservation team to a younger generation of leaders—some of whom are idealistic generalists. Not only is the "old guard" phasing out, the character of the leadership is becoming more cosmopolitan.

The front lines of conservation have been manned in the recent past by a preponderance of resource professionals whose leadership was fortified by considerable experience in applied ecology, which, through hands-on resource management in state and federal agencies, included broad administrative responsibilities. Increasingly, the conservation ramparts are being reinforced by replacements who had first become affiliated with the early leadership in various support capacities. A good number have come from the academic, legal, and social science fields. Some came as opportunists or as social activists; most came as amateur ecologists driven by compulsions arising out of reactions to insensitive, inappropriately designed, and abusive land and water resource developments.

Many new leaders are taking up the cudgels, often with significant first successes to their credit, and are moving into leadership positions with comparatively little practical experience in resource management. The result has been a broad infusion of theory into practicability, of idealism into dedication, of generalism into specialism. It seems evident that a potentially beneficial, stronger conservation force is being forged slowly with the passage of time, and that an abrasive melding of the various qualities is shaping a dynamic new leadership ethic. Both generalist and specialist are becoming increasingly interdependent, reflecting the great complexity of conservation problems in an increasingly interactive world ecosystem. To the extent that they learn to appreciate each other and to work in close harmony, their influence for public good will grow accordingly.

RICHARD H. STROUD
Editor, Second Edition

Preface to First Edition

THE MEN AND WOMEN WHOSE BIOGRAPHIES ARE PRESENTED IN *Leaders of American Conservation* were nominated by one or more member organizations of the Natural Resources Council of America. Criteria for making the nominations appear on page 13. Formed in 1947, the Council is a nonprofit, nonpolitical body of forty constituent associations and societies. Its objective is to advance the attainment of sound management of natural resources in the public interest. Its role is that of a service agency to its member organizations.

For the purpose of this book, the term "American conservation" is equated with conservation activities carried on principally inside the United States. Hence, most of the biographees are citizens or residents of the United States. But foreign nationals have been included, provided their careers or contributions have been intimately associated with education, management, or research in natural resources in the United States.

To be sure, the editors realize that many eminent conservationists in other nations have been students in United States institutions or have had keen scientific and professional interest in the development of natural resources in the United States. But to have included all such individuals would have inordinately lengthened the book. Thus, the editors perforce had to limit its geographic scope to conform to the practical exigencies of the project—in short, to what they were able to accomplish.

In the expanding annals of America, the lives and careers of most conservationists included are unlikely to be accorded permanent recognition by history. Yet what they did for their nation is too valuable to be forgotten. That is why this book was written. No comparable compilation has been made. Its reception will prove whether it was jusitified. Its aim is to provide a succinct and factual account of the career of each leader. The biographies are short to keep the volume a reasonable length. The length of a subject's sketch is not to be taken as a measure of his importance. In the case of some biographies, more extensive than others, it may simply mean that these persons either had longer or more varied careers, or that more information was available about them.

If *Leaders of American Conservation* is found useful as a reference work for workers and students concerned with this rapidly growing field, a more comprehensive, worldwide biographical directory would be in order. Its compilation might be undertaken by a qualified international organization; for example, the International Union for the Conservation of Nature and Natural Resources. For obvious reasons, the Natural Resources Council of America is ill-equipped to assay such a global project.

The contributors and editors undertook this book in the hope that it would be useful to the student, the research worker, the writer about resources, and the practicing conservationist. In no case is a biography intended to tell all that is known or may be found out about the subject. At the end of most sketches is at least one reference where additional or corroborative information may be obtained.

Serving with me on the Editorial Committee were my friends and conservation colleagues, James B. Craig, editor of *American Forests* magazine, and Daniel A. Poole, president of the Wildlife Management Institute. I thank them for their generous cooperation and encouragement. As a Committee, we are grateful to the contributors of the sketches whose efforts made the work possible.

Some readers may fail to find biographical sketches of certain individuals who they think should have been included. Such omissions are unintentional oversights, inevitable in a seminal undertaking of this kind. Nor can we hope to have avoided, in the first edition of this book, some errors. Every effort was made to keep them out; we hope to have kept them to a minimum. We urge reviewers and readers to call errors to the attention of the Editorial Committee. I make this appeal with the same sincerity as did Izaak Walton when he asked the reader's forbearance in his introduction to *The Compleat Angler*:

> I might say more, but it is not fit for this place; but if this Discourse which follows shall come to a second impression, which is possible, for slight books have been in this Age observed to have that fortune; I shall then for thy sake be glad to correct what is defective; but for this time I have neither a willingness nor leisure to say more, than to wish thee a *rainy evening* to read this book in, and *that the east wind may never blow when thou goest a fishing*. Farewell.

HENRY CLEPPER
Chairman of the Editorial Committee

GUIDELINES FOR NOMINATION OF INDIVIDUALS

(From 1971 Edition)

THE SUBJECTS OF THESE BIOGRAPHIES WERE CHOSEN BY THE MEMber organizations of the Natural Resources Council of America. Criteria for making the nominations were set forth by the council's editorial committee as follows:

Each biographee should be, or should have been, a person whose personal activities and career contributed in a distinctive way to the preservation or wise use of one or more resources. All varieties of service (administration, research, education, writing, and editing) may be considered, provided the contribution is of national or at least regional significance; and provided also that the individual making the contribution is recognized, by those competent to judge, as having rendered outstanding leadership or guidance in the advancement of resource knowledge and its application.

A basic requirement is that the contribution shall have been meritorious; that is, above and beyond the rendering of long and faithful service, or appointment to a high position in state or federal government, or election to a political office. An essential qualification for inclusion is the individual's performance of those acts that accomplished socially desirable results.

Under these criteria may be nominated many worthy individuals who once had decisive or influential roles in resource conservation but whose participation is now almost forgotten. Special effort should be made to identify such individuals, for this book is to be a history of dedicated involvement in American conservation.

Further considerations are:

A person's interest in conservation, however sincere or dedicated, is not alone a qualification.

The part-time enthusiast, the weekend or summer-vacation conservationist, is not the person who should be included among "leaders."

The political figure, however friendly he may be to conservationists and however favorable his voting record on conservation issues, should be passed over. As a rule, the only politicians nominated should be those whose political careers are noteworthy for important legislation. Remember, this book seeks to memorialize the authentic conservationist, not the professional politician. Thus, the conservationist who inspired great legislation or the person who drafted it, not necessarily the politician who introduced it, should be singled out.

A nomination should not be made because of the nominee's popularity. Nor should a nomination be used to accord honor to an otherwise obscure individual.

INTRODUCTION

THIS BOOK IS A BIOGRAPHICAL RECAPITULATION OF THE ONGOING conservation movement and the development of professional natural-resource management in the United States. It presents a chronicle and a cast that first emerged more than a century ago.

Not far beyond the edge of modern memory is an America with its resources in abundance, intact, and not in jeopardy. Only during the latter half of the 1900s did it become clear that the nation's pristine base was both finite and fragile. Even then, just a few persons fully recognized and openly espoused the imperative of judiciously husbanding the landscape and its wild living resources for the long-term benefit of America and its people. The insights of these scientifically minded individuals gained important focus, audience, and crusading impetus through the 1864 publication of *Man and Nature* by George Perkins Marsh. Marsh's monumental treatise explained how the removal of woods and other vegetative cover resulted in floods, soil erosion, and fluctuations in stream flow.

Action to halt the depletion of the fishery resource started in 1870 with the formation of the American Fisheries Society, an association of scientists and others interested in fish culture. It was the first native biological society organized to foster research and management of a natural resource. In 1871, creation of the United States Fish and Fisheries Commission was authorized by Congress with Spencer F. Baird of the Smithsonian Institution as commissioner. He was directed to investigate the conservation of food species of the nation's coasts and lakes.

One of the most conspicuous early examples of resource loss in the United States was the widespread devastation of forests by logging and fire. In 1873 the American Association for the Advancement of Science appointed a committee, with Franklin B. Hough as chairman, to alert Congress about worsening forest conditions. The result was the appointment in 1876 of Hough as an agent in the Division (now Department) of Agriculture to make an investigation of the forest situation. From this modest beginning grew the present Forest Service.

Meanwhile, in 1875, John Aston Warder of Ohio had called together a group of citizens to create an organization for forest conservation. They formed the American Forestry Association. Thus were set in motion two forces—one by action of government and the other by private citizens—that marked the beginning of the forest conservation movement in the United States.

Yet, the immediate influence of these developments on the officialdom of the government was negligible. Neither in the executive branch nor in the Congress was there much, if any, concern about the timber resource. It was the era of timber abundance; the prevailing belief was that the forests were inexhaustible. From 1877 to 1881 Carl Schurz, then secretary of the U.S. Department of the Interior, was almost the only high official in the federal government advocating legislation to stop forest destruction and to adopt a policy for forest renewal. He was little heeded.

Ravage of the forest resource—by settlers, land speculators, and the government itself—continued a few more decades. This period would be a notable scandal in American history had the course of despoliation not been gradually brought to a halt. Demands for a halt emanated not from legislators or the upper hierarchy of government, but from citizens—that is to say, from conservationists—organized for that purpose.

Soon after the national forest conservation movement was launched, action to aid wildlife resources was also started. In 1883 the American Ornithologists' Union, another citizens' organization, was formed and immediately began promoting the protection of game and nongame birds. A pioneer in this cause was George Bird Grinnell, who led the movement that resulted in the establishment in 1886 of the Division of Economic Ornithology and Mammalogy in the U.S. Department of Agriculture, the forerunner of the Bureau of Biological Survey and the current Fish and Wildlife Service of the U.S. Department of the Interior. The first director of the division was C. Hart Merriam, an ornithologist concerned about bird protection who was also active in the protection of all wildlife. In 1905 William Dutcher, for several years chairman of a national committee of state Audubon societies, incorporated the National Association of Audubon Societies, now the National Audubon Society, one of the nation's largest and most influential associations dedicated to conservation.

When another movement to preserve the country's scenic resources was started by a group of early conservationists, their motivation was wholly aesthetic rather than economic. John Muir, a legendary wilderness advocate, was the leading spokesman for safeguarding the natural environment, a cause that subsequently waxed into a program for national and state parks and for wilderness preservation. Although the Sierra Club, which he founded in 1892, was originally interested primarily in the protection of California's Sierra Nevada and its resources, the club's growth into a national organization dedicated to interpreting and defending all scenic resources followed logically from its beginnings.

The early conservation organizations were pitifully weak in membership and finances, but their determination was strong. Because of their vigilance and tenacity, they were able to influence events. Indeed, as a means to forward conservation reform, the citizen organization is possibly the strongest advocacy method ever devised. The indignation of such groups against the wasters and despoilers did not stop with vocal dissent, but became an aggressive movement that helped bring about the adoption of improvements in policies, by government agencies as well as by private corporations, for improved resource stewardship.

During the first decade of the present century, the movement for the conservation of renewable natural resources, and of the soil and water that support them, gathered momentum. The attention of the whole nation was drawn to the Governors' Conference on natural resources, held in the White House in May 1908 at the invitation of President Theodore Roosevelt. One result of the conference was the formation of the National Conservation Commission under the chairmanship of Gifford Pinchot. In addition, the first inventory of the nation's natural resources was presented in December of that year at the National Conservation Conference in Washington, D.C. The conservation crusade, so tentatively and obscurely begun in the 1870s, was now fairly launched.

From the start, the conservation movement attracted men and women who symbolized the social conscience of America. A few were national figures—Carl Schurz, Theodore Roosevelt, and Gifford Pinchot, for example. But the pioneer conservationists, by and large, were scarcely known to the general public. Even to our present generation they are almost wholly unknown. Yet they were the founders of a movement that has been one of the most glorious and most productive manifestations of our democratic republic.

The history of conservation is essentially the record of the struggles and successes of a few thousand men and women who, aware that certain conditions needed to be corrected or improved, devoted their time and talents to getting the job done. Only a small number were persons of prominence or influence. Many rose out of the relative obscurity of a business or a profession; few attained high office or public renown.

To be sure, Theodore Roosevelt is rightly esteemed as one of our pioneer statesmen in resource conservation. Gifford Pinchot is remembered as a national leader. When we think of soil conservation we immediately think of Hugh Bennett, another national figure, and Aldo Leopold's name brings to mind not only wildlife management but wilderness preservation as well. Likewise, John Muir has left his imprint on the annals of park and wilderness preservation.

Certain other figures of less historical prominence than those mentioned are still well remembered by today's generation of conservationists. From the recent past we recall Ovid Butler, influential editor of the magazine *American Forests*; Rachel Carson of *Silent Spring* fame; R. W. Eschmeyer, exponent of fisheries management; Edward H. Graham, soil conservationist and biologist; Henry S. Graves and William B. Greeley, spokesmen for forestry; Robert Marshall, wilderness enthusiast; Stephen T. Mather of the national parks; Olaus Murie, respected wildlife observer and writer; Fairfield Osborn, zoologist and foundation executive; Ernest F. Swift, expounder of resource philosophy; and Howard Zahniser, father of the wilderness system.

When we go back beyond a few decades, the imprint of those who helped start the conservation crusade and kept it a vital force in American affairs is much fainter. The debt we owe to the pioneers who founded and nurtured the movement is no less real because we have forgotten the precise character of their contributions. Of many names we may pick at random, contemporary conservationists may have difficulty identifying them by their professions, spheres of action, or specific services. For example, it is no longer easy to identify the roles of Edward A. Bowers, William H. Brewer, Austin Cary, Frederick V. Coville, Bernhard E. Fernow, Henry Gannett, W. J. McGee, T. Gilbert Pearson, John Wesley Powell, and Robert Sterling Yard. Yet these individuals made essential and enduring contributions to conservation.

In contrast to the homage rendered many early conservationists is the vilification they received when their efforts to safeguard a resource interfered with profit seekers. Few conservationists became authentic leaders without exposure to the contempt and derision of the exploiters of resources and their political allies. In our own time, the gentle and respected Rachel Carson was castigated and ridiculed by representatives of the chemical industry when she documented the losses of birds and other wildlife following the spraying of vegetation with certain persistent pesticides. She ventured to propose that greater care with the application of such chemicals be enforced, and that increased research be undertaken to seek alternate methods of control less dangerous to the natural environment.

Senator Boise Penrose of Pennsylvania, whose own career was not redolent of the rose, used to refer to Gifford Pinchot as "that damned tree doctor." Senator Henry M. Teller of Colorado, a former secretary of the Department of the Interior, declared in 1909, "I do not believe there is either a moral or any other claim upon me to postpone the use of what nature has given me, so that the next generation or generations may have an opportunity to get what I myself ought to get." These sorry examples could be continued; their purpose is to show that conservationists did not rise to positions of leadership without suffering the hostility of opponents and even defamation by them. It is not a pleasant matter, and we need not dwell on it.

Since the conservation movement began, the exploiters of resources have resented interference with their plans because such interference can be bad for business, which is doubtless true. Many continue to believe that exploitation without interference is still possible, which is certainly false. The history of this movement is replete with instances of exploiters whose main desire was to wrest riches from the resources; many had no more moral purpose than looters have. To be sure, it would be unfair to include all the commercial fishermen, lumbermen, livestock operators, mining interests, and water users in this category. But selfish waste and destruction of resources had to be stopped.

When reading about the lives of conservation leaders, one notes an attribute common to all. They have been and are today activated—one might say obsessed—by a notion of duty to society and the nation. Most have put their obligation to the cause above personal advantage. This is not to say that they have lacked ambition or have been indifferent to approbation. As in any group of spirited Americans, there have been conservationists with a thirst for glory, or at least for public recognition. The vast majority, however, have reached out not for applause or emolument but for opportunities to preserve and improve their native land.

The reader will observe that many of the conservationists listed in the pages that follow have been accorded honors of various sorts—honorary academic degrees, medals, and similar awards; election to office in scientific societies and citizens' associations; and having buildings, parks, and landmarks named for them. Considering their manifest services to their country, one realizes that these testimonies constitute modest recognition indeed.

No one who has studied the conservation movement in the United States can have failed to observe that certain individuals from time to time have dominated the action in its various sectors. It is revealing to note how often we find academicians among the activists, a fact that explains why some of the most profound influences on the course of conservation have flowed from the classroom, the laboratory, the museum, and the scientific society.

Of the thousands of men and women who contributed to the advancement of knowledge about resources and to their management in the public interest, a few hundred stand out. They stand out because of the particular nature of their contribution to a specific resource, or because of the significance of their influence on the attainment of a national goal or policy, or because their achievements and activities were or are noteworthy. These are the leaders of American conservation. This book has been compiled to grant them the recognition they deserve.

BIOGRAPHICAL SKETCHES

(ARRANGED ALPHABETICALLY)

ADAMS, ANSEL
(1902–1984)
Born February 20 in San Francisco, California. His formal education was erratic, primarily obtained through private instruction at home and through self-education in music and photography. Received honorary degrees from University of California, 1961; Occidental College, 1967; Yale University, 1973; University of Massachusetts, 1974; University of Arizona, 1975; Harvard University, 1981; and Mills College, 1982. Visiting Yosemite National Park every summer during his youth to photograph and explore, developed into ardent conservationist of Sierra Club, serving four years as custodian of Le Conte Memorial, the Sierra Club headquarters in Yosemite, and from 1934 as board member and club representative. His first portfolio of original photographs, *Parmelian Prints of the High Sierra*, issued in 1927, launched his career as foremost American photographer. In 1936 represented Sierra Club in Washington, D.C., and New York City. In 1938 published *Sierra Nevada: The John Muir Trail*, acclaimed for its pictorial beauty and effectiveness in Kings Canyon campaign. In 1941 was appointed photomuralist to U.S. Department of the Interior, and in 1946 founded first department of photography at California School of Fine Arts; also that year, received Guggenheim Fellowship, renewed in 1948 and 1959, enabling him to photograph national parks and monuments during their peaks of seasonal beauty. In 1955, in conjunction with Nancy Newhall, produced the famous exhibition and book of same name, *This Is the American Earth*, for Sierra Club. During 1956–57 was president of Trustees for Conservation, and in 1963 received Sierra Club's John Muir Award for his services to conservation. In 1966 was elected a fellow of American Academy of Arts and Sciences. In 1968 received Conservation Service Award from U.S. Department of the Interior. In 1969 was awarded the Progress Medal by Photographic Society of America, and in 1980 was awarded the Presidential Medal of Freedom in ceremonies at The White House. Received 1983 Special Achievement Award from National Wildlife Federation. Was cofounder of The Friends of Photography in 1967 and served until his death as chairman of its board of trustees. Was author and photographer-illustrator of numerous articles, books, portfolios, and technical manuals. The latter include his famous three-volume photography series, first published as five volumes in 1948, now completely revised: *The Camera*, 1980; *The Negative*, 1982; and *The Print*, 1983. His pictorial books include *Illustrated Guide to Yosemite Valley* (rev. 1963); *My Camera in Yosemite Valley*, 1949; *My Camera in the National*

Parks, 1950; *These We Inherit: The Parklands of America,* 1962; *Singular Images,* 1974; *The Portfolios of Ansel Adams,* 1977; *Yosemite and the Range of Light,* 1979; and *Examples: The Making of Forty Photographs,* 1983. Died April 22, 1984.

HOLT BODINSON
RICHARD H. STROUD

Ansel Adams, Interpreter of Nature: The Picture History of Photography. New York: Abrams, 1958.

Newhall, Beaumont, and Newhall, Nancy. *Masters of Photography.* New York: George Braziller, 1958.

Newhall, Nancy. *The Eloquent Light.* Sierra Club, 1963.

Who's Who in America, 42d ed., 1982–83.

ADAMS, CHARLES CHRISTOPHER

(1873–1955)

Born July 23 in Clinton, Illinois. Illinois Wesleyan University, B.S. (biology) 1895, Sc.D. (honorary) 1920; Harvard University, M.S. 1889; University of Chicago, Ph.D. (zoology) 1908. Was strong leader in ecology, especially during early years of development of this field in North America, emphasizing relation of human ecology to land use and urging broad ecological approach to problems of interrelationships of human ecology and public policies. Was assistant biologist at Illinois Wesleyan University, 1895–96; assistant entomologist, Illinois State Laboratory of Natural History, 1896–98; curator, University Museum, Michigan, 1903–6; director, Cincinnati Society of Natural History, 1906–7; and associate professor of animal ecology at University of Illinois State Laboratory of Natural History, 1908–14. Became assistant professor of forest zoology, New York State College of Forestry, Syracuse, in 1914, and was professor there during 1916–26. At same time, served as director of Roosevelt Wildlife Forest Experiment Station. In 1926 moved to New York State Museum, Albany, from which he retired as director in 1943. Was president of Association of Geographers in 1927. His bibliography includes more than 150 titles, mainly journal papers. His book *Guide to the Study of Animal Ecology* (1913) ranks among the important pioneer ecological treatises written in North America. Died May 22, 1955.

GEORGE SPRUGEL, JR.

American Men of Science (Biological Sciences), 9th ed., 1955.
Bulletin of the Ecological Society of America, vol. 37, no. 4, 1956.

ADAMS, JOHN HAMILTON
(born 1936)

Born February 15 in New York City. Michigan State University, B.A. 1959; Duke University Law School, Ll.B. 1962. Practiced law on Wall Street and in 1965 was appointed to United States Attorney's office in Southern District of New York. While at U.S. Attorney's office, became involved in a number of environmental issues, and in 1969 left U.S. Attorney's office to become founding staff member of Natural Resources Defense Council, Inc. Has served as executive director of the council from 1969 to present; during this period it has become the largest environmental public-interest law firm, with professional staff of more than forty lawyers and scientists. Also currently serves as president of Open Space Institute and is member of Catskill Center for Conservation and Development, League of Conservation Voters, and several other professional associations and commissions.

CHARLES H. CALLISON

ADAMS, SHERMAN
(born 1899)

Born January 8 in East Dover, Vermont. Dartmouth College, B.A. 1920, M.A. 1940, LL.D. 1953. Also awarded D.C.L. New England College, 1951; LL.D. University of New Hampshire, 1950; Bates College, 1954; Bryant College, St. Lawrence University, 1954; Center College, Kentucky, 1955; and University of Maine, Middlebury College, 1957. Began his career in forestry as treasurer, Black River Lumber Company, Vermont, 1921–22; and as manager, timberland and lumber operations, Parker-Young Company, Lincoln, New Hampshire, 1928–45. After disastrous New England hurricane of 1938, served on State Timber Salvage Committee. Was member of New Hampshire House of Representatives, 1941–44, serving as chairman of Committee on Labor, 1941–42, and as Speaker of the House, 1943–44. Helped frame and enact New Hampshire timber tax law, aided in formation of Northeast Forest Fire Compact, and improved forest policy in New Hampshire. Also helped improve working conditions of woodsmen. After election to Seventy-Ninth Congress in 1945, was author of law to create state forestry advisory boards. Was governor of New Hampshire, 1949–53, and chairman, New England Governors' Conference, 1951–52. As assistant to president of the United States, 1953–58, furthered cause of forest conservation at every opportunity, specifically at Fourth American Forest

Congress, 1953; at Southern Forest Fire Prevention Conference, 1956; and at annual forest fire prevention campaigns. Is life director of New England Lumber Manufacturers Association and president of Loon Mountain Recreation Corporation. Although not a professional forester, the esteem in which he is held by foresters is attested by his election to Society of American Foresters. Was formerly director of The American Forestry Association. Is author of *First-Hand Report* and articles for *Life* and other magazines.

KENNETH B. POMEROY

Who's Who in America, 42d ed., 1982–83.

AHERN, GEORGE PATRICK

(1859–1942)

Born December 29 in New York City. Graduated from United States Military Academy, 1882; law degree from Yale University, 1895. Served with U.S. Infantry in Dakota Territory, Minnesota, and Montana, 1882–98. Became interested in forestry about 1885. In 1894 advised Edward Bowers of General Land Office regarding creation of forest reserves in Montana; in 1896 guided Gifford Pinchot and Henry S. Graves through Montana and Idaho in search of potential forest reserves; in 1897 introduced and taught forestry courses at Montana Agricultural College, and obtained reservation of Gallatin Forest Reserve as demonstration forest. Served in Cuba and the Philippines in Spanish-American War. In the Philippines, organized Philippine Bureau of Forestry in 1900 and headed it until 1914. Succeeded in establishing Philippine School of Forestry. In 1914 was instrumental in assisting Ngan Han to set up Chinese Forest Service, and assisted in establishing school of forestry at Nanking University. During 1920s was active in the work of Tropical Plant Research Foundation. Was elected a fellow of Society of American Foresters in 1929. Wrote many articles, particularly on tropical forestry. Was active in controversy over public regulation of private cutting, and published two major books, *Deforested America* and *Forest Bankruptcy in America*, in support of such regulation. Was major figure in development of forestry both at home and abroad. Died May 13, 1942.

LAWRENCE RAKESTRAW

American Forests, February 1935.

Assembly, United States Military Academy, January 1943.

"Forestry Missionary," *Montana: The Magazine of Western History*, October 1959.

"George Patrick Ahern and the Philippine Bureau of Forestry, 1900–1914," *Pacific Northwest Quarterly*, July 1967.

Journal of Forestry. Obituary, July 1942.

AHLGREN, CLIFFORD ELMER
(born 1922)

Born April 22 in Toimi, Minnesota. Served in U.S. Coast Guard, 1941–44. University of Minnesota College of Forestry, B.S. (forest management) 1948; M.S. (forest ecology) 1953; Cornell College, Iowa, D.Sc. 1976. In 1948 was appointed director of research at Wilderness Research Foundation's Quetico-Superior Wilderness Research Center, and in 1969 became research associate at University of Minnesota College of Forestry. As exponents of wilderness research and management, he and his wife, Dr. Isabel Ahlgren, a botanist and ecologist, have greatly influenced wilderness conservation, both in Superior region of United States and in Quetico region of Canada. Through their lectures and writings, both in popular magazines and scientific journals, they are recognized resident experts in Boundary Waters Canoe Area and adjacent country. Their long-term investigations have been in three major fields: vegetational succession following disturbance of wilderness habitat; grafting and breeding of northern coniferous species; and ecological effects of fire on such species. He is active in The American Forestry Association, Society of American Foresters, Ecological Society of America, and American Phytopathological Society. Has presented invited papers in Spain, England, Norway, Canada.

HENRY CLEPPER

American Men and Women of Science (Physical and Biological Sciences), 15th ed., 1982.

ALBRIGHT, HORACE MARDEN
(born 1890)

Born January 6 in Bishop, California. University of California, B.L. 1912; Georgetown University Law School, LL.B. 1914; University of Montana, LL.D. 1956; University of California, LL.D. 1961; University of New Mexico, LL.D. 1962. In 1913 entered public service as confidential clerk to secretary of the Interior and advanced to assistant attorney, assigned to national park affairs, in 1916. From 1916 to 1933 remained in newly formed U.S. National Park Service, making significant contributions to early policy formulation, planning, development, and management of emerging national park system. In 1917 became assistant director of National Park Service, and in 1919 moved to the field as superintendent of Yellowstone National Park, his position for next ten years. While superintendent of Yellowstone, also served as field assistant to the director, 1920–26, and as assistant director (field), 1926–29. In 1929 became director of National Park Service and served in that capacity until 1933, when he retired from federal service to enter private business. The awards and recognition he has received for his contributions to conservation and park management are numerous and unique. In 1963 National Park Service established Horace M. Albright Training Center at Grand Canyon National Park. In 1961, University of California initiated Horace M. Albright Conservation Lecture Series, an annual lecture given by a leading conservation specialist; and in his honor, American Scenic and Historic Preservation Society established Horace M. Albright Scenic Preservation Award. His other awards include Distinguished Service Award of The American Forestry Association; Frances K. Hutchinson Medal of The Garden Club of America; Gold Medal of the Camp Fire Club of America; Theodore Roosevelt Medal for the Conservation of Natural Resources from Theodore Roosevelt Association; Pugsley Gold Medal of the American Scenic and Historic Preservation Society; Audubon Medal; and Cosmos Club Award. In 1980 was awarded The Medal of Freedom by the president of the United States. Has served as honorary vice-president of The American Forestry Association and of Sierra Club, and is honorary member of American Society of Landscape Architects. Following retirement from government, has served as director and trustee on boards of numerous national conservation organizations and has held the following offices: president (1952) and chairman (1952–61) of Resources for the Future; vice-president of Boone and Crockett Club; and chairman of Southern California Chapter of The Nature Conservancy (1964–65). Is author of numerous articles on resources and management and is coauthor with F. J. Taylor of book *Oh, Ranger!*

HORACE M. ALBRIGHT
HOLT BODINSON

Who's Who in America, 41st ed., 1980–81.

ALLEN, ARTHUR AUGUSTUS
(1885–1964)
Born December 28 in Buffalo, New York. Cornell University, B.A. (zoology) 1907, M.A. 1908, Ph.D. 1911. Began teaching at Cornell in 1910, and in 1926 became first full professor of ornithology in United States. His entire academic career was spent at Cornell, where he founded first ornithological laboratory in the country to achieve formal status as university department (1954). Retired from active teaching in 1953. Instrumental in placing ornithology in colleges and universities, he also awakened wide public enthusiasm and interest in preserving vanishing species of birds through his lectures, teaching, and written works. Was pioneer in color photography of birds and in recording songs and calls of North American birds. Was chairman of Cornell's Commission on Wildlife Conservation, president of Eastern Bird Banding Association, a founder of American Society of Mammalogists and of The Wildlife Society, and trustee of American Wildlife Institute. Was awarded *Outdoor Life* gold medal in 1924, and Burr award from National Geographic Society in 1948. Is author of many articles and nine books, the most important being his two volumes of *American Bird Biographies*, 1934, *The Book of Bird Life*, 1930 and 1961, and *Stalking Birds with a Color Camera*, 1951. Acknowledged as one of leading ornithological scientists of his generation, he has left invaluable legacy in vast store of knowledge he passed on to his students, many currently holding important positions in conservation throughout country. Died January 17, 1964.

EVE HERBST

New York Times. Obituary, January 18, 1964.

Who Was Who in America, 1961–68.

ALLEN, DURWARD LEON
(born 1910)
Born October 11 in Uniondale, Indiana. University of Michigan, B.A. 1932; Michigan State University, Ph.D. (zoology) 1937. Joined Michigan Department of Conservation in 1937; was biologist in charge of Swan Creek Wildlife Experiment Station for two years; and was transferred in 1939 to Rose Lake Wildlife Experiment Station. During World War II served in Medical Corps of U.S. Army. In 1946 joined U.S. Fish and Wildlife Service in Maryland and began wildlife investigations on agricultural lands; was assistant chief of Branch of Wildlife Research in

Washington, D.C., office, 1951–54. Was appointed associate professor of wildlife management in Department of Forestry and Conservation at Purdue University in 1954; has been professor there since 1957. Was assistant secretary general for Inter-American Conference on Renewable Natural Resources in 1948. Was recipient of medal of honor of Anglers Club of New York in 1956. During 1956–57 was president of The Wildlife Society; in 1969 received the society's Aldo Leopold Award. Previously had received two awards from the society for outstanding publications: one for territorial wildlife in 1945, the other for conservation education in 1955. Received 1983 Science Award from National Wildlife Federation. Is a fellow of American Association for the Advancement of Science. Is author of *Michigan Fox Squirrel Management*, 1943; *Pheasants Afield*, 1953; *Our Wildlife Legacy*, 1954; *The Life of Prairies and Plains*, 1967; and *Wolves of Minong*, 1979; was also editor of *Pheasants in North America*, 1956.

HENRY CLEPPER

American Men of Science (Physical and Biological Sciences), 11th ed., 1965.
World Who's Who in Science, 1968.
Who's Who in America, 42d ed., 1982–83.

ALLEN, EDWARD TYSON
(1875–1942)
Born in New Haven, Connecticut. Was tutored by his father, a former professor at Yale University. As ranger, entered U.S. Division of Forestry in 1898 to become one of first forest rangers in Pacific Northwest. Was state forester of California, 1905–6. During 1908–10, was district inspector in U.S. Forest Service and first district forester of Pacific Northwest Region. Helped organize Western Forestry and Conservation Association and served as its forester and manager for more than thirty years. Also organized western timberland owners for forest protection and created machinery for cooperation between federal, state, and private agencies in the five western states and British Columbia. In his forty-four years of service to forest conservation, he was called upon for advice and counsel in numerous capacities by Federal Trade Commission, Council of National Defense, National Lumber Manufacturers Association, and The American Forestry Association. In each instance, his vast knowledge of the art of forestry, economics, and forest industries marked him with stature of a statesman. Leadership in promoting harmonious working

relations between lumbermen and professional foresters was his primary contribution to conservation. Was charter member (1900) of Society of American Foresters, and a fellow since 1939. Was author of a forward-looking book, *Practical Forestry in the Pacific Northwest*, 1911. Died May 27, 1942.

SOCIETY OF AMERICAN FORESTERS

Allen, Shirley W. "We Present E. T. Allen." *Journal of Forestry*, 43:222–23, 1945.

Journal of Forestry. Obituary, 40:574–75, 1942.

ALLEN, ROBERT PORTER
(1905–1963)
Born April 24 in South Williamsport, Pennsylvania. Lafayette College, 1923–25; Cornell University, 1925. Served National Audubon Society for thirty years, as research associate and sanctuary director and, from 1955 to 1960, as research director. His life was dedicated to protection of vanishing species of rare birds. Instrumental in preventing extinction of whooping crane by discovering nesting grounds of the remnant wild flock in 1955 near Great Slave Lake, almost at Arctic Circle, he was leader in having whooping crane habitats in Texas and Canada proclaimed as refuges. Helped establish a working protection plan for flamingos and recommended methods of saving small surviving colonies of roseate spoonbills, thus helping to perpetuate the species. His monographs on whooping crane, roseate spoonbill, and American flamingo are standard authoritative works on these species. His most noted book, *On the Trail of Vanishing Birds*, 1957, won him 1958 John Burroughs medal for outstanding nature book of the year. Was also awarded William Brewster memorial medal by American Ornithologists' Union in 1957 and Nash Conservation Award in 1955. His important popular literary works include *The Flame Birds*, 1947, *Our Vanishing Wildlife*, 1957, and *Birds of the Caribbean*, 1961. His projected sixteen-volume series, "Birds of North America," was interrupted by his death on June 18, 1963. He left a priceless legacy in his research, in interest generated by his writings, and, above all, in rare species he helped save from extermination.

EVE HERBST

Audubon. September-October 1963.

New York Times. Obituary, June 29, 1963.

Who Was Who in America, 1961–68.

ALLEN, SHIRLEY WALTER

(1883–1968)

Born October 14 in Sherman, New York. Iowa State College, B.S. (agriculture) 1909, M.F. 1929. Entered U.S. Forest Service in 1909 as forest assistant in California; advanced to deputy supervisor of Lassen National Forest in 1912. Was professor of forestry extension at New York State College of Forestry at Syracuse during 1914–18, then worked for year with Forest Products Laboratory in Madison, Wisconsin. Returning in 1919 to Forest Service in California, was promoted year later to supervisor of Angeles National Forest. During 1922–23 was in lumber business in southern California and was briefly with Chamber of Commerce in Los Angeles. In 1924 began four years as forester for The American Forestry Association in Washington, D.C. In 1928 joined the faculty of School of Forestry and Conservation at University of Michigan, where he remained for three decades, retiring as professor emeritus of forestry in 1958. Throughout his career, was active in The Society of American Foresters, as associate editor of *Journal of Forestry,* 1927–28; as member of its council, 1940–41; as vice-president, 1942–45; and as president, 1946–47; was elected a fellow in 1948. In addition, held numerous advisory and consulting assignments, such as his appointment to official U.S. delegation to Second World Forestry Congress in Budapest in 1936. During 1935–38 was consultant to National Park Service, and subsequently to National Research Council. Was member of secretariat of Inter-American Conference on Natural Resources in 1948, and of Michigan Conservation Commission (chairman the last year) during 1953–58. Was a fellow of American Association for the Advancement of Science. As author of many articles on forestry, parks, wilderness, and general conservation, he was widely known for his books *An Introduction to American Forestry,* first published in 1938 and periodically revised, and *Conserving Natural Resources* (3d edition, 1966). Died in September 1968.

HENRY CLEPPER

American Men of Science (Physical and Biological Sciences), 11th ed., 1965.

Journal of Forestry. Obituary, 66 (12):947, December 1968.

ALPERIN, IRWIN MARK
(born 1919)
Born October 31 in Brooklyn, New York. Cornell University, B.S. (vertebrate zoology) 1940; New York University, M.S. (fishery biology) 1953. Served as temporary museum expert (ichthyology), New York State Museum and Science Service, in 1952, and as assistant, Fish Genetics Laboratory, American Museum of Natural History, 1952–53. Then joined Bureau of Marine Fisheries, New York State Department of Conservation, and advanced from aquatic biologist (marine) to program director and fisheries research biologist, 1953–66. During this period, was employed for interim year as fisheries research biologist at newly established Sandy Hook (New Jersey) Marine Laboratory of U.S. Bureau of Sport Fisheries and Wildlife, 1960–61. Was assistant director and chief marine biologist, Massachusetts Division of Marine Fisheries, 1966–71; and executive director, Atlantic States Marine Fisheries Commission, 1971. During his tenure as executive director, opened Washington, D.C., headquarters of the fifteen-state commission. Also administers the commission's Interstate Fisheries Management Program, which is concerned with development and implementation of Atlantic Coast regional fisheries management plans for many important recreational and commercial species. Serves as statutory member of three Atlantic Coast fishery management councils established by Fishery Conservation and Management Act of 1976 (P.L. 94–265). Has authored numerous technical and scientific papers in fisheries, marine science, and ichthyology; is certified fisheries scientist of American Fisheries Society; is active member of several marine resources-oriented and conservation organizations; and serves on several governmental advisory bodies.
ROBERT F. HUTTON

ANDREWS, CHRISTOPHER COLUMBUS
(1829–1922)
Born October 27 in Hillsboro, New Hampshire. After graduating from Harvard Law School, was admitted to bar in 1850 and began legal practice in Massachusetts. Moved to Minnesota in 1857 and practiced law; was elected to Minnesota State Senate in 1859, and was founder and coeditor of *St. Cloud Union* in 1861. Rose to rank of brevet major general during Civil War, returned to Minnesota in 1865, and was minister to Norway and Sweden from 1869 to 1877. His ministerial reports included information on Swedish forest culture. Was census supervisor in

Minnesota in 1880, and consul-general to Brazil from 1882 to 1885. Was early advocate of applying European (especially Swedish) forestry principles to American forests. After tragic Hinckley, Minnesota, forest fire in 1894, he gave his support and influence in Minnesota legislature to establish office of chief fire warden in 1895. Was chief fire warden (later forestry commissioner) from 1895 to 1911. His plan for reforestation of Minnesota included concept of multiple use. Campaigned successfully to get Congress to establish Minnesota National Forest in 1908 (now Chippewa National Forest). Influenced General Land Office to withdraw from entry lands, which became nucleus of Superior National Forest in 1909. Is considered the father of Quetico-Superior Wilderness Area because as early as 1905 he advocated creation of international park on Ontario-Minnesota border. Was secretary of Minnesota State Forestry Board, 1911–22. His *Recollections* was published in 1928. Died September 21, 1922.

Elwood R. Maunder

Dictionary of American Biography, 1928.

Who Was Who in America, 1897–42.

Widner, Ralph R., ed. *Forests and Forestry in the American States*. The National Association of State Foresters, 1968. Chapters 6 and 32.

Andrews, Horace Justin
(1892–1951)

Born October 31 at Sidnaw, Michigan. Was forestry graduate of University of Michigan in 1916; instructor in forestry at university for three years following graduation, with time out for service in Aviation Corps of U.S. Army in 1918. Also taught forestry at Iowa State College. In 1924 became director of Land Economic Survey for Michigan Department of Conservation, serving in that capacity until 1927, when he was appointed assistant state forester. Pioneering Land Economic Survey marked him as leader of movement in which economic surveys of forest resources were applied in all important forest regions of United States. In 1930 joined U.S. Forest Service as director of forest survey of Washington and Oregon, at Pacific Northwest Forest Experiment Station, Portland, Oregon. Remained there until 1938, when he returned to Michigan as research professor in wild-land utilization. In 1939 went back to Forest Service at Portland as assistant regional forester in charge of Division of State and Private Forestry of Pacific Northwest region; was appointed regional forester in 1943. Was member of Society of American Foresters, 1924. Died March 23, 1951.

SOCIETY OF AMERICAN FORESTERS

Journal of Forestry. Obituary, 49:388, 1951.

ARGOW, KEITH ANGEVIN
(born 1936)

Born September 3 in New Haven, Connecticut. Colorado College, B.A. (economics) 1958; University of Michigan, B.S. (forest management), M.F. (forestry) 1961; North Carolina State University, Ph.D. (political science and forestry) 1970. Served in U.S. Army, 1958–59. Was appointed research forester, U.S. Forest Service, Washington, D.C., in 1961, and conducted research in alternative methods of financing federal forest recreation programs. In 1963 transferred to Atlanta, Georgia, and Asheville, North Carolina, as project leader, Cradle of Forestry in America. Served as instructor of forestry (small private woodlands) at North Carolina State University, 1966–70, while conducting research on social action for land preservation. Was appointed district-ranger manager for Mount Rogers National Recreation Area, Virginia, and served there from 1970 to 1974. Was associate professor of forestry, Virginia Tech., 1974–78. Was executive director, Trout Unlimited, 1978–81. In 1981 founded American Resources Group in Washington, D.C., a forestry and environmental services firm that includes in its membership Land Conservation Fund of America, National Forestry Network, and Environmental Audit, Ltd., and also provides management services for National Woodland Owners Association. Is publisher of *Conservation News Digest* and *Woodland Report*, and is Washington, D.C., editor for *National Woodlands Magazine.* Has been member of board of directors of The American Forestry Association for twelve years and of executive committee of Natural Resources Council of America for two years. Was chairman of Virginia Chapter of The Nature Conservancy and of Committee on Natural Areas of the Society of American Foresters. Is member of Phi Beta Kappa and author of fifty-four articles and publications in forestry.

Who's Who in America, 42d ed., 1982–83.

ARNOLD, RICHARD KEITH

(born 1913)

Born November 17 in Long Beach, California. University of California, B.S. (forestry) 1937; Yale University, M.F. 1938; University of Michigan, Ph.D. 1950. During 1951–53 was fire research officer for California (now Pacific Southwest) Forest and Range Experiment Station at Berkeley, before joining forestry faculty of University of California, 1946–50 and 1951–55. In this assignment was manager of *Operation Firestop*, a cooperative project with U.S. Forest Service, Civil Defense Administration, Universities of California and Southern California, California Division of Forestry, and forest industries to develop new techniques in fire control. In 1955 returned to Pacific Southwest Forest and Range Experiment Station as chief of Division of Fire Research, and was appointed director of the station in 1957. Transferred to Washington, D.C., office of Forest Service in 1963; was director of Division of Forest Protection Research until 1966, when he went to University of Michigan as dean of School of Natural Resources. Returned in 1969 to Forest Service in Washington, D.C., as deputy chief in charge of research; directed national research program that included eight regional forest experiment stations, Forest Products Laboratory of Madison, Wisconsin, and Institute of Tropical Forestry in Puerto Rico. After retiring from Forest Service in 1972, was appointed professor at University of Texas where, until retiring in 1979, he served in various positions, including associate dean of Lyndon Johnson School of Public Affairs; director, Marine Science Institute; and assistant vice-president, research. Was associate editor of *Journal of Forestry*, 1956–58; was member of council of Society of American Foresters, 1964–69; was chairman of Forest Fire Working Group for the North American Forestry Commission, Food and Agriculture Organization of the United Nations, 1965–66; and was vice-president in 1959 of Association of State College and University Research Organizations. Is author of many papers published in scientific journals and has served on numerous national and international committees dealing with natural resources research.

R. KEITH ARNOLD
HENRY CLEPPER

Who's Who in America, 42d ed., 1982–83.

ASHE, WILLIAM WILLARD
(1872–1932)
Born June 4 in Raleigh, North Carolina. University of North Carolina, B. Litt. 1891; Cornell University, M.S. 1892. Was forester of North Carolina Geological Survey from 1892 to 1905, then worked for U.S. Forest Service from 1905 until his death in 1932. Was secretary of National Forest Reservation Commission and editor of its reports from 1918 to 1924. Was vice-president of Society of American Foresters in 1919. Was appointed member of Forest Service Tree Name Committee and served as chairman, 1930–32. An authority on forest types and vegetation, he discovered one hundred new species in the Southeast, including several kinds of trees. Determined much of acquisition policy of Forest Service for many years after Weeks Law (1911) went into effect. Did significant work on comparative costs of operating large and small timber. His experiments in getting gum out of trees with cups and gutters influenced development of system now used by naval-stores industry. Solved problem of successfully transplanting longleaf pine. Was prolific writer, and his scientific writings number 166 and include such subjects as botany, logging costs, forest economics, erosion, forest influences and forest types, land acquisition, and forest management. His monograph *Loblolly Pine* is regarded as model in its field. Died March 18, 1932.

SOCIETY OF AMERICAN FORESTERS

Dayton, William A., "William Willard Ashe," *Journal of Forestry*, 44:213–14, March 1946.

Journal of Forestry. Obituary, 30:652–53, May 1932.

AUDUBON, JOHN JAMES
(1785–1851)
Born April 26 in Santo Domingo (now Haiti). Reared in France, he developed an interest in natural history and a gift for drawing. In 1803 came to United States to enter business, and lived near Norristown, Pennsylvania, at Mill Grove, a farm his father had purchased. During next seventeen years, embarked on a number of business ventures, but study of birds and drawing of bird species became his main interests. Disposed of his capital to free himself from the obligation to pursue trade; in 1819, with hope of eventual publication of his work, he turned entirely to drawing of American birds. In 1824, with a nearly completed portfolio of watercolor paintings, he visited Philadelphia Academy of Sciences,

where he was advised to publish his work in England because engraving facilities there were better and he would escape resentment of George Ord, an influential but rival American ornithologist. *The Birds of America* in four volumes was published in England from 1827 to 1838, and its text, *Ornithological Biography*, in five volumes, from 1831 to 1839. During 1830s became world's pre-eminent ornithologist, and is still world's best known. During 1840s began work on American mammals, which was completed by his sons. His life ended before conservation became pressing need and cause, but his work, which was first cultural and scientific achievement by an American to receive full European recognition as greatest in its field, made lasting impression on Americans and paved way for conservationists who were to follow. In addition to writing aforementioned books, was author of *A Synopsis of the Birds of North America*, 1839, and *The Viviparous Quadrupeds of North America* (completed by his son), 1845–48. Died January 27, 1851.

NATIONAL AUDUBON SOCIETY

Concise Dictionary of American Biography, 1964.

Herrick, Francis Hobart. *Audubon the Naturalist*, 2 vols., New York: Dover Publications, 1968.

Who's Who in American History (Historical Volume), 1607–1896.

AVERY, CARLOS
(1868–1930)

Born January 25 in Minooka, Illinois. A newspaperman, he was owner and editor of *The Leader*, acquired in 1897 and published in Hutchinson, Minnesota. In 1905 was appointed to Minnesota Game and Fish Commission, which he headed for fourteen years. Becoming vice-president of American Game Protective Association in New York City in 1924, was advanced to presidency in 1928. In addition, served as editor of the association's bimonthly journal, *American Game*. During his career, held numerous offices, both elective and advisory, in conservation affairs. Was active in International Association of Game, Fish and Conservation Commissioners, which he served as secretary-treasurer for two decades. The secretary of U.S. Department of Agriculture appointed him a member of Federal Advisory Committee under Migratory Bird Treaty Act. Was president of American Fisheries Society during 1919–20 and was its secretary from 1924 until his death, at which time he was also chairman of National Committee on Wildlife Legislation. Was one of pioneers in securing state laws for hunting licenses as means of financing work of state game commissions and establishment of game refuges. Died October 5, 1930.

HENRY CLEPPER

American Game. Obituary, vol. 19, no. 6, November-December 1930.

New York Times. Obituary, October 6, 1930.

AYLWARD, DAVID ARCHER
(1882–1970)
Born November 15 in Salem, Massachusetts. Educated at Harvard University. Beginning in 1921 was active in reorganization of Massachusetts Division of Fisheries and Game and in recodification of state's game and fish laws. In 1929 became executive secretary of Massachusetts Fish and Game Association. Was instrumental in establishment in 1942 of the Parker River National Wildlife Refuge, a sanctuary for waterfowl along Massachusetts coast. When National Wildlife Federation was formed in 1936, was elected its first vice-president, and succeeded to presidency in 1937, an office he held for thirteen years, during which he successfully guided the federation through critical period in its development. Cooperated with other conservation leaders in attainment of numerous progressive goals, including Federal Aid in Wildlife Restoration Act of 1937, the earlier Fish and Wildlife Coordination Act of 1934, and other significant laws that formed basis for modern wildlife management practices. Died March 21, 1970.

E. WARNER SHEDD, JR.

AYRES, RICHARD EDWARD
(born 1942)
Born February 2 in Salem, New Jersey; grew up in Beaverton, Oregon. Princeton University, B.A. (honors) 1964; Yale University Law School, Ll.B. 1969; Yale University Graduate School of Political Science, M.A. 1969. In 1970 became a founding staff member of Natural Resources Defense Council, Inc., where he now serves as senior staff attorney. With the council, has concentrated on shaping and administrating nation's air pollution control laws. Has litigated widely in federal courts, including Supreme Court of the United States. Represented the council and led

settlement of largest air pollution enforcement case in history, resulting in reduction of sulfur oxides pollution from Tennessee Valley Authority by one million tons per year. At Natural Resources Defense Council, was appointed by President Carter to serve on National Commission on Air Quality, created by Congress to examine and make recommendations for change in Clean Air Act. President Carter also appointed him to Steel Tri Partite Commission, concerned with national industrial policy towards steel industry. Is chairman of National Clean Air Coalition, consisting of more than two dozen environmental, public-health, labor, civil rights, church, and civic organizations urging retention of strong clean air legislation in Congress. Is member of board of League of Conservation Voters. Belongs to several professional associations and has published widely on air pollution control.

CHARLES H. CALLISON

BAILEY, REEVE MACLAREN
(born 1911)
Born May 2 in Fairmont, West Virginia. University of Michigan B.A. 1933, Ph.D. (zoology) 1938. Was assistant, Biological Survey, New York Conservation Department, 1935–37; biologist, Biological Survey, New Hampshire Fish and Game Department, 1938; and instructor of zoology, Iowa State College, 1938–42, and assistant professor, 1943. Moved to University of Michigan as assistant professor of zoology in 1944, and became associate professor in 1950 and professor in 1959. Held parallel curatorial ranks in university's Museum of Zoology until retiring in 1982; is currently emeritus professor of zoology and emeritus curator of fishes. Was leader of Iowa Fisheries Research Unit, 1941–44, and has been research associate with The American Museum of Natural History, New York City, since 1964. Has participated in expeditions throughout United States, Bolivia, Bermuda, Guatemala, Paraguay, and Zambia. Served American Society of Ichthyologists and Herpetologists as editorial board member, 1946–49; vice-president, 1954; and president, 1959. Was council member of American Association for the Advancement of Science (AAAS), 1968–72, and president of American Fisheries Society (AFS), 1975–76. Is a fellow of American Institute of Fishery Research Biologists and of AAAS; is honorary member of AFS; and is member of Ecological Society of America, American Institute of Biological Sciences, Society of Systematic Zoologists, and American Society of Limnology

and Oceanography. His research interests include taxonomy, variation, distribution, ecology, nomenclature, and hybridization of freshwater fishes. Is author of more than one hundred articles, and is coauthor with M. O. Allum of *Fishes of South Dakota*, 1962. As chairman from 1949 to present of AFS committee on common names, he has been leader in stabilizing names of fishes, an effort that has resulted in publication of *A List of Common and Scientific Names of Fishes from the United States and Canada*, 1960, 1970, and 1980.

JAMES S. DIANA
GERALD R. SMITH

American Men and Women of Science (Physical and Biological Sciences), 14th ed., 1979.

Who's Who in America, 42d ed., 1982–83.

BAIRD, SPENCER FULLERTON
(1823–1887)
Born February 3 in Reading, Pennsylvania. Dickinson College, B.A. 1840, Sc.D. (honorary) 1856; Columbia University, LL.D. 1887; Harvard University, LL.D. 1887. In 1845 was appointed professor of natural history at Dickinson College, and in 1848 received grant from Smithsonian Institution—first grant made by Smithsonian for scientific exploration and field research—to explore bone caves of Pennsylvania. In July 1850 was appointed assistant secretary of Smithsonian; then, starting with his own personal collection, which he gave to the institution, he developed U.S. National Museum, and was in charge of explorations and collections made by government in expanding West. Became secretary of Smithsonian in 1878. Meanwhile, when new U.S. Commission of Fish and Fisheries was created in 1871, he was appointed its first commissioner, to serve without additional salary, which he did until his death. Established first marine laboratory in United States, at Woods Hole, Massachusetts, and started federal fisheries program to rehabilitate nation's fisheries resources. A prolific editor and writer, he was head of science department of *Harper's Magazine* and editor of *The Annual Record of Science and Industry*. His list of titles exceeds one thousand, covering such diverse fields as mammals, birds, reptiles, fish, geology, and travel. Two of his scientific works are still classics: *Mammals of North America* and *Birds of North America*. In 1850 became permanent secretary of American Association for the Advancement of Science, and in

1863 helped organize National Academy of Sciences. Held honorary memberships in fifteen foreign academies and scientific societies, and received decorations from Norway, Australia, France, and Germany. Died August 19, 1887.

HERBERT W. GRAHAM

Billings, J. S. *Memoir of Spencer Fullerton Baird, 1823–87.*

Biographical Memoirs, vol. 3. National Academy of Sciences, 1915.

Dall, W. H. *Spencer Fullerton Baird, A Biography.* Philadelphia: Lippincott, 1915.

Dictionary of American Biography, 1928.

Ridgeway, R. et al. *Biographical Memoirs of Spencer Fullerton Baird.* Annual Report of the Smithsonian Institution, 1888.

World Who's Who in Science, 1968.

BAKER, HUGH POTTER
(1878–1950)
Born January 20 in Saint Croix Falls, Wisconsin. Michigan State College, B.S. 1901; Yale University, M.F. (forestry) 1904; University of Munich, Doctor of Economics 1910; Syracuse University, LL.D. 1933; Rhode Island State College, LL.D. 1945; Boston University D.Sc. 1945; Amherst College, LL.D. 1947; University of Massachusetts, LL.D. 1947. Entering Division of Forestry, U.S. Department of Agriculture, in 1901, spent several years on part-time duty in the West making examinations of public-domain lands for forest reserves. In 1904 joined faculty of forestry at Iowa State College, leaving in 1907 to set up Department of Forestry at Pennsylvania State College. From 1912 to 1920 was dean of New York State College of Forestry at Syracuse, and established New York State Ranger School as unit of college. Left in 1920 to become executive secretary of American Paper and Pulp Association, and in 1928 was named manager of trade association department of U.S. Chamber of Commerce. In 1930 again returned to New York State College of Forestry as dean, then left in 1933 to become president of Massachusetts State College (now University of Massachusetts), retiring as president in 1947. During his incumbency, established professional curriculums in forestry and wildlife management. Was a fellow of American Association for the Advancement of Science and of Society of American Foresters. Wrote extensively on forestry and education. Died May 24, 1950.

HENRY CLEPPER

Journal of Forestry. Obituary, 48(7):516, July 1950.
National Cyclopaedia of American Biography, 1954.
Who Was Who in America, 1951–60.

BAKER, JOHN HOPKINSON
(1894–1973)
Born June 30 in Cambridge, Massachusetts. Harvard University, B.A.
1915. Began bird studies as boyhood hobby; became one of youngest
members of famed Nuttall Ornithological Club at Cambridge. Later, as
businessman in New York City, served as president of Linnaean Society
and as director of National Audubon Society (NAS), becoming chairman
of NAS's board in 1933. In 1934 abandoned successful brokerage business on Wall Street to assume full-time duties as chief executive officer of
NAS, first as executive director and, after 1944, as president. Retired as
president emeritus in 1959. An innovative leader, he started Audubon
Camps, summer workshops for teachers and other adults with courses
in natural history and ecology; the first was Audubon Camp of Maine,
which opened in 1936. Also initiated nature study centers for children,
the first being Audubon Center of Southern California in Los Angeles
County (1939), and NAS's annual nationwide lecture series known as
"Audubon Screen Tours" (1944). Instrumental in securing government
action to establish Everglades National Park, he was influential in other
national conservation policies for a quarter century. Under his direction
NAS established its own research program with emphasis on endangered
species, and produced or sponsored scientific monographs on ivory-
billed woodpecker, California condor, roseate spoonbill, whooping
crane, and West Indian flamingo. Was chairman of Fish and Wildlife advisory committee to secretary of U.S. Department of the Interior, 1948–
53; continued as member, 1957–60. Served also on board of trustees of
National Parks Association and on executive committee of Natural Resources Council of America. In 1969, National Audubon Society established in his honor the John H. Baker Scholarship Fund for Conservation
Education. Died September 21, 1973.

CHARLES H. CALLISON

Audubon, vol. 71:6, pp. 81–85.
National Audubon Society, staff biographies.
Who's Who in America, 1963.

BARBER, JOHN CLARK
(born 1925)
Born January 6 in Liberty, North Carolina. North Carolina State University, B.S. (forestry) 1950, M.S. 1951; University of Minnesota, Ph.D. 1961. Began his career in 1951 with U.S. Forest Service in Southeastern Forest Experiment Station, Asheville, North Carolina, as research forester specializing in hardwood silviculture. By 1964 his research and management abilities took him from research forester to project leader for seed, nursery, and genetics research in Macon, Georgia, and then to head of Institute of Forest Genetics, Gulfport, Mississippi. Moved to Washington, D.C., office in 1967 as branch chief in Timber Management Research, and in 1971 assumed post of assistant to deputy chief for research. In 1972 was appointed director, Southern Forest Experiment Station, New Orleans, with responsibility for Forest Service research in mid-South. In 1976 was named associate deputy chief of State and Private Forestry, which involved him in broad range of cooperative programs with states, other federal agencies, and private interests. In 1980 was selected to head twenty-one-thousand-member Society of American Foresters with national headquarters located in Bethesda, Maryland. As the society's executive vice-president, he has become recognized as principal spokesman for forestry in United States and abroad. Has authored more than forty publications dealing with tree breeding and improvement, seed certification, silviculture, forest management, and forestry research. In 1969 organized Second World Consultation on Forest Tree Breeding, held in Washington, D.C., and was actively involved in developing certification standards for forest tree seed. His professional activities include participation in International Poplar Commission, in North American Forestry Commission, and in International Union of Forestry Research Organizations. Has served on editorial board as an associate editor of *Journal of Forestry*. Also has served on several national committees of Society of American Foresters. Is member of The American Forestry Association, Forest Farmers Association, American Association for the Advancement of Science, Soil Conservation Society of America, and Sigma Xi, and is a fellow of Society of American Foresters.

WILLIAM E. TOWELL

Who's Who in America, 42d ed., 1982–83.

BARNES, WILL CROFT
(1858–1936)

Born June 21 in California. Following public-school education, served in U.S. Army, 1879–82, and was awarded Congressional Medal of Honor "for bravery in action with hostile Apache Indians." Engaged in open-range cattle business in Arizona and New Mexico, served in territorial legislatures of both states, and in 1907 entered U.S. Forest Service as grazing inspector. Gained intimate knowledge of western range conditions and the livestock business, and had wide acquaintance with stockmen. Had leading role in formulating range-management policy and developing range administration of national forests. From 1915 to 1928 was in charge of Branch of Grazing, Forest Service. For two years thereafter was secretary of U.S. Geographic Board, then resigned from government service to devote his time to writing. His published works are numerous and include many magazine articles descriptive of the West's rangelands and related resources. His books include *Western Grazing Grounds and Forest Ranges*, 1913; *Tales from an X-Bar Horse Camp*, 1920; *The Story of the Range*; and *Cattle*, 1930, of which he was co-author. Was persuasive exponent of range conservation and sound range administration. Although his accomplishments were practical rather than scientific, he was outstanding figure in introducing stability and efficiency to chaotic national forest range conditions of early 1900s. Died December 18, 1936.

HENRY CLEPPER

Who Was Who in America, 1897–1942.

BASKETT, THOMAS SEBREE
(born 1916)

Born January 23 in Liberty, Missouri. Central Methodist College, Missouri, B.A. (biology) 1937; University of Oklahoma, M.S. (zoology) 1939; Iowa State University, Ph.D. (zoology) 1942. Was research scholar at University of Oklahoma; extension specialist in wildlife conservation and assistant professor in zoology at Iowa State University; and assistant professor of wildlife management at University of Connecticut. In 1948 became leader of Missouri Cooperative Wildlife Research Unit as biologist for U.S. Bureau of Sport Fisheries and Wildlife. Served as chief of Division of Wildlife Research, 1968–73, and in 1973 returned as unit leader to Missouri, where he continues to serve. Has written more than seventy-two publications, and has guided students in publishing many other scientific papers. Missouri unit fostered fishery research before fisheries were established, and also pioneered research on bullfrogs that lead to scientific harvest management. Under his leadership important research on mourning dove has been pursued for more than twenty-five years; early studies in quail and dove biology provided hard data on impact of harvest and supported developing population management strategies. More recently, seven years of cooperative work have provided international leadership in assessing field habitats on stronger biological basis. U.S. Fish and Wildlife Service presented a unit award to Missouri unit for accomplishment in habitat evaluation work. Was editor of *Journal of Wildlife Management*, 1965–68; president of The Wildlife Society, 1971, vice-president of its National Capital Chapter, 1969, and chairman of five of the society's national committees. Is elected member of American Ornithologists' Union. Was named Distinguished Alumnus of Central Methodist College, Missouri, in 1965. Was selected by University of Missouri–Columbia Student Wildlife Club in 1972 for Outstanding Professional Award; and by University of Missouri Student Council of School of Forestry, Fisheries and Wildlife for Outstanding Faculty Award in 1979. Missouri Chapter of The Wildlife Society awarded him E. Sydney Stephens professional wildlife award in 1973. In 1977 received Meritorious Service Award from U.S. Department of the Interior.

SANDRA CLARK

Who's Who in America, 42d ed., 1982–83.

American Men and Women of Science (Physical and Biological Sciences), 15th ed., 1982.

BATES, CARLOS GLAZIER
(1885–1949)
Born October 14 in Topeka, Kansas. University of Nebraska B.S. (forestry) 1907. Joined U.S. Forest Service in 1907, advancing from forest assistant to principal silviculturist at time of his death. Was in charge of one of first forest experiment stations, Fremont Station in Colorado, from 1909 to 1927; was stationed that year at Forest Products Laboratory, Madison, Wisconsin, and at Lake States Forest Experiment Station, Saint Paul, Minnesota, from 1928. His research contributions, many of them pioneering, concerned prairie tree planting, forest and watershed influences, tree seed, physiological requirements of trees, shelterbelt in-

fluences, and genetics of forest trees. Was in charge of research that guided Prairie States Forest Project in Great Plains from 1933 to 1942. Devised instruments for measuring evaporation and stream sediments. Forest watershed influences study at Wagon Wheel Gap, Colorado, which he supervised in cooperation with U.S. Weather Bureau (1909–26), gained international recognition. In 1940 became a fellow in Society of American Foresters, after serving the society as vice-president in 1920, as chairman of Rocky Mountain Section in 1919, and as chairman of Minnesota Section in 1930. From 1925 through 1932 was associate editor of *Journal of Forestry* for dendrology, silvics, and silviculture. Was author of some sixty scientific papers and monographs. Died July 2, 1949.

PAUL O. RUDOLF

American Men of Science, 8th ed., 1949.

Journal of Forestry. Obituary, vol. 47, 1949; 54, 1956.

BEAN, MICHAEL J.
(born 1949)
Born July 3 in Fort Madison, Iowa. University of Iowa, B.S. (political science) 1970; Yale University Law School, J.D. 1973. Assistant editor, the Yale Law Journal 1972–73. Worked in private law practice with firm of Covington and Burling, 1973–76; was staff attorney of Environmental Law Institute, 1976; and was staff attorney and chairman of wildlife program of Environmental Defense Fund, 1977. Was consultant to U.S. Fish and Wildlife Service and to Council on Environmental Quality, 1976. At Environmental Defense Fund, he has been involved in efforts to amend Endangered Species Act and Marine Mammal Protection Act. Has participated in various lawsuits pertaining to administration of National Wildlife Refuge System; to programs of Tennessee Valley Authority and U.S. Army Corps of Engineers; and to implementation of laws to protect porpoises netted incidentally in tuna fisheries. Is member of International Council on Environmental Law, and of Commission on Environmental Policy, Law, and Administration of the International Union for Conservation of Nature and Natural Resources. Has served informally as counsel to nongovernmental conservation groups at meetings of parties to Convention on International Trade in Endangered Species of Wild Fauna and Flora. Has written reviews and articles on conservation topics that have appeared in various issues of the periodicals *Quarterly*

Review of Biology; *Natural History*; *Defenders*; *National Parks*; and *Atlantic Naturalist*. Is author of *The Evolution of National Wildlife Law*, 1977 (rev. 1983).

ENVIRONMENTAL DEFENSE FUND

BEAR, FIRMAN EDWARD
(1884–1968)
Born May 21 near Germantown, Ohio. Ohio State University, B.Sc. 1908, M.Sc. 1910; University of Wisconsin, Ph.D. 1917; University of Chile, D.Sc. (honorary); Rutgers University. D.Sc. (honorary). During his fifty years of professional activity, won national recognition as teacher, scientist, author, administrator, and conservationist. Taught at Ohio State, 1912–14 and 1916–26; West Virginia, 1914–16; and Rutgers, 1940–54. At West Virginia and Rutgers also served as chairman of soils departments. A prolific writer, was author or coauthor of seventy-eight scientific papers and several hundred semitechnical or popular articles. His first book, *Soils and Fertilizers*, 1924, served as a college text for more than forty years. Wrote *Theory and Practices in the Use of Fertilizers*, 1928; edited a monograph *Chemistry of the Soil*, 1955; wrote *Earth, The Stuff of Life*, 1961; and *Soils in Relation to Crop Growth*, 1965. Was science editor of *Country Home Magazine*, 1938–40, and editor-in-chief of *Soil Science*, 1940–66. As director of agricultural research for American Cyanamid Company, 1929–38, traveled widely in this country, Central America, and Europe. Served as president of Soil Science Society of America in 1943, of American Society of Agronomy in 1949, and of Soil Conservation Society of America in 1950. Spent twelve years on Secretary of Agriculture's Soil and Water Conservation Advisory Committee, six years on New Jersey State Soil Conservation Committee, was active board member of The Conservation Foundation, and served as special consultant on world food problems for U.S. Department of State. Was a fellow of American Association for the Advancement of Science, of American Society of Agronomy, and of Soil Conservation Society; and was honorary member of International Society of Soil Science. Died April 6, 1968.

GRANT F. WALTON

American Men of Science (Physical and Biological Sciences), 11th ed., 1965.
Soil Science. Obituary, vol. 105, no. 5, May 1968.
Who's Who in America, vol. 35, 1968–69.

BELDING, DAVID LAWRENCE
(1884–1970)
Born July 24 in Dover Plains, New York. Williams College, B.A. 1905; Harvard Medical School, M.D. 1914; Harvard University, M.A. 1915. Biologist for Massachusetts Fish and Game Commission (full-time and part-time) from 1905 to 1917. Was captain in U.S. Army Medical Corps, 1917–19. Held following positions: part-time biologist for Massachusetts Fish and Game Commission, 1919–22; research associate, Evans Memorial Hospital, 1919–46; director of laboratories at Massachusetts Memorial Hospitals, 1924–44; assistant professor of bacteriology at Boston University School of Medicine, 1920–24; professor of pathology and bacteriology, 1924–28, and professor of bacteriology and experimental pathology, 1928–49; member, Province of Quebec Salmon Commission, 1936–40; associate scientist at Woods Hole Oceanographic Institution, 1950–54; and collaborator for U.S. Fish and Wildlife Service Branch of Fishery Biology, 1950–57. In addition to books and papers on medical subjects, wrote *A Report upon the Mollusk Fisheries of Massachusetts*, 1909; *A Report upon the Quahaug and Oyster Fisheries of Massachusetts*, 1919; *The Soft-shelled Clam Fishery of Massachusetts*, 1930; *The Quahaug Fishery of Massachusetts*, 1931; *The Scallop Fishery of Massachusetts*, 1931; *A Report upon the Alewife Fisheries of Massachusetts*, 1921; and numerous papers in *Transactions of the American Fisheries Society* and elsewhere. A life member of American Fisheries Society, he was president, 1929–30, and was elected honorary member in 1967. Died December 5, 1970.

ROBERT F. HUTTON

American Men of Science (Physical and Biological Sciences), 11th ed., 1965.

BELLROSE, FRANK CLIFFORD
(born 1916)
Born August 20 in Ottawa, Illinois. University of Illinois, B.S. (zoology) 1938, Western Illinois University, Sc.D. 1974. Was game specialist of Illinois Natural History Survey from 1938 to his partial retirement in September 1982 as principal scientist. Since retiring has worked part time for that agency. His research was primarily on waterfowl. One of his earliest conservation efforts measured natural wood-duck cavities and modified early slab nest boxes for wood ducks. The new boxes were first installed in 1938 and thousands of the new design were eventually put

up. Played major role in stopping, in 1945, proposal by U.S. Army Corps of Engineers for series of dams and drainage projects in Illinois River Valley. His efforts resulted in proposal by an engineer to use levee districts for storage of flood water and for conservation. Has been regular contributor to conservation literature, authored new version of *Ducks, Geese and Swans of North America* (1976), and is working on book about wood ducks based on forty-three years of research. Has taught course in waterfowl management at Western Illinois University; has given seminars at universities; has taught at workshops for U.S. Fish and Wildlife Service; and has consulted on conservation problems with National Academy of Sciences, U.S. Fish and Wildlife Service, National Wildlife Federation, U.S. Air Force, and state departments of natural resources. Has been expert witness in state and federal courts on conservation issues, and has presented invited papers at national and international congresses and colloquia. His awards and honors include The Wildlife Society Publication (book) Award, 1976; Oak Leaf Award, The Nature Conservancy, 1977; American Motors Conservation Award, 1979; National Wildlife Federation Award, 1980; Conservation Service Award, U.S. Department of the Interior, 1980; and honorary member, The Wildlife Society, 1982.

GLEN C. SANDERSON

American Men of Science (Physical and Biological Sciences), 10th ed., 1960.

BENNETT, HUGH HAMMOND
(1881–1960)
Born April 15, near Wadesboro, North Carolina. University of North Carolina, B.S. 1903, LL.D. (honorary) 1936; Clemson Agricultural College, D.Sc. 1937; Columbia University, D.Sc. 1952. In 1903 joined Bureau of Soils, U.S. Department of Agriculture, and in 1909 was appointed soil survey inspector of southern and eastern divisions. In 1904 and 1905, during soil surveys in Virginia, became aware of accelerated soil erosion and decided that soil erosion was most serious agricultural problem. In November 1928 gave statement on the problem and on his plans for study and action to subcommittee of House of Representatives. As result, an appropriation of $160,000 was made available to U.S. Department of Agriculture for investigations of soil and water conservation; he was put in charge of work for Bureau of Chemistry and Soils. In September 1933, when Soil Erosion Service was set up as emergency

public-works agency in U.S. Department of the Interior, he was appointed the service's director. In April 1935, when Soil Conservation Service was created in U.S. Department of Agriculture, he was named as its first chief, and continued in this position until his mandatory retirement, at age of seventy, in April 1951. His term was extended one year so he could serve as special assistant to secretary of Agriculture. Was author of many technical articles and five books: *The Soils and Agriculture of the Southern States*, 1921; *The Soils of Cuba* (with R. V. Allison), 1928; *Soil Conservation*, 1939; *Elements of Soil Conservation*, 1947; and *This Land We Defend* (with William C. Pryor), 1942. A fellow of American Society of Agronomy and of American Association for the Advancement of Science, he was also founder, fellow, and president of Soil Conservation Society of America. Was chairman of Pan American Soil Conservation Commission. His awards included Frances K. Hutchinson Medal of The Garden Club of America, 1944; Medal of Merit, National Agricultural and Industrial Society of Cuba, 1947; Audubon Medal, National Audubon Society, 1947; Distinguished Service Medal, U.S. Department of Agriculture, 1947; Cullum Medal, American Geographical Society, 1948; Silver Medal, Federated Garden Clubs of New York State, 1949; and John Deere Gold Medal of American Society of Agricultural Engineers, 1949. Died July 7, 1960.

F. GLENNON LOYD

Brink, Wellington. *Big Hugh: The Father of Conservation*. New York: Macmillan, 1951.

Who Was Who in America, 1961–68.

BENNETT, LOGAN J.

(1907–1957)

Born August 29 in Festus, Missouri. Central College, Missouri, B.S. (biology) 1910; Iowa State College, M.S. 1932, Ph.D. (zoology) 1937. Was awarded doctoral degree after serving as game technician for Iowa State Conservation Commission in 1934, junior refuge manager of Trempealeau National Wildlife Refuge in Wisconsin in 1935, and leader of newly organized Iowa Cooperative Wildlife Research Unit. In latter two positions, was employee of U.S. Bureau of Biological Survey in which, with its successor agency, the Fish and Wildlife Service, he was to serve with distinction. With the bureau was organizer and leader of Pennsylvania Cooperative Wildlife Research Unit; biologist in charge of nationwide Cooperative Unit Program; and chief of Branch of Wildlife Research from 1948 until his retirement in 1953. Thereafter for nearly four years, was executive director of Pennsylvania Game Commission. As charter member of The Wildlife Society, served as its secretary in 1942, 1943, and 1946, and as president in 1947. Was also member of American Ornithologists' Union, American Society of Mammalogists, and Outdoor Writers Association of America. Received Winchester Award for Outdoorsman of the Year for 1956. Among his many technical writings, one of his best-known publications is *The Blue-Winged Teal—Its Ecology and Management*, 1938. Bird-dog fanciers will remember him for his book *Training Grouse and Woodcock Dogs*. Died September 12, 1957.

Daniel L. Leedy

Journal of Wildlife Management. Obituary, vol. 22, January 1958.

Benson, Arthur Ragnar
(born 1896)
Born October 16, in East Berlin, Connecticut. Attended Middletown (Connecticut) High School, 1915. As president of Associated Fishing Tackle Manufacturers from 1936 to 1953, assumed leadership in obtaining membership support for important Federal Aid in Fish Restoration Act in 1950 (popularly known as Dingell-Johnson Act), financed by ten-percent excise tax on fishing tackle manufactured by them. Helped convince fishing-tackle industry of its responsibility in conservation and proper utilization of sport fisheries resources and, as result, Sport Fishing Institute was founded in 1949. This institute, still the only broad-purview national fish conservation agency, was revolutionary development in that the industry recognized obligation to advance responsible husbandry of fisheries resources by reinvesting into fish conservation part of its income from sale of manufactured products used by anglers. Under his leadership, tackle manufacturers organized the institute as nonprofit, tax-exempt organization, professionally staffed, to carry out its now well-established program of research in fisheries biology, education in fish conservation problems and principles, and technical service to official agencies and key citizen groups. Served as its first president from 1949 to 1959, during the institute's critical formative years, and is currently president emeritus. Was also first president of Sport Fishery Research Foundation from 1962 to 1967, and continues on its board of

trustees. Was trustee of North American Wildlife Foundation from 1946 through 1976. In February 1968 was elected to Sporting Goods Hall of Fame by National Sporting Goods Association "for his work behind the scenes in field of conservation"; was only man ever so honored for any reason other than for development of manufactured product. Is life member of both American Fisheries Society and Izaak Walton League of America, and is honorary life member of Sport Fishing Institute.

RICHARD H. STROUD

BERG, NORMAN ALF

(born 1918)

Born March 14 in Burlington, Iowa. University of Minnesota, B.S. 1941; Harvard University, Masters in Public Administration, 1956. Began his professional career in 1941 as vocational agricultural instructor in Minnesota. His work with Soil Conservation Service, U.S. Department of Agriculture, began in 1943. Served in several positions in Idaho and South Dakota, with three years leave for service in World War II as U.S. Marine. Was moving force in getting conservation irrigation farming techniques applied widely in southern Idaho. Was named assistant to administrator of Soil Conservation Society in Washington, D.C., in 1960. Following three years of service as deputy administrator for field services in 1968, was named associate administrator in 1969. Was appointed chief in 1979 and retired in 1982. Received U.S. Department of Agriculture's Distinguished Service Award in 1973, and National Wildlife Federation's Conservation Award in 1980 for "outstanding contributions to the wise use and management of the nation's natural resources." As charter member of Senior Executive Service, was recipient of Presidential Rank Award (Meritorious Executive) in 1980. Chaired U.S. Section, Great Lakes Land Use Reference Group, of the International Joint Commission of the United States and Canada from 1972 to 1978. Is charter member and a fellow of Soil Conservation Society of America, and member of Cosmos Club. Serves as senior advisor to American Farmland Trust; as Washington representative for Soil Conservation Society of America; and as supervisor of Anne Arundel Conservation District in Maryland.

SOIL CONSERVATION SOCIETY OF AMERICA

Who's Who in America, 42d ed., 1982–83.

BERRYMAN, JACK HOLMES

(born 1921)

Born July 28 in Salt Lake City, Utah. Westminster College, Salt Lake City, A.A. 1940; University of Utah, B.S. and M.S., 1947. Served in U.S. Navy, 1941–45. Served as wildlife biologist with Utah Fish and Game Department, 1947–50, before joining Federal Aid Division of U.S. Fish and Wildlife Service in Albuquerque, then transferred to Minneapolis in 1953. In 1959, as associate professor in College of Natural Resources, established wildlife extension program at Utah State University. In 1965 returned to Fish and Wildlife Service in Washington, D.C., where he was responsible for reorganization of animal control activities and development of wildlife enhancement and pesticide monitoring programs, and subsequently established Office of Extension Education. On retirement in 1978 became executive vice-president of International Association of Fish and Wildlife Agencies, where he coordinates activities. Is member of Phi Sigma, Sigma Xi, Xi Sigma Pi, American Fisheries Society, Washington Biologists Field Club, and The Wildlife Society, of which he was successively regional representative, vice-president, and president, 1964–65. Received Minnesota Award for "outstanding contribution to the profession of wildlife management," 1960; American Motors Conservation Award, 1976; and Distinguished Service Award of U.S. Department of the Interior, 1979.

JOHN S. GOTTSCHALK

American Men and Women of Science (Physical and Biological Sciences), 15th ed., 1982.

BERTRAND, GERARD ADRIAN

(born 1943)

Born July 7 in Boston, Massachusetts. University of New Hampshire, B.A. (zoology) 1965; Florida State University, M.S. (biology) 1967; Oregon State University, Ph.D. (biological oceanography) 1970; University of Wisconsin, J.D. (environmental law) 1975. Undertook research and earned advanced biology degrees on interrelationship of marine animal populations. During law school, worked for University of Wisconsin Sea Grant Office and wrote book on Green Bay's coastal and environmental needs. Acted as ecological advisor to chief of U.S. Army Corps of Engineers, and was influential in formulating the corp's original environmental policies and guidelines. Using these guidelines, was able to have major

53

impact on reshaping water projects in several states, such as halting Cross Florida Barge Canal Project. Was senior scientist for President's Council on Environmental Quality under presidents Nixon, Ford, and Carter; worked on issues such as control of poisons on public lands, wetlands protection, and control of trade in wildlife. From 1977 to 1980 served as chief of international affairs for U.S. Fish and Wildlife Service. His activities included helping to develop wildlife conservation programs in more than fifty nations. As member of delegations to international commissions and conferences, worked for international cooperation and treaties for protection of endangered species, including Indian elephants, tigers, the great bustard, Siberian cranes, and marine mammals. Has served since 1980 as president of Massachusetts Audubon Society. Was chairman and is now member of executive committee of American Committee for International Conservation, which represents in North America the International Union for Conservation of Nature and Natural Resources. Also serves as trustee of variety of other environmental and cultural organizations, including Ocean Research and Education Society, Animal Welfare Institute, Fauna and Flora Preservation Society, and Massachusetts Cultural Alliance.

JAY COPELAND

BESLEY, FRED WILSON
(1872–1960)
Born February 16 in Vienna, Virginia. University of Maryland, B.A. 1892, Sc.D. 1912; Yale University School of Forestry, M.F. 1904. Was teacher in public school, 1892–1900; student assistant in Bureau of Forestry, U.S. Department of Agriculture, 1901–2; and returned to Bureau of Forestry, 1904. Was appointed state forester of Maryland in 1906, and worked in that position until retiring in 1942; held national record for continuous service, having served for thirty-six years. During this period, maintained political independence of the agency and established high standards of service for employees under his direction. Was associate professor of forestry, University of Maryland, 1923–42, and professor of forest management, University of West Virginia, 1943–45. Was member of Society of American Foresters for fifty-two years, and elected a fellow in 1940. Served as treasurer of the society, 1922–24; chairman of Allegheny Section, 1927; and member of the society's council for three terms, 1934 to 1937. Was president of Yale Forestry School Alumni Associa-

tion, 1925–26; president of Association of State Foresters, 1925–26; director of The American Forestry Association; and member of numerous state and federal boards and committees. After retiring as state forester, acquired timber holdings in Maryland, managing them through Besley and Rogers Forest Land Company. Died November 8, 1960.

SOCIETY OF AMERICAN FORESTERS

American Men of Science, 8th ed., 1949.

Journal of Forestry. Obituary, vol. 59: 55, 1961.

BETHEL, JAMES SAMUEL
(born 1915)
Born August 13 in New Westminster, B.C., Canada. University of Washington, B.S. (forestry), 1937; Duke University, M.F. 1939, D.F. 1947. Served in U.S. Army Air Force, 1942–46. Was instructor in forestry, Pennsylvania State University, 1939–41; assistant professor of biology, Virginia Polytechnic Institute and University, 1941–42; and director of Wood Products Laboratory, North Carolina State College, 1949–59. Headed special projects in science education, National Science Foundation, 1959–62. At University of Washington was professor of forestry, 1962–64, and dean of College of Forestry, 1964–81. As consultant to United Nations Food and Agriculture Organization, was advisor to government of Yugoslavia, 1952; was also consultant to U.S. Economic Development Administration in Puerto Rico, 1956. Was member of President's Council on Environmental Quality, 1971; Committee on Effects of Herbicides in Vietnam for National Academy of Sciences, 1971; Committee on Environmental Problems Affecting National Materials Policy, 1972–73; and board of Agriculture and Renewable Resources for Commission on Natural Resources, 1973. Is a fellow of Institute of Wood Science for American Association for Advancement of Science and of Society of American Foresters. Held presidency of Institute of Wood Engineers, 1958–59; of Society of Wood Science and Technology, 1960–61; and of Association of State Colleges and Universities Research Organizations, 1969–70. Has been active in Institute of Biological Sciences, International Society of Tropical Foresters, and Association of Tropical Biologists. Is author (with Panshin, Harrar, and Baker) of *Forest Products*, 1962.

HENRY CLEPPER

American Men and Women of Science (Physical and Biological Sciences), 15th ed., 1982.

Who's Who in America, 38th ed., 1974–75.

BIRGE, EDWARD ASAHEL
(1861–1950)
Born September 7 in Troy, New York. Williams College, B.A. 1873, M.A. 1875; Harvard University, Ph.D. 1878; University of Pittsburgh, Sc.D. 1897; Rensselaer Polytechnic Institute, Ph.D. 1924; University of Wisconsin, LL.D. 1905; University of Missouri, Ph.D. 1919. During fifty years at University of Wisconsin—from instructor in 1875 to retirement as president in 1925, and fifteen years as president emeritus—he, together with Chancey Juday, laid much of foundation of limnology. His were the first detailed accounts of summer stratification of temperature and oxygen; first description of wind-induced water movements in stratified lakes (introducing term *thermocline*); first systematic measurement of penetration of solar radiation; and first to introduce concept of heat budgets. His pioneering studies with Juday on chemical composition of plankton, dissolved gases, and regional differences in water chemistry laid basis for understanding and conservation of lake environments. Was commissioner of fisheries in Wisconsin, 1895–1915; director, Wisconsin Geological and Natural History Survey, 1897–1919; president, American Microscopical Society, 1902; president, American Fisheries Society, 1906–7; commissioner of forestry, 1907–15; and member of Wisconsin Conservation Commission, 1908–15. His bibliography lists sixty-eight titles, which include thirty-eight papers under single authorship and twenty-one coauthored with Juday. Died June 9, 1950.

CLIFFORD H. MORTIMER

Mortimer, C. H. *An Explorer of Lakes*. Madison: University of Wisconsin Press, 1956.

Sellery, G. C. *A. E. Birge, A Memoir*. Madison: University of Wisconsin Press, 1956.

BLAIR, WILLIAM DRAPER, JR.
(born 1927)
Born May 2 in Charlotte, North Carolina. Princeton University, B.A. (with honors) 1949. Served in active duty with U.S. Marine Corps Re-

serve, 1945–46. Was reporter and foreign correspondent for *Baltimore Sun*, 1949–53. Became assistant international editor for *Newsweek*, 1953, and subsequently was London correspondent, 1953–55; Bonn bureau chief, 1955–57; and Paris bureau chief, 1957–59. Was director of media services, U.S. Department of State, 1959–70, and deputy assistant secretary for public affairs in that agency, 1970–80. Received U.S. Department of State's highest honor award for distinguished public service, 1980. Was member of board of governors, The Nature Conservancy, 1972–80, and chairman, 1975–77; president, Audubon Naturalist Society of the Central Atlantic States, 1968–70, and member of board of directors, 1966–73; and president, The Nature Conservancy, 1980. During his tenure The Nature Conservancy has protected hundreds of outstanding natural areas and launched several programs of national significance, such as National Critical Areas Conservation Program; National Endangered Species Program; Rivers of the Deep South Program; R. K. Mellon National Wetlands Program; and Trade Lands Program.

THE NATURE CONSERVANCY

Who's Who in America, 42d ed., 1982–83.

BOLEN, ERIC GEORGE
(born 1937)
Born November 24, in Plainfield, New Jersey. University of Maine, B.Sc. (wildlife management) 1959; Utah State University, M.S. 1962, Ph.D. 1967. Was employed as assistant biologist for Vermont Game Department in summers of 1957, 1958, and 1961, and with U.S. Fish and Wildlife Service in summers of 1959 and 1960. Served as instructor of biology at Texas A&I University, 1965–66. In 1966 was appointed to faculty of Texas Tech University, where he served as assistant professor of wildlife management, 1966–69; associate professor, 1969–72; professor, 1973 and from 1978 to present; and associate dean of Graduate School, 1978 to present. Has been honored both for research and for teaching at Texas Tech and, in 1981, was named its Paul Whitfield Horn Distinguished Professor. Initiated graduate program in wildlife management there. From 1973 to 1978 worked as assistant director of Rob and Bessie Welder Wildlife Foundation, Sinton, Texas, and held several adjunct professorships during that period. Is member of many scientific organizations; served as president of Southwestern Association of Naturalists, 1976–77; president of Texas Chapter of The Wildlife Society, 1974–75;

and editor of The Wildlife Society Bulletin, 1975–78. As author of more than 120 publications, mostly on waterfowl and other game birds but ranging from plant ecology to soil mites, he is recognized authority on whistling ducks and their allies. Has served as consultant to a number of organizations and has traveled widely on five continents in pursuit of his research interests.

J. KNOX JONES, JR.

American Men and Women of Science (Physical and Biological Sciences), 15th ed., 1982.

BOOTHBY, CHARLES LAURENCE
(born 1935)

Born May 8 in Livermore, Maine. University of Maine, B.S. (agronomy) 1958, M.P.A. 1975. Joined U.S. Soil Conservation Service in 1958 and worked in three field offices in Maine, developing conservation plans with farmers and assisting them with installation of soil and water conservation measures. In 1964 was named executive director of Maine Soil and Water Conservation Commission, where he assisted in drafting and passage of Site Location of Development Law, Registration of Dams Act, and Land Use Regulation Law. As administrator of state agency's activities, directed technical site reviews and conducted public hearings on establishment of water levels at dams, in addition to administering construction contracts for conservation districts. In 1977 was named executive secretary of National Association of Conservation Districts, where he serves in Washington, D.C., headquarters, analyzing proposed environmental and natural resources legislation, preparing background papers and testimony, and monitoring administrative rules and regulations regarding environmental programs. Has been active in Soil Conservation Society of America, serving as president of Northern New England Chapter and council member of D.C. Chapter. Was national president of Association of State Soil Conservation Administrative Officers in 1973. Served as representative to Natural Resources Council of America. Is private consultant in land use and conservation to Norlands Foundation, Livermore, Maine.

NATIONAL ASSOCIATION OF CONSERVATION DISTRICTS

BORDEN, THOMAS BRADLEY

(born 1927)

Born May 2 in Houston, Texas. Purdue University, B.S. (forest management) 1952, M.S. (conservation education) 1957. Served as district forester, Illinois Department of Conservation, 1952–54; forester, Trees for Tomorrow, Wisconsin, 1954–55; assistant state forester, South Dakota Department of Game, Fish and Parks, 1957–59; state forester, Colorado State Forest Service, since 1959; and assistant director, Colorado State University Experiment Station, 1969. Was elected president of Society of American Foresters for 1982–83 term; was vice-president, The American Forestry Association, 1983; and was president of National Association of State Foresters. Is member of other conservation organizations, especially in the West, and has written widely for conservation magazines and forestry journals.

HENRY CLEPPER

BOWERS, EDWARD AUGUSTUS

(1857–1924)

Born August 2 in Hartford, Connecticut. Yale University, B.A. 1879, LL.B. 1881. Was lawyer and judge in Dakota Territory, 1882–86; for three years was inspector of public lands for U.S. Department of the Interior; and was assistant commissioner of General Land Office, 1893–95. Practiced law in New Haven from 1898, and from 1901 to 1917 lectured on forest law at Yale University Forest School. One of America's pioneer forest conservationists, he was director and twice secretary of The American Forestry Association. As early as 1887, prepared detailed plan for reservation from sale and exploitation of nation's vast acreage of public timberlands. His report, *The Present Condition of the Public Lands*, at joint meeting of The American Forestry Association and American Economic Association in December 1890, brought about demands for reform in public-lands protection from theft and trespass. Is credited with drafting act of March 3, 1891, that provided for creation of forest reserves (now national forests); the act was named by Gifford Pinchot as "most important legislation in the history of forestry." In addition, was influential in initiating events leading to act of June 4, 1897, which provided for administration of forest reserves and made it possible to practice forestry on them. Author of numerous papers and speeches on resource conservation, he was effective critic of government's neglect of public lands and timber, and exponent of action leading to their eventual management in the public interest. Died December 8, 1924.

HENRY CLEPPER

Who Was Who in America, vol. 4, 1961–68.

BOX, THADIS WAYNE
(born 1929)
Born May 9 in Llano County, Texas. Southwest Texas State College, B.S. 1956; Texas A&M University, M.S. 1957, Ph.D. 1959. Operated private ranch in central Texas. Taught and did range research in Utah, 1959–62. Established Department of Range and Wildlife at Texas Tech University and served as associate professor and professor, 1962–68. Established International Center for Arid and Semi-Arid Land Studies at Texas Tech University, 1968–70. From 1970 to present has served as dean of College of Natural Resources at Utah State University. Has conducted research on range-wildlife relationships for Welder Wildlife Foundation in Sinton, Texas, and served as research scientist for Commonwealth Scientific and Industrial Research Organization in Australia. In 1967 received E. Harris Harbison Award for distinguished teaching from Danforth Foundation and has received special awards for teaching or research from Texas Tech, Utah Environmental Council, and Utah Association of Soil Conservation Districts. Served as consultant for numerous international and bilateral organizations on range-livestock and livestock-wildlife relationships in Africa, South America, and Asia. Is author or coauthor of almost two hundred scientific and professional publications dealing with range and wildlife management, and coauthor of textbook in McGraw-Hill's American Forestry series, *Range Management*, 1975.

LAURENCE R. JAHN

American Men and Women of Science (Physical and Biological Sciences), 15th ed., 1982.

Who's Who in America, 42d ed., 1982–83.

BRADLEY, HAROLD CORNELIUS
(1878–1976)
Born November 25 in Oakland, California. University of California, B.A. 1900; Yale University, Ph.D. (chemistry) 1905. In 1905 taught

chemistry at Yale University Medical School. Beginning in 1906 taught physiological chemistry at University of Wisconsin until his retirement in 1949. During part of his career, was director of research at Woods Hole Marine Laboratory in Massachusetts. From 1908 to 1914 was volunteer aid to John Muir in attempt to prevent flooding of Hetch Hetchy Valley of California. In 1912 wrote first article on ecological changes involving soil erosion from overuse, which was published in Sierra Club *Bulletin*; also contributed articles to other journals and conservation magazines. In 1952 began first of several trips on Colorado River and its tributaries; his findings were used in Sierra Club campaign in opposition to construction of dams in Dinosaur National Monument. In 1955 started a campaign for clean-up of litter in national parks, forests, and desert areas; his efforts resulted in an educational program whereby many visitors now carry out their litter. Served as member of board of directors of Sierra Club, 1951–61; was president, 1957–59; and honorary president from 1974 until his death in 1976. Received John Muir Award of the Sierra Club in 1966, and was appointed to Hall of Fame for Skiiers in 1968 for pioneering mountain and cross-country skiing in Sierra Nevada and midwestern areas. Died January 4, 1976.

LUELLA K. SAWYER

American Men of Science (Physical and Biological Sciences), 10th ed., 1960.

Sierra Club Handbook, 1967.

Who's Who in America, 1950–51.

BRADLEY, PRESTON
(1888–1983)
Born August 8 in Linden, Michigan. Hamilton College of Law, D.C.L.; Lake Forest College, LL.D.; Yankton College, LL.D.; Meadville Theological School, University of Chicago, D.D.; Lincoln Memorial University, L.H.D. Was one of "Fifty-Four Founders" of Izaak Walton League of America in Chicago in 1922 and gave this national organization its name. Served three terms as president of the league, was elected honorary president in 1968, and was elected to its Hall of Fame in 1960. Founded Peoples Church of Chicago in 1912 and was its pastor until 1980. Conducted more than fifty years of continuous broadcasting on Chicago radio stations and made numerous television appearances; his sermons and broadcasts dealt much with natural resource conservation. Was honored

in 1967 by proclamation of governor of Illinois and mayor of Chicago designating October 20 as Preston Bradley Day. Was life member of Chicago Art Institute, Adventurer's Club, and Chicago Historical Society, and served for forty-six years as member of board of Chicago Public Library. Published *Liberalist*, a church magazine, for forty-seven years, and authored ten books and numerous special articles, many dealing with environmental problems. Died June 1, 1983.

JACK LORENZ

Who's Who in America, 41st ed., 1980–81.

BRANDBORG, STEWART MONROE
(born 1925)
Born February 2 in Lewiston, Idaho. University of Montana, B.S. (wildlife technology) 1949; University of Idaho, M.S. (wildlife management) 1951. Was employed by U.S. Forest Service; Idaho Cooperative Wildlife Research Unit, University of Idaho; and Idaho Department of Fish and Game, 1942–53. One of his studies, *Life History and Management of the Mountain Goat in Idaho* (1954), was first definitive investigation of this species. As assistant conservation director of National Wildlife Federation, 1954–60, he was responsible for conservation-education projects and prepared and edited its *Conservation Report*. Was elected to council of The Wilderness Society in 1956; became director of special projects in 1960 and executive director in 1964. Was associated with development of Wilderness Act of 1964 from its introduction as bill in 1956. With its enactment, led and directed citizen mobilization programs in more than thirty states to organize wilderness teams that worked to bring many dozens of unprotected areas into National Wilderness Preservation System. Work with citizen groups was principal focus of his leadership of The Wilderness Society, 1964–76. His interest in training and mobilization of citizen leaders has continued: from 1982 to 1984 he was national coordinator for program of regional environmental leadership conferences sponsored by heads of major national conservation organizations. His commitment to grassroots leadership development has combined with his work for protection of wilderness, the National Park, Wildlife Refuge and National Forest Systems, and other public lands in major national campaigns in U.S. Congress and in various agencies of government. Also played active roles for protection of human environment and wildlife. Served in 1977 as special assistant to assistant

secretary of U.S. Department of the Interior for Fish, Wildlife and Parks, and as special assistant to director of National Park Service, designing and directing the service's public participation programs from 1978 through 1980. Was an organizer and first co-chairman, 1970–75, of Urban Environment Conference, for which he continues to serve on its board. Is secretary-treasurer of Human Environmental Center, and has been member of executive committee of Natural Resources Council of America.

Stewart M. Brandborg

Who's Who in America, 42d ed., 1982–83.

Brandwein, Paul Franz
(born 1914)
Born April 2 in Austria. New York University, B.A. 1934, M.S. 1937, Ph.D. (botany) 1940; Colorado College, D.Sc. 1952. Was high-school science teacher for twelve years, eight of which he chaired the department. Began science editing in 1946 for Harcourt, Brace and World; two years later left the classroom for an editorial position. Became senior editor and eventually senior vice-president of now Harcourt Brace Jovanovich. Along way, held number of concurrent positions: director of education, The Conservation Foundation; director, Pinchot Institute of Conservation Studies; and adjunct professor of conservation and education, University of Pittsburgh. Through his widely used text series in science and social studies and influence of conferences held at Pinchot Institute, he strongly influenced nature and amount of basic conservation concepts included in American school texts. Created conceptual framework for Ekistics program, which is basic conservation program for California schools. Brought his concerns for conservation education to many curricula and to teacher-training reform projects during 1960s and 1970s. Among his publications most significantly affecting conservation education are *Teaching Science Through Conservation* (with M. Munzer), *Concepts in Science* (text series), *Concepts in Social Studies* (text series), and *People and Environment* (with M. Brennan). Is member of American Association for the Advancement of Science; The American Phytopathology Society; The National Association for Research in Science Teaching; National Science Teachers Association; and Conservation Education Association. His direct contributions are at least matched by his influence on colleagues, stimulating them to apply their best critical thinking

skills to design and develop conservation curricula and instructional strategies and materials of high quality.

CHARLES E. ROTH

American Men and Women of Science (Physical and Biological Sciences), 14th ed., 1979.

BREWER, GEORGE EMERSON, JR.
(1899–1968)

Born November 13 in New York City. Yale College, B.A. 1922. Taught English at Yale University, 1922–25, at University of Buffalo, 1926–27, and at Columbia University in 1928. During 1930s lived in Massachusetts, and was associated with Federal Theater, 1936–38. During World War II was lieutenant colonel in U.S. Army Air Force. In 1948 participated in establishment of The Conservation Foundation in New York City (now with headquarters in Washington, D.C.). As vice-president until his retirement in 1965 (trustee thereafter), he was active in formulating its educational program. Served as governor of Pinchot Institute for Conservation Studies and was director of National Parks Association. Helped organize and later held position of director of Student Conservation Association. Was member of advisory committee of Hudson Valley Conservation Commission and was trustee of Association for Protection of Adirondacks. Was author of many articles on conservation topics, and coauthor and producer of *Yours Is the Land* and *Living Earth*, a series of educational films distributed for The Conservation Foundation by Encyclopaedia Britannica films. Died February 20, 1968.

THE CONSERVATION FOUNDATION

BREWER, WILLIAM HENRY
(1828–1910)

Born September 14 in Poughkeepsie, New York. Yale University, Ph.B. 1852, A.M. 1859, LL.D. 1903; Washington and Jefferson College, Ph.D. 1880. After teaching chemistry and geology at Washington College, Pennsylvania, from 1858 to 1860, assisted in geological survey of California, 1860–64. Returned to Yale Sheffield Scientific School as professor of agriculture in 1864, and retired in 1903 in emeritus status. Was one of small group of scientists concerned about destruction of nation's timber. For ninth census of 1870, prepared special report, "The Woodlands and Forest Systems of the United States," published in *Statistical Atlas* of 1874; it contained most of knowledge about forests available at that time. As early as 1873, gave lectures on forests and forestry at Yale, probably first such instruction ever offered in an American university. During 1870s and 1880s helped bring to attention of government the need for forest conservation. Was member of committee of American Association for the Advancement of Science that memorialized the government in 1874, resulting in appointment of first forestry agent in U.S. Department of Agriculture and beginning of forestry as function of federal government. Was member of Forest Commission of 1896, appointed by National Academy of Sciences at request of the secretary of U.S. Department of the Interior, to make recommendations for a federal forest policy. Was active in The American Forestry Association, and one of early associate members of Society of American Foresters. Was author of more than one hundred papers on agricultural, geological, and related subjects, and editor of *Botany of California* (1876), one of first botanical treatises of that state. Died November 2, 1910.

HENRY CLEPPER

National Cyclopaedia of American Biography, 1906.

Who Was Who in America, 1897–1942.

BREWSTER, WILLIAM
(1851–1919)
Born July 5 in Wakefield, Massachusetts. Amherst College, A.M. (honorary) 1880; Harvard University, A.M. (honorary) 1899. Left his career in banking in 1880 to assist in developing collection of birds and mammals at Boston Society of Natural History. In 1885 was head of Department of Mammals and Birds at the Cambridge, Massachusetts, Museum of Comparative Zoology, and after 1900 was curator of Department of Birds. Was founder of Nuttall Ornithological Club in Cambridge in 1873, and its president for many years. One of three organizers of American Ornithologists' Union in 1883, he was president from 1895 to 1898. Was organizer also of one of first Audubon societies; was later director of National Association of Audubon Societies; and was long the president of Massachusetts Audubon Society. For years was director of Massachusetts Fish and Game Department, and was a founder of American Game Protective and Propagation Association in 1911. Maintained private museum of ornithology at Cambridge, and wildlife sanctuary near

Concord, where he studied ecology of birds and small mammals. Wrote more than three hundred scientific and literary papers, as well as books and bulletins, but is best remembered for his book *Bird Migration*, 1886. His writings comprise important additions to literature of American ornithology, the development of which he notably influenced. Was a fellow of American Association for the Advancement of Science and of American Academy of Arts and Sciences. The William Brewster memorial (gold) medal was created by American Ornithologists' Union in 1919 in his honor, to be awarded periodically to authors of works on birds of Western Hemisphere. Died July 11, 1919.

NATIONAL AUDUBON SOCIETY

Dictionary of American Biography, 1929.

National Cyclopaedia of American Biography, 1932.

Who Was Who in America, 1897–1942.

"William Brewster, 1851–1919." *Bird Lore*, 21(5):277–86, September-October 1919.

BRIGGS, SHIRLEY ANN
(born 1918)
Born May 12 in Iowa City, Iowa. University of Iowa B.A. (art and botany) 1939, M.A. (art) 1940. Was instructor of art, North Dakota Agricultural College, 1941–43; illustrator, Martin Aircraft Corporation, 1943–45; information specialist, U.S. Fish and Wildlife Service, 1945–48; chief of graphics section, U.S. Bureau of Reclamation, 1948–53. Worked on diorama production for Smithsonian Institution, 1953–54, and for National Park Service, 1955–56. Edited and illustrated books on natural history, 1948–63. Started *Atlantic Naturalist* magazine for Audubon Naturalist Society of Central Atlantic States in 1946; was editor, 1946–69; and vice-president for publications, 1956–69, producing booklets on natural history of region. Has conducted winter and breeding bird-population studies in Glover-Archbold Park from 1959 to present, recording decrease in Neotropical migrants. Helped establish Rachel Carson Council in 1965; has been secretary since 1965 and executive director since 1970, guiding the council's work as international information center on toxic contaminants of environment. Was member of Pesticide Policy Advisory Committee, Environmental Protection Agency, 1975–77; Advisory Panel on Monitoring Environmental Con-

taminants in Food, Office of Technology Assessment, 1978–79; and advisory committee for Conference on Pesticides and Human Health of Society for Occupational and Environmental Health, 1979. Has been member of executive committee, Natural Resources Council of America, 1977–79 and 1980 to present; secretary, 1981–82. Since 1962 has taught course on conservation philosophy in United States, in Graduate School of U.S. Department of Agriculture. From Audubon Naturalist Society received Paul Bartsch Award in 1972, and was made honorary vice-president in 1975.

RACHEL CARSON COUNCIL

Who's Who in America, 42d ed., 1982–83.

BROMFIELD, LOUIS
(1896–1956)

Born December 27 in Mansfield, Ohio. Student at Cornell University College of Agriculture and Columbia University School of Journalism; Marshall College, Litt.D. (honorary). During World War I served both in French Army and with American Expeditionary Forces. Internationally known author, soil conservationist, and scientific farmer, he lived abroad until 1938, collecting material for his many books and extensive writings; year later purchased Malabar Farm in Pleasant Valley, Ohio. There developed his philosophy of agriculture and conservation, summed up in several of his books, notably *Pleasant Valley*, 1945; *Malabar Farm*, 1948; *Out of the Earth*, 1950; and *From My Experience*, 1955. In addition to his conservation writings, gave thousands of talks on radio and television, and before live audiences throughout the world. Was active promoter and vice-president of Friends of the Land organization. Besides awards and honors, including Pulitzer Prize conferred on him for his literary attainments, received wide recognition for his conservation work, including Audubon Medal of National Audubon Society and France K. Hutchinson Medal of The Garden Club of America. Died March 18, 1956.

H. T. MARSHALL

Anderson, David. *Louis Bromfield*. New York: Twayne Publishers, 1964.

Oxford Companion of American Literature, 4th ed., 1965.

Who Was Who in America, 1951–60.

BROWER, DAVID ROSS
(born 1912)

Born July 1 in Berkeley, California. University of California, 1930–31; honorary degrees from Hobart-Smith Colleges 1967, Claremont College Graduate School 1971, Starr King School of the Ministry 1971, University of Maryland 1973, University of San Francisco 1973, Colorado College 1973. Was editor, University of California Press, 1941–52; executive director, Sierra Club, 1952–59, and honorary vice-president, 1971. Was chairman, Natural Resources Council of America, 1955–57; director, North Cascades Council, 1957; secretary, Trustees for Conservation, 1960–61 and 1964–65; president, Friends of the Earth, 1969–79, and chairman, 1979; founder, League of Conservation Voters, 1969, and on steering committee, 1979; director, Environmental Liaison Board, Nairobi, 1975–81; president, Conference on Fate of the Earth, 1982; and president, Earth Island Institute, 1982. Was conservation lecturer in Finland, Sweden, Kenya, Italy, Australia, New Zealand, Japan, Czechoslovakia, 1971–83. Initiated, designed, and was general editor of Sierra Club series "Exhibit Format" (20 vols.) and Friends of the Earth series "The Earth's Wild Places" (10 vols.), as well as many other books and films; was editor of *Sierra Club Bulletin*, 1946–69. Was leader in movements to keep dams out of Dinosaur National Monument and Grand Canyon; to establish Kings Canyon, North Cascades, and Redwood national parks, and Point Reyes National Seashore; and to establish National Wilderness Preservation System and Outdoor Recreation Resources Review. Received numerous awards, including honorary memberships in National Parks Association, The Mountaineers, Appalachian Mountain Club, and Sierra Club; and awards from California Conservation Council (1953), National Parks Association (1956), Carey-Thomas Award (1964), Paul Bartsch Award (1967), and John Muir Award of the Sierra Club (1977). Is principal subject of *Encounters with the Archdruid* (John McPhee, 1971).

DAVID R. BROWER

David R. Brower, Environmental Activist, Publicist, and Prophet; oral history, Bancroft Library, University of California, 1980.

Who's Who in America, 42d edition, 1982–83.

Sierra Club Handbook, 1967.

Who's Who in the West, 1968.

BROWN, CARL BARRIER
(1910–1963)
Born November 12 in Salisbury, North Carolina. University of North Carolina, B.S. 1929; University of Cincinnati, M.A. (geology) 1931. Was assistant geologist with Virginia Geological Survey, 1931–32; surveyor in Bureau of Chemistry and Soils, U.S. Department of Agriculture, 1932–33; and junior geologist with U.S. Geological Survey, U.S. Department of the Interior, 1934. Joining U.S. Soil Conservation Service in 1934, was successively junior engineer, assistant engineer, associate geologist, geologist, senior soil conservationist, and research specialist (sedimentation). From 1950 until his death, served as assistant chief of operations, director of Planning Division, and assistant to assistant administrator for watersheds. As one of principal architects of legislation that gave life to small watershed idea, he was for several years in charge of the agency's sedimentation research. After passage of Flood Control Act of 1936, concentrated on watershed protection problems, and was instrumental in development of small watershed conservation techniques. Was consultant to the secretary of Agriculture, Bureau of the Budget, and congressional committees during planning and drafting of legislation that became Small Watershed Protection and Flood Prevention Act of 1954; after its enactment, was one of its leading implementers. In recognition of his work in 1959, received Superior Service Award of U.S. Department of Agriculture. Was author of *The Control of Reservoir Silting*, a Department of Agriculture publication, and wrote seventy-five other papers on sedimentation, watershed protection, soil conservation, water supply, flood prevention, and geology. Was member of World Bank Agricultural Mission of Japan in 1954, and of American Society of Civil Engineers, American Geophysical Union, and Soil Conservation Society of America. Died May 5, 1963.

F. GLENNON LOYD

Who's Who in Engineering, 8th ed., 1959.

BROWN, CLAUDEUS JETHRO DANIELS
(1904–1979)
Born August 15 at Farr West, Utah. Brigham Young University B.S., M.S. (zoology); University of Michigan, Ph.D. (limnology) 1933. Conducted fisheries surveys in Utah, Washington, and Oregon in 1934–35 for U.S. Bureau of Fisheries; served as instructor in zoology, Montana State Uni-

versity, 1935–37; and was assistant director of Institute for Fisheries Research, Michigan Department of Conservation, 1937–44, his principal responsibilities being day-to-day operation of the institute and supervision of lake and stream surveys. During 1944–45 served as chief of Technical Section of the Washington State Pollution Commission; and was in charge of reservoir investigations in Portland, Oregon, office of U.S. Fish and Wildlife Service, 1945–47. While on zoology faculty at Montana State University, organized curriculum in fish and wildlife management, conducted in-service training courses for fish and game personnel in Montana and Wyoming, and directed research for fifty-six master's and fourteen doctoral students, as well as writing a book, *The Fishes of Montana*. On leave from Montana State, served with Food and Agriculture Organization of the United Nations in Paraguay, 1956–57, and with Ford Foundation in Egypt, 1963–64 and 1966. Retired as emeritus professor in 1972. Served as executive secretary, editor, and president of American Microscopical Society; as president of American Fisheries Society; and on editorial board of American Society of Limnology and Oceanography. Was charter member of The Wildlife Society; a fellow of American Institute of Fishery Research Biologists; a member of Fisheries Society of British Isles; and member of numerous other professional societies. Was author of more than fifty papers in fisheries and limnology. His broad experience in research, academia, and with state and federal fisheries agencies made him especially effective in the training of fisheries biologists. Died December 18, 1979, in Prescott, Arizona.

JOHN L. FUNK
ROBERT F. HUTTON

American Men and Women of Science (Physical and Biological Sciences), 14th
  ed., 1979.

BROWN, JANET WELSH
(born 1931)
Born September 20 in Albany, New York. Smith College, B.A. (government) magna cum laude and Phi Beta Kappa, 1953; Fulbright Award (Burma) 1953–54; Ford Fellowship for Graduate Studies 1954–55; Yale University, M.A. (southeastern Asian studies) 1955; New York University, graduate studies (government and public administration) 1955–58; The American University, Ph.D. (international relations and organization) 1964. Was faculty member in Social Science Division of Sarah Law-

rence College, 1956–58; professor of political science and international relations at Federal City College (now University of the District of Columbia), 1958–73, serving as department chairperson, 1969–70 and 1973; assistant professor of government at Howard University, 1964–68; director, Office of Opportunities in Science, American Association for the Advancement of Science, 1973–79; and executive director of Environmental Defense Fund, 1979 to 1984. Has been principal investigator on several research projects for National Science Foundation and National Institutes of Health, and has served on various boards and in many advisory positions. Was commissioner, Scientific Manpower Commission, 1973–79, and president, 1975–76; member of executive council of Federation of Organizations of Professional Women, 1974–77; and member of editorial board, *Science 80, 81,* and *82.* Current responsibilities include service on boards of Independent Sector of Urban Environment Conference (co-chair) and of League of Conservation Voters.

Louis S. Clapper

Brown, Lester Russell
(born 1934)
Born March 28 in Bridgeton, New Jersey. Rutgers University, B.S. (agricultural science) 1955; University of Maryland, M.S. (agricultural economics) 1959; Harvard University, M.P.A. 1962. Entered U.S. Department of Agriculture in 1959 as agricultural analyst, and joined the secretary's staff in 1964 as his advisor on foreign agricultural policy. Was administrator of International Agricultural Development Service, 1966–69; and a senior fellow with Overseas Development Council, 1969–74. Since 1974 has been president of and senior researcher with Worldwatch Institute. Is author of *Man, Land and Food,* 1963; *Seeds of Change,* 1970; *World Without Borders,* 1972; *In the Human Interest,* 1974; *By Bread Alone,* 1974; *The Twenty-Ninth Day,* 1978; *Building a Sustainable Society,* 1981; and numerous Worldwatch papers on food, population, economic, and resource issues. Received Arthur S. Flemming Award, 1965, as "one of ten outstanding young men in the federal government"; U.S. Department of Agriculture's Senior Service Award, 1965; Christopher Award, 1980, for *By Bread Alone;* Ecologia Firenze Prize, 1981, for *The Twenty-Ninth Day;* A. H. Boerma Award; and Special Conservation Award, 1981, from The National Wildlife Federation; also was selected in 1966 by U.S. Jaycees as one of "ten outstanding young

men in America." Is member of Council on Foreign Relations; U.S. Committee for UNICEF; and board of directors of Overseas Development Council.

American Men and Women of Science (Physical and Biological Sciences), 15th ed., 1982.

Who's Who in America, 42d ed., 1982–83.

BROWN, WILLIAM Y.
(born 1948)
Born August 13 in Artesia, California. University of Virginia, B.A. (biology) 1969; Johns Hopkins University, M.A.T. 1970; University of Hawaii, Ph.D. (zoology) 1973; Harvard University Law School, J.D. 1977. While a graduate fellow of National Science Foundation at University of Hawaii, 1971–73, studied ecology of sooty tern and brown noddy on Rabbit Island near Oahu. Was assistant professor of biological sciences at Mount Holyoke College, 1973–74; and worked for Environmental Protection Agency, 1974; Council on Environmental Quality, 1975; and U.S. Fish and Wildlife Service, 1976–77. Was executive secretary of federal interagency Endangered Species Scientific Authority, 1977–81; and has been senior scientist in wildlife program of Environmental Defense Fund since 1981. Is actively involved in acid rain studies, wetlands protection, endangered species preservation, Antarctic conservation, and other conservation issues. Serves on U.S. Department of State's Antarctic Advisory Committee; federal Ad Hoc Scientific Group on Antarctica; and official U.S. Delegation to meetings of parties to Convention on the Conservation of Antarctic Marine Living Resources. Has written extensively on zoology and conservation in various scientific journals, books, periodicals, and conference proceedings.

ENVIRONMENTAL DEFENSE FUND

BROWNING, BRYCE COGSIL
(born 1894)
Born June 19 in Adamsville, Ohio. Was educated at Muskingum College, LL.D. His career in conservation began in 1927 with his appointment as manager of Zanesville, Ohio, Chamber of Commerce, which, under his

leadership, undertook campaign to establish Muskingum Watershed Conservancy District. The conservancy's proposal went beyond conventional flood-control projects; it incorporated concepts of total watershed protection, and multiple uses of reservoirs with emphasis on soil conservation, forestry, and public recreation. When Conservancy District was established near New Philadelphia, Ohio, June 3, 1933, he was appointed its secretary-treasurer. During his incumbency, the cooperative federal-state-local undertaking involved sixty thousand acres in eighteen counties and had attained international recognition. Before retiring in 1965 he had been active in other national and regional conservation bodies. Is a former director and honorary life member of The American Forestry Association; past president of Ohio Forestry Association; and honorary life member of Soil Conservation Society of America. Served as member of Ohio Natural Resources Commission, 1949–58, then held four-year membership on Ohio Water Commission. In 1949 received The American Forestry Association's award for public service in conservation; in 1956, Friends of the Land awarded him Hugh Bennett gold medal for conservation service; and in 1958 received Ohio Farm Bureau agricultural service award, and award of recognition by Ohio Forestry Association. On December 14, 1968, became first living person to be installed as member of Ohio Conservation Hall of Fame.

JOSEPH W. PENFOLD

BROWNING, GEORGE MONROE
(born 1908)

Born December 4 in Verona, Missouri. University of Missouri, B.S. (agriculture) 1932; University of West Virginia, M.S. (agriculture) 1934; Ph.D. (soils) 1938. From 1934 to 1935 was soil scientist in West Virginia for U.S. Soil Erosion Service. In 1935 became soil conservationist for U.S. Soil Conservation Service, in charge of soil and water conservation research, serving first in West Virginia, then shifting to Iowa in 1941. Joined Iowa State University staff in 1947 as research professor of soils; was advanced to assistant director of Agricultural Experiment Station in 1949 and to associate director in 1951. In 1967 was appointed regional director of Association of North Central Agricultural Experiment Stations. Is author of more than fifty technical articles and bulletins dealing with soil structure, tillage, soil and water-loss measurements, and other phases of soil and water conservation. Is recognized for his leadership in development of soil erosion factors used universally for estimating run-off and erosion. In 1958 represented state agricultural experiment stations in study of national soil and water conservation research needs. In 1965 was co-chairman of joint U.S. Department of Agriculture–State Agricultural Experiment Station task force, which prepared report evaluating and projecting agricultural research needs for the decade ahead. Report was submitted to and approved by Congress. Is charter member and fellow of Soil Conservation Society of America, of which he was president, 1963–64; a fellow of American Society of Agronomy; and member of Soil Science Society of America.

FRANK W. SCHALLER

American Men of Science (Physical and Biological Sciences), 11th ed., 1965.

Who's Who in America, 37th ed., 1972–73.

BRUCE, DONALD
(1884–1966)
Born July 23 in Newtonville, Massachusetts. Yale University, M.F. 1910. Served five years with U.S. Forest Service in Montana, starting as forest assistant and advancing to forest supervisor. Spent six years as assistant and associate professor of forestry at University of California. After serving in France during World War I as captain on staff of Tenth Engineers, spent seven years as part-time consultant with Forest Service in Washington, D.C., in charge of forest measurements for purpose of improving methods of forest-mensuration research and in training promising research foresters. From 1923 until his death, was partner in consulting firm Mason and Stevens (now Mason, Bruce and Girard). When firm was known as Mason and Stevens, he was in charge of branch office in Washington, D.C. His sound advice and assistance to industrial forest owners in pine regions of western United States in combining selective cutting practices with profitable utilization methods was important contribution to conservation. Is author of numerous Forest Service bulletins and articles in periodicals, and his best-known work, *Forest Mensuration*, written with F. X. Schumacher, has been standard college textbook since 1935. With James W. Girard, wrote *Board Foot Volume Tables for Sixteen-Foot Logs*, *Board Foot Volume Tables for Thirty-Two-Foot Logs*, and *Board Foot Volume Tables Based on Total Height*, standard references known to all professional foresters. In 1961 published *Prism Cruis-*

ing in Western United States and Use Thereof. Died October 16, 1966.

CARL A. NEWPORT

American Men of Science (Physical and Biological Sciences), 11th ed., 1955.

BUCHHEISTER, CARL WILLIAM
(born 1901)

Born January 20 in Baltimore, Maryland. Johns Hopkins University, B.A. 1923; Pace College, LL.D.; Bowdoin College, L.H.D. Beginning in 1925 taught in private schools in Baltimore and Long Island, New York, and was also for eight years founder-director of boys' camp in New Hampshire. From 1936 to 1939 was executive director of Massachusetts Audubon Society, and beginning in 1936 was for two decades director of Audubon Camp of Maine, a summer workshop for teachers and adult leaders. In 1940 was appointed assistant director of National Audubon Society, New York City; was advanced to senior vice-president in 1959; and retired in 1966 as president emeritus. Active in other ornithological and conservation organizations, he has been on board of directors of Audubon Society of Canada; was honorary vice-president of The American Forestry Association in 1963; was member of Citizens Committee for Outdoor Recreation Resources Review Commission; was chairman of Natural Resources Council of America, 1964–66; is on board of directors of National Parks and Conservation Association and of Wildfowl Foundation, Inc.; and is honorary director of The Student Conservation Association. Received Distinguished Service Award of The American Forestry Association (1973); Award of Honor of Natural Resources Council of America (1979); and Frances K. Hutchinson Medal of The Garden Club of America (1980). The Carl W. Buchheister National Bird Garden was dedicated at National Arboretum, Washington, D.C., in 1982. Is lifelong field naturalist who has written extensively for *Audubon* magazine and other conservation publications, and is popular lecturer on nature subjects. His career has been notable for his ardent defense of wildlife and its environment, and for his effective exposition through public education of the national value of natural resources.

CARL W. BUCHHEISTER
HENRY CLEPPER

Who's Who in America, 37th ed., 1972–73.

BURNHAM, JOHN BIRD
(1869–1939)
Born March 16 in Newcastle, Delaware. Trinity College, Connecticut, B.A. 1891, D.Sc. (honorary) 1939. From 1891 to 1897 was business manager of *Forest and Stream Magazine* in New York City, resigning his position to join first Klondike gold rush. In 1898 purchased farm in Willsboro, New York, which he operated as Highlands Game Preserve. Early in 1905 was appointed chief game protector of state of New York, and three years later was named deputy commissioner of fish and game; in 1911 became acting commissioner. In that year, was selected by founders of American Game Protective and Propagation Association to become its first president. In 1915 was member of three-man committee selected to codify New York's fish and game law. One of first objectives of American Game Protection and Propagation Association was to secure enactment of strong federal law for protection of migratory birds. Became organizer of public support for such a law, which became reality with enactment of Weeks-McLean Act on March 4, 1913. Was named chairman of advisory committee to U.S. Department of Agriculture on Migratory Bird Law established by new law. When constitutionality of Weeks-McLean Act was challenged, he again led campaign to obtain ratification of Migratory Bird Treaty with Great Britain for Canada. Also served as chairman of U.S. Forest Service Committee on Game in National Forests, and was member of Committee on Game and Fur-bearing Animals of National Conference on Outdoor Recreation of 1924. In 1921 led expedition to Siberia to collect specimens of unclassified Marco Polo sheep for American museums. His book *The Rim of Mystery* is account of expedition. In 1926 was awarded gold medal of Camp Fire Club of America. Died September 24, 1939.

JAMES B. TREFETHEN

"John Bird Burnham, 1869–1939." *American Wildlife*, 28(6):244–46, November-December 1939.

Who Was Who in America, 1897–1942.

BURROUGHS, JOHN
(1837–1921)
Born April 3 near Roxbury, New York. Ashland Collegiate Institute and Cooperstown Seminary; Yale University, Litt.D. (honorary) 1910; Colgate University, L.H.D. 1911; University of Georgia, honorary docto-

rate, 1915. After teaching school for eight years was clerk in U.S. Department of Treasury, Washington, D.C., from 1863 to 1973. In 1874 bought farm at Esopus, New York, but continued as national bank examiner until 1884. Wrote many books and nature essays, published in nation's foremost literary journals. Through his writings, aroused wide public interest in natural world and ornithology in particular. Although not technically a biologist, he was accurate observer and contributed to scientific as well as popular information about flora and fauna of Hudson River Valley and Catskill Mountains. Had rare ability to express his love of nature in clear, poetic language, which met enthusiastic response in thousands of readers. Wrote twenty-seven books, among them: *Wake Robin*, 1871; *Winter Sunshine*, 1875; *Birds and Poets*, 1877; *Locusts and Wild Honey*, 1879; *Fresh Fields*, 1884; *Signs and Seasons*, 1886; *Indoor Studies*, 1889; *Walt Whitman: A Study*, 1896; *The Light of Day*, 1900; *John James Audubon*, 1902; *Literary Values*, 1904; *Ways of Nature*, 1905; *Camping and Tramping with Roosevelt*, 1907; *Leaf and Tendril*, 1908; and *The Summit of the Years*, 1913. Was elected member of American Academy of Arts and Letters. In 1926, John Burroughs medal was created in his honor to be awarded periodically by The American Museum of Natural History. Died March 29, 1921.

Eve Herbst

Chapman, Frank M. "John Burroughs," *Bird Lore*, vol. 23, no. 3.

Concise Dictionary of American Biography, 1964.

Dictionary of American Biography, 1929.

Fisher, Clyde. "With John Burroughs at Slabsides." *Natural History*, vol. 31, no. 5.

National Cyclopaedia of American Biography, 1:247–48, 1898.

Who Was Who in America, 1897–1942.

Wiley, Farida, ed. *John Burroughs' America: Selections from the Writings of the Hudson River Naturalist*.

BUTLER, OVID MCQUOT

(1880–1960)

Born July 14 in Indianapolis, Indiana. Butler University, B.A. 1902, D.Sc. (honorary) 1956; Yale Forest School, M.F. 1907. Entered U.S. Forest Service in 1907, assigned to Boise National Forest in Idaho and later to Ogden, Utah, district office, where he was assistant chief and chief of

Division of Forest Management. At outbreak of World War I, made investigations of lumber distribution with reports published by Forest Service; and in 1922 was named assistant director of Forest Products Laboratory in Madison, Wisconsin. In same year, was appointed forester by
The American Forestry Association; was executive secretary and editor,
1923–45; and was executive director emeritus from 1948 until his death.
As editor of *American Forests*, was one of nation's most influential exponents of forestry and resource conservation; the association was in
forefront of every national movement for improved resource management and development of parks and recreation. Was a fellow and president (1928) of Society of American Foresters; U.S. delegate to 1936
World Forestry Congress in Budapest; member of advisory board of National Arboretum; and member-at-large of National Council, Boy Scouts
of America. Was named in 1950 as "one of the ten most influential men
in American forestry"; and in 1952 received The American Forestry Association's Distinguished Service Award. Was author of hundreds of articles and editorials on forestry and conservation, and author-editor of
books *American Conservation, Rangers of the Shield,* and *Youth Re-
builds,* all published in 1935. Died February 20, 1960.

FRED E. HORNADAY

New York Times. Obituary, February 21, 1960.

BUTLER, WILLIAM A.
(born 1940)
Born December 10. Stanford University, B.A. 1963; Yale, J.D. 1969;
Harvard, Ph.D. 1971. From 1967 to 1970 was teaching assistant at Yale
and then worked as law clerk for several firms. Beginning in 1970, served
as general counsel and twice as acting executive director for Environmental Defense Fund. Currently is vice-president for government relations and counsel in charge of Washington, D.C., office for National Audubon Society. In addition to having legal training, is graduate biologist
and postgraduate ornithologist. His wide-ranging knowledge stood him
in good stead during protracted administrative proceedings that resulted
in rulings requiring U.S. Department of Agriculture and Environmental
Protection Agency to curb use of long-lasting hard pesticides DDT and
aldrin/dieldrin. For these efforts, was first winner of Resources Defense
Award presented by National Wildlife Federation. Is member of Admin-

istrative Conference of the U.S. and of various study panels for National Academy of Sciences.

LOUIS S. CLAPPER
PAUL C. PRITCHARD

CAHALANE, VICTOR HARRISON

(born 1901)

Born October 17 in Charlestown, New Hampshire. Massachusetts Agricultural College, B.S. (landscape gardening), 1924; Yale University, M.F. (forestry) 1927. During graduate studies at University of Michigan, also was instructor in School of Forestry and Conservation, followed by employment as deer investigator for Michigan Department of Conservation, 1929–30. From 1931 to 1934 was director of Cranbrook Institute of Science. In 1934 began his career in U.S. National Park Service as wildlife technician; became chief of Wildlife Division in 1939. When wildlife studies in national parks were transferred to U.S. Fish and Wildlife Service in 1940, he was put in charge of section on national park wildlife. In 1944 returned to National Park Service as chief of Biology Branch, a position he held until retirement in 1955. During his national park career, he was leader in pioneering and developing philosophy of habitat protection and management through ungulate population controls. At same time, contributed substantially to worldwide wildlife conservation through his active participation in International Union for the Conservation of Nature, as well as writing *Meeting the Mammals* and *Mammals of North America*. Participated in preparing *Fading Trails*, and conducted study and wrote *A Biological Survey of Katmai National Monument*. In 1955 became assistant director of New York Museum, and there continued his prolific writings, retiring from this position in January 1967. As extra-career contributions, served as first secretary of The Wildlife Society, 1937–39, and became its president in 1940. Served as advisor to National Parks Board of Trustees of the Union of South Africa in 1950–51; president of National Parks Association, 1959–60; president of Defenders of Wildlife, 1963–71; vice-chairman of American Committee for International Wildlife Protection, 1960–70; vice-president of Adirondack Mountain Club, 1962–68. Other publications include *National Parks, A World Need*; *The Imperial Collection of Audubon Animals*; *The Quadrupeds of North America* (editor), and *Alive in the Wild* (editor). Is currently member of New York State Forest Practice Board.

C. GORDON FREDINE

American Men and Women of Science (Physical and Biological Sciences), 12th ed. (vol. 1), 1971.

Who's Who in America, 39th ed., 1976–77.

CAIN, STANLEY ADAIR
(born 1902)
Born June 19 in Jefferson County, Indiana. Butler University, B.S. 1924; University of Chicago, M.S. 1927, Ph.D. (plant ecology) 1930; University of Montreal, Sc.D. (honorary) 1959. From instructor in botany at Butler University, advanced to associate professor; became assistant professor at Indiana University, and Waterman instructor from 1933 to 1935. At University of Tennessee, rose from assistant professor to professor. In 1940 was chosen a Guggenheim fellow. In 1945 was chief of science section at U.S. Army University in France, and from 1946 to 1950 was botanist at Cranbrook Institute of Science. Was professor of conservation at University of Michigan, and chairman of its Department of Conservation from 1950 to 1961. From 1965 to 1968 served as assistant secretary of U.S. Department of the Interior in charge of wildlife and national parks. Is currently on faculty of University of California, Santa Cruz. In 1938 held office of treasurer of Ecological Society of America; later became vice-president and president. Has served as member of advisory board of The Conservation Foundation, and was ecological expert on Technical Assistance Mission to Brazil for UNESCO in 1955. In 1956 was chairman of panel on environmental biology for National Science Foundation. Three years later, was vice-president of International Botany Congress held in Canada, and in 1959 received distinguished achievement award from Michigan. Was member of Michigan Conservatory and served as its chairman. Was member and chairman of advisory board of National Parks, Historical Sites, Buildings, and Monuments; member of advisory board of U.S. Department of the Interior; and chairman of ad hoc committee of International Biological Program of National Academy of Science, 1963–64. Has served as secretary and as vice-president of American Association for the Advancement of Science. The Botanical Society of America presented him a certificate of

merit in 1956. Is author of many books and papers, including *A Manual of Vegetation Analysis* and *Plant Geography.*

THE CONSERVATION FOUNDATION

American Men and Women of Science (Physical and Biological Sciences), 14th ed., 1979.

Who's Who in America, 40th ed., 1978–79.

CALLISON, CHARLES HUGH
(born 1913)
Born November 6 in Alberta, Canada. University of Missouri School of Journalism, B.J. 1937. Started employment in 1937 as newspaperman in Kansas and Missouri; joined staff of Missouri Conservation Commission in 1941 as education and information specialist. After helping to establish the commission's magazine, *Missouri Conservationist,* became its editor. Resigned in 1946; was named executive secretary of Conservation Federation of Missouri, a league of sportsmen's and conservation organizations, and edited quarterly *Missouri Wildlife.* In 1951 was appointed to staff of National Wildlife Federation in Washington, D.C., serving from 1953 as secretary and director of conservation. There gained recognition as authority on federal and state laws and policies affecting natural resources. Was editor of information bulletin *Legislative News Service,* issued to the forty member organizations by Natural Resources Council of America, and from 1957 to 1959 was chairman of the council. In 1960 was appointed assistant to president of National Audubon Society in New York City, and in 1966 was elected as the society's executive vice-president, continuing as such until retiring in 1978. Contributes to "National Outlook," a current report on national and state conservation matters; to *Audubon* magazine, the society's bimonthly organ; and also serves on magazine's editorial board. In 1978 founded Public Lands Institute, which in 1981 became a division of Natural Resources Defense Council with Callison as its director. His official appointments to conservation bodies have included Advisory Committee on Fish and Wildlife of U.S. Department of the Interior; chairmanship of Legislative Committee of the International Association of Game, Fish and Conservation Commissioners; Federal Water Pollution Control Advisory Board; President Nixon's Task Force on Natural Resources and the Environment, 1968–69; and New York State Environmental Board. Has written

widely on conservation subjects, such as in the book *Man and Wildlife in Missouri*, a history of Missouri's Conservation Commission; is editor of *America's Natural Resources* (revised edition 1967), sponsored by Natural Resources Council of America.

CHARLES H. CALLISON
HENRY CLEPPER

Who's Who in America, 42d ed., 1982–83.

CARHART, ARTHUR HAWTHORNE
(1892–1978)
Born September 28 in Mapleton, Iowa. Iowa State College, B.S. (landscape engineering) 1916. Following service in U.S. Army during World War I, was employed in 1919 as recreation engineer by U.S. Forest Service and was assigned to Rocky Mountain District with headquarters in Denver. Made land-use studies and management plans for recreational development in national forests of Colorado, Minnesota, and elsewhere. Leaving Forest Service in 1922 for private practice in landscape architecture and city planning, returned to government employment in 1938 as first director of federal aid to wildlife restoration program in Colorado Game and Fish Department. During World War II was information specialist for Office of Price Administration in Denver. A prolific writer, he was author of hundreds of published articles and twenty-five books, including *Water or Your Life, Timber in Your Life, The National Forests, Planning for Wild Land Management, Fresh Water Fishing*, and *Hunting North American Deer*. His writings earned him award from Authors League; Founders Award of Izaak Walton League of America in 1956; Jade of Chiefs Award of the Outdoor Writers Association of America; and Distinguished Service Award of American Forest Products Industries, Inc. in 1964. Conceived and promoted establishment of Conservation Library Center of Denver Public Library and was its consultant since its creation in 1960 until his death. Died November 30, 1978.

JOSEPH W. PENFOLD

Who's Who in America, 1968–69.

CARLANDER, KENNETH DIXON
(born 1915)
Born May 25 in Gary, Indiana. University of Minnesota, B.A. 1936, M.S.

1938, Ph.D. 1943. Joined Minnesota Department of Conservation as aquatic biologist in 1938; resigned in 1946 (after two years' leave of absence for military service) to become assistant professor of zoology and leader of cooperative fishery research unit at Iowa State University. In years since, has guided upwards of one hundred graduates (thirty-three with doctorates) in fisheries science, many of whom hold important positions in government, industry, and education; was appointed Distinguished Professor in 1974. Under auspices of Ford Foundation, spent year (1965–66) helping to organize proposed Institute of Aquatic Resources associated with University of Alexandria, United Arab Republic. In 1978 assisted Satya Wacana Christian University in Salatiga, Java, Indonesia, in fisheries education and research. Active in affairs of his profession, he is member of more than twenty scientific and educational organizations, and has held offices in many of them. Editorially assisted seven scientific periodicals dealing with research in fisheries biology. Has served American Fisheries Society in numerous capacities, including president in 1961–62, for more than twenty-five years. The society gave him its Award of Excellence in 1979 and elected him honorary member in 1981. Was president of Iowa Academy of Science in 1980 and was made a Distinguished Fellow in 1980. Was author or coauthor of more than two hundred technical and semipopular articles in fields or ornithology, herpetology, and fisheries, and compiled *Handbook of Freshwater Fishery Biology* and *First Supplement*, 1950, 1953, 3d edition, vol. 1., 1968; vol. 2, 1977; vol. 3 in preparation. This prodigious work by one of America's foremost conservation educators is unquestionably the most comprehensive single-source document for information on biology of North American freshwater fishes.

KENNETH D. CARLANDER
JOSEPH H. KUTKUHN

American Men and Women of Science (Physical and Biological Sciences), 15th ed., 1982.

Who's Who in America, 42d ed., 1982–83.

Who's Who in the World, 5th ed., 1980–81.

World Who's Who in Science, 1968.

CARLTON, FRANK EBERLE
(born 1933)
Born October 31 in Jacksonville, Florida. Emory University, M.D. 1961.

Had urological residency at Massachusetts General Hospital. In 1973 founded National Coalition for Marine Conservation as national, non-profit activist organization committed to conservation of oceanic game fish, serving as first president (1973–83) and then as vice-chairman. The same year, organized and cofounded (with Christopher M. Weld) Marine Resources Conservation Foundation to develop centralized source of information on fisheries and marine affairs. Also in 1973 was appointed conservation/sport-fishing advisor to International Commission for the Conservation of Atlantic Tunas, and was appointed by President Gerald Ford as U.S. commissioner, 1975–83. From 1973 until 1977 was Georgia commissioner to Atlantic States Marine Fisheries Commission. Was appointed by the secretary of U.S. Department of Commerce to Marine Fisheries Advisory Committee in 1974, and served as vice-chairman and chairman of Recreational Fisheries Subcommittee; in 1975 was appointed by the secretary of U.S. Department of State to Fisheries Section of Ocean Affairs Advisory Committee. Was cofounder (with R. H. Stroud) of Marine Recreational Fisheries Symposium in 1976, serving as vice-chairman and then as chairman from 1977 to present. Was member of Atlantic Salmon Treaty Working Group in 1980, 1981, and 1982, negotiating international convention for conservation of Atlantic salmon. Following treaty ratification, was appointed by President Ronald Reagan as U.S. commissioner to North Atlantic Salmon Conservation Treaty Organization in 1983. Is former chairman of Conservation Committee of Savannah (Georgia) Sport Fishing Club, and is member and past chairman of advisory panel of South Atlantic Fishery Management Council. Is author of several papers on optimum yield in recreational fisheries management, fisheries legislation, and allocation of living marine resources.

KENNETH HINMAN

CARPENTER, FORREST ALMON
(born 1914)
Born November 27 in Wallowa, Oregon. Attended Oregon State College, 1931–32 and 1935–36. Was employed by U.S. Corps of Engineers on dam construction project, Fort Peck, Montana, 1936–37, and at Malheur National Wildlife Refuge, Burns, Oregon, 1937–41. After several months at Upper Mississippi River Wild Life and Fish Refuge, Winona, Minnesota, moved to Minneapolis regional office of U.S. Fish and Wild-

life Service as assistant regional refuge supervisor, 1941–58, except for brief periods from 1946 to 1948 with U.S. Navy during World War II, and as refuge manager, Des Lacs National Wildlife Refuge, Kenmare, North Dakota. Served as regional refuge supervisor of eleven-state Fish and Wildlife Service region, from 1958 until retiring in 1973. During nearly thirty-six years of federal employment, was associated with national wildlife refuge program, intimately participating in its development from infant organization to current world-renowned system. Did much of groundwork in developing policies and drafting legislation that govern refuge system. Played major role in selecting and training a corps of some four hundred refuge managers who are now leaders in management of nation's wildlife resources. After retirement, was instrumental in establishing nonprofit watchdog organization, National Wildlife Refuge Association. Has served continuously as president and executive officer, and as editor of organization's newsletter *Blue Goose Flyer*. Has been member of The Wildlife Society since 1946. Was awarded U.S. Department of the Interior Meritorious Service Award, and American Motors Corporation Conservation Award in 1979, and was named 1981 Alaska Conservationist of the Year by National Audubon Society.

CARSON, RACHEL LOUISE
(1907–1964)
Born May 27 in Springdale, Pennsylvania. Pennsylvania College for Women, B.A. 1929, D. Litt. (honorary) 1952; Johns Hopkins University, A.M. 1932; Oberlin College, D.Sc. (honorary) 1952; Drexel Institute of Technology, D. Litt. (honorary) 1952; Smith College, D. Litt. (honorary) 1953. In 1931 was employed as staff biologist at University of Maryland, and in 1936 was appointed aquatic biologist in Bureau of Fisheries, U.S. Department of the Interior. The bureau was merged with Biological Survey of U.S. Department of Agriculture to become U.S. Department of the Interior's Fish and Wildlife Service, for which she was designated editor-in-chief in 1949, and from which she resigned in 1952 to devote her remaining career to writing. In addition to her widely read contributions to periodical publications on biological, ecological, and conservation subjects, was author of *Under the Sea Wind*, 1941; *The Sea Around Us*, 1951; *The Edge of the Sea*, 1956; and her enormously popular *Silent Spring*, 1962. One of the leading authors on natural history of the present century, she probably had as much influence as any contemporary conservationist on developing concern by thinking Americans about

their environment. Her books have been published throughout world in many languages. *Silent Spring*, her best-known and most controversial work, documents massive injury to ecosystem caused by unwise use of pesticides. She urged not that pest control be abandoned, but that more research be undertaken to enable pesticides to be used safely and to find alternate techniques for pest control. The book finally alerted Americans to threats to their environment. For it and her previous writings, she was accorded many honors. In 1950, American Association for the Advancement of Science conferred on her its science writing award. In 1952 received John Burroughs medal from John Burroughs Memorial Association; Frances K. Hutchinson Medal of The Garden Club of America; Distinguished Service Award of U.S. Department of the Interior; and Henry G. Bryant gold medal of Geographical Society of Philadelphia. In addition, received Audubon Medal of National Audubon Society; gold medal of New York Zoological Society, conservationist of the year award of National Wildlife Federation in 1963; and other honors and citations, both literary and scientific. In 1969 Coastal Maine Refuge was named Rachel Carson National Wildlife Refuge by U.S. Department of the Interior. Died April 14, 1964.

NATIONAL AUDUBON SOCIETY

National Cyclopaedia of American Biography, 1960.

Who Was Who in America, 1961–68.

Who's Who of American Women, 1964–65.

CARY, AUSTIN F.
(1865–1936)
Born July 31 in East Machias, Maine. Bowdoin College, B.A. 1887, M.A. 1890, D.Sc. 1922; studied entomology and biology at Johns Hopkins and Princeton universities from 1888 to 1891. Taught at Bowdoin College, 1887–88, then worked as land crusier and topographical surveyor, and made entomological studies in Maine and New Hampshire. Some of his reports were published by state of Maine and by *Paper Trade Journal*. Made several trips abroad, usually to Germany, to study forestry practices. In 1898 was employed by Berlin Mills Company in New Hampshire, the first company forester in America, but was only partially successful in converting company to conservative cutting practices. Left to teach at Yale Forest School, 1904–5, and then at Harvard, 1905–9. In 1909 became superintendent of forests in New York State. In 1910 began

his long employment with U.S. Forest Service, until his retirement in 1935, and from 1917 worked wholly in the South. His official title was logging engineer, but he functioned as roving extension forester. A believer in individual enterprise, spent most of his time with private landowners, inducing them to manage their holdings with intention of producing continuous crops of timber. Was so successful in allying forestry practice with business that he was known as father of forestry in the South, and is remembered as one of most influential proponents of industrial forestry in this century. The present well-managed condition of many New England and southern woodlands is result of his teaching the possibilities of good forest practices through on-the-ground demonstrations and through articles, speeches, and letters. As author of numerous papers in trade journals and forestry magazines, wrote long-used *Manual for Northern Woodsman*, 1909. Died April 28, 1936.

DAVID C. SMITH

Hewyard, Frank. "Austin Cary, Yankee Peddler in Forestry." *American Forests*, June 1955.

Smith, David Clayton. *A History of Maine Lumbering*, 1860–1930. Doctoral Thesis, Cornell University, 1965.

White, Roy Ring. "Austin Cary, the Father of Southern Forestry." *Forest History*, vol. 5, no. 1 (Spring), 1961.

———. *Austin Cary and Forestry in the South*. Doctoral Thesis, University of Florida, 1961.

Who Was Who in America, 1897–1942.

CHAMBERS, CHARLES McKAY, JR.
(born 1941)
Born June 21 in Hampton, Virginia. University of Alabama, B.S. 1962, M.S. 1963, Ph.D. (physics) 1964; Harvard University, National Science Foundation Postdoctoral Fellow (mathematics) 1965; George Washington University, J.D. (with honors in administrative law) 1976, and postgraduate work in economics and management, 1976–77. Was aerospace engineer with National Aeronautics and Space Administration in Huntsville, Alabama, 1962–63; research and teaching associate in physics and then associate professor of mathematics at University of Alabama, 1963–69; director and treasurer of University Associates, Washington, D.C., 1969–72; and associate dean and professor at George Washington University, 1972–77. As associate dean of Office of Interdisciplinary Pro-

gram Planning and Development, conceived and implemented special master's degree programs in diverse areas, including oral biology, forensic pathology, and health-care administration. In 1977 joined Council on Postsecondary Accreditation, for which he served as general counsel and acting president. At the council much of his work involved liaison with Postsecondary Education Subcommittee of House Education and Labor Committee; Education, Arts, and Humanities Subcommittee of Senate Labor and Human Resources Committee; and U.S. Department of Education. Worked toward 1981 reauthorization of Higher Education Act and developed key amendments on accreditation contained in the act. Has published extensively on many topics and has been active in numerous scientific and academic societies. Became executive director of American Institute of Biological Sciences on June 1, 1983. Is currently (1983–84) president of American Association of University Administrators.

LOUIS S. CLAPPER

American Men and Women of Science (Physical and Biological Sciences), 15th ed., 1982.

CHAPLINE, WILLIAM RIDGELY, JR.
(born 1891)

Born January 10 in Lincoln, Nebraska. University of Nebraska, B.S. (forestry and agronomy) 1913. Joined U.S. Forest Service and studied range problems in western states, 1913–20; was headquartered in Washington, D.C., and became chief, Office of Grazing Studies, 1920–25, responsible for range investigations, surveys, and management-plan development and application. With passage of McSweeney-McNary Act in 1928, Division of Range Research was formed, including supervision of thirty full-time scientists stationed throughout United States. Duties included responsibility for planning, developing, directing, and coordinating range and associated watershed research of federal government. By 1946 wildlife considerations became important, and soon thereafter Division of Range Research became Division of Range and Wildlife Habitat Research. Cooperative investigations were expanded with U.S. Fish and Wildlife Service, state fish and game departments, and universities. Thus he was pioneer in range, watershed, and wildlife habitat research and first person to direct these activities under Forest Service Experiment Station program. Served during 1951–52 as executive secretary of organizing committee, U.S. Department of State, for Sixth International Grassland Congress. Retiring from Forest Service in 1952, established Section of Forest Conservation in Food and Agricultural Organization of the United Nations, Rome, Italy, involving global contacts and technical guidance in grazing, watershed management, and shifting cultivation. Served as professor in second international graduate pasture-management course in Uruguay in 1954. Range inspections followed in Argentina, Chile, and Peru, 1955. Was range-management consultant to government of Spain, 1956–57; and professor of range course for internationals at Colorado State University, 1967. For nineteen months in 1967–69, traveled to twenty-five countries (mainly in Africa, Asia, Australia, and New Zealand) for investigating and consulting under auspices of U.S. departments of State and Agriculture and of Food and Agricultural Organization of the United Nations. Has participated in seven International Grassland congresses, and ten other international conferences. Is author of numerous publications, articles, and technical reports, primarily in field of range research and management.

LLOYD W. SWIFT

American Men and Women of Science (Physical and Biological Sciences), 15th ed., 1982.

CHAPMAN, FRANK MICHLER
(1864–1945)
Born June 12 in Englewood, New Jersey. Attended Englewood Academy; Brown University, Sc.D. (honorary) 1913. Became self-educated in ornithology while employed in bank for six years; left bank to devote himself entirely to collecting and cataloging bird skins. In 1888 was appointed assistant to curator of ornithology and mammalogy of American Museum of Natural History in New York City, beginning fifty-four years of active service at the museum during which he advanced to associate curator in 1901, to curator of birds in 1908, and to chairman of bird department from 1920 until his retirement in 1942. As one of founders of National Audubon Society in 1905, served continuously on its board of directors for thirty-two years. In 1899 founded magazine *Bird Lore*, which he edited and published for thirty-six years, giving it to National Audubon Society in 1935 to be published subsequently, as it is today, as *Audubon*. Started traditional Christmas bird count, an annual survey of winter bird life still sponsored by Audubon Society. Is credited also with persuading President Theodore Roosevelt to issue proclamation in 1903

that set aside Pelican Island in Florida as first federal bird reservation, thus starting national wildlife refuge system. Active in American Ornithologists' Union, he was president in 1911 and was elected a fellow. For his literary and scientific contributions to ornithology, was elected to National Academy of Sciences, and was recipient of the academy's Elliot medal in 1918. In addition, received first award of Linnaean medal by Linnaean Society of New York in 1912; medal of Theodore Roosevelt Memorial Association in 1928; and John Burroughs medal of The American Museum of Natural History in 1929. Was author of 225 articles in periodicals, and also wrote seventeen books, among most important of which were *Handbook of Birds of Eastern North America*, 1895 and subsequent editions; *The Distribution of Bird Life in Columbia*, 1917; *The Distribution of Bird Life in Ecuador*, 1926; and *Autobiography of a Bird Lover*, 1933. Died November 15, 1945.

CHARLES H. CALLISON

Auk, 67:307–15, July 1950.

National Academy of Sciences Biographical Memoirs, 25:111–45, 1948.

National Cyclopaedia of American Biography, 1950.

Twentieth Century Authors. New York: H. W. Wilson Company, 1942 (and 1st supplement, 1955).

Who Was Who in America, 1943–50.

CHAPMAN, HERMAN HAUPT
(1874–1963)

Born October 8 in Cambridge, Massachusetts. University of Minnesota B.S. 1896, B.Agr. 1899, D.Sc. 1947; Yale University M.F. 1904. While superintendent of Minnesota Agricultural Experiment Station at Grand Rapids, 1898–1903, helped obtain passage of Morris Act of 1902, which started system of national forests in Minnesota. After two years as forest assistant in Forest Service, 1904–5, was appointed instructor at Yale School of Forestry; in 1911 was named Harriman professor of forestry, the position he filled with distinction for three decades. From 1917 to 1919 was on leave of absence with Southwestern Region of the Forest Service; and in 1927–28 conducted field studies in Lake States for Forest Taxation Inquiry. For many years was director of The American Forestry Association. In 1922 was elected a fellow of Society of American Foresters; served as president, 1934–37; and in 1948 was awarded Sir William

Schlich memorial medal for outstanding service to forestry. Was first chairman of the Society's Committee on Accrediting Schools of Forestry, which in 1937 established bases for accreditation of professional forestry education. Later, was chairman of the Society's Committee on Ethics, which drafted canons of professional ethics adopted in 1948. A prolific writer, he was author of textbooks on forest finance, management, mensuration, and valuation. In addition, wrote numerous bulletins and hundreds of periodical articles on forestry. On his retirement from his Yale professorship, was consultant in forest management and policy, and continued working for advancement of forestry. For half-century was one of most influential foresters in America. Died July 13, 1963.

HENRY CLEPPER

American Men of Science (Physical and Biological Sciences), 10th ed., 1960.

"Chapman Retires." *Journal of Forestry.* September 1943.

"Herman Haupt Chapman Retires," *Yale Forest School News,* July 1943.

CHEPIL, WILLIAM STEPHAN
(1904–1963)
Born January 1 in Gimli, Manitoba, Canada. University of Saskatchewan, B.S.A. 1930, M.S. 1932; University of Minnesota, Ph.D. 1940. Was officer in charge, Dominion Substation, Regina, Saskatchewan, from 1931 to 1936. In 1936 was apppointed agricultural scientist at Dominion Soil Research Laboratory at Swift Current, Saskatchewan, where he studied mechanics of wind erosion and developed methods and equipment (including laboratory and portable wind tunnels and rotary sieves) for studying wind erosion and soils. In 1946 began assignment as soil reclamation specialist with United Nations Relief and Rehabilitation Administration Mission to China, for which he received meritorious service citation from Chinese government. In 1948 became professor of soils at Kansas State College and soil scientist, Agricultural Research Service, U.S. Department of Agriculture, on soil-erosion project. In 1953 was made officer in charge of soil-erosion research in Manhattan, Kansas, and in 1961 was appointed research investigations leader for soil erosion in Southern Plains Branch of Soil and Water Conservation Research Division of Agricultural Research Service. Regarded as world authority on wind erosion and its control, he has had his research reported in more than one hundred scientific publications. With his associates, developed universal wind-erosion equation to determine erodibility of fields and,

conversely, requirements for reducing erosion. Also developed wind-erosion climatic factor for United States and method of predicting dust storms and wind-erosion potential. Was elected a fellow of American Society of Agronomy in 1962. Died September 6, 1963.

ORVILLE W. BIDWELL

American Men of Science (Physical and Biological Sciences), 10th ed., 1960.

CLAPP, EARLE HART
(1877–1970)
Born October 15 in North Rush, New York. Cornell University, 1902–3; University of Michigan, B.A. (forestry) 1905, Sc.D. (honorary) 1928. Joined U.S. Forest Service as forest assistant in 1905. Was in charge of forest management, 1907–8; and was associate district forester, Southwestern District, 1908–11; forest inspector (silviculture), 1911–15; assistant chief in charge of research, 1915–35; associate chief, 1935–39; and acting chief, 1940–42. Retired in 1945 after four decades of service. Was appointed Forest Service representative to Agricultural War Board in 1941. In 1930 was elected a fellow of Society of American Foresters, and in 1960 was awarded its council's Gifford Pinchot Medal for distinguished service to forestry. Was author of many government and scientific publications, particularly the report published by American Tree Association in 1926, *A National Program of Forest Research*, which provided basis for McSweeney-McNary Act of 1928 and thus broadened scope of forestry research in America. Was editorial director of monumental Copeland report, *A National Plan for American Forestry*, issued by Senate in 1933. During his career, was advocate of acquisition of private forestlands by public agencies and of regulation of private forest management by federal and state governments. Was principal architect of Forest Service's nationwide system of forest experiment stations and of its forestry research policy. Died July 1, 1970.

HENRY CLEPPER

American Men of Science (Physical and Biological Sciences), 11th ed., 1965.

CLAPPER, LOUIS SHIRLEY
(born 1916)
Born November 10 in Saint Louis, Missouri. University of Missouri

School of Journalism, B.J. 1938. His professional career began in 1938 with employment on sport staff of *Kansas City Journal* writing weekly hunting and fishing column. After serving in U.S. Navy during World War II, became coeditor and publisher of *Donelson* (Tennessee)) *Diary*, a suburban weekly newspaper. When Tennessee Game and Fish Commission was set up under new model law in 1949, became its first public-relations officer; subsequently developed the commission's information-education program, became assistant director, and for two extended periods served as acting director. During latter period, was coeditor of *Tennessee Conservationist* magazine, and wrote news releases, including column "Outdoors in Tennessee." Served from 1952 to 1954 as secre-tary-treasurer of forerunner of American Association for Conservation Information and is honorary life member of that organization. Also was secretary-treasurer of National Water Safety Congress, 1956–58, and served in similar capacity for Tennessee Outdoor Writers Association for several years. In April 1958 joined Washington, D.C., staff of National Wildlife Federation and served as conservation director, responsible for the organization's liaison with Congress and executive-branch agencies, and for publication of *Conservation News* and *Conservation Report*. From origins of *National Wildlife* magazine in 1962 and of *International Wildlife* magazine in 1971, served as Washington editor and contributed "Washington Reports" to each. At retirement in 1982 was vice-president for national affairs, in charge of the federation's international program. Long edited Natural Resources Council of America's *Legislative News Service* and contributed to its *Executive News Service*. Served on Presi-dent's Water Pollution Control Advisory Board and on U.S. National Commission for UNESCO. Has received awards or citations from Na-tional Association of Conservation Education and Publicity (1951), American Association of Conservation Information (1957), Water Safety Congress (1958), Tennessee Game and Fish Commission (1958), Sport Fishing Institute (1966), Izaak Walton League of America (1970), Inter-national Association of Fish and Wildlife Agencies (1981), The Wildlife Society (1982), and Gulf Oil Corporation (1983). Served Natural Re-sources Council of America as member of executive committee, vice-chairman, and chairman (1979–81), and has served as executive secre-tary since January 1982.

Louis S. Clapper
Thomas L. Kimball

CLARK, WILSON FARNSWORTH
(born 1921)
Born February 25 in Schenectady, New York. Middlebury College, B.A. 1942; Cornell University, Ph.D. (conservation education) 1949. Was research chemist on Manhattan (A-bomb) project, 1945–47, and extension wildlife conservationist, Extension Service, Cornell University, 1949–54. Subsequently joined faculty of Eastern Montana College, Billings, and remained there until retiring in 1981. Then joined staff of Custer National Forest as writer, editor, historian, and environmental-education specialist, 1981 to present. Has served on numerous resource-related boards, among them Montana State Advisory Board, Bureau of Land Management (1968–75), Montana State Board of Natural Resources and Conservation (1973–80), board of governors, Pinchot Institute for Conservation Studies (1964–68), and editorial review board, *Journal of Environmental Education* (1963–80). Has been heavily involved in numerous professional and citizens' organizations, among them Conservation Education Association (1954–80), Montana Conservation Council (1954–75), and Soil Conservation Society Education Committee (1968–72). Was founder and director of Billings Public Schools' Environmental Education Program "Exploring the World," which operated sixth-grade program successfully for ten years (1966–75) and earned national award. Has written numerous articles on environmental education for various journals, bulletins, and newsletters, and has two books to his credit. Also has received several distinguished achievement awards, among them awards from Montana Association of Soil Conservation Districts, 1966; Rocky Mountain Center on Environment, 1975; Bureau of Land management, 1975; Montana State Board of Natural Resources, 1980; and Distinguished Professor Award for Community Services from Eastern Montana College, 1979.

JUNE McSWAIN

American Men and Women of Science (Physical and Biological Sciences), 14th
ed., 1979.

CLAWSON, MARION
(born 1905)
Born August 10 in Elko, Nevada. University of Nevada, B.S. (agriculture) 1926, M.S. 1929; Harvard University, Ph.D. (economics) 1943. Worked for nearly twenty-four years in service of U.S. government, beginning in

Bureau of Agricultural Economics, U.S. Department of Agriculture, from 1929 to 1946, directing extensive studies of agricultural development on major irrigation projects. In 1947 was appointed regional administrator in Bureau of Land Management, U.S. Department of the Interior; was named director a year later and held directorship for five years, 1948–53. From 1953 to 1955 was economic consultant in Israel, and has been on assignments to Chile, India, the Middle East, Pakistan, and Venezuela. Since 1955 has fulfilled various roles, including acting president for Resources for the Future, Inc. Has studied intensively the effect of urban expansion on rural countryside. Was consultant to Ford Foundation in 1960 and 1962, and to Natural Resources Agency in California during 1964–65. In 1947 was vice-president and is currently a fellow of American Agricultural Economic Association; is charter member of Society for Range Management; and was executive secretary of Society for International Development, 1959–62, and vice-president, 1963–66. Is author, coauthor, or editor of more than thirty books, among them *Western Range Livestock Industry*, 1950; *Uncle Sam's Acres*, 1951; *The Federal Lands*, 1957, and *Soil Conservation in Perspective*, 1965, both with Burnell Held; *Economics of Outdoor Recreation* (with Jack L. Knetsch), 1966; *Forests For Whom and For What?*, 1975; and *New Deal Planning: The National Resources Planning Board*, 1981.

MARION CLAWSON
HENRY CLEPPER

American Men of Science (Social and Behavioral Sciences), 11th ed., 1965.

Who's Who in America, 41st ed., 1980–81.

CLEMENT, ROLAND CHARLES
(born 1912)

Born November 22 in Fall River, Massachusetts. Studied wildlife management and forestry at Stockbridge School of Agriculture, University of Massachusetts; Brown University, B.A. 1949; Cornell University, M.S. (wildlife conservation) 1950. While serving with U.S. Air Force Weather Service during World War II, conducted investigations in ornithology and subarctic ecology in Labrador. Was executive secretary of Audubon Society of Rhode Island from 1950 to 1958. Joined staff of National Audubon Society, New York City, in 1958 to serve successively as membership director to 1962, as staff biologist to 1967, and vice-president from 1967 to 1977, when he retired. Was Audubon Society's spokesman during long chemical-insecticides controversy; served on U.S. Forest Service's advisory committee on California condor; was chairman of Corps of Engineers' environmental advisory board; was Western Hemisphere secretary for International Council for Bird Preservation; and was chairman of U.S. Department of the Interior Committee on Nongame Wildlife Policy. Has served as director of Environmental Defense Fund, World Wildlife Fund–U.S., and was awarded Richard King Mellon Fellowship at Yale University's School of Forestry and Environmental Studies, 1983. Is author of numerous articles for scientific and popular journals, and editor of *A Gathering of Shorebirds*, 1960; Was contributor to *Life Histories of North American Birds*, U.S. National Museum, and to W. E. Clyde Todd's *Birds of the Labrador Peninsula*.

CHARLES H. CALLISON
ROLAND C. CLEMENT

American Men and Women of Science (Physical and Biological Sciences), 14th ed., 1979.

CLEMENTS, FREDERIC EDWARD
(1874–1945)

Born September 16 in Lincoln, Nebraska. Educated in biological sciences at University of Nebraska, Ph.D. 1898, LL.D. 1940. During and following his graduate studies, held appointments at University of Nebraska, starting as assistant in botany and advancing to full professor of plant physiology. For ten years, starting in 1907, was head of Department of Botany, University of Minnesota. Thereafter was with Carnegie Institution until retiring in 1941. During this period directed research in origin of plant species by means of physical factors in their environment, primarily from field stations at Piles Peak in Colorado and Santa Barbara in California. After leaving Carnegie Institution his studies were continued from Santa Barbara with private funds. Was consultant and collaborator to several federal agencies, and active member of Botanical Society of America, American Association for the Advancement of Science (fellow), and many other professional societies. His writings were mainly in botany and ecology. His book *Plant Succession*, 1916, a basic work in ecology, has served as guide for foresters, soil scientists, and others in natural resources conservation. Was coauthor of *Plant Ecology*, 1929, with J. E. Weaver, and *Bio-ecology*, 1939, with Victor E. Shelford. His wife, as illustrator and assistant in investigations and publications, contributed to his work and to their effective scientific team. As noted botanist and ecologist, he was regarded as national and international authority in these fields. Died July 26, 1945.

LLOYD W. SWIFT

National Cyclopaedia of American Biography, 1948.

CLEPPER, HENRY EDWARD
(born 1901)
Born March 21 in Columbia, Pennsylvania. Pennsylvania State Forest Academy, Mont Alto (subsequently a unit of Pennsylvania State University), B.F. 1921. Entered Pennsylvania Department of Forests and Waters, in which he was employed for fifteen years, first as field forester and later as assistant chief of Bureau of Research and Education; then followed year as information specialist in Washington, D.C., office of U.S. Forest Service. In 1937 was appointed executive secretary of Society of American Foresters; except for two-year leave of absence with War Production Board during World War II, he served in this position and as managing editor of *Journal of Forestry* for twenty-eight years until his retirement in 1966. Helped establish the society's quarterly journal *Forest Science* in 1955 and research series "Forest Sciences Monographs" in 1959. Is author of more than one hundred articles and bulletins on forestry and related resources, many historical in nature. Was editor and coauthor of *Forestry Education in Pennsylvania*, 1957; coeditor and coauthor of *America's Natural Resources*, 1967; author of *American Forestry—Six Decades of Growth*, 1960; editor and coauthor of *Careers in Conservation*, 1963, 1979, and of *Origins of American Conservation*, 1966; coauthor of *The World of the Forest*, 1965; editor of *Leaders in American Conservation*, 1971; author of *Professional Forestry in the United States*, 1971, *Crusade for Conservation*, 1975, and *Famous and Historic Trees*, 1976; editor (with R. H. Stroud) of *Marine Recreational Fisheries*, 1976–81, of *Black Bass Biology and Management*, 1975, and of *Predator-Prey Systems in Fisheries Management*, 1979. From 1957 to 1965 was advisor to Forestry Committee of Food and Agricultural Organizations of the United Nations at the organization's biennial conferences in Rome. From 1970 through 1971 was consulting editor of American Fisheries Society, and during first quarter of 1972 was its acting executive secretary. Served as consulting editor to Sport Fishing Institute from 1974 to 1981. Is a fellow of Society of American Foresters, and in 1957

received its Gifford Pinchot Medal. Also received The American Forestry Association's John Aston Warder Medal and, in 1965, the award of American Forest Products Industries, Inc., for distinguished service to forestry.

HENRY CLEPPER
ARTHUR B. MEYER
RICHARD H. STROUD

Who's Who in America, 42d ed., 1982–83.

CLIFF, EDWARD PARLEY
(born 1909)
Born September 3 at Heber City, Utah. Utah State University, B.S. (forestry) 1931, D.Sc. (honorary) 1965. As career forester with U.S. Forest Service beginning in 1931, was assistant ranger, Wenatchee National Forest, Washington; in charge of wildlife management, Pacific Northwest Region, Portland, Oregon, from 1935; supervisor, Siskiyou and Fremont national forests in Oregon, 1939–44; assistant chief, Division of Range Management, Washington, D.C., 1944–46; assistant regional forester, Intermountain Region, Ogden, Utah, 1946–50; regional forester, Rocky Mountain Region Denver, 1950–52; assistant chief, Forest Service, 1952–62, and chief, 1962–72. After retiring from Forest Service, served as consultant to National Commission on Materials Policy, 1972–73, and as international forestry consultant (from 1973 to present) completed sixteen projects involving work and travel in United States and twenty-one countries in Latin America, Africa, Asia, Near East, and southern Europe. Is charter member of American Society of Range Management and The Wildlife Society, a fellow of Society of American Foresters, and member of The American Forestry Association, The Nature Conservancy, Forest History Society, International Society of Tropical Foresters, American Society of Landscape Architects (honorary), Boone and Crockett Club (emeritus), National Wildlife Federation (international associate), National Association of Civilian Conservation Corps Alumni, and National Arbor Day Foundation (honorary trustee). Was chairman, 1963–65 and 1970–71, of North American Forestry Commission of Food and Agriculture Organization of the United Nations; and head of U.S. delegation to Sixth World Forestry Congress in Madrid, 1966, vice-president of the congress, and member, U.S. delegation to Fifth, Seventh, and Eighth World Forestry congresses in Seattle, 1960,

Buenos Aires, 1972, and Jakarta, 1978. Received distinguished service awards from Utah State University in 1958, the U.S. Department of Agriculture in 1962, and Tuskegee Institute in 1970; Career Service Award from National Civil Service League in 1968; Outstanding Achievement Award from International Association of Fish, Game and Conservation Commissioners in 1972; Gifford Pinchot Medal from Society of American Foresters in 1973; and Bernhard Eduard Fernow Award from American Forestry Association in 1983.

EDWARD P. CLIFF
WILLIAM E. TOWELL

Who's Who in America, 40th ed., 1978–79.

CLUSEN, CHARLES M.
(born 1946)
Born October 11 in Manitowoc, Wisconsin. University of Michigan, B.S. (conservation) 1969, teaching fellowship in Department of Resource Planning and Conservation, 1969–70. In summers during college was employed with National Park Service and Montana Forest Service. Was project director for advanced-studies program in environmental and population education, and director of Division of Environmental and Population Affairs, Institute for the Study of Health and Society, Atlanta, Georgia, 1970–71. Was assistant to conservation director and to executive director, Sierra Club, 1971–72; subsequently served there as assistant conservation director, 1972–74; Washington, D.C., representative, 1974–76; and associate director, Washington, D.C., office, 1976–79. Has been conservation director of The Wilderness Society, 1979 to present, and was chairman of Alaska Coalition, which coordinated efforts leading to enactment of Alaska Lands bill, 1978–79. Is member of boards of American Rivers Conservation Council and River Conservation Fund; member of board, former co-chairman, and secretary-treasurer of Urban Environment Conference; member of board, former vice-chairman, and secretary-treasurer of Human Environment Center; and member of National Wildlife Refuge Study Task Force, U.S. Fish and Wildlife Service.

THE WILDERNESS SOCIETY

CLUSEN, RUTH CHICKERING
(born 1922)

Born June 11 in Bruce, Wisconsin. University of Wisconsin–Eau Claire, B.S. (education) 1945. As long-time advocate of global approach to environmental problem solving, served as U.S. delegate to US-USSR Joint Committee on Environmental Protection held in Moscow in 1974. Two years earlier, had participated in U.S. Conference on the Human Environment in Stockholm, which saw initiation of U.N. Environmental Programme. Her environmental work has also included acting as international environmental consultant under 1971 U.S. Department of State grant, and as environmental consultant to U.S. Department of the Interior, The Conservation Foundation, U.S. Chamber of Commerce, and Wisconsin Department of Natural Resources. Has served on board of Joint Center for Urban Environmental Studies and Environmental Protection Agency's Management Advisory Committee for the Municipal Construction Division. Chaired Environmental Quality Committee of League of Women Voters of the United States, 1966–74, and was president, 1974–78, when the league first sponsored presidential debates. Her work on the league's national board helped assure the group's continuing involvement with environmental issues. In 1978 was appointed assistant secretary for environment, U.S. Department of Energy. In 1977 Natural Resources Council of America awarded her its Award of Honor for outstanding work for better environment. In March 1978 was named International Conservationist of 1977 by National Wildlife Federation, and honorary member of Water Pollution Control Federation. Became honorary vice-president of The American Forestry Association in 1978, and won 1978 Distinguished Alumnus Award of American Association of State Colleges and Universities. Also holds honorary degrees from Colgate University, Wayne State University, St. Mary's College, and Northland College.

LEAGUE OF WOMEN VOTERS OF THE UNITED STATES

Notable Americans, 9th ed., 1976–77.
Who's Who in America, 42d ed., 1982–83.

COFFMAN, JOHN DANIEL
(1882–1973)

Born May 10 in Allentown, Pennsylvania. Yale University M.F. 1909. Entered U.S. Forest Service in California in July 1909 as forest assistant in Inyo and Shasta national forests; was promoted to deputy supervisor of Trinity National Forest in 1911; and advanced to supervisor of California (now Mendocino) National Forest in 1916. In 1928 transferred to National Park Service as fire-control expert, Berkeley, California, and in 1933 was assigned to Washington, D.C., headquarters, where he was named chief forester of newly created Branch of Forestry. Filled this position until his retirement in 1952, when he received Distinguished Service gold medal honor award of U.S. Department of the Interior. Returned to California as consulting forester in forest protection and recreational forestry. Was elected a fellow of Society of American Foresters in 1936, and served on the society's council, 1946–47. Died June 28, 1973.

HENRY CLEPPER

American Men of Science (Physical and Biological Sciences), 10th ed., 1960.

COLBY, WILLIAM EDWARD
(1875–1964)
Born May 28 in Benicia, California. Hastings College of Law, LL.B. 1898; University of California, LL.D. 1937; Mills College, LL.D. 1937. Specialized in mining and forest law; was lecturer on mines at Stanford University, and on mines and waters at University of California. Was associated with John Muir in battle over Yosemite Valley and Hetch Hetchy Dam. Initiated Sierra Club high trips in 1901, and led them until 1929, taking people into wilderness to learn for themselves the values they contained. Contributed substantially to saving Sierra redwoods, enlarging Sequoia National Park, and establishing Kings Canyon and Olympic national parks. Was first chairman of California State Park Commission, 1927–37; during his tenure, twelve million dollars was expended in purchase of more than fifty new parks for California State Park System, including Point Lobos Reserve, Calaveras Big Trees, Bull Creek Flat, and other outstanding redwood areas. Drafted forest-fire law for California. Conceived of idea for the 185–mile John Muir Trail, which runs from crest of Sierra Nevada to summit of Mount Whitney. Was author of articles on law of mines and mining. Wrote for Sierra Club *Bulletin* and was editor of *John Muir's Studies in the Sierra*. After retiring from forty-nine years on Sierra Club board, was made honorary president. The Colby Award, established in his name, is presented annually to Sierra Club member who has done outstanding conservation work for

the club. Was first to receive John Muir Award, set up in 1961 by Sierra Club. Was also member of American Alpine Club, Boone and Crockett Club, and Save-the-Redwoods League. Died November 9, 1964.

MICHAEL McCLOSKEY

Sierra Club Handbook, 1967.

Who Was Who in America, 1961–68.

COLLINGWOOD, GEORGE HARRIS
(1890–1958)

Born May 27 in Fayetteville, Arkansas. Michigan State College, B.S.F. 1911; University of Michigan, M.A. 1917. Was ranger for U.S. Forest Service in Arizona, 1911–12. Was appointed assistant extension professor of forestry in Cornell University College of Agriculture, 1916; resigned in 1923 to be extension forester for U.S. Department of Agriculture, and helped develop federal farm forestry extension program cooperatively with state colleges of agriculture. In 1928 was appointed forester for The American Forestry Association; for next twelve years directed the association's educational program cooperatively with federal and state agencies, forest industries, and private woodland owners. As eloquent speaker and persuasive writer, carried conservation message throughout America. In many appearances before congressional and state legislative committees, was recognized as informed spokesman for the public's interest in resources. In 1940 became chief forester for National Lumber Manufacturers Association, and helped establish industry-wide conservation program. Was forest products specialist for national housing agencies, 1946–47; research consultant to Hoover Commission in 1948; and research consultant to U.S. Chamber of Commerce, 1949. In that year was appointed to Library of Congress Legislative Reference Bureau as specialist in forestry and natural resources. Throughout his career, was one of best-known foresters in America; his knowledge of forestry policy and legislation was encyclopedic. Among his numerous writings, including bulletins and magazine articles, is popular book *Knowing Your Trees*, 1937. Was a fellow of American Association for the Advancement of Science and of Society of American Foresters. Died April 2, 1958.

HENRY CLEPPER

CONDRA, GEORGE EVERT
(1869–1958)
Born February 2 near Seymour, Iowa. University of Nebraska, B.S. 1896, M.A. and Ph.D. 1902. Was crusader in field of scientific investigation of natural resources and their utilization. As chairman of Nebraska Conservation Commission, participated in Joint Conservation Congress held in Washington, D.C., in December 1908. This congress gave marked impetus to developing conservation movement. Was organizer and director of Conservation and Survey Division of University of Nebraska, and also state geologist from 1918 to 1954. Was member of Nebraska State Soil Conservation Committee, serving as chairman and assisting in organization of Nebraska's Soil and Water Conservation Districts. In cooperation with U.S. Geological Survey, instituted program of groundwater investigation that is one of longest-running cooperative programs in any state. Scientific and professional organizations of which he was member included Geological Society of America, American Association of State Geologists, American Paleontological Association, American Soil Survey Association, Nebraska Academy of Science, Nebraska Reclamation and Nebraska Irrigation associations, and Permian Section International Geological Congress. Received Kiwanis Award for Distinguished Service in 1945. Was author of more than forty scientific publications and of textbooks *Geography of Nebraska* and *Geography and Agriculture of Nebraska*. Was early contributor to conservation movement. Died August 7, 1958.

ROBERT W. EIKLEBERRY
D. E. HUTCHINSON

CONNAUGHTON, CHARLES ARTHUR
(born 1908)
Born May 25 in Placerville, Idaho. University of Idaho, B.S. (forestry) 1928, Ph.D. (honorary) 1965; Yale University, M.F. 1934. Held increasingly responsible positions with U.S. Forest Service in administration, then silviculture and watershed management research, and became director of Rocky Mountain Forest and Range Experiment Station in 1936. Then served as director of Southern Forest Experiment Station, and in 1951 became regional forester of Southern Region with responsibilities for national forest management and state and private forestry programs. Held similar positions for California Region and Pacific Northwest Re-

gion. Retired from U.S. Forest Service in 1970. Is author of numerous articles and pamphlets on silviculture, watershed management, and multiple-use forestry, and has been frequent speaker at conferences and university commencements. Represented Society of American Foresters as visiting scientist lecturer in 1967–68, and has long been active with that organization, giving leadership in sections and committees, and serving as council member and president (1960–61). Was elected a fellow in 1959, and was awarded highest professional honor bestowed by the society, the Sir William Schlich Memorial Medal Award, in 1968. Has been director of The American Forestry Association since 1956, and became president in 1971. Has contributed much to advancement of conservation and forestry programs in technical and administrative fields. Of even greater long-term consequence has been his leadership in harmonizing and reconciling competitive uses of forested lands, and his ability to develop understanding among competing user interests. Among his greatest achievements was his leadership in raising of funds to establish permanent home for Society of American Foresters and headquarters for Renewable Natural Resources Foundation.

SOCIETY OF AMERICAN FORESTERS

American Men and Women of Science (Physical and Biological Sciences), 12th ed. (vol. 1), 1971.

Who's Who in America, 37th ed., 1972–73.

COOLIDGE, HAROLD JEFFERSON
(born 1904)
Born January 5 in Boston, Massachusetts. Harvard University, B.S. 1927; Cambridge University, 1927–28; George Washington University, Sc.D. (honorary) 1959; Seoul National University, Sc.D. (honorary) 1965; Brandeis University, Sc.D. (honorary) 1970. In 1926 was assistant zoologist for Harvard African expedition to Liberia and Belgian Congo. Two years later was assistant mammalogist and head of Indo-China division of Kelley-Roosevelt's Field Museum expedition. In 1929 became assistant curator of mammals, and in 1946 associate mammalogist, at Museum of Comparative Zoology at Harvard University. Has served both as secretary and chairman of American Committee for International Wildlife Protection. In 1937 was organizer and executive of Asiatic Primate expedition to Siam and Borneo. As executive director of Pacific Science Board of National Academy of Sciences–National Research

Council since 1946, he has helped to plan and organize various Pacific Science congresses, and was secretary-general of Tenth Congress in 1961. Was secretary of National Parks Association for thirteen years, collaborator with U.S. National Park Service, and director of World Wildlife Fund–U.S. In 1953 began consulting for Bernice Pauahi Bishop Museum in Honolulu, Hawaii. Has been active in International Union for Conservation of Nature and Natural Resources, serving as chairman of Survival Service Commission, International Committee on National Parks, and as president during 1966–72. In 1960 was presented Seventy-fifth Anniversary Medal of Merit by University of Arizona. Served as member of organizing committee of Sixteenth International Zoological Congress. In 1962 served as chairman for First World Conference on National Parks in Seattle. The Garden Club of America presented him the Frances K. Hutchinson Medal in 1963; New England Society in 1964 honored him with Reginald Townsend Award; and Smithsonian Institution gave him Browning Award in 1978. Received 1966 Conservation Award of African Safari Club of Washington. Has served on advisory council of Conservation Foundation, and is a fellow of New York Zoological Society. Is author of *A Revision of the Genus Gorilla*, *Three Kingdoms of Indo-China*, and *The Indo-China Forest Ox, or Kouprey*; also has written many scientific and conservation papers.

THE CONSERVATION FOUNDATION
HAROLD J. COOLIDGE

American Men and Women of Science (Physical and Biological Sciences), 14th ed., 1979.

Who's Who in America, 42d ed., 1982–83.

COOPER, TOBY
(born 1944)
Born October 8 in Los Angeles, California. University of Michigan, B.S. (biology/zoology) 1966; M.S. (zoology) 1969; Ph.D. candidacy (wildlife management) 1970 to present. Served on steering committee of Michigan's Teach-In on the Environment, 1970, and co-chaired ENACT, 1970. Was a founding board member of Ann Arbor Ecology Center. Joined faculty of Principia College as instructor in biology and environmental studies, 1971–72. Was six-month volunteer for demonstration organic farming project at University of California, Santa Cruz, 1972. Joined staff of National Parks and Conservation Association, 1973–75. Joined

staff of Defenders of Wildlife as wildlife programs coordinator in 1975; became programs director in 1977 and director of national issues in 1983. Authored numerous articles, staff reports, and columns of magazines *National Parks, Defenders, Frontiers, Backpacker,* and others.

DEFENDERS OF WILDLIFE

COOPER, WILLIAM SKINNER
(1884–1978)

Born August 25 in Detroit, Michigan. Alma College, B.S. (botany and ecology) 1906, D.Sc. (honorary) 1930; Johns Hopkins University, 1970; University of Chicago, Ph.D. 1911; University of Colorado, D.Sc. (honorary) 1961. Concurrent with his biological studies, developed intense interest and expertise in geomorphology, which later contributed greatly to his recognition of geology-vegetation relationships. Was lecturer in ecology at Stanford University, 1914–15; became instructor of botany at University of Minnesota in 1915, and advanced to professor. Retired in 1951 as emeritus professor of botany, but has continued active research on dunes and their associated vegetation. As member of numerous scientific expeditions to southern Alaska, played important role in having Glacier Bay set aside as national monument. Served as member of Committee on Preservation of Natural Conditions, National Research Council. Was vice-president in 1927, president in 1936, and named eminent ecologist in 1963 of Ecological Society of America. Was awarded Certificate of Merit by Botanical Society of America in 1956. Was author of numerous scientific papers and monographs in botany and geomorphology; one of his more important papers, *The Fundamentals of Vegetational Change,* 1926, was clear expression of his concept of vegetation dynamics, a concept now taken for granted by most ecologists. Died October 8, 1978, in Boulder, Colorado.

GEORGE SPRUGEL, JR.

American Men of Science (Physical and Biological Sciences), 11th ed., 1965.

Bulletin of the Ecological Society of America, vol. 44, no. 4, 1963; vol. 60, no. 1, 1979.

COTTAM, CLARENCE
(1899–1974)

Born January 1 in St. George, Utah. Brigham Young University, B.S.

(biology) 1926, M.S. 1927; George Washington University, Ph.D. 1936. After serving as instructor in biology at Brigham Young University, 1927–29, was junior biologist in Bureau of Biological Survey, U.S. Department of Agriculture, 1929–31; assistant biologist, 1931–35; and senior biologist in charge of food habits, Division of Wildlife Research, 1935–40. Also held latter position at U.S. Fish and Wildlife Service, 1940–42, and was in charge of economic wildlife investigations, Division of Wildlife Research, 1942–44; became assistant to the director, 1944; chief of Division of Wildlife Research, 1944–46; and assistant director, 1946–54. Was dean of College of Biological and Agricultural Sciences at Brigham Young University, 1954–55, and director, Welder Wildlife Foundation, from 1955 until his death. His awards include honorary award of Utah Academy of Sciences, Arts and Letters in 1948, and of Laval University in 1952; Aldo Leopold Award of The Wildlife Society in 1955; Distinguished Service Award in Conservation and Forestry of Utah State University in 1957; National Audubon Conservation Distinguished Service Medal in 1961; Poage Humanitarian Ward, Society of Animal Protection, 1962; Frances K. Hutchinson Medal of The Garden Club of America, 1962; and Paul Bartsch Award, Audubon Naturalist Society, 1962. Was president of The Wildlife Society, 1949–50; of Texas Ornithological Society in 1957; and of National Parks Association, 1960–63. Author of many scientific papers, he is possibly best known for his book *Food Habits of American Diving Ducks*, 1939, and for his consummate skill and effectiveness in championing environmental needs and wise use of natural resources. Died March 30, 1974.

GEORGE SPRUGEL, JR.
JAMES G. TEER

American Men of Science (Physical and Biological Sciences), 11th ed., 1965.

Who's Who in America, 38th ed., 1974–75.

COVILLE, FREDERICK VERNON
(1867–1937)

Born March 23 in Preston, Chenango County, New York. Cornell University, B.A. (botany) 1887. After graduation served briefly in geological survey of Arkansas, but returned to Cornell to teach botany until 1888. Thereafter his professional career was with U.S. Department of Agriculture, becoming botanist and also curator of National Herbarium. Was active in development of National Arboretum, and was acting director for a few years. His *Botany of the Death Valley Expedition*, published in 1893, is regarded as classic on desert vegetation. Was authority on American *Juncaceae*, and his publications on these grasslike plants were standard references. During his career pioneered in a number of areas, such as seed laboratory in U.S. Department of Agriculture; formulation of policy on grazing use on national forestlands; selection and breeding of commercial varieties of blueberries; and founding of Tucson, Arizona, desert botanical laboratory of Carnegie Institution. Was assigned to cooperative interagency effort with U.S. Department of the Interior in 1897, and in connection with grazing use of public lands has been credited with starting first sustained national movement toward range management. In 1898 began field appraisals in the Northwest, and as outgrowth of this work, was one of first to show that proper controls were needed. By 1904 had outlined proposed regulations, subsequently incorporated in grazing regulations for public lands. Was coauthor of 1923 edition of *Standardized Plant Names*. Was active in professional and scientific societies. Died January 9, 1937.

LLOYD W. SWIFT

National Cyclopaedia of American Biography, 1939.

Talbot, M. W., and Cronemiller, F. P. "Some Beginnings of Range Management." *Journal of Range Management*, vol. 14, March 1961.

COX, THOMAS RICHARD
(born 1933)
Born January 16 in Portland, Oregon. Oregon State University, B.S. 1955; University of Oregon, M.S. 1959, Ph.D. 1969. Following several years of high-school teaching, obtained summer appointments at University of Oregon and at Lewis and Clark College, 1966–70. Received full-time appointment at San Diego State University in 1967, and became professor of history in 1974. Served on board of directors of Forest History Society, 1974–82, and on editorial board of *Journal of Forest History*, 1972 to present; was its president 1978–80, and visiting scholar, 1979–80. Has been prolific writer in field of forest and conservation history, with topics ranging from lumber industry to state parks. His articles won Forest History Society's Blegen Award for excellence in 1974 and 1982. His most important work is *Mills and Markets: A His-*

tory of the Pacific Coast Lumber Industry to 1900 (1974), which won Emil and Kathleen Sick Award for Western history.

HAROLD K. STEEN

Who's Who in America, 42d ed., 1982–83.

COX, WILLIAM THOMAS
(1878–1961)
Born January 25 near Glenwood, Minnesota. University of Minnesota, B.S. (forestry) 1906. In 1901 became student assistant in U.S. Department of Agriculture's Bureau of Forestry, and forest assistant in 1905. In 1907 was promoted by Bureau of Forestry to rank of assistant forester in charge of silviculture and management. In 1911, at Minnesota Forestry Board's request, organized state's forest service and became Minnesota state forester until 1924. Was refuge manager, Upper Mississippi National Wild Life Refuge, 1925–28. Between 1929 and 1931 assisted Brazil in organizing its National Department of Forestry; also explored its Amazonian forests. From 1931 to 1933 was Minnesota's conservation commissioner. In 1935 became Federal Resettlement Administration's regional biologist for Minnesota and the four states surrounding it. Between these activities, worked as forestry and/or wildlife consultant to private owners of forest property. During World War II headed joint American-British Mission engaged in obtaining from South America supplies of balsa and mahogany needed by American Navy and Royal Air Force. From 1946 to 1959 wrote column entitled "Wild Animals of Field and Forest," which appeared in Saint Paul's biweekly newspaper, the *Farmer*, published by Webb Publishing Company. Was a fellow, Society of American Foresters; and author of *Biennial Reports*, Minnesota State Forest Service, 1912–22, *Wild Animals of Field and Forest*, and *Fearsome Creatures of the Lumberwoods*. In 1952 received National Association of Conservation, Education and Publicity's annual award for "meritorious service to state, national, and international progress." Died January 25, 1961.

J. H. ALLISON

CRAFTS, EDWARD CLAYTON
(1910–1980)

Born April 14 in Chicago, Illinois. Attended Dartmouth College; University of Michigan, B.S. (forestry) 1932, M.F. 1936, Ph.D. 1942, Sc.D. 1969. Was forest officer for twenty-nine years in U.S. Forest Service with assignments in Utah, Arizona, New Mexico, and California before moving to Washington in 1944; chief, Division of Forest Economics Research for number of years; and assistant chief in charge of program development, legislation, and congressional relations for ten years. Directed numerous policy studies including a five-year appraisal of nation's timber supply, which was published in 1958 as *Timber Resources for America's Future*. Was first director of Bureau of Outdoor Recreation, U.S. Department of the Interior, 1962–69. Was executive director of President's Council on Recreation and Natural Beauty; executive officer of Lewis and Clark Trail Commission; and secretary of the Interior's alternate representative on National Advisory Council on Historic Preservation and National Forest Preservation Commission. Served as chairman of federal interagency study team that explored all resource potentials of North Cascade Mountains to determine how these federal lands could best serve the public interest; the findings and recommendations for management and administration of the area appear in *North Cascades Study Report*, published in 1965. Received Distinguished Service Award of both Department of the Interior and U.S. Department of Agriculture, and Distinguished Service Award from American Institute of Park Executives. Was official representative to two World Forestry congresses and a fellow of Society of American Foresters. Died December 22, 1980.

WILLIAM E. TOWELL

Who's Who in America, 38th ed., 1974–75.

CRAIG, JAMES BARKLEY
(born 1912)

Born September 30 in West Hebron, Washington County, New York. Kent State University, B.A. 1936. Began his professional career as reporter on *Akron* (Ohio) *Times Press*, followed by similar experience on *Athens* (Ohio) *Messenger* and *Cumberland* (Maryland) *News*. Served in Pacific Area with Forty-first Infantry Division in World War II. Returned to newspaper work with *Cumberland Times* and became interested in conservation of natural resources. In 1947 became assistant editor of

American Forests, published by The American Forestry Association of Washington, D.C. In 1950 was named manager of New York City News Bureau of American Forest Industries, Inc. Returned to *American Forests* as editor in 1953, was elected secretary of The American Forestry Association in 1956, and retired in 1977. In 1960 was named to steering committee of National Watershed Congress and served as chairman of its award committee. As result of his extensive travels, has written hundreds of articles on conservation and more than 160 editorials, many of which have been reprinted in periodicals, in textbooks, and in *Congressional Record*. His courageous exposé of mining-claim abuses led to correction of situation in Multiple-Use Mining Act of 1955. The weight of his pen has been leveled impartially on fire bugs, grazers, lumbermen, litterbugs, and polluters whenever there was just cause. During his editorship, *American Forests* grew in readership and in coverage of entire range of natural resources. In 1959 was cited by Kent State University for distinguished service in his chosen field.

KENNETH B. POMEROY

International Authors and Writers Who's Who, 1976.

Who's Who in America, 39th ed., 1976–77.

CRAIGHEAD, FRANK COOPER, JR.

(born 1916)

Born August 14 in District of Columbia. Pennsylvania State University, B.A. 1939; University of Michigan M.S. 1940, Ph.D. 1950. Has held numerous positions, including with U.S. Forest Service, U.S. Fish and Wildlife Service, New York Zoological Society, National Geographic Society, and U.S. Department of Defense. Until his recent retirement, served for ten years as senior research associate at State University of New York at Albany. Currently is president of Craighead Environmental Research Institute in Moose, Wyoming. Though recognized as one of world's leading authorities on grizzly bear, he has studied variety of wildlife species and populations. Has written more than seventy-five popular and technical articles on natural resource subjects. Coauthored with his brother, John J. Craighead, *Hawks in the Hand* (1937), *How to Survive on Land and Sea* (1943), *A Field Guide to Rocky Mountain Wild Flowers* (1954), and *Hawks, Owls and Wildlife* (1956). Also wrote documentary book *Track of the Grizzly* (1979). He and his brother were first to use radiotracking and satellite biotelemetry techniques in wildlife research, and both were instrumental in initiating National Wild and Scenic Rivers System. They were subjects of two documentary films produced by National Geographic Society—*Grizzly* (1967) and *Wild River* (1970). Received citation from secretary of the Navy in 1947 for pioneering work in survival training. In 1970 received Pennsylvania State University Distinguished Alumnus Award, and was made the university's first alumni fellow in 1973. Was awarded National Geographic Society's John Oliver La Gorce gold medal in 1979 for his work in use of biotelemetry and UHF radio location using satellite technology in wildlife and wildlife-habitat management.

RICHARD E. MCCABE

CRAIGHEAD, JOHN JOHNSON
(born 1916)
Born August 14 in District of Columbia. Pennsylvania State University, B.A. 1939, University of Michigan M.S. 1940, Ph.D. 1950. Served in U.S. armed forces during World War II. Was free-lance wildlife researcher and writer early in his career. Assumed leadership of Montana Cooperative Wildlife Research Unit at University of Montana in 1952 and served in that capacity until his retirement in 1977. Is now professor emeritus of zoology and forestry at University of Montana, and director of privately funded Wildlife-Wildlands Institute, currently conducting research studies on wilderness habitat, raptors, grizzly/brown bear biology, satellite-tracking technology, and further development of techniques for mapping vegetation of large wilderness ecosystems using satellite multi-spectral imagery and computer analysis. At University of Montana, trained numerous graduate students specializing in population work on Canada geese, raptors, elk, and bears. Is recognized for his definitive research, spanning twenty-five year period, on biology of grizzly bear. He and his brother, Frank C. Craighead, Jr., pioneered radio-tracking and satellite biotelemetry techniques, and were leaders in originating National Wild and Scenic Rivers System. Has coauthored with his brother *Hawks in the Hand* (1937), *How to Survive on Land and Sea* (1943), *A Field Guide to Rocky Mountain Wild Flowers* (1954), and *Hawks, Owls and Wildlife* (1956), plus five monographs and more than eighty scientific papers. His monograph *A Definitive System for Analysis of Grizzly Bear Habitat and Other Wilderness Resources*, which received The Wildlife Society's 1983 Monograph of the Year Award, presents methodology for evaluating vegetative land-form characteristics of large expanses of

remote wilderness by means of computer technology and LANDSAT multispectral imagery. Is member of Phi Beta Kappa, Phi Kappa Phi, Phi Sigma Biological Society, Sigma Kai, and a fellow of American Association for the Advancement of Science. Served as vice-president of The Wildlife Society, president of Montana Wilderness Association, and is on advisory board of The Nature Conservancy and of American Wilderness Alliance. In recognition of his contributions to field of wildlife biology, received Arthur S. Einarsen Award (1977); American Motors Award (1978); Pennsylvania State University Distinguished Alumus Award (1970); and Alumni Fellow Award (1973). With his brother, was selected by National Geographic Society as subject for two documentary films— *Grizzly* (1967) and *Wild River* (1970). Has been member of Outstanding Educators of America since 1973, and was awarded National Geographic Society's John Oliver La Gorce gold medal (1979) for pioneering in use of biotelemetry, and for vegetation mapping and animal location using satellite technology.

RICHARD E. McCABE

CUTLER, MALCOLM RUPERT

(born 1933)

Born October 28 in Plymouth, Michigan. University of Michigan B.S. (wildlife management); Michigan State University, M.S., and Ph.D. 1973. In 1957 became executive secretary of Wildlife Conservation, Inc., Boston, Massachusetts. From 1958 until 1962 was chief of education division, Virginia Commission of Game and Inland Fisheries; from 1962 until 1965 worked for National Wildlife Federation, first as assistant chief of its conservation education division, and in 1964 as managing editor of *National Wildlife* magazine. After receiving his doctorate, joined faculty of Michigan State University as assistant professor of resource development and extension specialist in resources policy. In 1977 President Jimmy Carter appointed him assistant secretary for conservation, research, and education at U.S. Department of Agriculture, where he oversaw review and evaluation of nation's national forest roadless areas for possible designation as wilderness. Was senior vice-president of National Audubon Society, 1980—84. Became executive director of The Environmental Fund in 1984.

JOHN C. BARBER

Who's Who in America, 41st ed., 1980—81.

DAMBACH, CHARLES ARTHUR
(1911–1969)
Born December 31 in Cleveland, Ohio. The Ohio State University, B.S. (agriculture) 1937, M.S. (entomology) 1941, Ph.D. (animal ecology) 1945. Was associate regional biologist with U.S. Soil Conservation Service, Washington, D.C., 1937–42; assistant, then acting director of Ohio Cooperative Wildlife Research Unit, 1942–45; and associate professor of zoology at Ohio State University, director of its conservation curriculum, and director of Conservation Laboratory for Teachers, 1945–50. Became chief, Division of Wildlife, State of Ohio Department of Natural Resources, 1950–55. Was director of Ohio State University's Natural Resources Institute, coordinating natural resource activities of ten departments, 1955–68. Conceptualized and was first director of the university's School of Natural Resources, coordinating development of instruction, research, and public-service programs, and administering Ohio Biological Survey, 1968–69. Was a fellow of Society of American Foresters; Soil Conservation Society of America; American Association for the Advancement of Science; and Ohio Academy of Science. Was actively involved in many other national, state, and local conservation, natural-resource, and civic organizations, including a number of national-level advisory groups. Received Conservation Education Association's Outstanding Key Man award in 1969, and authored more than thirty papers in national and regional journals, including *Journal of Wildlife Management*, *Journal of Forestry*, *Journal of American Water Works Association*, and *Journal of Soil and Water Conservation*. Died October 30, 1969, in Columbus, Ohio.

JOHN F. DISINGER

American Men of Science (Physical and Biological Sciences), 11th ed., 1965.

Who's Who in America, vol. 35, 1968–69.

DAMTOFT, WALTER JULIUS
(1890–1976)
Born November 11 in Southport, Connecticut. Yale University Sheffield Scientific School, Ph.B. 1910; Yale Forest School, M.F. 1911; North Carolina State College at Raleigh, Doctor of Forest Science (honorary) 1954. Worked for U.S. Forest Service as field assistant, forest assistant, and forest examiner in Colorado, 1911–12, and in North Carolina, 1913–19, where he appraised lands for Pisgah National Forest under Weeks

Law. Joined Champion Paper and Fibre Company, Canton, North Carolina as chief forester in 1920. Served in that capacity with additional duties as assistant secretary, 1933; assistant secretary-treasurer, 1946; and assistant secretary-treasurer and director of general wood and woodlands department from 1951 until retiring in 1958. As first industrial forester in the South, was spokesman and leader for many forest industry and conservation programs throughout his career. Took important part in organization of Southern Pulpwood Conservation Association in 1939 (president in 1942–43) and Forest Farmers Association. Was member of North Carolina Board of Conservation and Development for many years, and served as its vice-chairman and chairman of forestry committee. Was trustee and vice-president of American Forest Products Industries; director of American Pulpwood Association; director and vice-president of The American Forestry Association; council member of Society of American Foresters, 1944–47, of which he was elected a fellow in 1951; and served many other conservation and industrial organizations in various capacities. In 1951 was head of Pulp and Paper Branch, Forest Products Division, Economic Stabilization and Administration, Washington, D.C. Received Certificate of Commendation from Forest Farmers Association in 1959. Died November 22, 1976.

ELWOOD L. DEMMON

American Men of Science (Physical and Biological Sciences), 11th ed., 1965.

DANA, SAMUEL TRASK
(1883–1978)
Born April 21 in Portland, Maine. Bowdoin College, B.A. 1904; Yale University, M.F. 1907. Honorary doctorates were awarded by Syracuse University in 1928, by Bowdoin in 1930, and by Yale University and University of Michigan in 1953. Entered U.S. Forest Service in 1907 and moved from forest assistant to assistant chief of Office of Silvics and Forest Investigations. Following service in World War I as captain in U.S. Army, returned to Forest Service and became assistant chief of research in 1920. Was forest commissioner of Maine, 1921–23. Returned to Forest Service as director of Northeastern Forest Experiment Station, 1923. Was appointed dean of School of Forestry and Conservation at University of Michigan in 1927 (renamed School of Natural Resources in 1950); there pioneered development of forestry and natural resources education, and retired in 1953 as dean emeritus. Served as treasurer,

vice-president, and president of Society of American Foresters; was twice editor-in-chief of *Journal of Forestry*, for a total of six years. Was chairman of American delegation to First World Forestry Congress; member of Task Force on Natural Resources of the First Hoover Commission on Reorganization of the Executive Branch of Federal Government; and presidentially appointed member of Outdoor Recreation Resources Review Commission. His major books were *Forest and Range Policy*, 1956; *California Lands* (with Myron Krueger), 1958; *Minnesota Lands* (with John H. Allison and Russell N. Cunningham), 1960; and *Forestry Education in America* (with Evert W. Johnson), 1963. Was advisor to secretary of Agriculture on strip-mining policy; consultant to U.S. Forest Service for planning its forest recreation research program; consultant to The American Forestry Association on Redwood National Park policy; consultant to Bureau of Outdoor Recreation on education in outdoor recreation; and advisor on forestry education to Yale University, University of Florida, and North Carolina State University. Received Sir William Schlich Memorial Medal of Society of American Foresters; American Forest Products Industries award for Distinguished Service to Forest Industry; medal for outstanding service in international forestry at Sixth World Forestry Congress; sesquicentennial medal of University of Michigan; and John Aston Warder Medal of The American Forestry Association. Died May 8, 1978.

R. KEITH ARNOLD
HENRY CLEPPER

American Men of Science (Physical and Biological Sciences), 11th ed., 1965.

Who's Who in America, 40th ed., 1978–79.

DARLING, FRANK FRASER
(1903–1979)
Born June 23 in Scotland. Midland Agricultural College, national diploma in agriculture; University of Edinburgh, Ph.D. 1930, D.Sc. 1938; University of Glasgow, LL.D. (honorary); Williams College, D.Sc. (honorary). From 1930 to 1934 served as chief officer of Imperial Bureau of Animal Genetics. In 1944 became director of West Highland Survey and served until 1950. In 1947 Royal Scottish Geographical Society presented him with Mungo Park Medal, and in 1950 became a Rockefeller special research fellow. Beginning in 1953, for five years served as senior lecturer on ecology and conservation at University of Edinburgh. From

1959 to 1972 was director of research and vice-president of The Conservation Foundation, Washington, D.C. In 1959 became honorary trustee of Royal National Parks of Kenya. In 1967 was elected vice-president of International Union for the Conservation of Nature and Natural Resources. In 1969 was Knighted by Queen Elizabeth. Was a fellow of Royal Society of Edinburgh and of Institute of Biology, and member of British Ecological Society. Participated in numerous surveys and studies of wildlife and land use in Africa, Alaska, Great Britain, and elsewhere. Wrote numerous scientific publications and is known for the following books: *Wild Life Conservation*, 1934; *A Herd of Red Deer*, 1937; *Wild Country*, 1938; *Wild Life of Britain*, 1943; *Pelican in the Wilderness: Odyssey of a Naturalist*, 1956; *The Unity of Ecology*, 1963; and *The Nature of a National Park*, 1968. Died October 22, 1979.

THE CONSERVATION FOUNDATION

Directory of British Scientists, London, 1964–65.

Who's Who in America, 1968–69.

DARLING, JAY NORWOOD
(1876–1962)
Born October 21 in Horwood, Michigan. Beloit College, Wisconsin, Ph.D. 1900, Litt.D.; Drake University, LL.D. Began his career as reporter in Sioux City, Iowa, soon drawing sketches to accompany stories. His gift for political cartooning was basis for half-century career that gave him fame and fortune with the simple pen name "Ding." In 1906 joined *Des Moines Register*, an association lasting for most of his career. In 1917 his cartoons were syndicated through *New York Herald Tribune*, eventually appearing in 130 daily newspapers. For five years was also editorial cartoonist for *Collier's Weekly*. His satirical pen won Pulitzer Prize for cartooning in 1923 and 1942. His strong interest in conservation of natural resources was often reflected in his drawings, which continued to bring national attention to crises in soil erosion, pollution, and other misuses of land and wildlife resources. Was particularly concerned about wildlife problems and the destruction of irreplaceable waterfowl habitat. This interest caused him to take leave of absence from newspaper work to serve as chief of Biological Survey (forerunner of U.S. Fish and Wildlife Service) during 1934–35. Was leading organizer and first president of National Wildlife Federation, which he conceived as potentially largest and most broadly interested citizens' conservation organi-

zation in nation. Devised world-famous wildlife conservation stamps produced by the federation. Received Theodore Roosevelt Gold Medal award and Pulitzer Prize, 1923. Because of his longstanding interest, the J. N. "Ding" Darling Foundation was instrumental in organization and passage of Lewis and Clark Trail Commission, which planned the historical trail from Saint Joseph, Missouri, to Pacific Coast, to be marked and set aside for historical and recreational purposes. Sanibel Island in Florida, one of his favorite bird-watching locations, was set aside and renamed J. N. "Ding" Darling Wildlife Refuge in his memory. Was author of *Ding Goes to Russia*, 1931, and *The Cruise of the Bouncing Betsy*, 1937. Died February 12, 1962.

JAMES D. DAVIS

Who Was Who in America, 1961–68.

DASMANN, RAYMOND FREDRIC
(born 1919)
Born May 27 in San Francisco. University of California at Berkeley, B.A. 1948, M.A. 1951, Ph.D. (zoology) 1954. Worked as forest guard for U.S. Forest Service and California Division of Forestry, 1939–41, and was with U.S. Army in Southwest Pacific, 1941–45. Was research assistant and associate at Museum of Vertebrate Zoology and the School of Forestry, University of California, 1948–55. After teaching biology at University of Minnesota, Duluth, 1953–54, served as assistant to associate professor and head of game management at Humboldt State College, California, 1954–59. From 1959 to 1961 was Fulbright research biologist at National Museums of Southern Rhodesia. Was lecturer in zoology at University of California, Berkeley, in 1961; returned in 1962 to Humboldt State College, where he became professor of wildlife management and chairman of Division of Natural Resources. Was director of environmental studies of The Conservation Foundation, 1966–70; senior ecologist for International Union for Conservation of Nature and Natural Resources, 1970–77; and professor and board chairman of environmental studies at University of California, Santa Cruz, since 1977. Is a fellow of California Academy of Sciences; and has been president of California section and national president of The Wildlife Society. Is member of American Society of Mammalogists; Ecological Society of America; Faunal Preservation Society; and Association of Tropical Biology. In 1966–67 served as consultant to UNESCO. His writings include the fol-

lowing books: *Pacific Coastal Wildlife*, 1957; *Environmental Conservation*, 1959, 1976; *Wildlife Biology*, 1964, 1981; *African Game Ranching*, 1963; *The Last Horizon*, 1963; *The Destruction of California*, 1965; *A Different Kind of Country*, 1969; *No Further Retreat*, 1971; *Planet in Peril*, 1972; *Ecological Principles for Economic Development*, 1972; *The Conservation Alternative*, 1975; and *California's Changing Environment*, 1981.

THE CONSERVATION FOUNDATION
RAYMOND F. DASMANN

American Men and Women of Science (Physical and Biological Sciences), 15th
ed., 1982.

Who's Who in America, 42d ed., 1982–83.

DAVIS, DEAN WILLIAM
(1894–1963)
Born February 15 in West Plains, Missouri. University of Missouri, B.A.
1915, B.J. 1916. Before entering military service during World War I,
was engaged in newspaper work on *Cleveland* (Ohio) *Leader*. After war,
became businessman. First became active in organized conservation
work when he served as county chairman during 1936 campaign of
Conservation Federation of Missouri to take the state Game and Fish
Department out of politics. This movement established Missouri Conservation Commission as nonpolitical state agency dedicated to management of forest and wildlife resources under constitutional amendment
that established a model law. Was elected as director of Conservation
Federation of Missouri in 1938 and served as its president, 1946–49. In
1951 received Missouri's Master Conservationist award. Was also active
nationally, serving as member of board of directors of The National
Wildlife Federation, 1948–51, and as vice-president during 1952 and
1953. Traveled widely to give state affiliates of the federation a national
viewpoint in same manner as he had labored to give county chapters in
Missouri a statewide outlook. Was particularly effective in opposing construction of dams on clear-water streams of the Ozarks, and in arousing
public support for protection of Florida Key deer. Died January 30,
1963.

LOUIS S. CLAPPER
National Cyclopaedia of American Biography, 1965.

DAVIS, HERBERT SPENCER
(1875–1958)
Born March 28 in Oneida, New York. Wesleyan University, Ph.B. 1899; Harvard University, Ph.D. 1907. Was instructor and assistant professor at Washington State College, 1901–6, and professor of zoology at University of Florida, 1907–22. Joined U.S. Fish and Wildlife Service as fish pathologist, and in 1929 became chief of aquaculture investigations, serving in that capacity until his retirement in 1944. Was then chief fish pathologist for Oregon State Game Commission, 1945–47, after which he became research associate at University of California, Berkeley. Was responsible for establishment of experimental fisheries stations at Leetown, West Virginia; Pittsford, Vermont; and Convict Creek, California. Pioneered early experimental dietary work with trout in hatcheries and conducted some of first research directed toward perfecting superior strains of fishes. His major work dealt with diseases and parasites of fishes, and his publication *Care and Disease of Trout*, 1935, became most-used resource at fish hatcheries throughout world. His *Culture and Diseases of Game Fishes*, 1953, was his last and most comprehensive publication. Was president of American Fisheries Society, 1932–33. Died July 15, 1958.

RICHARD J. GRAHAM

American Men of Science, 7th ed., 1944.

Transactions of the American Fisheries Society, vol. 88, no. 2, 1959.

DAVIS, KENNETH PICKETT
(1906–1982)
Born September 2 in Denver, Colorado. University of Montana, B.S.F. 1928; University of Michigan, M.F. 1932, Ph.D. (forest management) 1940. Employed as district ranger in U.S. Forest Service, 1928–31, then silviculturist at Northern Rocky Mountain Forest and Range Experiment Station, 1931–40; and as assistant and then chief of Division of Forest Management Research, Washington, D.C., 1940–45. Was dean of School of Forestry at Montana State University, 1945–49. In 1949 was appointed professor of forest management and in 1950 chairman of Department of Forestry at University of Michigan School of Natural Resources. Was acting dean of School of Natural Resources in 1966. In 1967 was appointed David T. Mason Professor of Forest Land Use at School of Forestry and Environmental Studies, Yale University, retaining

that position until his retirement in 1974. In addition to his official duties, was president of Montana Conservation Council, 1948–49; member of Michigan Board of Registration of Foresters, 1956–62; chairman of Wood Section, Michigan Natural Resources Council, 1954–61; and Fulbright lecturer at University of Helsinki in 1963. Long active in Society of American Foresters, he was chairman of Washington, D.C., Northern Rocky Mountain, and Wisconsin-Michigan sections; chairman of Forest Practices Committee, 1945–56; acting editor of *Forest Science*, 1957–58; member of the society's council, 1958–61; vice-president, 1966; president, 1970; and was elected a fellow, 1961. In 1976 received Sir William Schlich Memorial Award in recognition of his contributions to advancement of forestry. The University of Montana awarded him its Distinguished Alumnus Award in 1979. Also received Distinguished Alumnus Award from University of Michigan in 1980. Was author of more than one hundred articles and other publications. Especially noteworthy are his books *American Forest Management: Regulation and Valuation*, 1954, 1966; *Forest Fires: Control and Use*, 1959 and (with A. A. Brown) 1973; and *Land Use*, 1976. Died November 29, 1982, in Bryn Mawr, Pennsylvania.

SOCIETY OF AMERICAN FORESTERS

American Men and Women of Science (Physical and Biological Sciences), 15th ed., 1982.

Who's Who in America, 41st ed., 1980–81.

DAVIS, WATERS SMITH, JR.
(1899–1958)
Born October 30 in Galveston, Texas. Graduated Williams College 1922. His business career began when he was made vice-president of Comet Rice Company. For number of years, held seat on New York Stock Exchange and was member of brokerage firm of Lapham and Davis. In 1940 returned to League City, Texas, and assumed management of his family's ranch holdings, League Davis properties, which included extensive operations in lumber, grain, cotton, and cattle industries. Made experiments in management of lands and grasses. In 1944 was elected district supervisor of his local Brazoria-Galveston Soil Conservation District. In 1947 Texas Association of Soil Conservation Districts elected him president. Began writing *Texas Topsoil*, probably the first newsletter devoted to development of soil conservation districts. In 1950 was

elected president of National Association of Soil Conservation Districts, served five consecutive terms, and until his death was treasurer and director. In 1954 began series of terms as general chairman of five National Watershed congresses. Was awarded Hugh Hammond Bennett gold medallion in 1958 by Friends of the Land. His own National Association selected him as Conservation Man of the Year in 1954. He was made honorary life member of Soil Conservation Society of America in 1952. Died November 15, 1958.

DAVID STEWART, JR.

Who's Who in the South and Southwest.

DAY, ALBERT MERRILL
(1897–1979)

Born April 2 in Humboldt, Nebraska. University of Wyoming, B.S. (biology) 1922. Began as leader in Division of Predator and Rodent Control, U.S. Bureau of Biological Survey, in Wyoming, from 1918 to 1930, then became assistant chief and chief of that division, in Washington, D.C., serving 1930–38. Was first chief of Division of Federal Aid in Wildlife Restoration, 1938–42, and nurtured that agency to early prominence. Served Fish and Wildlife Service, U.S. Department of the Interior, as assistant director, 1942–46, and director, 1946–53. Was director of wildlife research for Arctic Institute of North America, 1954–57; director of Oregon Fish Commission, 1958–60; executive director of Pennsylvania Fish Commission, 1960–64; and conservation consultant, 1965–79. Served as member or advisor for several international fisheries commissions; for U.S. Section, United Nations Conference on Law of the Sea; and for special advisory committee to secretary of the Interior. Was national director of Izaak Walton League of America, 1945–52, and honorary member of The Wildlife Society. Contributed to professional and popular journals, and was author of *North American Waterfowl*, 1949, and coauthor of chapter in *Waterfowl Tomorrow*, 1964. Died January 21, 1979.

PHILIP A. DUMONT

American Men of Science (Physical and Biological Sciences), 11th ed., 1965.

DAYTON, WILLIAM ADAMS
(1885–1958)
Born December 14 in New York City. Williams College, B.A. 1905, M.A. 1908. Was plant ecologist and dendrologist with U.S. Forest Service for more than forty-five years, from 1910–55, and advisor after retirement. Pioneered in range research on national forests, was in charge of range forage investigations, and conducted field work in many parts of country. Was transferred from the West to Washington, D.C., in 1914; became chief of new Division of Dendrology and Range Forage Investigations in 1942. Under his supervision, Forest Service herbarium, founded by him in 1910, became largest collection of range plants in nation, with more than 120,000 specimens. In 1943 served as dendrologist with forest survey in Costa Rica. Was authority on range plants and leader in standardization of English plant names. Received gold medal of Massachusetts Horticultural Society and Distinguished Service Award of U.S. Department of Agriculture. Was member of more than twenty scientific societies, serving several as president or other officer. Was delegate to Seventh International Botanical Congress at Stockholm, Sweden, in 1950, and section chairman at Sixth International Grassland Congress, State College, Pennsylvania, in 1952. Was author of *Important Western Browse Plants*, 1931; *Range Plant Handbook* (with others) 1937; *Standardized Plant Names* (2d ed., with Harlan P. Kelsey), 1942; *The Forests of Costa Rica* (with others), 1943; *Notes on Western Range Forbs*, 1960; and more than 150 scientific articles, bulletins, notes, and reviews. Died October 20, 1958.

ELBERT L. LITTLE, JR.

American Men of Science, 9th ed., 1955.

Taxon 8: 185–87; portrait, 1959.

Who Was Who in America, 1951–60.

DeCOSTER, LESTER ALLEN
(born 1935)
Born May 2 in Hartford, Maine. University of Maine, B.S. (forestry) 1959. Was appointed that year as service forester in Maine Forestry Department; in 1962 worked on first aerial direct-seeding reforestation projects in the state; in 1964 was named assistant supervisor of information and education for the department. Was also executive secretary

of Maine Forest Products Council and edited newsletter. In 1969 became regional manager for New England at Bangor for American Forest Products Institute, and in 1972 helped organize National Outstanding Tree Farmer contest. In 1982 became vice-president in Washington, D.C., of Resources Division of American Forest Institute. As such, edits bimonthly magazine *American Tree Farmer* and *American Tree Farm System*, which has been managed by the institute for forty years. Comprising this system are 85 million acres of private forest owned by 48,000 tree farmers in all 50 states under general supervision of 45 state tree-farm committees. Is active in The American Forestry Association, Society of American Foresters, Public Relations Society of America, and Outdoor Writers Association.

HENRY CLEPPER

DENNEY, RICHARD NELSON
(1923–1981)

Born February 21 in Tucson, Arizona. Colorado A&M College (subsequently Colorado State University), B.S. (forestry, range management, and wildlife management) 1948, M.S. (wildlife research and management) 1951. Joined Colorado Game and Fish Department as wildlife technician in 1949 and later became regional game manager, wildlife researcher, and, in 1963, assistant state game manager. Also served on graduate faculty of Colorado State University, 1961–66. In 1966 became forestry officer (wildlife) for FAO–UNDP Kenya Range Management Project in Nairobi. Served as independent wildlife consultant, 1971–74, often working for American Humane Association, and spent austral summer of 1973–74 as guest scientist for National Science Foundation in Antarctic. In 1974 rejoined Colorado Division of Wildlife as nongame mammal specialist, and became big-game manager for the division, 1976–78. After serving briefly as general manager of consulting firm, was selected in 1978 as executive director of The Wildlife Society, a position he held until his death in 1981. Was named Colorado Conservationist of the Year in 1965 and was active in The Wildlife Society, serving as president of Colorado Chapter, 1972–74, and of Central Mountains and Plains Section, 1974–75. Was member of several professional and conservation organizations, served on numerous committees and advisory councils, authored more than one hundred popular and technical articles and papers, and appeared as host or cohost of several "Wild Kingdom" television programs. Died December 6, 1981.

HARRY E. HODGDON

DICKENSON, RUSSELL ERRETT
(born 1923)

Born April 12 in Melissa, Texas. Northern Arizona University, B.S. 1947, D.Sc. (honorary) 1982. Served in U.S. Navy and Marine Corps during World War II. Joined staff of National Park Service as park ranger at Grand Canyon National Park in Arizona, 1946. In subsequent field assignments as ranger, chief ranger, and superintendent, served at Chiricahua National Monument, Arizona; Big Bend National Park, Texas; Glacier National Park, Montana; Grand Teton National Park, Wyoming; Zion National Park, Utah; and Flaming Gorge National Recreation Area, Utah. Has also served as chief of Division of Resource Management and Visitor Protection in Midwest Regional Office in Omaha. Also held three important managerial posts: director of National Park Service's Pacific Northwest Region, covering Alaska, Washington, Oregon, and Idaho; deputy director of the service, based in Washington, D.C.; and director of the service's National Capital Region. In 1967 became chief of new areas studies and master planning in the service's headquarters, Washington, D.C. In 1980 became director of National Park Service. Received U.S. Department of the Interior's Meritorious Service Award in 1971, and its Distinguished Service Award in 1972; Cornelius Amory Pugsley Gold Medal Award of the American Scenic and Historic Preservation Society in 1975; Northern Arizona University's Distinguished Alumni Award in 1978; Award for Excellence of National Society for Park Resources in 1981; and George Washington Medal of U.S. Capitol Historical Society in 1982. A year later, became first American to receive Golden Flower of Rheydt Award from Germany, presented once every two years for preserving environment on national and international level.

PAUL C. PRITCHARD
MARY LOU PHILLIPS

DILG, WILL H.
(1867–1927)

Born in 1867 in Milwaukee, Wisconsin. As writer for outdoor magazines, was founder in January 1922 of Izaak Walton League of America in Chicago. Originally established by group of fifty-four men, the league was started with object of improving land and water conservation in the public interest. Among its first projects was fight to preserve clean waterways and combat stream pollution. Now a national organization of fifty-five thousand members, with active local chapters throughout the country, the league works to advance management of all resources and total quality of environment. As the league's first president until 1926, he helped save from commercial exploitation that portion of Superior National Forest in Minnesota now included in Boundary Waters Canoe Area. Also conceived plan for creating Upper Mississippi Wild Life and Game Refuge and set up Izaak Walton League Fund to save starving elk in Jackson Hole, Wyoming. In 1952 the league dedicated to him the Will H. Dilg Memorial, now in Prairie Island City Park, Minnesota. Died March 8, 1927.

ROBERT L. HERBST

DIXON, JOSEPH SCATTERGOOD
(1884–1952)

Born March 5 in Cherokee County, Kansas. Educated in biological sciences at Throop Academy, graduating in 1908; graduate studies at Stanford University and University of California, Berkeley. Was member of Alexander expedition to Alaska during 1907–8, and of Harvard expedition to Alaska and Siberia during 1913–14, collecting biological data. Was assistant curator of mammals at Museum of Vertebrate Zoology at Berkeley, 1915–18, and economic mammalogist at the museum, 1918–31. In 1931 joined George Melendez Wright to start Wildlife Division in National Park Service, U.S. Department of the Interior, for which he was field naturalist from 1931 to 1946, the year he retired. Was member of Ornithologists Union, and honorary member of Cooper Ornithological Club; vice-president, president, and member of board of governors of American Society of Mammalogists; member of The Wildlife Society; and fellow and, in 1937, vice-president of California Academy of Sciences. Was regional director in 1936 of First North American Wildlife Conference, which led to founding of National Wildlife Federation. Published numerous scientific articles on economic mammalogy, ornithology, and ecology, and was author of *Birds and Mammals of Mount McKinley National Park*, no. 3 of National Park Service's "Fauna Series," and coauthor of "Fauna Series" no. 1; collaborated with Joseph Grinnell and Jean M. Linsdale in *Fur-Bearing Mammals of California*, 1937; and was coauthor with Lowell Sumner of *Birds and Mammals of the Sierra Nevada*, 1953. Died June 23, 1952.

BEN H. THOMPSON

American Men of Science, 8th ed., 1949.

DODGE, MARCELLUS HARTLEY
(1881–1963)
Born in 1881. Columbia University, B.A. 1903. Served as president and chairman of board of Remington Arms Company, maintaining close personal interest in conservation affairs throughout his life. Was member of American Game Protection Association; of board of directors of American Wildlife Institute, 1935–45; and trustee of North American Wildlife Foundation, 1946–63. Was largely responsible for rallying support of sporting arms and manufacturing industry for Pittman-Robertson Federal Aid in Wildlife Restoration Act, a major factor in enactment of that milestone legislation. Support of the industry for retention of 11 percent excise tax on sporting firearms and ammunition and its application to wildlife conservation was vital consideration when act was being considered by Congress in 1937. In 1959 suggested that national wildlife refuge be created in Great Swamp of Morris County, New Jersey, and donated substantial funds to North American Wildlife Foundation to initiate project. North American Wildlife Foundation acquired and donated the land to federal government by 1964; the refuge was dedicated in May 1964. Died December 25, 1963.

JAMES B. TREFETHEN

Who Was Who in America, 1961–68.

Who's Who in America, 1962–63.

DOREMUS, THOMAS EDWARD
(1874–1962)
Born in 1874. For many years was an industrialist and officer of du Pont

Company, devoting much of his time to furthering cause of conservation. In 1911 was one of founding members of American Game Protective and Propagation Association, and became member of its board of directors in 1912. From 1935 to 1945 was trustee of American Wildlife Institute (predecessor of Wildlife Management Institute) and of North American Wildlife Foundation. With establishment of the latter organization in 1945, became treasurer, serving in that capacity until his death. In 1935 was instrumental in launching The National Wildlife Federation. Also helped obtain private funds with which to start Cooperative Wildlife Research Unit Program, a student training program involving U.S. Department of the Interior, state conservation agencies, land-grant colleges, and American Wildlife Institute (later, Wildlife Management Institute). Played prominent role in passage of Federal Aid in Wildlife Restoration Act of 1937 by developing support for its enactment among members of sporting arms and ammunition manufacturers. Was awarded Nash Conservation Award in 1955. Died September 23, 1962.

JAMES B. TREFETHEN

DOUGLAS, MARJORY STONEMAN
(born 1890)
Born April 7 in Minneapolis, Minnesota. Wellesley College, B.A. 1912; University of Miami, Litt.D. (honorary) 1960. Was reporter and assistant editor for *Miami Herald*, 1915–22, and book editor, 1941–47. During World War I worked in publicity department of American Red Cross in France, 1917–20. After war traveled around Europe writing news articles about child refugee relief, then returned to *Miami Herald* as assistant editor. In 1925 commenced to write fiction, and for next thirteen years was successful short-story writer. Was instructor in department of English, University of Miami, Coral Gables, Florida, 1925–29. Was active member of original committee set up in 1927 to push for Everglades National Park. In early 1940s turned to novels and regional histories, and wrote *The Everglades: River of Grass*, 1947 (rev. 1978). Continues to work for preservation and repair of Everglades. Was editor, University of Miami Press, 1960–63, and has been director emeritus since 1963. Is founder and, since 1970, president of Friends of the Everglades, and leader of Coalition to Repair the Everglades. Was named Conservationist of the Year by Florida Audubon Society in 1975; Conservationist of the Year by Florida Wildlife Federation in 1976; and received Nash Conser-

vation Award from American Motors Corporation in 1977. Is currently
working on biography of author-naturalist W. H. Hudson.

NATIONAL AUDUBON SOCIETY

Contemporary Authors, New Revision Series, vol. 2, 1981.

DRAKE, GEORGE LINCOLN
(1889–1979)
Born April 7 in Laconia, New Hampshire. Pennsylvania State University,
B.S. (forestry) 1912. From 1912 to 1930 was with U.S. Forest Service in
Alaska, Oregon, and Washington as forest examiner, deputy supervisor,
logging engineer, and assistant regional forester. Was employed in 1930
by Simpson Logging Company as its first professional forester; served as
general superintendent of logging and forestry work, retiring as vice-
president in 1954. Joined Society of American Foresters in 1918, was
president, 1952–53, and was elected a fellow in 1953. As representative
of West Coast Lumbermen's Association and Pacific Northwest Loggers
Association, helped draw up forest practice rules under National Industrial Recovery Act of 1933. The rules initiated the application of forestry
on industrial timberlands of the West. Among his many activities and
offices in behalf of improved forest management, he was member of
board of Washington Forest Fire Association, 1930–54; director of Pacific Logging Congress, 1932–37 (president during latter year); member
of Western Forestry and Conservation Association for four decades, and
president in 1948. Was originator of Shelton Cooperative Sustained
Yield Unit, a pooling of private and national forests totaling 260,000
acres under coordinated management plan for the years 1947–2047. Was
a founder and vice-president of South Olympic Tree Farm established in
1941. Received awards from Washington State University in 1950, The
American Forestry Association in 1954, and Pennsylvania State University in 1957. Died April 5, 1979.

HENRY CLEPPER

DRURY, NEWTON BISHOP
(1889–1978)
Born April 9 in San Francisco, California. University of California, B.L.
1912, LL.D. 1947. From 1912 to 1918 was instructor in English at Uni-

versity of California. Following military service in World War I, opened public-relations firm in San Francisco. In 1920 was instrumental in founding Save-the-Redwoods League, which he served as executive secretary from 1920 to 1940; through his early leadership, crusade to preserve coastal groves became national movement. In 1927 helped write legislation creating California State Park Commission, and from 1929 to 1940, concurrent with his duties in the league, served as the commission's acquisition officer and executive secretary. During this period, fifty-six state parks were established. In 1940 was appointed director of National Park Service, a position he held until 1951. During his administration, became widely known in conservation circles for his tenacious opposition to special-interest demands, especially during critical years of World War II. From 1951 to 1959 was chief of California Division of Beaches and Parks. Following his retirement in 1959, returned to Save-the-Redwoods League as secretary until 1971. Awards received for his accomplishments in conservation and park development include: Conservation Award of the Trustees of Public Reservations; Pugsley Gold Medal of the American Scenic and Historic Preservation Society; Distinguished Service Award of The American Forestry Association; Conservation Award of the National Audubon Society; and Frances K. Hutchinson Medal of The Garden Club of America. Also was honorary member of American Society of Landscape Architects and of Society of American Foresters; fellow, American Institute of Park Executives; and honorary vice-president of Sierra Club. Two California redwood groves—Drury Brothers Grove in Prairie Creek State Park and Newton B. Drury Grove in Humboldt Redwoods State Park—have been designated as living memorials to him. Died December 14, 1978.

HOLT BODINSON
JOHN B. DEWITT

Shankland, Robert. *Steve Mather of the National Parks.* New York: Alfred A. Knopf, 1951.

Who's Who in America, 40th ed., 1978–79.

Who's Who in the West, 1969.

DULEY, FRANK LESLIE
(1888–1978)
Born December 21 in Grant City, Missouri. University of Missouri, B.S.A. 1914, A.M. 1915; University of Wisconsin, Ph.D. 1923. At Uni-

versity of Missouri, where he was on faculty from 1915 to 1925, helped in 1917 to set up first plots in this country to study effects of cropping systems on run-off and erosion. Still maintained, these plots, together with Old Sandborn experimental field, were designated as national monument in 1965 by U.S. Department of the Interior. From 1925 to 1933 was professor of agronomy at Kansas State College. Was then made regional director in Kansas of one of first groups of soil erosion projects started in United States; after three years with U.S. Soil Conservation Service in Kansas, became leader of research team in soil and moisture conservation in Lincoln, Nebraska, retiring from federal service in December 1958. From 1959 to 1964 was employed by Colorado State University and assigned to project of Agency for International Development at University of Peshawar, West Pakistan, where he also served as principal of its new agricultural college. Was a fellow of American Association for the Advancement of Science, American Society of Agronomy, and Soil Conservation Society of America (president in 1947). U.S. Department of Agriculture conferred on him Superior Service Award in 1955 for his work in originating and developing stubble mulch system of farming for water and wind-erosion control. Wrote numerous articles on soil and water conservation. Died April 11, 1978.

D. E. HUTCHINSON

American Men of Science (Physical and Biological Sciences), 11th ed., 1965.

DUNLAP, LOUISE CECIL
(born 1946)
Born February 7 in Lancaster, Pennsylvania. Duke University, B.A. (political science) 1968. Served as intern in Department of Housing and Urban Development, 1968–70; legislative assistant to president, National Parks and Conservation Association, 1970–71; and assistant legislative director, Friends of the Earth, 1971–72, where she was assistant legislative director of Campaign to Stop the SST. Became a founder and board member of Environmental Policy Center in 1972, and was nationally recognized by President Jimmy Carter in 1977 for organizing nationwide citizens' coalition, which worked successfully for more than six years for enactment of first federal law to regulate strip-mining of coal. When Environmental Policy Center, of which she was president since 1976, became Environmental Policy Institute through 1982 merger, she became first woman chief executive officer of major national environmental or-

ganization. In addition to working on energy and environmental public policies before Congress and executive branch since 1970, authored *An Analysis of the Legislative History of the Surface Mining Control and Reclamation Act of 1975, Twenty-first Annual Rocky Mountain Mineral Law Institute* (Matthew Bender, 1976). Is board member of Environmental Policy Institute, League of Conservation Voters, National Clean Air Coalition, Clean Water Action Project, and Coast Alliance.

ENVIRONMENTAL POLICY INSTITUTE

DUNN, PAUL MILLARD
(born 1898)

Born October 15 in Lennox, South Dakota. Iowa State College, B.S. 1923, M.S. (forestry) 1933. Was assistant and associate state forester in Missouri from 1926 to 1931, before joining faculty of Utah State University School of Forest Range and Wildlife Management; was dean there from 1938 to 1942 and also state forester and fire warden for Utah. While dean of School of Forestry at Oregon State College from 1942 to 1954, was also director of Oregon Forest Products Laboratory, 1942–53, and of College Forest Experiment Station, 1950–54. During 1952–53, took leave of absence on assignment with Food and Agriculture Organization of the United Nations to assist government of Chile to establish curriculum in forestry at University of Chile. Joined Saint Regis Paper Company as technical director of forestry in 1955, and in 1962 was advanced to vice-president (forestry and timberlands), a position he held until his retirement in 1968; thereafter continued as forestry consultant. Returned to faculty of School of Forestry, Oregon State University, as professor of forestry, 1968–73. In Society of American Foresters served as chairman of Intermountain and Columbia River sections and of Division of Education; member of the society's council, 1946–49; president, 1962–63; and a fellow in 1959. Received Gifford Pinchot Medal in 1975. Is also a fellow of American Association for the Advancement of Science and of Utah Academy of Arts, Sciences, and Letters. Was president of Forest History Society in 1967–68 and of The American Forestry Association, 1968–70. Was president of Southern Pulpwood Conservation Association and director of American Pulpwood Association. Was member of Cooperative Forestry Research Advisory Committee for U.S. Department of Agriculture, 1964–74, and of advisory committee for Northeastern Forest Experiment Station, 1955–76. Is trustee of Oregon State University Foundation, the Western Forestry Center, and Keep Oregon Green Association. Received Iowa State University Alumni Association's Distinguished Achievement Award in 1968, and Western Forestry and Conservation Award for Lifetime Service in 1971.

SOCIETY OF AMERICAN FORESTERS

JAMES R. LYONS

American Men and Women of Science (Physical and Biological Sciences), 12th ed., vol. 2, 1972.

Journal of Forestry. Forestry News, vol. 65:912, 1967.

Who's Who in America, 38th ed., 1974–75.

DUTCHER, WILLIAM

(1846–1920)

Born January 20 in Stelton, New Jersey. Following education in local public schools, engaged in insurance business. His avocation was wildlife (especially bird) conservation, for which cause he made a notable and lasting contribution. After joining American Ornithologists' Union in 1883, became in 1884 a member of its Committee on Bird Protection, which in 1886 drafted prototype state law for protection of nongame birds. Was made chairman of this committee in 1896, the year that marks beginning of existing Audubon movement. By 1903, Audubon law protecting songbirds had been passed in twenty-six states. Having encouraged formation of regional Audubon societies, which by 1905 had increased to more than forty, he founded in that year the National Association of Audubon Societies (now National Audubon Society) and was elected organization's president, an unsalaried post he held until his death. The society, which sixty-five years later is one of nation's largest and most influential citizens' bodies devoted to preservation and wise use of all natural resources, has approximately eight thousand members and a strong network of chapters throughout United States. Dutcher was for years an indefatigable worker for laws to protect bird life, and through many personal visits to state legislatures he obtained enactment of legislation regulating or prohibiting market hunting and the killing of song and insectivorous birds. Was administrator of fund to employ wardens to protect seabirds and plumed herons. In 1910 was successful in obtaining passage of New York Plumage Act, which closed the state (the nation's center of millinery trade) to all American wild bird plumage and to foreign plumage from birds of the same families. This law was precursor of Weeks-McLean Act passed by Congress in 1913 and of Migratory Bird Treaty Act of 1918, which saved untold millions of birds from market hunting for their plumage and which prohibited their importation into United States. Although without scientific education in biology, he was recognized by scientific societies for his crusading work. Active in New York Zoological Society, he was elected also to New York Academy of Sciences and was a fellow of American Association for the Advancement of Science. The Camp Fire Club of America presented him with its gold medal for his accomplishments in bird conservation. Died July 2, 1920.

JEANNE GOODWIN

Auk. October. 1921.

Bird Lore, September-October, 1920.

New York Times, Obituary, 21:4, July 4, 1920.

Who Was Who in America, 1897–1942.

DUTTON, WALT LEROY
(1889–1976)
Born May 1 near Alliance, Nebraska. Oregon Agricultural College (now Oregon State University), B.S. (forestry) 1913. That year, entered U.S. Forest Service in Pacific Northwest and advanced successively through positions of forest guard, assistant forest ranger, forest ranger, grazing examiner, assistant forest supervisor, forest supervisor, and district forest inspector. Was transferred to Washington, D.C., office in 1936 as chief (now director) of Division of Range Management. In this position, made an outstanding record in curtailing destructive grazing use and improving range and watershed conditions on the national forests through reduction in numbers of permitted livestock, better handling of the grazing animals, installation of structural range improvements, and range reseeding. Much of reduction in grazing use was accomplished in face of opposition from organized livestock industry and hostile committees of Congress. Retired in 1953 and spent eighteen months with British Colonial Service as range and forestry consultant in African colonies. In 1955 was member of United Nations team making economic survey of possibilities for increasing agricultural production in Argentina. In 1948–49 served two years on three-man Pan-American Committee on Conservation Awards. In 1949 received U.S. Department of Agriculture

Superior Service Award "for outstanding service to public welfare through effective administration and leadership in field of range management, resulting in critically needed improvement of range land in the national forests with respect to forage, water run-off, and soil conservation." Also in 1949 received U.S. Department of Agriculture Certificate of Merit in which he was commended "for performance substantially exceeding the requirements of his position." In 1951 was assigned to Army of Occupation in Japan as special advisor on pasture and forestry activities. As life member and one of founders of American Society of Range Management, he served on its board of directors, 1949–51. Was member of Society of American Foresters from 1918 until his death. Died February 13, 1976.

LLOYD W. SWIFT

DYSART, BENJAMIN CLAY
(born 1940)
Born February 12 in Columbia, Tennessee. Vanderbilt University B.S. (civil engineering) 1961; M.S. (environmental engineering) 1964; Georgia Institute of Technology Ph.D. (civil engineering) 1969. Was staff engineer, Union Carbide Corporation, Columbia, Tennessee, 1961–62 and 1964–65. Was trainee for Federal Water Pollution Control Administration, Georgia Tech, 1965–67. At Environmental Systems Engineering Department, Clemson University, was assistant professor, 1968–79; associate professor, 1970–75; water resources engineering graduate-program coordinator, 1970–73, and director, 1973–75; and professor from 1976 to present. Served as scientific advisor to assistant secretary of the Army for civil works, 1975–76. Was named McQueen Quattlebaum Professor of Environmental Engineering, 1982. Has been director of National Wildlife Federation since 1974; member of its executive committee since 1976; president since 1983; and was vice-president, 1978–83. Served as vice-president, South Carolina Wildlife Federation, 1969–73, and president, 1973–74. Was member of Secretary of the Army's Lock and Dam 26 Special Task Force, 1975–76; Civil Works Advisory Board, Department of the Army, 1975–76; U.S. Department of Energy's Southern States Energy Board Environmental Task Force, 1978–81; Scientific Evaluation Panel on Oil Pollution, National Oceanic and Atmospheric Administration, 1980; and Nonpoint Source Pollutant Task Force, Environmental Protection Agency, 1979–80. Was secretarial ap-

pointee, Outer Continental Shelf (OCS) Scientific Committee, U.S. Department of the Interior, 1979–82; secretarial appointee, OCS Advisory Board, 1979–82; gubernatorial appointee, Heritage Advisory Board, South Carolina Wildlife and Marine Resources Department, 1974; member, Environmental Quality Control Advisory Board, South Carolina Department of Health and Environmental Control, 1979 to present, and chairman, 1981–82. Named South Carolina Wildlife Conservationist of the Year, 1979. Author or coauthor of more than 150 published works and presentations on environmental and water resources engineering, pollution control, and resource public policy.

NATIONAL WILDLIFE FEDERATION

EDDY, SAMUEL
(1897–1972)
Born March 29 in Decatur, Illinois. James Millikin University, B.A. 1924; University of Illinois, A.M. 1925, Ph.D. (zoology) 1929. Was instructor and assistant professor at Millikin University, 1924–26; teaching assistant in zoology at University of Illinois; and assistant aquatic biologist for Illinois Natural History Survey, Urbana, 1926–29. From assistant professor of zoology, University of Minnesota, 1929–38, became associate professor, 1938–44, professor, 1944–64, and was honorary curator of fishes at James Ford Bell Museum of Natural History, University of Minnesota, during 1960s. Was in charge of fisheries research for Minnesota Department of Conservation and was consultant for biological surveys to Minnesota Division of Game and Fish, 1937–40. Was vice-president of Ecological Society of America in 1953. His books included two textbooks on comparative anatomy; was coauthor of *Taxonomic Keys to Common Animals of North Central States*, 1950, and was author of *How to Know the Fresh-Water Fishes of the United States*, 1957. Conducted surveys in Illinois and Minnesota, and worked in areas of fish taxonomy and growth.

LAURENCE R. JAHN
J. C. UNDERHILL

American Men of Science (Physical and Biological Sciences), 11th ed., 1965.

Who's Who in America, 1964–65.

World Who's Who in Science, 1968.

EDGE, MABEL ROSALIE
(1877–1962)

Born November 3 in New York City. Private-school education; Wagner College, Staten Island, New York, Litt.D. (honorary) 1948. Active in votes-for-women movement, became interested in conservation following adoption of women suffrage amendment in 1920. One of her early concerns was for wild birds, and she launched successful personal campaign within National Audubon Society for change in society's leadership. In 1929 created Emergency Conservation Committee and for three decades was its crusading chairman. Supported by many small contributions, it published more than one million copies each of one hundred different pamphlets on resource issues. Under aegis of this committee, campaigned for waterfowl hunting laws and regulations, against U.S. Biological Survey's policies of predator poisoning, and for creation of Olympic and Kings Canyon national parks. One of her most notable reforms was establishment of Hawk Mountain Sanctuary in southeastern Pennsylvania. In 1934, having solicited necessary funds, she obtained one-year lease on Hawk Mountain, where for decades shooters had annually slaughtered thousands of migrating birds of prey. Later was able to exercise option to purchase some two square miles of wooded property, which became nucleus of present sanctuary and first created for birds of prey. It is now administered by Hawk Mountain Sanctuary Association, which she organized in 1936 and of which she was director and president until her death. A militant activist in conservation movement of mid-twentieth century, she also helped obtain victory that abolished baiting and use of live decoys in waterfowl hunting and resulted in other reforms in wildlife management. Died November 30, 1962.

JEANNE GOODWIN

Hawks Aloft: The Story of Hawk Mountain. New York: Dodd, Mead Company, 1947.

New York Times. Obituary, December 1, 1962.

New Yorker. April 17, 1948.

Who's Who in America, 1954–55.

EDMINSTER, FRANK CUSTER
(1903–1977)

Born December 26 in Ithaca, New York. Cornell University, B.S. 1926,

M.S. (ornithology) 1930. For seven years was research biologist with New York State Conservation Department. Was instructor in game management at Cornell University, 1936–37. Joining U.S. Soil Conservation Service in 1937 as regional biologist, advanced to New York state conservationist and finally to recreation specialist. Retired in 1966 from U.S. Department of Agriculture after twenty-eight years of distinguished service during which he gained national reputation in integrated fields of land and wildlife management. Pioneered in management of farm ponds for fish production and in use of shrubs as tools of land management. Was chairman of Northeast Board of Agricultural Examiners for U.S. Civil Service Commission, 1946–57. Served as secretary of The Wildlife Society, 1940–42, and in 1947 was co-recipient of the society's award for outstanding wildlife publication of year. Was elected a fellow of Soil Conservation Society of America and was chairman of that society's committee on wetland management. Following retirement from government service, served as consulting ecologist. Authored more than one hundred scientific and popular publications. His major books include *The Ruffed Grouse*, 1947; *Fish-Ponds for the Farm*, 1947; and *American Game Birds of Field and Forest*, 1954. Died December 22, 1977.

LAWRENCE V. COMPTON

American Men of Science (Physical and Biological Sciences), 11th ed., 1965.

EHRLICH, PAUL RALPH
(born 1932)
Born May 29 in Philadelphia, Pennsylvania. University of Pennsylvania, B.A. (zoology) 1953; University of Kansas, M.A. 1955, Ph.D. 1957. Has conducted numerous research projects and served as field officer in Canadian Arctic and Sub-Arctic, and is Bing Professor of Population Studies at Stanford University. Is world-renowned population biologist and honorary president of Zero Population Growth, and author of international best seller, *The Population Bomb*, 1968, 1971, which played major role in triggering worldwide ecological movements during early 1970s. Also has either authored or coauthored, among other books, *The End of Affluence*, 1974; *The Golden Door*, 1979; *Ecoscience*, 1977; *Extinction*, 1981; and hundreds of scientific articles. Travels extensively worldwide as scientist and environmental spokesman and has been prime spokesperson for Conference on Biological Consequences of Nuclear War, emphasizing wildlife protection, resource conservation, population stabili-

zation, and need in America to reduce energy/resource consumption and fertility levels and to establish immigration reforms. Has won awards and fellowships from Sierra Club (John Muir Award), American Academy of Arts and Sciences, American Association for the Advancement of Science, and National Science Foundation. Has been professionally affiliated with many organizations and is advisory editor on numerous professional journals.

ZERO POPULATION GROWTH

American Men and Women of Science (Physical and Biological Sciences), 15th ed., 1982.

Who's Who in America, 42d ed., 1982–83.

Who's Who in the World, 6th ed., 1982–83.

EICHER, GEORGE JOHN
(born 1916)
Born August 27 in Bremerton, Washington. Washington State University, Utah State University, Oregon State University, B.S. 1941. Was party leader, Bristol Bay, Alaska research project, U.S. Bureau of Fisheries, 1939–41. In 1943 became Arizona's first fish biologist and headed its fish research and management until 1947, when he returned to Bristol Bay, Alaska, as project leader in charge of salmon research for U.S. Fish and Wildlife Service; also led research project in Southeastern Alaska on ocean mortality of pink salmon, 1950–55. In 1956 became chief biologist for Portland General Electric Company in Portland, Oregon, and later founded and managed that company's environmental department. In 1978 founded environmental consulting firm, Eicher Associates. Was founding president of Association of Power Biologists; president of American Fisheries Society, 1964–65; and has been active in American Institute of Fishery Research Biologists, The Wildlife Society, American Society of Limnology and Oceanography, Fishery Society of the British Isles, Pacific Fisheries Biologists, New York Academy of Sciences, and other organizations. In Arizona developed new system of aquatic weed control, made finding that trout could thrive in Salt River desert reaches, and pioneered lake rehabilitation and rough fish control. In Bristol Bay, Alaska, using aerial photography, made important findings influencing sockeye salmon spawning populations; supervised construction of first salmon ladder in Bristol Bay region, and was first to chemically treat an Alaska lake for fisheries management purposes. Is best known as de-

signer of fish passage facilities and developed several innovations in designs that have proven highly effective, and has designed fish passage and protection facilities in United States, Argentina, and Australia. Has published more than sixty papers on fisheries science and management. During and after holding presidency of American Fisheries Society, led efforts to augment interest and membership in the society (thereby making possible a paid executive staff) and to establish local society chapters. Is honorary life member of the society.

ROBERT F. HUTTON

American Men and Women of Science (Physical and Biological Sciences), 15th ed., (vol. 2), 1982.

Who's Who in America, 42d ed., 1982–83.

ELDREDGE, INMAN FOWLER
(1882–1963)
Born March 24 in Camden, South Carolina. Attended Clemson College, Biltmore Forest School, Bachelor of Forestry 1909; North Carolina State College, Doctor of Forest Science (honorary). In 1905 entered U.S. Forest Service as student assistant; was appointed forest assistant in 1906, and in 1909 was made forest examiner assigned to timber sales. Later that year became supervisor of newly created national forests in Florida, and for eight years administered half-million acres of government timberland. During this period developed new techniques of conservative turpentining, now in general use throughout naval-stores region. In 1917, at outbreak of World War I, was commissioned in U.S. Army and served as captain in Tenth Engineers (Forestry) in France. After war, returned to Forest Service as chief of Division of Timber Management in Eastern Region; subsequently was forest inspector of management and timber sales on all national forests on chief forester's staff in Washington, D.C. His Forest Service career was interrupted in 1926, when he took industrial employment to manage Suwanee Forest in longleaf pine region of southeast Georgia. Returned to Forest Service in 1932 as regional director of forest survey of the South at Southern Forest Experiment Station in New Orleans. In 1944 retired from Forest Service but continued work as private forest consultant. Was member of board of Charles Lathrop Pack Foundation and of Southern Division of Natural Resources Planning Board. Was member, Society of American Foresters, 1911, a fellow,

1942, and member of its council, 1940–43. Received Gifford Pinchot Medal, 1956. Died April 15, 1963.

SOCIETY OF AMERICAN FORESTERS

Journal of Forestry. Obituary, 61: 470, 1963.

EMBODY, GEORGE CHARLES
(1876–1939)
Born November 23 in Auburn, New York. Colgate University, M.S. (aquatic biology) 1901; Cornell University, Ph.D. (biology) 1910. Taught science at Delaware Literary Institute, New York, early in his career; became high-school teacher at Bradford, Pennsylvania, professor of science at Butler College, professor of biology at Randolph-Macon College, and later was assistant professor in aquaculture at Cornell University. Served as conservation biologist for New Jersey Fish Commission, then became biologist-advisor in fisheries for New York Conservation Department. In 1932 was biologist in charge of trout investigations in California. Was president of American Fisheries Society in 1924. Among his many papers on fisheries, his work in fish culture and trout field studies is the work for which he will be remembered most. Was pioneer in area of fish population harvest and dynamics, and is recognized as one of foremost early leaders in fisheries ecology. Died February 17, 1939.

ELWOOD A. SEAMAN

Who Was Who in America, 1897–1942.

ENGLISH, PENNOYER FRANCIS
(1894–1958)
Born February 21 in Farmington, Washington. Oregon State College, B.S. (zoology) 1919; Texas A&M College, M.S. 1925; University of Michigan, Ph.D. (wildlife management) 1934; also did graduate work at University of Chicago and Ohio State University. Nearly all his professional career was spent as university educator. Was assistant in zoology at Oregon State College, 1919–21; assistant professor of biology at Texas A&M College, 1921–24; professor of biology at St. Teresa College, Minnesota, 1924–26; associate professor of biology at Texas A&M College, 1926–31; biologist for Michigan Department of Conservation,

1933–35; associate professor of wildlife management at University of Connecticut, 1935–38; and professor of wildlife management at Pennsylvania State University, 1938–58. Was charter member of The Wildlife Society, its secretary from 1943 to 1946, its tenth president in 1946, and was elected honorary member in 1956. Other professional affiliations included Society of American Mammalogists, Cooper Ornithological Society, Wilson Ornithological Club, and American Ornithologists' Union. Was author of more than fifty scientific papers on wildlife management and conservation. As teacher and research worker, guided and directed graduate programs of some sixty wildlife management students. One of first in United States to be trained in wildlife management, he helped found wildlife profession. Died October 8, 1958.

ROBERT G. WINGARD

American Men of Science (Biological Sciences), 9th ed., 1955.

Journal of Wildlife Management. Obituary, vol. 23, July 1959.

ERRINGTON, PAUL LESTER

(1902–1962)

Born June 14 in Bruce, South Dakota. South Dakota State College, B.S. 1930; University of Wisconsin, Ph.D. (zoology) 1932. Was employed by Iowa State University during his entire professional career: as research assistant professor of zoology, 1932–38; research associate professor of zoology, 1938–48; and professor of zoology, 1948–62. His major research concerned food habits of avian and mammalian predators; effects of predation on prey populations; and automatically adjusting trends in population mechanisms of vertebrates. Spent a year (1958–59) in Scandinavia under auspices of Swedish government, Guggenheim Foundation, and National Science Foundation. Was selected twice by The Wildlife Society for outstanding writing on terrestrial wildlife: in 1941 for *The Great Horned Owl and Its Prey in North-Central United States,* 1940 (bulletin of Iowa Agricultural Experiment Station, with Frances Hamerstrom and F. N. Hamerstrom, Jr.), and in 1947 for "Predation and Vertebrate Populations," 1946, in *Quarterly Review of Biology.* In 1962 The Wildlife Society awarded him the Aldo Leopold Medal, the highest honor the society can bestow. Award was especially fitting, since he had received his graduate training under supervision of Professor Leopold at University of Wisconsin. A memorial fund at Iowa State University in Errington's name supports lectures by distinguished scientists. His bibliography includes more than two hundred titles. His better-known publications are *Of Men and Marshes*, 1957; *Muskrats and Marsh Management*, 1961; *Muskrat Populations*, 1963; *Predation and Life*, 1967. Died November 5, 1962.

THOMAS G. SCOTT

American Men of Science (Physical and Biological Sciences), 10th ed., 1960.

Iowa State Journal of Science. Bibliography, 38(4):447–58, 1964.

Journal of Wildlife Management. Obituary, 27(2):321–24, 1963.

ESCHMEYER, REUBEN WILLIAM
(1905–1955)
Born June 29 in New Knoxville, Ohio. Heidelberg College, Tiffin, Ohio, B.A. 1927; University of Michigan, A.M. 1931, Ph.D. (fisheries) 1937. Began his professional career as fisheries biologist for Institute of Fisheries Research, Michigan Conservation Department, where he was in charge of lake investigations for eight years, until 1938; there pioneered use of rotenone as management tool for improving fishing in public waters by eliminating existing fish populations and starting over, and in improvement of lake and pond fish habitat. In 1938 joined staff of Biological Readjustment Division (later renamed Fish and Game Branch), Tennessee Valley Authority, as associate aquatic biologist in charge of fisheries work; remained there for twelve years, becoming assistant chief of that division (later branch) in 1947. Organized and directed research program that resulted, in 1944, in abandoning closed season on warmwater game fishes in multipurpose TVA reservoirs, and in near-doubling of total catch without harm to future supply, a concept since applied in varying degrees throughout most of United States. In 1950 was selected as first executive vice-president of Sport Fishing Institute, Washington, D.C., a newly organized, national conservation organization; developed program emphasizing conservation education, research in fisheries biology, and improvement of professional standards in fisheries science. Understanding close dependence of fish on proper soil and forest conditions, he showed conservationists and sportsmen basic similarity between managing fish populations and managing land crops. Was consulted by state fish and conservation commissions for advice on modernizing their state fisheries programs. Was founding editor of Sport Fishing Institute's monthly *Bulletin*, wrote important essays on fish conservation subjects, particularly those grouped together in *Fish Conser-*

vation Fundamentals; *Land, Water and Fishing*; and *Conservation Chart and Text*. In addition to series of ten children's conservation books, was author or coauthor of more than fifty scientific fisheries papers; wrote chapters on fish conservation for conservation textbooks; and was junior author (with Carl L. Hubbs) of *The Improvement of Lakes for Fishing*, 1938, and senior author (with George S. Fichter) of *Good Fishing*, 1959. Died May 21, 1955. Was installed posthumously in Ohio Conservation Hall of Fame in August 1967.

RICHARD H. STROUD

American Men of Science, 8th ed., 1949.

Journal of Wildlife Management. Obituary, 19(4):483–84, October 1955.

Sport Fishing Institute Bulletin. Obituary, 44:1–2, July 1955.

EVANS, CHARLES FLOYD
(1885–1963)
Born February 26 at Muscoda, Wisconsin. University of Wisconsin, B.A. 1909; Yale University School of Forestry, M.F. 1912. Reported for duty with U.S. Forest Service in 1912 and was assigned to Targhee National Forest at Saint Anthony, Idaho, for two years and at Vernal, Utah, for three years. Was forest supervisor of Challis National Forest at Mackay, Idaho, 1918–22, and then assistant chief of operations in Ogden, Utah, regional office. Moved to New Orleans, Louisiana, in March 1927 as district inspector for Division of State Cooperation of the Forest Service, administering fire protection and tree seedling provisions of Clarke-McNary Act. From 1929 to 1934 served in similar capacity for southeastern states from base in Asheville, North Carolina. When southern regional office of Forest Service opened in Atlanta, Georgia, in July 1934, he became assistant regional forester in charge of State and Private Forestry Division for eleven states, performing outstanding service in this position until retiring in 1950. During this period, provided leadership and guidance in these programs. Was active worker in Society of American Foresters from 1921 until after retirement; served as chairman of Gulf States, Appalachian, and Southeastern sections; was national councilman, vice-president, and president during 1950–51; and elected fellow in 1950. The American Forestry Association honored him in 1950

with its Distinguished Service to Conservation Award. Died September 7, 1963.

JOHN W. COOPER

Journal of Forestry. Obituary, November 1963.

EVANS, MICHAEL BROCK
(born 1937)
Born May 24 in Columbus, Ohio. Princeton University, B.A. (history) 1959; University of Michigan Law School, LL.B. 1963. Spent four years in private law practice, including environmental law, 1963–67. Was appointed to position of northwest conservation representative for Sierra Club and Federation of Western Outdoor Clubs in 1967, responsible for interests of fifty organizations in four Northwest states, Northwest Canada, and Alaska. Was primarily responsible for organization of nearly thirty new environmental organizations, including Washington, Oregon, and Idaho environmental councils; initiated some of first environmental law proceedings by intervening in Federal Power Commission proceedings in opposition to dams in Hells Canyon; was active in campaigns to establish North Cascades National Park, additions to Three Sisters Wilderness in Oregon, Alpine Lakes Wilderness in Washington, Hells Canyon National Recreation area, and others. In 1973 became director of Washington, D.C., office of Sierra Club, participating in or leading campaigns on Alaska oil pipeline; Big Cypress Swamp Preserve, Florida; Boundary Waters Canoe Area, Minnesota; Congaree Swamp, South Carolina; Clean Air Act; Alaska natural gas pipeline; Forest Management Act; Eastern Wilderness Act; Mount Saint Helens National Monument; Energy Mobilization Board; and others. Initiated or participated in efforts to bring together environmentalists with often competing interests: National Homebuilders, labor, electric utilities, forest products industry, Army Corps of Engineers, and oil companies. In 1980 became associate director of Sierra Club and, in 1981, vice-president for national issues, National Audubon Society. Authored many articles in various publications, including those in which he was featured columnist for *Audubon* and *Sierra* magazines; two law-review articles, one on nuclear power issues for *Oregon Law Review*, 1974, and one on meaning of wilderness as force in American cultural history for *Idaho Law Review*, 1981. Received Environmentalist-of-the-Year Award from Washington Environ-

mental Council, 1972; and John Muir Award of the Sierra Club, 1981. Was member of executive committee, Natural Resources Council of America, 1973–77, and chairman, 1977–79; board of directors, Sierra Club, 1981–82; board of directors, Human Environment Center; steering committee, League of Conservation Voters; and executive committee, OSHA/Environmental Network.

MICHAEL B. EVANS

EVENDEN, FREDERICK GEORGE
(1921–1982)
Born April 11 in Woodburn, Oregon. Oregon State University, B.S. 1943, Ph.D. (zoology) 1949. In 1948 was appointed research biologist in U.S. Fish and Wildlife Service Office of River Basin Studies, Sacramento, California. In 1953 became executive director of Sacramento Science Center and Junior Museum. From 1956 to 1963, while in private business, was active conservationist. Created Conservation Committee for Golden Empire Council, Boy Scouts of America, and served as its chairman for several years; was on Chamber of Commerce Natural Resources Committee; and was president of Sacramento Audubon Society. In 1963 was selected by The Wildlife Society, Washington, D.C., as its first full-time executive secretary; and became executive director in 1968 until retiring in 1978. Was editor of *The Wildlife News*, 1964–69, and 1973–74, as well as editor of *The Wildlifer*, 1974–78. Served as chairman of International Association of Fish and Wildlife Agencies' Professional Improvement Committee, 1966–68; American Ornithologists' Union's Committee on Conservation, 1966–69; and on Boy Scouts National Conservation Committee, 1963–78, where he was instrumental in creation of Conservation of Natural Resources and Mammalogy merit badges. Was member of board of Consulting Experts on Rachel Carson Trust for Living Environment, 1967–69; vice-chairman of Renewable Natural Resources Foundation, 1970–78; secretary-treasurer of American Committee for International Conservation, 1978–79; and treasurer, Natural Resources Council of America, 1973–78. Was a fellow of American Association for the Advancement of Science. Received California Conservation Council Honor Award in 1958, and Boy Scouts Silver Beaver award in 1959. Authored numerous scientific articles and notes on natural resources subjects. Died February 20, 1982.

HENRY CLEPPER

American Men and Women of Science (Physical and Biological Sciences), 14th ed., 1979.

Who's Who in America, 42d ed., 1982–83.

Wildlife Society Bulletin, vol. 10, no. 2, 1982.

EVERMANN, BARTON WARREN
(1853–1932)
Born October 24 in Albia, Monroe County, Iowa. Indiana University, B.S. 1886, A.M. 1888, Ph.D. 1891, LL.D. 1927; University of Utah, LL.D. 1922. From 1886 to 1891 was professor of biology at Indiana State Normal School. Joining U.S. Bureau of Fisheries in 1891, was advanced to chief of Division of Statistics and Methods of Fisheries in 1902; became assistant in charge of scientific inquiry the following year; and was in charge of Alaska Fisheries Service, 1910–14, before retiring from federal service. While in government, also served as United States fur seal commissioner in 1892; was special lecturer at Stanford University, 1893–94; and was lecturer on fish and game protection at Cornell University, 1900–03, and at Yale University, 1903–6. In 1914 became director of California Academy of Sciences, San Francisco, and in 1922, director of Steinhart Aquarium; held these offices until his death. Was coauthor (with David Starr Jordan) of *The Fishes of North and Middle America*, 4 vols., 1896–1900; *American Food and Game Fishes*, 1902; *A Checklist of the Fishes and Fishlike Vertebrates of North and Middle America*, 1896. Wrote or contributed to 196 publications on fishes, including *Fishes of the Philippines*, 1906; *The Golden Trout of the Southern High Sierras*, 1906; *The Fishes of Alaska*, 1907; and *Fishes of Peru*, 1915. His wide interest as naturalist is revealed in 191 other publications, including 59 on birds. Management policies that he advocated for Alaska seal herd have helped conserve this valuable species, once on verge of extinction. Died September 27, 1932.

ROBERT V. THURSTON

Dictionary of American Biography, 1944.

National Cyclopaedia of American Biography, 1906.

Webster's Bibliographical Dictionary, 1961.

Who Was Who in America, 1897–1943.

World Who's Who in Science, 1968.

FARQUHAR, FRANCIS PELOUBET
(1887–1974)
Born December 31 in Newton, Massachusetts. Harvard University, B.A. 1909; University of California, LL.D. (honorary) 1967. Was in professional practice as certified public accountant from 1918 to 1959. Worked for enlargement of Sequoia National Park, 1919–26, and as representative of Sierra Club, appeared in behalf of this movement before Congressional committees. Was president of Sierra Club, 1933–35, and 1948–49; served on board of directors, 1924–51; was appointed honorary vice-president, 1969–74; and received the club's John Muir Conservation Award in 1965. From 1936 to 1950 served on Committee on Registration of Historic Sites for California Department of Natural Resources. Was editor of *Sierra Club Bulletin*, 1926–46; *American Alpine Journal*, 1956–59; *Up and Down California*, 1960–1964; *The Journal of William H. Brewer*, 1930; and *Mountaineering in the Sierra Nevada* by Clarence King, 1935. Authored *Place Names of the High Sierra*, 1926; *Yosemite, The Big Trees and the High Sierra: A Selective Bibliography*, 1948; and *History of the Sierra Nevada*, 1965. In addition, wrote numerous articles on western mountains and history, including several for *Encyclopedia Britannica*. Received Henry T. Wagner Medal from California Historical Society in 1965 for mountaineering, and was director of Save-the-Redwoods League. Died November 21, 1974.

LUELLA K. SAWYER

Sierra Club Handbook, 1967.

FELL, GEORGE BRADY
(born 1916)
Born September 27 in Elgin, Illinois. University of Illinois, B.S. (botany) 1938; University of Michigan, M.S. (wildlife management) 1940. Taught high-school science in 1940–41; did technical and manual conservation work in civilian public service for four years; was public-health laboratory technician in Rockford, Illinois, for three years; and soil conservationist with U.S. Soil Conservation Service for one year. In 1949, as chairman of Illinois State Academy of Science Conservation Committee, promoted establishment of Illinois natural area preservation program. In 1949 became vice-president of Ecologists Union and then played principal part in developing that organization into The Nature Conservancy, for which he served consecutively from 1950 to 1958 as vice-president,

secretary, and executive director. During that time, guided organization through early stages of its development and establishment of its structure and progam. Served as vice-president of Wild Flower Preservation Society, 1959–64. Organized Natural Land Institute in 1958 and has served as its director since that time. Initiated and secured enactment of legislation creating Illinois nature preserves system and Illinois Nature Preserves Commission, serving as its secretary, 1964–70, and executive secretary, 1970–82. Drafted and secured passage of Illinois Conservation District Act in 1963 and Illinois Natural Areas Preservation Act in 1981. Participated in organizing Natural Areas Association and served as its first secretary-treasurer, 1978–83.

GEORGE B. FELL

American Men and Women of Science (Physical and Biological Sciences), 15th ed., 1982.

FERNOW, BERNHARD EDUARD
(1851–1923)
Born January 7 in the province of Posen, Prussia. Studied law at the University of Konigsberg; then completed the prescribed curriculum in forestry for government service at Hanover-Muenden Academy and was licensed in 1869; University of Wisconsin, LL.D. 1896; Queen's University, LL.D. 1903; University of Toronto, LL.D. 1920. Before coming to United States in 1876, had been with Prussian Forest Service. From 1878 to 1885 managed large private forest in Pennsylvania and became active in public forestry causes; was also secretary of American Forestry Association, 1883–95. In 1886 was appointed chief of Division of Forestry, U.S. Department of Agriculture, and served until 1898. Was largely responsible for law of 1891 that authorized president to set apart portions of timbered public domain as forest reserves, the basic act from which present national forest system evolved. As chief forester, laid foundations on which was built present organization of U.S. Forest Service. In addition, created intelligent public interest in forestry and in need for education and research. From 1898 to 1903 was director of New York State College of Forestry at Cornell University, where he organized first professional forestry curriculum in Western Hemisphere. In 1904 gave series of lectures on forestry at Yale University, engaged also in consulting practice, and in 1907 helped start Department of Forestry at Pennsylvania State College. In 1907 went to University of Toronto, where he organized

Faculty of Forestry, and in 1919 retired with emeritus status. In 1902, while at Cornell, was responsible for establishment of *Forestry Quarterly*, of which he was editor from 1903 to 1916. After its merger with *Proceedings* of Society of American Foresters, through which it became *Journal of Forestry*, was editor-in-chief from 1917 to 1923. His contributions to literature of forestry are exceptional in number and quality; his bibliography totals 250 published papers, bulletins, and three books: *Economics of Forestry*, 1902; *A Brief History of Forestry*, 1913; and *Care of Trees*, 1910. Fernow Hall at Cornell was named for him and dedicated in his honor in 1922. One of pioneer leaders of profession of forestry in America, he had dominant role as administrator, educator, author, and editor. Gave the turn of this century its start in education for the profession, and remained educational leader as long as he lived. Died February 6, 1923.

HENRY CLEPPER

Dictionary of American Biography, 1931.

Journal of Forestry, Obituary, 21:306–37, 1923.

Rodgers, Andrew Denny, III. *Bernhard Eduard Fernow: A Study of North American Forestry*. Princeton, New Jersey, 1951.

FISHER, SHERRY ROBERT
(born 1907)
Born May 23 in Des Moines, Iowa. Iowa State University, 1927–28; University of Arizona, 1928–30. Served in U.S. Air Force during World War II. Was commissioner and chairman, Iowa State Conservation Commission, 1958–64, and member of Citizens Committee for the Outdoor Recreation Resources Review Commission, 1959–63. Made original presentation to National Park Service for Hoover Memorial, established in 1961 at West Branch, Iowa, assisting their complementary land-acquisition program. Was principal founder of J. N. "Ding" Darling Foundation in 1962, serving as trustee, 1962–84, and president and chairman, 1962–74; assisted in establishing J. N. "Ding" Darling National Wildlife Refuge on Sanibel Island, Florida. Played key leadership role in originating Lewis and Clark Trail Plan in 1962–63 by organizing and chairing several meetings that generated support for passage by Congress in 1964 of PL 88–630, creating Lewis and Clark Trail Commission; served as member and chairman of the Commission, 1966–71. Was member of Advisory Council to the Public Land Law Review Commis-

sion, 1964–70; national chairman of fisheries committee of Izaak Walton League of America, 1968–69; and member of Iowa State Soil Conservation Committee 1971–73, spearheading new tree-planting and water-quality programs. Served as appointed member of Lewis and Clark Historic and Mormon National Historic Trails advisory councils from 1981 to present. Helped originate cooperative program in Iowa State Extension Department by establishing new conservation teaching modules in 1982. Received Silver Beaver Award of the Boy Scouts of America in 1955; Conservationist of the Year Award of Des Moines Chapter of Izaak Walton League of America in 1964; and Conservationist of the Year awards from Iowa Wildlife Federation and from National Wildlife Federation in 1970.

HORACE M. ALBRIGHT

FORBES, STEPHEN ALFRED
(1844–1930)
Born May 29 in Stephenson County, Illinois. Attended Bush Medical College in Chicago but did not take his degree. Indiana University awarded him doctorate in 1884 by thesis and examination. His first publications appeared in 1870. In 1872 was appointed curator of museum established by State Natural History Society at Normal, Illinois; when it became State Laboratory of Natural History in 1877, was appointed its head. In 1885 became professor of zoology and entomology at University of Illinois; director of State Laboratory of Natural History; and state entomologist. Was professor of zoology for twenty-five years, and concurrently professor of entomology for thirteen years and dean of College of Science for sixteen years. When State Laboratory of Natural History and State Entomologist's Office were united in 1917 to form Illinois Natural History Survey, he became the first chief, a position he held until his death. Often called the father of ecology, his interests covered all biology. Altogether, wrote more than fifty papers and reports on such diverse subjects as crustacea, foods of fishes, foods of birds, ornithology, taxonomy and distribution of fishes, economic entomology, elm trees, forestry survey, and river biology. His best-known works are *The Lake as a Microcosm*, Illinois Natural History Survey Bulletin 15(9):537–50, and two-volume work (with R. E. Richardson) entitled *The Fishes of Illinois*. Died March 13, 1930.

GEORGE W. BENNETT

A Century of Biological Research, Illinois Natural History Bulletin 27(2):94–97.

FORBUSH, EDWARD HOWE
(1858–1929)
Born April 24 in Quincy, Massachusetts. His formal education was limited, and he learned ornithology and taxidermy by working. At age of sixteen was appointed curator of ornithology of Worcester Massachusetts Natural History Museum. Following collecting expeditions in Florida, was cofounder of Naturalists' Exchange. In 1888 led collecting expedition to Pacific Northwest, Western Canada, and Alaska. In 1893 served on committee of Massachusetts Board of Agriculture, studying destructive gypsy moth, and in 1903 was designated ornithologist to the board. In 1908 was named state ornithologist, and in 1920 was appointed first director of Division of Ornithology in Massachusetts Department of Agriculture. Retired in 1928. His investigations contributed much to scientific knowledge of the control by birds of insects injurious to agricultural and tree crops. Among his lasting contributions are Massachusetts wildlife and conservation laws, which he inspired and which served as models for legislation in other states. A founder of Massachusetts Audubon Society, he was also a fellow of American Ornithologists' Union. Was on Advisory Board of U.S. Department of Agriculture for migratory bird treaty of 1913 between Canada and United States. Among his important writings are *Useful Birds and Their Protection*, 1907, and his monumental *Birds of Massachusetts and Other New England States*, 1925 and 1927. Died March 7, 1929.

NATIONAL AUDUBON SOCIETY

Edward Howe Forbush: A Biographical Sketch. Proceedings of the Boston Society of Natural History, 39(2):33–72, 1928.

"In Memoriam: Edward Howe Forbush." *Auk*, 47(2):137–46, April 1930.

National Cyclopaedia of American Biography, 1931.

Who Was Who in America, 1897–1942.

FOSBERG, FRANCIS RAYMOND
(born 1908)
Born May 20 in Spokane, Washington. Pomona College, B.A. (botany) 1930; botanist at Los Angeles Museum for two years; University of Ha-

waii, M.A. (botany) 1935; University of Pennsylvania, Ph.D. (botany) 1939. On Bishop Museum Mangarevan Expedition, 1934, his earlier interest in island ecology became focused on atolls. Was U.S. Department of Agriculture botanist, 1939–46, working on U.S. Economic Survey of Micronesia; had Guggenheim Fellowship, 1947–48; was visiting professor, University of Hawaii, 1948; taught at George Washington University, 1948–49; and did research at Catholic University, 1949–50. During World War II, was senior botanist on Colombian Chinchona Mission, locating trees that made possible the revival of wild quinine industry when Far Eastern sources were cut off. From 1951 to 1966 was botanist with U.S. Geological Survey. Joined Smithsonian Institution as advisor on tropical botany in 1966, became curator of botany in 1970, and was made botanist emeritus in 1978. His part in dozens of symposia, expeditions, and special missions has enabled him to assemble more than 64,000 collections of herbarium material. Has written some 600 articles and books, several being standard texts. With special concern for threatened species of plants and animals, he stresses interaction of ecosystems and interdependence of species. Served as chairman of Committee on Conservation in Micronesia for Pacific Science Board of the National Research Council; and had leading role in Pacific Science Congresses, Man and the Biosphere Program of UNESCO, and its predecessor, International Biological Program. With two colleagues, aroused sufficient international concern to thwart U.S.-British plan to destroy unique life of Aldabra Island for an air base, and continues to try to preserve the other unspoiled high coral island, Henderson. Received Gregory Medal of Pacific Science Association in 1971; George Davidson Medal of the American Geographical Society in 1972; and Browning Award in 1979.

Shirley A. Briggs

American Men and Women of Science (Physical and Biological Sciences), 12th ed. (vol. 2), 1972.

Foster, Charles Henry Wheelwright
(born 1927)
Born March 18 in Boston, Massachusetts. Harvard University, B.A. (English) 1951; University of Michigan, B.S. (forestry) 1953, M.S. (wildlife management) 1956; Johns Hopkins University, Ph.D. (geography and environmental engineering) 1969; Suffolk University, D.P.A. (honorary) 1971; Yale University, M.A. (honorary) 1977. Served in U.S. Army

1945–47. Was executive secretary of Wildlife Conservation, Inc., 1953–55; consultant to Massachusetts Water Resources Commission, 1956–59; commissioner of Massachusetts Department of Natural Resources, 1959–66; president of The Nature Conservancy, 1966–67; advisor to The Conservation Foundation, 1968–69; chairman of board of New England Natural Resources Center, 1970–71; and first secretary of Massachusetts Executive Office of Environmental Affairs, 1971–74. Was professor of environmental policy at University of Massachusetts; senior staff member at Arthur D. Little, 1975–76; dean of Yale School of Forestry and Environmental Studies, 1976–81; visiting scholar at Stanford University, 1981–83; and president of W. Alton Jones Foundation in Charlottesville, Virginia, from 1983 to present. Has been trustee or member of numerous natural resource and environmental organizations and advisory bodies, including Cape Cod National Seashore Advisory Commission; Atlantic States Marine Fisheries Commission; New England Interstate Water Pollution Control Commission; Massachusetts Historical Commission; International Commission for the Northwest Atlantic Fisheries; Public Land Law Review Commission; National Science Foundation Advisory Committee on the Assessment of Research on Natural Hazards; Massachusetts Governor's Council on Resouce Management Policy and Council on Solid Waste; The Conservation Foundation; Woods Hole Oceanographic Institution; and Board of Overseers of Harvard College. Is a fellow of American Association of the Advancement of Science, and member of Society of American Foresters, Soil Conservation Society of America, and The American Forestry Association.

THE CONSERVATION FOUNDATION

American Men and Women of Science (Physical and Biological Sciences), 15th ed., 1982.

Who's Who in America, 42d ed., 1982–83.

FOX, ADRIAN CASPER
(born 1905)
Born January 28 near Leeds, North Dakota. Educated in agriculture, forestry, botany, and entomology at North Dakota State College, M.S. 1932. Began his career as assistant county agent before joining U.S. Soil Conservation Service (SCS) in 1935 as assistant forester at Huron, South Dakota. In 1935 became biologist at Park River, North Dakota, where he directed wildlife conservation and game management programs in

SCS demonstration projects and Civilian Conservation Corps camps throughout state. Served from 1942 to 1955, except for thirty-three months in military service, as head of educational relations work for seven-state region consisting of Montana, Wyoming, Colorado, North Dakota, South Dakota, Nebraska, and Kansas. In 1955 was transferred, in charge of this work nationally, to Washington, D.C., office of SCS, where he served until his retirement in December 1965. Served on board of directors of Conservation Education Association and American Nature Study Society; was advisor to youth programs and education committees of National Association of Soil and Water Conservation Districts, and member of Conservation Education Committee for Soil Conservation Society of America; Izaak Walton League of America, and National Association of Biology Teachers. Received Nebraska Conservation Trophy in 1949 and Award of Merit from National Association of Conservation and Publicity in 1950. In 1964 was awarded American Motors Conservation Award for professional conservationists. Is author of numerous articles and publications; and coauthor of *Teaching Soil and Water Conservation*, of which a million and a half copies have been distributed to teachers and other youth leaders by U.S. Department of Agriculture.

ALBERT B. FOSTER

FRANK, BERNARD
(1902–1964)
Born March 7 in New York City. Cornell University, B.S. (forestry) 1925, M.F. 1929. First year of his career was spent as forester for pulp and paper company in Quebec, and in 1926 was assistant in forest utilization at Cornell. Entering U.S. Forest Service in 1927, was assigned to economic studies, and in 1931 was transferred to Lake States Forest Experiment Station at Saint Paul for research. From 1934 to 1945 was on forestry staff of Tennessee Valley Authority; returned to Forest Service in Washington, D.C., in 1945 as assistant chief of Division of Watershed Management Research until his retirement in 1959. Set up program of watershed management research in India on assignment for Food and Agriculture Organization of United Nations. In 1960 joined faculty of School of Forestry of Colorado State University as professor of watershed management. A charter member of The Wilderness Society, founded in 1935, Frank was on its Governing Council from its inception. Was a

fellow of Society of American Foresters and of Soil Conservation Society of America, as well as member of editorial board of *Journal of Soil and Water Conservation*, and was active on other scientific and conservation bodies. Was coauthor of *Water, Land and People*, 1950; author of *Our National Forests*, 1955; and wrote more than one hundred papers and bulletins on all aspects of forestry management, recreation, soil erosion, and flood control. Died November 15, 1964.

MICHAEL NADEL

Living Wilderness. Winter 1964–65, no. 87.

FRANKLIN, THOMAS MICHAEL
(born 1950)
Born June 20 in Washington, D.C. University of Maryland, B.S. (wildlife management) 1972. Did graduate studies in administrative sciences at University of Maryland and Johns Hopkins University. In 1973 joined Urban Wildlife Research Center as wildlife biologist and in 1977 became its executive director. In 1983 was appointed field director of The Wildlife Society. Has served as liaison with American Planning Association and as co-chairman of Program Committee representing The Wildlife Society for Forty-Ninth North American Wildlife and Natural Resources Conference. Has served on executive committee of Natural Resources Council of America, and on board of directors of National Institute for Urban Wildlife (formerly Urban Wildlife Resources Council, UWRC) and Center for Urban Environmental Studies. Was program chairman for first Urban Fishing Symposium in 1983. Under his leadership, the UWRC received Gulf Oil Conservation Award and Natural Resources Council of America Award of Achievement in 1982. Has served on governmental and private sector wildlife advisory councils and has authored or coauthored numerous publications on urban and suburban wildlife and fish conservation.

HARRY E. HODGDON

FREDERICK, KARL TELFORD
(1881–1963)
Born February 2 in Chateaugay, New York. Princeton University, B.A. 1903, A.M. (economics) 1904; Harvard Law School, LL.B. 1908. Was

editor of *Harvard Law Review*, 1906–8, was admitted to New York Bar in 1909, and practiced law throughout his active career. As member of United States pistol and revolver teams, won individual pistol world championship at 1920 Olympic Games in Belgium. Was a founder of New York State Conservation Council, serving as its president from 1935 to 1942, and thereafter until his death as chairman of its board of directors. For twenty-six years was director of The American Forestry Association and chairman of its executive committee for most of that period. Long active in Camp Fire Club of America, was its vice-president in 1926 and president in 1927 and 1928, and received the club's Medal of Honor in 1956. Was a founder of American Game Protective Association and early leader of The National Wildlife Federation, serving as director from 1939 to 1948 and as vice-president from 1949 to 1953. In 1927 was elected to board of directors of National Rifle Association; to its presidency, 1934–36; and to its executive council in 1937; and was awarded honorary life membership in 1958. For many years was member of American Olympic Committee. As member of National Crime Commission's Committee on Firearms, devoted much study to formulation of Uniform Pistol Law, which was approved by American Bar Association and adopted by a number of states. Frederick Peak in Yellowstone National Park was named for him in 1966. Died February 11, 1963.

RICHARD PARDO

FREDINE, CLARENCE GORDON
(born 1909)
Born August 15 in Saint Paul, Minnesota. Hamline University, Saint Paul, B.S. (biology) 1932; University of Minnesota, graduate study (zoology) 1932–35. Was biologist supervisor, ECW/CCC, Minnesota State Forests, 1935–36; biologist, Game and Fish Division of the Minnesota Conservation Department, 1935–41; and assistant professor in wildlife at Purdue University, 1941–47. Was regional supervisor, River Basin Studies, U.S. Fish and Wildlife Service, Atlanta, Georgia, 1947–52. Made significant contribution to knowledge about America's wetlands habitats as wildlife research biologist supervisor, 1952–55. Transferred in 1955 to National Park Service as principal naturalist (biology), where his interest in application of ecological principles influenced the Service's research and wildlife-management programs. As principal park planner, served in

Mission 66 program, 1962–64. Became chief of National Park Service Division of International Affairs in 1964. Helped organize and expand student conservation program, and helped develop the service's policy leading to increased international activities. Assisted in establishment of Latin American Committee on National Parks, and organized Inter-American Conference on Renewable Natural Resources in Argentina and Joint United States–Japan Park Management Panel. Was executive secretary of The Wildlife Society, 1960–63; vice-president, 1966–67; and was elected honorary member in 1964. Received U.S. Department of the Interior Distinguished Service Award in 1967. Coauthored *Wetlands of the United States: Their Extent and Their Value to Waterfowl and Other Wildlife*, 1956. After serving as staff director for Second World Conference on National Parks, 1972, retired from National Park Service in 1973. As volunteer, was assistant editor of *Parks Magazine*, 1973–78. Was president, Washington Biologists Field Club, 1973–76, and executive director of Renewable Natural Resources Foundation, 1975–81. Subsequently became coordinator of volunteer advisory staff for American Fisheries Society; received its Distinguished Service Award in 1983.

FRED G. EVENDEN
C. GORDON FREDINE

American Men of Science (Physical and Biological Sciences), 11th ed., 1965.

Who's Who in America, 42d ed., 1982–83.

FREEMAN, RAYMOND LEE
(born 1919)
Born June 13 in Earlham, Iowa. Iowa State University, B.L.A. 1942. Served in U.S. Army, 1942–46. Began thirty-year career with National Park Service, in water resources planning programs at Omaha, Nebraska, 1946–53. Was assistant chief, River Basin and Water Resource Studies in Washington, D.C., headquarters office until 1953–55, when he was designated to serve on staff of Mission 66 program, which was instrumental in developing long-range plans and programs for National Park Service. Served as assistant regional director for National Capital Parks, 1962–66, then became deputy assistant director in 1966 and deputy associate director in 1968. Was responsible for formulation and implementation of major planning, design, and construction programs for National Park Service. In 1971 became associate director of Office of Field Operations, interpreting policy, establishing programs, and evalu-

ating management and operations of National Park Service facilities. Served as president of American Society of Landscape Architects (ASLA), 1971–73. As assistant director of Office of Development in National Park Service, 1973, was responsible for direction of park planning, environmental impact statements, interpretive media, and design and construction of projects. Since retiring from federal service in 1978, has served as director of government affairs to ASLA. Has been visiting lecturer to Texas A&M University, Cornell University, Syracuse University, University of Virginia, and Iowa State University. Was presented with U.S. Department of the Interior's Meritorious Service Award, 1966, and invested as distinguished fellow of ASLA, 1967. Received U.S. Department of the Interior's Distinguished Service Award, 1971, and Landscape Architecture Foundation's Le Gasse Award, 1982. Has been involved actively with International Federation of Landscape Architects (IFLA) as ASLA senior delegate to IFLA Grand Council, chairman of International Committee on Legislation, and special assistant to president of IFLA.

AMERICAN SOCIETY OF LANDSCAPE ARCHITECTS
Who's Who in America, 42d ed., 1982–83.

FRITZ, EMANUEL
(born 1886)
Born October 29 in Baltimore, Maryland. Cornell University, M.E. 1908; Yale University, M.F. 1914. Began his professional career in forestry under state forester of New Hampshire. Joined U.S. Forest Service in 1915 in Northern Rocky Mountain Region; transferred in 1916 to Fort Valley Forest Experiment Station in Arizona. Then followed two years with U.S. Army Air Service in France as officer with 639th Aero Squadron (mechanics). Joined faculty of University of California School of Forestry in 1919 and taught wood technology and forest products. Then began half-century of study of ecology of California redwoods, and silvicultural practices and economics of the redwood industry. As forestry advisor to California Redwood Association, influenced adoption of selective cutting practices by industry. Long a member of Society of American Foresters, was member of its council, 1934–36; associate editor, 1928–30; chief editor, 1930–33; and was elected a fellow in 1951. Received distinguished achievement award in 1955 from Western Forestry and Conservation Association. A founder of Redwood Region Logging Congress, he was its manager for twenty-two years. Served as coun-

cilor of Save-the-Redwoods League since 1933. Is currently director of Forest History Society, Inc. Is author of nearly two hundred articles on forestry, forest policy, wood technology, and lumbering, and of book *California Coast Redwood*, an annotated bibliography published in 1957. Retired from the university in 1954.

PAUL CASAMAJOR

American Men of Science (Physical and Biological Sciences), 11th ed., 1965.
Who's Who in the West.

FROME, MICHAEL
(born 1920)
Born May 25 in New York City. Studied at City College, New York; George Washington University; and Pan-American Airways School, University of Miami. Following service in U.S. Army Air Corps, 1942–45, was staff writer on *Washington Post* (D.C.), 1945–46, and worked in public relations for American Automobile Association, 1947–57. On becoming free-lance writer in 1958, first devoted much attention to tourism, then enlarged his horizons to studies and articles about natural resources, people, and their environment. In 1967 began contributing monthly articles to *American Forests* magazine and in 1968 to *Field and Stream*, remaining with those periodicals for six and seven years, respectively. Subsequently contributed weekly column ("Environmental Trails") to *Los Angeles Times* for five years. In 1983 was appointed environmental editor and columnist of *Western Outdoors*. Among his books are *Whose Woods These Are: The Story of the National Forests*, 1962; *Strangers in High Places: The Story of the Great Smoky Mountains*, 1966, reissued in 1980; Rand Mc-Nally *Park Guide*, annually since 1967; *The National Forests of America* (coauthor with Orville L. Freeman), 1968; *The Varmints*, 1969; *The Forest Service*, 1972, reissued in 1983; *Battle for the Wilderness*, 1974; and *The National Parks* (with David Muench), 1977 and 1979. As lucid interpreter of natural resources and defender of endangered environment, he has written knowledgeably about forests, soil, water, wildlife, and outdoor recreation as they relate to human culture. In 1978 served as visiting professor of environmental studies at Pinchot Institute for Conservation Studies; and 1982–84 as visiting associate professor at College of Forestry, University of Idaho. In 1982 delivered Wilderness Resource Distinguished Lecture at University

of Idaho. Is leading author and critic of contemporary policies, public, and private, that affect America's resource heritage.

HENRY CLEPPER

FROST, SHERMAN LEWIS
(born 1909)
Born May 22 in New Haven, Connecticut. University of Connecticut, B.S. 1931; Yale University School of Forestry, M.F. 1933. Served with Civilian Conservation Corps Camp in Connecticut and with U.S. Forest Service in Colorado, New Mexico, Louisiana, and Texas, 1933–36. Was in charge of information and education with Texas Forest Service, also serving as secretary-treasurer of Texas Forestry Association, 1936–48. Helped organize and served as first chairman of Southern States Forestry Educational Council; was executive director of The American Forestry Association, 1948–52; was involved in consulting, research, and writing for National Geographic Society and The Conservation Foundation, 1952–54; and was research director for Ohio Forestry Association, drafting water conservation plan for Ohio and making studies of conservancy districts and watershed programs, 1954–56. Worked in Ohio Department of Natural Resources, generally at deputy director level, in capacities related to water planning and to planning and research in environmental assessment, geological survey, lands and soil, soil and water districts, recreation planning, scenic rivers, natural areas, and engineering, 1956–72; and was executive secretary of Ohio Water Commission, 1960–72. Since then, has been on special assignments with Ohio Environmental Protection Agency; Ohio Agricultural Research and Development Center; Great Lakes and Ohio River Basin commissions; Ohio State University; and Ohio Department of Natural Resources; and was member of Ohio Environmental Board of Review, 1976–81. Is a fellow of Ohio Academy of Science, and was editor of American Association of School Administrators' textbook, *Conservation in the People's Hands* (1962).

JOHN F. DISINGER

GABRIELSON, IRA NOEL

(1889–1977)

Born September 27 at Sioux Rapids, Iowa. Morningside College, B.A. (biology) 1912, LL.D. 1941; Oregon State College, D.Sc. 1936; Middlebury College, D.Sc. 1959; Colby College, D.Sc. 1969. After teaching high-school biology at Marshalltown, Iowa, 1912–15, joined Bureau of Biological Survey in U.S. Department of Agriculture, and worked mainly in West for next two decades in field and supervisory positions involving economic ornithology, food habits research, rodent control, and game management. In 1935 transferred to Washington, D.C., as assistant chief of Division of Wildlife Research, becoming chief of Bureau of Biological Survey that same year; in 1940 was appointed as first director of Fish and Wildlife Service in U.S. Department of the Interior. Served as deputy coordinator of fisheries during World War II, with responsibility of sustaining seafood production essential to conduct of the war. Appointed as U.S. Delegate to International Whaling Conference by U.S. Department of State in 1946; resigned government service that same year to assume presidency of Wildlife Management Institute, a post he held until 1970, when he became board chairman. As United States delegate in 1948, helped found International Union for the Conservation of Nature and Natural Resources. In 1961 helped to organize and became president of World Wildlife Fund (United States) and trustee of World Wildlife Fund (International). Served on advisory committee of Outdoor Recreation Resources Review Commission; was member of secretary of the Interior's Advisory Committee on Fish and Wildlife for many years, and was later member of Secretary's Advisory Board on Wildlife Management. Was chairman of Citizens Committee on Natural Resources; chairman of Coordinating Committee on the Potomac River Valley; member of National Conservation Committee, Boy Scouts of America; and member of Committee on Pest Control and Wildlife Relationships, National Academy of Sciences–National Research Council. Directed staff studies of organization and operation of wildlife departments in thirty-one states and two Canadian provinces. Authored *Western American Alpines*, 1932; *Wildlife Conservation*, 1941; *Wildlife Refuges*, 1943; and *Wildlife Management*, 1951. Coauthored *Birds of Oregon*, 1940; *The Birds of Alaska*, 1958; *Birds: A Guide to the Most Familiar American Birds*, 1949; and edited *Fisherman's Encyclopedia*, 1951, and *New Fish Encyclopedia*, 1964. Received Distinguished Service Medal of U.S. Department of the Interior in 1948; Aldo Leopold Memorial Award Medal of The Wildlife Society in 1953; Audubon Medal of the National Audubon

Society in 1949; Hugh H. Bennett Medal of Friends of the Land in 1958; Distinguished Service Award of The American Forestry Association in 1962; and U.S. Department of the Interior's Conservation Service Award in 1964. Died September 7, 1977.

DANIEL A. POOLE

American Men and Women of Science (Physical and Biological Sciences), 12th ed. (vol. 2), 1972.

Who's Who in America, 39th ed., 1976–77.

GANNETT, HENRY
(1846–1914)
Born August 24 in Bath, Maine. Harvard University, S.B. 1969, M.E. 1870; Bowdoin College, LL.D. 1899. As topographer on geographical surveys in West, 1872–79, became chief geographer in 1882 for Geographical Survey, U.S. Department of the Interior, serving that bureau with distinction until his death. Was chairman for twenty years of U.S. Geographic Board, established in 1890. Aided in formation of National Geographic Society in 1883, was its first secretary, and was president, 1910–14. Was also a founder of Geographical Society of America and associate editor of the society's *Bulletin*, and a founder of Association of American Geographers. Following passage of act of 1897 that provided for administration and protection of forest reserves (then under jurisdiction of U.S. Department of the Interior), was put in charge of their mapping and classification. His duties included making estimate of timber stand, which was reported to be 1.39 billion board feet in twelfth census of 1900. Assigned by President Theodore Roosevelt to supervise compilation of first inventory of natural resources ever made in United States, he edited National Conservation Commission's monumental three-volume report published in 1909. Was author of books on geography, including *Manual of Topographic Surveying*, and of several statistical atlases of United States. Died November 5, 1914.

HENRY CLEPPER

Dictionary of American Biography, 1931.

National Geographic Magazine. Obituary, 26(6):609–13, December 1914.

Who Was Who in America, 1897–42.

GARNER, MARY MARTIN

Born in Little Rock, Arkansas. George Washington University Law School, J.D. 1942. Admitted to practice before courts of District of Columbia and United States Supreme Court. From 1944 to 1974 served as attorney in Office of the General Counsel, U.S. Department of Agriculture, and as deputy director of Division of Natural Resources. Since 1975 has served as legal consultant to National Association of Conservation Districts, conducting research and writing in soil and water conservation district law, state erosion and sediment control legislation, and related topics. Serves on Governing Council of the International Bar Association, as assistant secretary in Inter-American Bar Association, and as chairman of International Law Council of Federal Bar Association. Was principal drafter of Model State Act for Soil Erosion and Sediment Control, published by Council of State Governments in its 1973 Suggested State Legislation; Model State Act has resulted in passage of similar laws in twenty-one states and District of Columbia. Was presented National Association of Conservation Districts Distinguished Service Award in 1972; Federal Bar Association's Earl W. Kintner Award for Distinguished Service in 1979; and Inter-American Bar Foundation's Distinguished Service Award in 1982. Her writings on soil conservation law have appeared in *Journal of Soil and Water Conservation, The Agricultural Law Journal,* and *Federal Bar News and Journal.*

NATIONAL ASSOCIATION OF CONSERVATION DISTRICTS

GARRATT, GEORGE ALFRED

(born 1898)

Born May 7 in Brooklyn, New York. Michigan Agricultural College, B.S. 1920; Yale University, M.F. 1923, Ph.D. 1933; University of the South, D.Sc. 1957; Michigan State University, LL.D. 1972. His career has been largely devoted to teaching and educational administration, including forty-one years on faculty of Yale University. Taught forestry at Michigan Agricultural College, 1921–22; and at University of the South, 1923–25. In 1925 joined faculty of Yale School of Forestry, where his specialty was wood technology; became Manufacturers' Association professor of lumbering in 1939, and Pinchot professor of forestry in 1955. Was assistant dean, 1936–39, and dean from 1945 until 1965. Retired in 1966 as dean and Pinchot professor of forestry emeritus. During World War II was chief of division of technical service training at U.S. Forest Service Forest Products Laboratory in Madison, Wisconsin; later was director of packaging training center, U.S. Transportation Corps in Paris, France. For the latter service was awarded United States Medal of Freedom. Was member of Connecticut State Park and Forest Commission, 1949–71 (chairman 1950), and of Connecticut State Council on Agriculture and Natural Resources, 1959–71 (chairman 1961–65). Served on national forestry research advisory committee, U.S. Department of Agriculture, 1958–64. Was member of program planning committees of Third, Fourth, and Fifth American Forest congresses; charter member of Forest Products Research Society (vice-president 1948, president 1949); a fellow, Society of American Foresters (vice-president 1956–57, president 1958–59, council member 1960–61). Was director, The American Forestry Association, 1970–75, and a fellow, Canadian Institute of Forestry. Was charter member, Society of Wood Science and Technology, and director of study of forestry education in Canada sponsored by Canadian Institute of Forestry. Received Sir William Schlich Medal of the Society of American Foresters in 1966; distinguished service award of American Forest Products Industries, Inc. in 1967; and John Aston Warder Medal of The American Forestry Association in 1981. Is author of *Mechanical Properties of Wood*, 1931; *Wood Preservation* (with G. M. Hunt), 1938, 1953, 1967; and *Forestry Education in Canada*, 1971.

JESSE H. BUELL
GEORGE A. GARRATT

American Men and Women of Science (Physical and Biological Sciences), 15th ed., 1982.

Yale Forest School News. Deanship Succession, vol. 53, April 1965.

Who's Who in America, 41st ed., 1980–81.

GIFFORD, JOHN CLAYTON
(1870–1949)
Born February 8 at Mays Landing, New Jersey. Swarthmore College, B.S. 1890; graduate studies in botany at University of Michigan and Johns Hopkins University; University of Munich, Bavaria, D.Oec. (economics) 1899. Taught botany at Swarthmore College, 1890–94. While employed as forester for New Jersey Geographical Survey during 1885–96, was founding editor of magazine *New Jersey Forester*, subsequently named

American Forests, which became official organ of The American Forestry Association. In 1900 joined faculty of New York State College of Forestry at Cornell University, the first collegiate institution in America to offer professional curriculum in forestry. When it was discontinued three years later, he became special agent for U.S. Bureau of Forestry (now Forest Service) on survey of forests of Puerto Rico. Subsequently traveled in West Indies, Central and South America, and Mexico, studying tropical forests and fruit-bearing trees. For two decades was professor of tropical forestry and conservation at University of Miami; in addition to his university teaching, lectured widely in public schools and before civic organizations. Joined Society of American Foresters in 1902; was elected a fellow in 1942. Was a fellow also of American Association for the Advancement of Science. Was author of one of first books on forest management—*Practical Forestry*, 1901—and thereafter wrote many articles and several books on agriculture, forestry, and horticulture, among them *The Everglades of Florida*, 1911, and his last, *Living by the Land*, 1945. Died June 25, 1949.

HENRY CLEPPER

Journal of Forestry, 45(6):455–56, June 1947.

Who Was Who in America, 1943–50.

GILL, THOMAS HARVEY
(1891–1972)

Born January 21 in Philadelphia. University of Pennsylvania, B.A. 1913; Yale University, M.F. 1915; University of the Andes, Venezuela, honorary doctorate 1953. Joined U.S. Forest Service in Wyoming in 1915 as assistant ranger; ranger, 1916–17; and supervisor, 1922, in charge of public relations in Washington, D.C., office, 1922–25. Was forester for The American Forestry Association and associate editor of *American Forests and Forest Life*, 1925. Was appointed in 1926 as executive director of Charles Lathrop Pack Forestry Foundation, continuing until its liquidation in 1960. Was first lieutenant in U.S. Army Air Service during World War I. Long active in Society of American Foresters, he was chairman of Committee on International Relations for seven years; elected fellow in 1948; and awarded Sir William Schlich Memorial Medal in 1954 for outstanding contributions to forestry. International services include membership (1944) on Technical Committee on Forestry and Forest Products of United Nations Interim Commission on Food and Agriculture, and advisor on forestry (1945) at Food and Agriculture Organization of the United Nations' organizing conference in Quebec. Was delegate to all six World Forestry congresses: Rome 1926, Budapest 1936, Helsinki 1949, India 1954, Seattle (as member of organizing committee) 1960, and Madrid 1966. Other international bodies, including Japan 1951, Formosa 1952, and the Philippines 1959, have sought his advice on forests and related natural resources. Was president and founder of International Society of Tropical Foresters; currently is executive director of International Union of Societies of Foresters. Was awarded Merito Civico Forestal by Mexico; Distinguished Service Cross by Germany; Chevalier, Merite Agricole, by France; honorary diploma by Mexican Institute of Renewable Resources; and Bernhard E. Fernow Award by The American Forestry Association and Deutscher Forstverein. Was author of numerous articles on forestry and natural resources, and of books *Forests and Mankind* (coauthor), 1929; *Tropical Forests of the Caribbean*, 1931; *The Forestry Directory* (coeditor), 1943, 1949; *Land Hunger in Mexico*, 1951; and other works, including fiction. Died May 21, 1972.

HENRY CLEPPER

Who's Who in America, 1968–69.

GILLETT, CHARLES ALTON
(1904–1981)
Born October 24 in Auburn, New York. Cornell University, B.S. 1925, M.S. 1929. Appointed extension forester in North Dakota in 1925, served two years, then in 1929 became extension forester in Arkansas. In 1933, as first state forester of Arkansas, built up forestry organization and fire control system during next six years. In 1939 was employed by Seaboard Air Line Railroad as industrial forester, engaging in educational work with landowners, schools, and youth organizations in area served by railroad. American Forest Products Industries, Inc. (AFPI), which had been founded three years earlier in Washington, D.C., by forest industries as medium for public education, engaged him in 1944 as chief forester. AFPI's primary purpose was to inform American people about economic contributions of forest products to general welfare and about progess in private forestry under free enterprise. After three years as chief forester, was promoted to position of managing director. Under his administration, the tree-farm movement, which was started in 1941,

grew to seventy million acres. The 32,000 tree farms in system formed world's greatest voluntary forest-growing enterprise. In addition, successfully directed *Keep America Green* fire prevention campaign, together with cooperative 4–H club forestry program under which more than one million boys and girls conducted 4–H forestry projects. Thus for two decades he was national exponent of industrial forestry policy and interpreter of private forestry progress. After retiring in 1967, continued for two years as consultant to AFPI (by then renamed American Forest Institute). Died December 21, 1981, in Seminole, Florida.

HENRY CLEPPER

Charles A. Gillett. "Profile of a Forester." *American Forests*, July 1967.

GLASCOCK, HARDIN ROADS, JR.
(born 1921)
Born November 7 in Muncie, Indiana. University of Washington, B.S. (forest management) 1947. Following graduation, was employed by nonoperating forest owners in state of Washington. In 1951 became district forester for Industrial Forestry Association in Eugene, Oregon. In 1958 was appointed forest counsel for Western Forestry and Conservation Association, Portland, Oregon. Served as chief executive officer of Society of American Foresters (SAF), and editor-in-chief of *Journal of Forestry*, 1966–78. During his tenure, SAF reorganized for greater effectiveness; strengthened its finances; instituted departments of science programs, resource policy, and public affairs; expanded educational activities; increased membership by one third; and established permanent headquarters at Bethesda, Maryland. Led development of *Forest Policies*, a comprehensive statement of principles approved by SAF membership in 1967. Was instrumental in 1972 in founding Renewable Natural Resources Foundation at Bethesda, serving as its first elected board chairman. Since 1978 has been part-time forest consultant, tree farmer, writer, and visiting lecturer out of Corvallis, Oregon. Under his continuing chairmanship, Foundation has converted former Gilbert H. Grosvenor estate into Renewable Resources Center, funded and built new office building housing member societies, instituted resource policy program, and begun publication of *Renewable Resources Journal*. Has written numerous articles interpreting land-use policies and multiple use of natural resources. Has served as forestry advisor to Food and Agriculture Organization of United Nations, and as member of numerous resource

boards, advisory panels, committees, and task forces at regional, national, and international levels. Is a fellow of American Association for the Advancement of Science and SAF, and life member of The American Forestry Association.

HARDIN R. GLASCOCK, JR.

Journal of Forestry, 63(10):808, October 1965.

Journal of Forestry, 76(8):456 and 529, August 1978.

Who's Who in America, 42d ed., 1982–83.

GODDARD, MAURICE KIMBALL
(born 1912)
Born September 13 in Lowell, Massachusetts. University of Maine, B.S. (forestry) 1935, Sc.D. (honorary) 1966; University of California, M.S. 1938; Waynesburg College, Sc.D. (honorary) 1959. Became instructor in forestry at Pennsylvania State College in 1935. Was in military service, 1942–46. Was appointed director of Mont Alto Branch of Pennsylvania State School of Forestry in 1946, and of School of Forestry at Pennsylvania State University in 1952. As secretary since 1955 of Department of Forests and Waters, Commonwealth of Pennsylvania, obtained much favorable resource-use legislation with impact on timber, minerals, water, recreation, and wildlife; promoted statewide park program and seventy-million-dollar bond issue to support it. In his position as secretary of Forest and Waters and Power Resource Board, served on Geographic Board, Governor's Executive Board, Sanitary Water Board, and several other official boards and councils. Was director of The American Forestry Association and of Pennsylvania Forestry Association; was member of Commonwealth Industrial Research Corporation, four river basin committees, several other commissions and boards, and President's Public Land Law Review Commission. In Society of American Foresters, became member in 1935, a fellow in 1963, chairman of Allegheny Section in 1951, chairman of Committee on Civil Service in 1952–53, and member of the society's council for two terms, 1956–59. In 1981 received the society's Gifford Pinchot Medal, for outstanding contributions to administration and professional development of forestry.

SOCIETY OF AMERICAN FORESTERS

GORDON, SETH EDWIN
(1890–1983)

Born April 2 in Richfield, Pennsylvania. Graduated Pennsylvania Business College, 1911; University of Michigan, D.Sc. (honorary) 1953. After brief career in teaching and business, joined Pennsylvania Game Commission as game protector in 1913, was appointed assistant secretary of the commission in 1915, and became secretary and chief game protector in 1919. In 1926 became conservation director of Izaak Walton League of America. Was president of American Game Association, 1931–34, and first secretary of American Wildlife Institute in 1935. In 1936 became executive director of Pennsylvania Game Commission, until 1948, when he became private conservation consultant. Was then engaged by California Wildlife Conservation Board to advise on funds allocated to California Department of Fish and Game, was appointed director of that department in 1951, serving until 1959. Was member of Forest Research Advisory Committee to U.S. Secretary of Agriculture, 1952–62, and of President's Water Pollution Control Advisory Board to the Surgeon General of the United States, 1958–61. Was trustee and vice-president of North American Wildlife Foundation, 1947–75; member of Conservation Committee of the Boy Scouts of America, 1956–64; and general counsel from 1963 (also honorary life member and past president) of International Association of Game, Fish and Conservation Commissioners (later International Association of Fish and Wildlife Agencies), and in 1982 was elected general counsel for life. Was memorialized by International Association in 1970 when it established annual Seth Gordon Conservation Award. Was honorary member and past president of American Fisheries Society; past vice-president of The American Forestry Association; director of National Rifle Association of America for twenty-four years; and honorary member of Outdoor Writers Association of America and Western Association of State Game and Fish Commissioners. Received Founders Award of Izaak Walton League of America in 1959; was its honorary national president in 1961–62; and was elected to its Hall of Fame, 1969, and as national life member, 1978. Was honorary life member of Camp Fire Club of America and recipient of Aldo Leopold Medal of The Wildlife Society in 1967. Had one of longest continuous careers of any of pioneer conservationists. Among his greatest contributions was his participation in drafting of Model Game Law of 1934, which established criteria for modern wildlife administration. Was one of first wildlife administrators to develop realistic regulations for deer, and was instrumental in obtaining public acceptance of modern principles of game management. Died June 22, 1983.

C. R. GUTERMUTH

Who's Who in America, 42d ed., 1982–83.

GORDON, WILLIAM GEORGE
(born 1931)
Born July 15 in Corty, Pennsylvania. Mt. Union College, B.S. 1953; University of Michigan, M.S. (fisheries) 1957; did graduate work in various studies at University of Michigan, 1961–66. Served as fisheries biologist with Great Lakes Research Station, Sandusky, Ohio, 1957–79, directing Exploratory Fishing and Gear Research Station, Bureau of Commercial Fisheries, Sandusky, Ohio, 1959–79; served as deputy base director of Exploratory Fishing and Gear Research Station of Bureau of Commercial Fisheries, Ann Arbor, Michigan, 1961–66. Then moved to Washington, D.C., where he served on staff of Program Planning and Budget Office of Bureau of Commercial Fisheries, 1966–70. Was deputy regional director of Northeast Region of National Marine Fisheries Service, Gloucester, Massachusetts, 1970–75; director of Office of Resource Conservation and Management of the National Marine Fisheries Service, 1975–81; and has served as assistant administrator (director) for fisheries of the National Oceanic and Atmospheric Administration, Department of Commerce, Washington, D.C., from 1981 to present. Is author or coauthor of twenty-eight scientific publications. Is member of Phi Sigma and Sigma Xi. Has served on many international fisheries delegations in Europe, the South Pacific, the Orient, and North and Central America. Has been on numerous occasions an advisor to Food and Agricultural Organization of the United Nations. Is active member of American Fisheries Society, The American Forestry Association, International Association of Fish and Wildlife Agencies, and Boy Scouts of America. Is best known as effective, innovative leader in marine fisheries management and development.

ROBERT F. HUTTON

GOTTSCHALK, JOHN SIMISON
(born 1912)

Born September 27 in Berne, Indiana. Earlham College, B.A. 1934, LL.D. 1966; University of Indiana, M.A. 1943. Was employed as park ranger with Indiana Conservation Department in 1930, later becoming park naturalist and superintendent of fisheries. During World War II, was production laboratory director in Schenley penicillin plant. Began his federal career as fisheries biologist for U.S. Fish and Wildlife Service. Organized Federal Aid in Fish Restoration program in 1951, and was successively chief of Division of Sport Fisheries, regional director in Northeast Region, and, in 1964, director of Bureau of Sport Fisheries and Wildlife. Initiated first formal federal endangered species program, several innovative waterfowl management programs including "point system" bag limit, and search for lead-shot substitute. Left U.S. Department of the Interior in 1970 to become assistant to director of National Marine Fisheries Service for recreational fisheries and environmental programs. Retired from government service in 1973 and was appointed executive vice-president of International Association of Fish and Wildlife Agencies (IAFWA). Represented Interior Department and the association at numerous international meetings, and served as member of Survival Service and Ecology commissions of International Union for the Conservation of Nature and Natural Resources, and as member of International Migratory Bird Committee. In 1979 became legislative counsel for IAFWA and in 1981, on retirement from active duties, became its counsel. Was vice-president of The Wildlife Society; president of American Fisheries Society, Washington Biologists' Field Club, and Citizen's Program for the Chesapeake Bay; and member of board of directors of The National Wildlife Federation. Received Conservation Award of the Nash Motor Company in 1955; John Pearce Award of the Northeast Wildlife Society in 1965; the Distinguished Service Award of the U.S. Department of the Interior in 1971; Special Conservation Award of The National Wildlife Federation in 1973; Seth Gordon Award of the IAFWA in 1975; and Aldo Leopold Medal of The Wildlife Society in 1976. Is honorary member of both The Wildlife Society and American Fisheries Society.

JOHN S. GOTTSCHALK

American Men and Women of Science (Physical and Biological Sciences), 15th ed., 1982.

Who's Who in America, 42d ed., 1982–83.

GRACIE, JAMES W.
(born 1942)

Born February 13 in Baltimore, Maryland. Johns Hopkins University, B.S. (chemistry) 1970. In 1971 helped to form Maryland Trout Unlimited Chapter, served as chapter newsletter editor for eight years, held every office from secretary to president, and served on chapter board for ten consecutive years. Was first chairman of Middle Atlantic Council of Trout Unlimited, which he helped to form. Served as first chairperson and helped put together Trout Unlimited Water Quality Surveillance Program in which more than forty Trout Unlimited chapters across country participated. Has been active in resource-oriented projects at chapter and council levels, designing and directing many of outstanding resource activities conducted by Maryland Chapter in past decade. Spearheaded successful effort to eliminate discharge of toxic chlorine into natural trout waters in Maryland. Also instigated and spearheaded effort in Maryland General Assembly that led to passage of Storm Water Management law, which requires developers to maintain characteristics of run-off after development. At national level of Trout Unlimited, became first chairman of Resource Management and Protection Committee and served in that capacity for six years. Headed Trout Unlimited task force on Alaska Lands. Instigated effort to develop a program to improve grassroots involvement on national resource issues. Was elected president for 1983 of Trout Unlimited.

ROBERT L. HERBST

GRAHAM, EDWARD HARRISON
(1902–1966)

Born November 30 in New Brighton, Pennsylvania. University of Pittsburgh, B.S. 1927, Ph.D. (botany) 1932. For three years was curator of botany at Carnegie Museum of Natural History, Carnegie Institute, Pittsburgh. Then in 1937 joined U.S. Soil Conservation Service, U.S. Department of Agriculture, and advanced successively from biologist to chief of Division of Biology, and finally to assistant administrator for international programs. Retired in 1964 from federal government after twenty-seven years of distinguished service, during which he was active leader in conservation and scientific community. Was lecturer in land-management ecology in Graduate School of U.S. Department of Agriculture from 1942 to 1952, at Harvard University in 1949, and was a Guggenheim

fellow in 1954. Represented United States at numerous scientific conferences in Mexico, Venezuela, Denmark, France, Scotland, and Greece.
Served as president of Soil Conservation Society of America; was consultant to Nature Conservancy of Great Britain; chairman of Commission on Ecology of the International Union for the Conservation of Nature and Natural Resources; and member of United States National
Committee for the International Biological Program. Following his retirement from government service, was consultant to Ford Foundation
and senior associate of The Conservation Foundation. Author of numerous scientific papers and monographs, he will long be remembered for
his two books *The Land and Wildlife*, 1947, and *Natural Principles of
Land Use*, 1944. Died May 16, 1966.

HENRY CLEPPER

American Men of Science (Physical and Biological Sciences), 11th ed., 1965.

Journal of Wildlife Management. Obituary, vol. 30, July 1966.

GRANGER, CHRISTOPHER MABLEY
(1885–1967)
Born November 25 in Detroit, Michigan. Michigan State University, B.S.
(forestry); doctor of forestry (honorary) 1932. Began career of nearly
forty-five years with U.S. Forest Service as forest assistant on Sequoia
National Forest in California. After assignments as deputy supervisor
and supervisor of various national forests in Colorado and Wyoming,
became assistant regional forester for operation in Denver in 1916. After
serving as major in Army Engineers' forestry unit during World War I,
became regional forester for Pacific Northwest Region in 1919, with its
important national-forest and state and private forestry cooperative programs. Transferred to Washington, D.C., in 1930; developed nationwide
forest survey authorized by 1928 McSweeney-McNary Act, which pro-
duces basic forest resource information for private forestry enterprise
and for public forest policy. In 1933 administered Forest Service's part of
Civilian Conservation Corps program. In 1935 was named assistant
chief of Forest Service for administration of national forests. In 1952
received U.S. Department of Agriculture's Distinguished Service Award.
Michigan State University conferred on him its Alumni Award for Distinguished Service in 1949. Was chief of American delegation and co-
president of Third World Forestry Conference in Helsinki in 1949, and
president of Society of American Foresters, 1932–34. Remained active

in promoting forest conservation after retiring in 1952. Died November 21, 1967.

GORDON D. FOX

American Men of Science (Physical and Biological Sciences), 10th ed., 1960.

GRANT, KENNETH ELVARD
(born 1920)

Born March 19 in Rollinsford, New Hampshire. University of New Hampshire, B.S. (agriculture) 1941; Harvard University, M.P.A. 1964. Became U.S. Soil Conservation Service employee in March 1945, after serving in U.S. Army Air Corps from December 1941 to October 1945. In New Hampshire rose from junior soil scientist to state conservationist in twelve years; there served as head of the service's work from January 1959 until enrolling in Harvard's Littauer School of Public Administration in 1963. Was promoted and transferred to Washington, D.C., as associate administrator of agency in 1967, becoming its administrator in January 1969. Was in forefront of the service's efforts to apply its farm-proven techniques of soil and water conservation and development to achieve environmental improvement, to assist urbanizing areas with acute land- and water-management problems, and to assist multicounty areas to gain economic and social betterment. Helped initiate nation's first resource conservation and development project (Lincoln Hills) in southern Indiana. While heading the service's work in New Hampshire, also served as U.S. Department of Agriculture's representative on Connecticut River Basin Comprehensive Study. During his Indiana assignment, had leadership for the department's part of Ohio River Basin Comprehensive Framework Survey, the first of its kind completed in United States, as well as leadership in Wabash River Basin Comprehensive Study. Was member of team that made trips to West Pakistan in 1967 and 1968 to advise government of Pakistan on erosion, sedimentation, and water management. Received U.S. Department of Agriculture's Distinguished Service Award, 1969; became a fellow in Soil Conservation Society of America, 1969; and is member of American Society for Public Administration and of Conservation Committee of the Boy Scouts of America.

F. GLENNON LOYD

Who's Who in America, 39th ed., 1976–77.

GRAVES, HENRY SOLON
(1871–1951)
Born May 3 in Marietta, Ohio. Yale College, B.A. 1892, after which he studied forestry in Europe, the second native American to prepare for forestry career. Yale University, M.A. 1900, LL.D. 1940; Harvard University, M.A. 1911; Lincoln Memorial University, LL.D. 1923; Syracuse University, LL.D. 1923. Appointed in 1898 as assistant chief of Division of Forestry (now Forest Service), U.S. Department of Agriculture, under Gifford Pinchot. Resigned in 1900 to become director of Yale University School of Forestry. Returning to Forest Service as chief forester in 1910, held post until 1920. When United States entered World War I, was commissioned as temporary lieutenant colonel, Corps of Engineers, to set up forestry operations for production of Army's timber needs in France. Returning in 1922 as dean of Yale School of Forestry, won recognition as foremost forestry educator in America. Retired as dean emeritus in 1939. From 1929 to 1931 directed Forest Education Inquiry, which established standards of professional instruction. Was twice president of The American Forestry Association, 1923–24 and 1934–36; and president of Society of American Foresters, 1912. In 1944 the society awarded him the Sir William Schlich Memorial Medal and in 1950 the Gifford Pinchot Medal. Was chairman of Committee on Forestry and Forest Products that planned for inclusion of forestry in work program of Food and Agriculture Organization of the United Nations. French government honored him with medal of Order *Merite Agricole* in recognition of his distinguished service to forestry. Was author of *Forest Mensuration*, 1906, and *Principles of Handling Woodlands*, 1911, both pioneer textbooks; coauthor of *Forest Education*, 1932, and *Problems and Progress of Forestry in the United States*, 1947. Died March 7, 1951.

HENRY CLEPPER

"Henry Solon Graves, 1871–1951." *Journal of Forestry.* May 1951.

Who Was Who in America, 1951–60.

GREELEY, WILLIAM BUCKHOUT
(1879–1955)
Born September 6 in Oswego, New York. University of California, B.S. 1901, LL.D. 1927; Yale University, M.F. 1904, M.A. 1927. Entered Bureau of Forestry (now U.S. Forest Service) in 1904; successively promoted to supervisor of Sequoia National Forest, 1906; regional forester,

Northern Rocky Mountain Region, 1908; and chief, Branch of Forest Management, Washington, D.C., office, 1911. During World War I was major (later lieutenant colonel) in charge of forestry operations for American Expeditionary Forces in France. Returned to Forest Service in 1919, and a year later was appointed chief. During eight years of his administration, under Clark-McNary Act of 1928, fundamental forest policy of United States was established, providing for federal-state cooperation in fire control, reforestation, and farm forestry extension. Net area of national forests was enlarged to nearly 160 million acres. In May 1928 he became secretary-manager of West Coast Lumbermen's Association at Seattle. While in this position, was influential in advancing forest management and protection on lands of forest industries. Retired in 1946, but continued leadership in forestry by chairing board of American Forest Products Industries, Inc. Was president of Society of American Foresters in 1915, elected a fellow in 1918, and received Sir William Schlich Memorial Medal for distinguished service to forestry in 1946. Was director of The American Forestry Association for thirty-four years. Author of *Forests and Men*, 1951, and *Forest Policy*, 1953, he was frequent contributor to scientific and popular magazines on natural resources subjects. Died November 30, 1955.

Henry Clepper

Morgan, George, T., Jr., *William B. Greeley, A Practical Forester, 1879–1955*. St. Paul, Minn.: Forest History Society, 1961.

"William Buckhout Greeley, 1879–1955," *Journal of Forestry*, January 1956.

GREEN, SAMUEL BOWDLEAR
(1859–1910)
Born September 15 in Chelsea, Massachusetts. Massachusetts Agricultural College at Amherst, B.S. 1879, graduate student in horticulture, 1880–81. Was horticulturist for Houghton Farm Agricultural Experiment Station at Cornwall, New York, 1881–84, and superintendent of horticulture at Massachusetts Agricultural College, 1886–88. In 1888 became horticulturist for University of Minnesota's Agricultural Experiment Station, and professor of horticulture and forestry in 1897 at the university. Was member of executive board of Minnesota Horticultural Society, 1892–1910, and served as president, 1907–10. Also served as president of board of administration of Farmers Institute of Minnesota and as member of executive committee of Minnesota State Forestry As-

sociation. In 1899 became member of Minnesota State Forestry Board, which legislature had authorized to oversee state forestlands. Successfully worked toward creation of Division of Forestry in University of Minnesota (1903), transfer of administration and protection of Itasca Park to the State Forestry Board (1907), and creation of Cloquet Experimental Forest (1909). Was appointed professor of forestry and dean of College of Forestry at University of Minnesota in 1910. Wrote many books and articles, including *Forestry in Minnesota*, 1898, and *Principles of American Forestry*, 1903. Was associate editor of *Farm and Fireside* from 1888 until his death. Early recognized need for practice of forestry and was largely responsible for introduction of higher education for forestry and horticulture in Minnesota. Died July 11, 1910.

ELWOOD R. MAUNDER

Allison, John H. "The Story of Samuel Green," *Conservation Volunteer*, September/October, November/December, 1967.
Dictionary of American Biography, 1960.
Who Was Who in America, 1897–1942.

GREGG, FRANK
(born 1925)
Born December 15 in Denver, Colorado. University of Colorado, B.A. (journalism) 1949. Was editor of *Colorado Outdoors*, Colorado Game and Fish Department, 1951–55, and *Outdoor America*, Izaak Walton League of America, 1957–61. Wrote extensively on policy issues in water, public-lands and wildlife management, and outdoor recreation resources. Was executive director, Izaak Walton League of America, 1957–61; helped organize conservation interests in support of strong federal water pollution control program. As staff assistant to secretary of the Interior, 1961–63, developed concept of Land and Water Conservation Fund legislation. Was executive director of Citizens Committee for the Outdoor Recreation Resources Review Commission report, 1963–65, and vice-president for public policy programs, The Conservation Foundation, 1965–67. Was presidential appointment as founding chairman of New England River Basins Commission in 1967, serving under three presidents through 1977; developed the commission as effective instrument for federal-state cooperation in natural resources planning and management. At Bureau of Land Management, 1978–80, was first director to serve under Federal Land Policy and Management Act.

His administration emphasized strengthened consideration of environmental values, increased energy production, equality of access for all interests, and strengthened science programs. Was visiting professor at University of Arizona and consultant to Conservation Foundation on public-land policy, 1981–83; and has been director of School of Renewable Natural Resources, University of Arizona, from 1983 to present. Is author of both popular and scholarly publications on natural resources policy, planning, institutions, management, and administration. Is member of The Wildlife Society. Received Joseph W. Penfold Award of Izaak Walton League of America in 1971, and Caldwell Award of Division of Landscape Resources, University of Arizona, in 1983; and was nominee for Rockefeller Public Service Award in 1981.

FRANK GREGG

GRIFFITH, GEORGE ALLISON
(born 1901)
Born March 19 in Vaughnsville, Ohio. Graduated from International College, Fort Wayne, Indiana, in 1921. Most of his business career was with Wayne Knitting Mills of Fort Wayne until 1944, when he moved to Grayling, Michigan. As dedicated nonprofessional conservationist with particular interest in preserving trouts and their environment, and in perpetuating sport of trout angling, was effective in promoting improved methods for trout and stream management as member of Izaak Walton League of America and of Federation of Sportsmen's Clubs in Indiana and Michigan. Governor of Michigan in 1950 appointed him to Michigan Conservation Commission, where he served until 1961; in 1954 was chairman of the commission, and of its Fish Conservation Committee from 1955 to 1961. On July 16, 1959, on Au Sable River in Grayling, Michigan, founded Trout Unlimited, a national, nonprofit, nonpolitical organization of conservation-minded fishermen dedicated to preserving clean waters, and to continuing and improving high-quality fishing by supporting and encouraging legislation, regulations, and research programs based on sound biological and ecological knowledge. In 1961 was elected president of Trout Unlimited, an office he held until 1964, when he became its board chairman. As result of his leadership, Trout Unlimited had grown by 1983 to organization with international membership in excess of thirty thousand. In 1963 was appointed to special commission to study functions and structure of Michigan Conservation Depart-

ment; recommendations resulting from this study were responsible for reorganizing the department into highly efficient operation of state government. Has written numerous articles dealing with water quality and trout management for *Trout* magazine, the official organ of Trout Unlimited. Was inducted into Fishing Hall of Fame in 1983.

ROBERT L. HERBST

GRINNELL, GEORGE BIRD
(1849–1938)
Born September 20 in Brooklyn, New York. Yale University, B.A. 1870, Ph.D. (osteology) 1880, Litt.D. (honorary) 1921. Between 1870 and 1875 was member of important scientific and exploratory expeditions in the West, including expedition through Black Hills in 1874 and reconnaissance of Yellowstone National Park in 1875. During these missions, became interested in culture and welfare of American Indian, annually returning to the West for many years to expand his knowledge. In 1876 became editor of *Forest and Stream* magazine, rising to senior editor and publisher in 1880, positions he held until 1911. In this capacity, in 1876 launched sustained campaign against market hunting for realistic game laws. Movement culminated in enactment of Migratory Bird Treaty with Great Britain in 1916 and with adoption of strong regulatory control of hunting in all states. In winter of 1893, had investigation made of game poaching in Yellowstone National Park; resulting articles led directly to enactment by Congress of Yellowstone Park Protection Act of 1894, a keystone of national park legislation. In summer of 1885, explored country in Montana now known as Glacier National Park, and through his writings was largely responsible for its inclusion in 1910 in national park system. A quiet and modest man who preferred to work behind the scenes, he had clear influence on much of pioneer legislation affecting national parks, national forests, and wildlife. In 1886 founded Audubon Society of New York, first such state organization in America and forerunner of National Audubon Society, which he served as director for twenty-six years. Was a founding member of Boone and Crockett Club in 1887, was president from 1918 to 1927, and in 1927 was named honorary president for life. Served on first advisory board for Federal Migratory Bird Law. As fellow of American Ornithologists' Union, was also president of National Parks Association, and was trustee of The American Museum of Natural History in New York City. In 1925 was

awarded Theodore Roosevelt Gold Medal of Honor for his contribution to cause of conservation. Was author or coauthor of nearly thirty volumes, ranging from adventure books for boys to scholarly works on Indian life and customs. Died April 11, 1938.

JAMES B. TREFETHEN

Dictionary of American Biography, vol. 22, supp. 2, 1958.
Who Was Who in America, 1897–1942.

GUTERMUTH, CLINTON RAYMOND
(born 1900)
Born August 16 in Fort Wayne, Indiana. Attended University of Notre Dame, 1918–19. Graduate American Institute of Banking 1927, postgraduate 1928. University of Idaho, D.Sc. (honorary) 1972. Was director of education, Indiana Department of Conservation, 1934–40, and director of fish and game, 1940–42. Became executive secretary, American Wildlife Institute, 1945–46; and vice-president of Wildlife Management Institute, 1946–71. Was trustee and secretary-treasurer of North American Wildlife Foundation, 1945–73; founder and first secretary, treasurer, and president, World Wildlife Fund–U.S., 1961–73, and honorary president for life, 1973; and retired trustee and member of executive committee of World Wildlife Fund International, 1971–73. Has been director and president, Wildfowl Foundation, Inc., 1956 to present; and trustee and president, Stronghold, Inc. (Sugarloaf Mountain, Maryland), 1947 to present. Is a founder and first secretary, Natural Resources Council of America, 1946–57; was chairman, 1959–61; became honorary life member, 1971; and was founding member of steering committee, National Watershed Congress, 1954–73, and chairman, 1958–62. Served on secretary of U.S. Department of the Interior's Advisory Committee on Fish and Wildlife, 1948–53 and 1957–61; and on secretary of U.S. Department of Agriculture's Committee on Wildlife, 1965–69. Was appointed to National Advisory Council, Public Land Law Review Commission, 1964–70; was director of executive committee, Citizens Committee on Natural Resources, 1954–78; director of American Committee for International Wild Life Protection, 1950–72; and trustee of The Wildlife Society, 1951–79, now trustee emeritus. Was director, National Rifle Association of America; first vice-president, 1971–73; president, 1973–75; and was elected executive council for life, 1975. Was director and president, National Institute for Urban Wildlife, 1976–83, and now

honorary chairman. As secretary of North American Wildlife Foundation, initiated campaigns that raised more than $3 million in private donations to acquire lands deeded to federal government to establish Great Swamp (New Jersey), Key Deer (Florida), and Cedar Point (Ohio) national wildlife refuges. Published numerous articles on conservation, including statewide survey report *Where to Go in Indiana: Official Lake Guide*, 1938; was first editor of Wildlife Management Institute's biweekly *Outdoor News Bulletin*, 1947–48; and contributing author, *The Fisherman's Encyclopedia*, 1950, and *The Standard Book of Fishing*, 1950. Was program chairman of annual North American Wildlife and Natural Resources Conferences, 1946–70. Received Aldo Leopold Medal from The Wildlife Society, 1957; Distinguished Service Award, National Association of Soil Conservation Districts, 1959; Fishing Hall of Fame, 1958; fellow, American Association for Advancement of Science, 1959; Watershed Man of the Year Award, National Watershed Congress, 1963; National Service Award, Keep America Beautiful, 1965; Meritorious Service Award, Michigan United Conservation Clubs, 1968; Distinguished Service Award, The National Wildlife Federation, 1969; Horace M. Albright Medal, American Scenic and Historic Preservation Society, 1970; Citizens of Year Award, The American Forestry Association, 1971; Order of the Golden Ark Medal, HRH Prince of The Netherlands, 1972; Hunting Hall of Fame, 1975; National Conservation Award, African Safari Club, 1977; Gold Medal for Eminent Service, Camp Fire Club of America, 1977; Award of Honor, Natural Resources Council of America, 1980; and Audubon Medal, National Audubon Society, 1982.

DANIEL A. POOLE

Who's Who in America, 42d ed., 1982–83.

HAFENRICHTER, ATLEE LAWRENCE
(1897–1973)
Born October 12 near Plainfield, Illinois. Northwestern College, B.A. 1922; University of Illinois, Ph.D. 1926. In 1926 became head of Department of Botany and Bacteriology at Baker University and, simultaneously, served as investigator for Division of Ecology, Carnegie Institution of Washington. From 1929 to 1933 was assistant professor of farm crops and assistant in Agricultural Experiment Station at Washington State University. His career in conservation began in 1933 when he was

appointed as agronomist in U.S. Department of the Interior Soil Erosion Service, which became Soil Conservation Service in U.S. Department of Agriculture in 1935. Shortly after his transfer, became chief of Regional Nursery Division and progressed steadily until he was regional plant materials specialist for the thirteen western states, including Alaska and Hawaii; was technically responsible for testing vegetation of all kinds in eight plant materials centers in field evaluation plantings, and on farms and ranches under actual use. More than one hundred new species and varieties are in use and in commercial production from twenty-five thousand plants that were tested. Is author of numerous scientific papers, state experiment station and federal bulletins, monographs, chapters in textbooks, and U.S. Department of Agriculture yearbooks. Presented papers to Sixth and Seventh International Grassland congresses, served as chairman of section at Eighth Congress, and was coauthor of paper given at Ninth. In 1947 received Superior Service Award and in 1963 Distinguished Service Award from U.S. Department of Agriculture. In 1955 was elected a fellow of American Society of Agronomy, and in 1964 an honorary member of Soil Conservation Society of America. Retired in 1967. Died May 20, 1973.

H. WAYNE PRITCHARD

American Men of Science (Physical and Biological Sciences), 11th ed., 1965.
Who's Who in the West, 1963–74.

HAGENSTEIN, WILLIAM DAVID
(born 1915)
Born March 8 in Seattle, Washington. University of Washington, B.S.F. 1938; Duke University, M.F. 1941. After working as entomological field aide for U.S. Department of Agriculture in 1938, was logging superintendent for Eagle Logging Company in 1939, and Civilian Conservation Corps foreman, U.S. Forest Service, in 1940. Was forester for West Coast Lumbermen's Association in 1941–43 and 1945–49, with interim service during World War II as senior forester in Foreign Economic Administration, attached to construction units of U.S. Army in Guadalcanal and U.S. Navy in Guam. Spent last six months of World War II in Costa Rica developing American quinine plantation. In 1949 became manager of Industrial Forestry Association, and executive vice-president in 1956–80; became president of W. D. Hagenstein and Associates, Inc., 1980. Has served variously as consulting forest engineer for U.S. Navy in the

Philippines in 1952; was MacMillan lecturer in forestry at University of British Columbia in 1952, and Benson memorial lecturer at University of Missouri in 1966. Has been on executive committee of Northwest Forest Pest Action Council since 1949 and has been chairman of the council's Timber Disaster Committee since 1962. As trustee of Washington State Forestry Conference since 1948, has also been advisory trustee of Keep Washington Green Association and trustee of Keep Oregon Green Association, both since 1958. Has served on Advisory Committee of Pacific Northwest Forest and Range Experiment Station since 1954; was director of Foundation for American Resource Management, 1963–67; and vice-president and on executive committee of Western Forestry Center in 1965. As life member of The American Forestry Association, was honorary vice-president, 1966–69. In Society of American Foresters, has been chairman of Division of Private Forestry, 1955; associate editor of *Journal of Forestry*, 1946–53; council member, 1958–63; president 1966–69; and in 1963 was elected a fellow. Is author of numerous articles and other publications on forestry, and is coauthor of textbook *Harvesting Timber Crops*, 1966. Received Forest Products Industry National Award for forest management in 1968 from National Forest Products Association.

SOCIETY OF AMERICAN FORESTERS

Who's Who in America, 42d ed., 1982–83.

HAIR, JAY DEE
(born 1945)
Born November 30 in Miami, Florida. Clemson (South Carolina) University B.S. (biology) 1967; Clemson M.S. (zoology) 1969; University of Alberta, Canada, Ph.D. (zoology) 1975. Served in U.S. Army, 1970–71. Became assistant professor, wildlife biology, Clemson University, 1973; associate professor, zoology and forestry, administrator of Fisheries and Wildlife Sciences, North Carolina State University, 1977. Served as special assistant to assistant secretary, Fish and Wildlife and Parks, and to director, U.S. Fish and Wildlife Service, U.S. Department of the Interior, 1978–1980, to coordinate development of national fish and wildlife policy. Has been executive vice-president, National Wildlife Federation, from 1981 to present. Has been member, Acid Rain Clearinghouse Professional Advisory Council; American Association for the Advancement of Science; American Fisheries Society; board of directors of Amer-

ican League of Anglers; Boy Scouts of America National Conservation
Committee; Ecological Society of America; International Commission
on Ecology; National Coordinating Committee on Fish and Wildlife in
Federal Water Resources Projects (1981); National Petroleum Council
(U.S. Department of Energy secretarial appointee); Natural Resources
Council of America; Society of American Foresters; and The Wildlife
Society. Was board member of South Carolina Wildlife Federation,
1974–1977, and president, 1976–77. Was chairman, Fish and Wildlife
Task Force, National Academy of Sciences Study Committee, 1979–81.
Named Outstanding Young Man of America by U.S. Jaycees, 1975;
South Carolina Governor's Wildlife Conservationist of the Year, 1977;
and North Carolina Governor's Conservationist of the Year, 1980. Was
certified as wildlife biologist by The Wildlife Society, 1980. Received
North Carolina Governor's Award for public service, 1983. Is author of
numerous articles on resource ecology and management, including *Measurement of Ecological Diversity*, and was editor of *Ecological Perspectives of Wildlife Management*.

NATIONAL WILDLIFE FEDERATION

International Men of Achievement, 1981.

Who's Who in America, 42d ed., 1982–83.

HALL, WILLIAM LOGAN
(1873–1960)
Born May 28 in Holden, Missouri. Kansas State College, B.S. 1898, M.S.
(horticulture and forestry) 1899. Joining in 1899 the Bureau of Forestry
(now Forest Service), U.S. Department of Agriculture, he served succession of assignments, including supervision of tree planting, making forest
survey in Hawaii, directing Branch of Forest Products, and becoming
first district (now regional) forester in eastern United States. Was influential in securing establishment in 1910 of Forest Products Laboratory
in Madison, Wisconsin. During World War I served in U.S. Army Corps
of Engineers, and in 1919 returned to Forest Service and worked on
plans that culminated in Clarke-McNary Act of 1924. Late in 1919 resigned from Forest Service and entered private business as consultant.
Served numerous lumber and paper companies in the South and West,
and concurrently built up extensive timber property in Arkansas. Thus
contributed significantly to advancement of both public and private forestry in United States during formative decades of forest conservation

movement. His professional career spanned sixty years. As charter member of Society of American Foresters in 1900, served it as secretary-treasurer, 1903–7; as president in 1913; and as member of its council, 1918–19. Was elected a fellow of the society in 1939 and was presented with Gifford Pinchot medal for distinguished service to forestry in 1954. Died October 2, 1960.

SOCIETY OF AMERICAN FORESTERS

Journal of Forestry, 43:771, 1945.

Journal of Forestry. Obituary, 58:904, 1960.

HAMILTON, WILLIAM JOHN, JR.
(born 1902)
Born December 11 in Corona, New York. Cornell University, B.S. 1926, M.S. 1928, Ph.D. (zoology) in 1930. Was appointed assistant biologist at Cornell in 1926, and had advanced to professor of zoology in Department of Conservation by 1947; retired as emeritus professor in 1963. Had concurrent appointment as research associate in mammalogy at The American Museum of Natural History in New York City. Has been chairman of Science Advisory Committee of Edward Niles Huyck Biological Station since 1939. Was member of Advisory Committee for Environmental Biology, National Science Foundation, 1956–58. Served as vice-president of American Society of Mammalogists, 1949–50, and as president, 1950–51. Was secretary of Ecological Society of America, 1939–41, and president, 1955. His chief research interests were in fields of mammalogy and herpetology with emphasis on food habits of North American vertebrates, vertebrate populations, and life histories, and he was strong advocate of basing conservation practice on results of sound scientific studies. A prolific writer, his scientific publications number more than 150, plus many review articles. Was author of *Mammals of Eastern United States*, 1943, and coauthor of book *Conservation in the United States*, 1939. His *American Mammals*, 1939, was first definitive treatment in a single book of all mammal families of North American continent, and served for many years as bible of American mammalogy.

GEORGE SPRUGEL, JR.

American Men and Women of Science (Physical and Biological Sciences), 15th ed., 1982.

Bulletin of the Ecological Society of America, vol. 35, no. 4, 1954.

HARDTNER, HENRY ERNEST
(1870–1935)
Born September 10 in Pineville, Louisiana. Educated in bookkeeping at Soules' College. Began lifelong career in forestry in 1892 as part-owner and secretary-treasurer of Nugent-Hardtner and Company, Nugent, Louisiana. During succeeding decade, experienced ups and downs of contemporary American lumbermen as he bought one tract after another of virgin timber, cut each one, and moved on to another. Subsequently organized Urania Lumber Company, became interested in growing trees as crop, and gradually became known as father of southern forestry. In December 1908 was designated Louisiana delegate to Joint Conference on Conservation, Washington, D.C. Experience made him active advocate for Louisiana Commission on Natural Resources, the first in South; became the first chairman. Also was named chairman of newly organized Conservation Commission. After election to state legislature in 1910, became strong force for pioneering forestry legislation. Lands devoted to forestry were valued at one dollar per acre for forty years for taxation purposes. Another law established severance tax on timber. Meanwhile, pioneered in fire prevention by organizing fire protection system on ninety thousand acres belonging to his company. Launched great reforestation program by planting thirty thousand acres of cutover land around Urania. As long-time member of American Forestry Association, cooperated with Forest Service in early research experiments, and became host of Yale School of Forestry for its annual spring field classes. Was associate member of Society of American Foresters; president, Southern Forestry Congress; president, Louisiana Forestry Association; chairman, forestry commitee, Southern Pine Association; chairman, Southern Forest Research Advisory Committee; and member of conference committee on Article X of the Lumber Code, 1934. Died August 7, 1935.

KENNETH B. POMEROY

Forests and People, 13(1):56–57, 124–25, 1963.
Journal of Forestry, 33:885–86, 1935.

HARPER, VERNE LESTER
(born 1902)
Born August 13 in Monroe, South Dakota. University of California, B.S. 1926, M.S. 1927; Duke University, Ph.D. 1943; North Carolina State

University, D.Sc. (honorary) 1967. Began U.S. Forest Service career in gum-naval-stores research in Florida in 1927; successively became division chief, forest management, Southern Forest Experiment Station, New Orleans, 1935–36; assistant division chief, forest management research, Washington, D.C., 1937–42; assistant chief, division of forest economics research, 1943–44; director, Northeastern Forest Experiment Station, Philadelphia, Pennsylvania, 1945–50; and deputy chief (research), Washington, D.C., 1951–65. Became professor of forestry, University of Florida, 1966, and professor emeritus, 1973. Was member of U.S. delegation to conferences of United Nations Food and Agriculture Organization in 1951, 1953, 1957, 1959, and 1965; chairman Latin-American Forestry Research Commission, 1958–61; chairman, executive committee, Fifth World Forestry Congress, Seattle, Washington, 1960; and vice-chairman, U.S. delegation to Sixth World Forestry Congress, Madrid, Spain, 1966. Also was member of International Union of Forest Research Organizations, 1956–62, and vice-president, 1962–65. Elected president, International Union of Societies of Foresters, 1969–74. As member of Society of American Foresters Committee on International Relations from 1953 to 1966 (chairman in 1956), obtained funds to compile English portion of multilingual forestry terminology and grants to assist American Foresters in attending foreign schools. Primarily responsible for establishment of North American Forestry Commission in U.N. Food and Agriculture Organization. His work with Latin-American officials in 1954 resulted in establishment of Latin-American Research and Training Institute at Merida, Venezuela. Was elected honorary member of Finnish Society of Foresters and a fellow of American Society of Foresters; and was awarded Distinguished Service Award of U.S. Department of Agriculture, and Bernhard E. Fernow Award for Distinguished Service to International Forestry. Is author of numerous scientific articles dealing with turpentine production of southern pines, forest management, silviculture, timber resources, range management, watershed management, wood utilization, and international relations in forestry.

VERNE L. HARPER
KENNETH B. POMEROY

American Men and Women of Science (Physical and Biological Sciences), 15th ed., 1982.

Who's Who in America, 39th ed., 1976–77.

Hartzog, George Benjamin, Jr.
(born 1920)
Born March 17 in Colleton County, South Carolina. American University, B.S. (business administration) 1953. Honorary degrees from Washington University (LL.D.) 1971, Wofford College (LL.D.) 1972, Lincoln College (L.H.D.), 1972, and University of Arizona (LL.D.) 1972. Read law under supervision of Hon. J. M. Moorer, 1939–42. Admitted to practice before Supreme Court of South Carolina, 1942; Supreme Court of the United States, 1949; Supreme Court of Missouri, 1963; U.S. District Court for the District of Columbia, 1970; Supreme Court of Virginia, 1974. Served in U.S. Army, 1940–41 and 1943–46. Was appointed attorney and administrator with Bureau of Land Management and National Park Service, U.S. Department of the Interior, 1946; assistant superintendent of Rocky Mountain National Park, 1955–57, and Great Smoky National Park, 1957–59; and superintendent of Jefferson National Expansion Memorial, Saint Louis, 1959–62. Entered private employment as executive director, Downtown Saint Louis, 1962–63. Was associate director of National Park Service, 1963, and director, 1964–72. Is author of three volumes of National Park Service administrative manual series. Received Meritorious Award Certificate from William A. Jump Memorial Foundation, 1956; Special Service Award of Greater Saint Louis Federal Business Association, 1962; Distinguished Service Award of U.S. Department of the Interior, 1962; Alumni Recognition Award of The American University, 1966; Cornelius Amory Pugsley Gold Medal Award, 1967; and George B. Hartzog, Jr. Award from Clemson University, 1979. Is trustee, American Museum of Immigration, A Christian Ministry in the Historical Parks, and Marjorie Merriweather Post Foundation; and member, board of directors, White House Historical Association, White House Preservation Fund, and Yosemite Institute and World Resources Cooperation.

George B. Hartzog
William E. Towell

Who's Who in America, 40th ed., 1978–79.

Harville, John Patrick
(born 1918)
Born January 13 in Eureka, California. San Jose State College, B.A. (bio-

logical sciences) 1940; Stanford University, M.A. (biology) 1949, Ph.D. (biology) 1955. Was teacher of biology, photography, and physical sciences in several California high schools, 1941–46; instructor of biological sciences at San Mateo Junior College, California, 1946–47; and member of faculty of San Jose State College 1945. Was science faculty fellow of National Science Foundation, 1959–60, studying research and education in fisheries on Pacific Coast. As senior fishery biologist for Fisheries Research Institute of University of Washington at Lake Iliamna, Alaska, conducted research on sockeye salmon, 1960–62. Traveled to the Philippines as U.S. Peace Corps science advisor, where he also conducted field researches into ecological characteristics of endemic cyprinid fishes of Lake Lanao, Mindanao, 1962–64. Returned to San Jose State College, where he resumed his faculty responsibilities in departments of Biology and Science Education, 1964–71. During this tenure, was organizer and first director of Moss Landing Marine Laboratory, California, 1966–70, and Sea Grant program director at that laboratory, 1970–71, where he supervised ecological investigations of Monterey Bay. Served as executive director of Pacific Marine Fisheries Commission, 1971–83. Was member of California Advisory Commission on Marine and Coastal Resources; Advisory Committee to the San Francisco Conservation and Development Commission; and Marine Advisory Committee of California Department of Fish and Game. Served as nonvoting member of Pacific and North Pacific Fishery Management Councils and consultant to Marine Fisheries Advisory Committee of the National Oceanic and Atmospheric Administration.

LAWRENCE D. SIX

American Men and Women of Science (Physical and Biological Sciences), 15th ed., 1982.

HAWES, AUSTIN FOSTER
(1879–1962)
Born March 17 in Danvers, Massachusetts. Tufts College, B.A. 1901; Yale University, M.F. 1903. Attracted to U.S. Bureau of Forestry (now Forest Service), he was among early student assistants in that organization. Was appointed state forester of Connecticut in 1904, and was state forester of Vermont from 1909 to 1917. Returned to Forest Service during World War I, serving in various capacities related to war effort. Became state forester of Connecticut again in 1921, retiring from that po-

sition in 1944. Organized statewide system of fire protection, promoted acquisition of extensive state forests, provided for their management for wood production and recreation, and fostered a successful program of extension work generally resulting throughout the state in intelligent and favorable public sentiment toward forestry. From 1933 to 1941, using Civilian Conservation Corps to degree exceeding most other states, he carried out forest improvement work over large areas of state forestlands. Retired as state forester in 1944. Was active in Association of State Foresters and president in 1927. Was elected a fellow of Society of American Foresters in 1939 in recognition of his leadership in advancement of sound state forestry administration in public interest. Was coauthor with R. C. Hawley of both *Forestry in New England*, 1912, and *Manual of Forestry*, 1918. Died May 10, 1962.

JESSE H. BUELL

"Austin F. Hawes Retires." *Yale Forest School News*. April 1944.
Journal of Forestry. Obituary, September 1962.

HAWLEY, RALPH CHIPMAN
(1880–1971)
Born March 5 in Atlanta, Georgia. Amherst College, B.A. 1901; Yale University, M.F. 1904. After a year with U.S. Bureau of Forestry and another as assistant state forester of Massachusetts, joined faculty of Yale Forest School in 1906 and began lifetime career in teaching; this was at strategic period when forestry movement was gaining momentum in United States and there was great need for technically trained foresters. His major work at Yale was in silviculture and forest protection. Succeeded in 1933 to Morris K. Jessup professorship of silviculture and held that position until his retirement in 1948. Recognized importance of fieldwork in training of foresters, and was instrumental in making arrangements with New Haven Water Company whereby Yale School of Forestry cooperatively managed its forestlands, eventually covering twenty thousand acres, and used them for training and research. Was chairman of committee of Society of American Foresters that designated and described forest types recognized in United States; and of committee of same society that published book *Forest Terminology*. Was elected a fellow of Society of American Foresters in 1942. Served twelve years as associate editor of *Journal of Forestry*. Is coauthor (with A. F. Hawes) of *Forestry in New England*, 1912, and *Manual of Forestry*, 1918; and is

author of *Practice of Silviculture*, 1921 and later editions, and *Forest Protection*, 1937. Died January 19, 1971.

JESSE H. BUELL

American Men of Science (Physical and Biological Sciences), 10th ed., 1960.

Yale Forest School News, October 1948.

HAY, KEITH GEORGE
(born 1928)
Born June 30 in Newton, Kansas. Wentworth Military Academy 1948; University of Kansas, B.S. (zoology) 1950; Colorado State University, M.S. (wildlife management) 1955; University of Colorado, nondegree graduate work (environmental education), 1960–61. Served in U.S. Army, 1950–53. Was employed by Colorado Game and Fish Department, 1955–63, first as wildlife conservation officer, later becoming assistant editor of *Colorado Outdoors Magazine*, big-game biologist, and public information officer. In his last four years, produced and hosted the department's weekly outdoor TV program on KRMA–TV Denver. In 1963 joined U.S. Department of the Interior's Bureau of Outdoor Recreation, where he researched and coauthored book (1966) on recreational attributes of Lewis and Clark expedition route and initiated Land and Water Conservation Fund grants-in-aid program in mid-continent region. Employed by U.S. Bureau of Sport Fisheries and Wildlife in 1966 as assistant chief, Office of Conservation Education, organized first national symposium on urban wildlife and edited its proceedings, *Man and Nature in the City*, 1968. Became conservation director for American Petroleum Institute, 1970. In that capacity, successfully established and maintained productive liaison between petroleum industry and leadership of national conservation/environmental organizations. His field trips for industry, government, and conservation leaders to energy facilities throughout United States and England have been lauded for their objectivity and educational value. Has served on U.S. Department of the Interior's Outer Continental Shelf Environmental Studies Committee; and on board of directors of Citizens Committee on Natural Resources and of International Union for the Conservation of Nature and Natural Resources Commission on Education. Has chaired New England Marine Industries Council and Washington Conservation Roundtable, and is currently chairman of National Institute for Urban Wildlife. Received Lewis and Clark Trail Commission's Jefferson Medal in 1966, and Amer-

ican Motors Conservation Award in 1974. Has been frequent contributor to *Ranger Rick* nature magazine, and authored National Wildlife Federation's book *The Beaver's Way* (1973) and American Petroleum Institute's book *Fish and Offshore Oil Development* (1984). An active member of The Wildlife Society, International Association of Fish and Wildlife Agencies, and Outdoor Writers Association of America, he is certified wildlife biologist and has published more than one hundred technical and popular papers in field of wildlife biology and energy/environmental problems.

LAURENCE R. JAHN

HAZZARD, ALBERT SIDNEY

(1901–1979)

Born July 30 in Buchanan, New York. Cornell University, B.A. 1924, Ph.D. (zoology) 1931. Was instructor in zoology at Cornell, 1924–31; associate aquatic biologist in U.S. Bureau of Fisheries, 1931–35; chief fisheries biologist and director of Michigan Institute for Fisheries Research, 1935–55; assistant executive director of Pennsylvania Fish Commission, 1955–63; and fisheries consultant, 1963–79. Was elected president of American Fisheries Society, 1950–51, and honorary life member, 1970; was active in Society of Ichthyologists and Herpetologists. Served for many years, commencing in 1959, on Board of Scientific Advisors of Trout Unlimited, and in 1963 received its first annual Trout Conservation Award. While employed in Pennsylvania and advising Trout Unlimited, actively promoted philosophy that, with use of artificial lures and high size limits, live release of most fish caught was best approach to trout management. Was effective teacher, especially among youth groups, in his later years. Albert S. Hazzard Memorial Fund was established in his honor by American Fisheries Society. Authored numerous scientific papers, including *Natural History of Fishes*, *Ecology of Fishes*, *Fish Management Methods*, and *Pennsylvania Fishes*. Died January 11, 1979.

C. GORDON FREDINE
ROBERT E. OLSON

American Men of Science (Physical and Biological Sciences), 11th ed., 1966.

Fisheries. Obituary, Vol. 4, No. 2:59–60, 1979 (American Fisheries Society).

HEADY, HAROLD FRANKLIN
(born 1916)
Born March 29 in Buhl, Idaho. University of Idaho, B.S. 1938; New York State College of Forestry, M.S. 1940; University of Nebraska, Ph.D. 1949. Was range conservationist for U.S. Soil Conservation Service, White Salmon, Washington, 1941; assistant professor at New York State College of Forestry, Syracuse, 1942, and at Montana State University, Bozeman, 1942–47; associate professor, Texas A&M University, College Station, 1947–51; on faculty, University of California at Berkeley, 1951–81: professor of forestry, 1962, associate dean of College of Natural Resources, 1974–77, assistant vice-president of Agricultural and University Services, associate director of Agricultural Experiment Station, 1977; and pasture consultant, Food and Agriculture Organization, Saudi Arabia, 1962–63. Was Guggenheim fellow, 1958–59. Currently is part-time consultant. Has written four books and numerous research papers on ecological relationships and methods of sampling of grasslands and deserts, influence of domestic and wild animals on vegetation, and on range management. Is member of Xi Sigma Pi, Alpha Xi Sigma, Sigma Xi; charter member, fellow, Renner award recipient, and former president of American Society for Range Management.

CLARE W. HENDEE
ROBERT D. WILLIAMSON

Who's Who in America, 42d ed., 1982–83.
American Men and Women of Science (Physical and Biological Sciences), 15th ed., 1982.

HEALD, WELDON F.
(1901–1967)
Born May 1 in Milford, New Hampshire. Graduated with degree in architecture from Massachusetts Institute of Technology, but turned to writing as career, concentrating on conservation. Was author of 754 pieces of literature that appeared in 146 different publications. His specialties were history, ecology, preservation of mountains, wilderness, deserts, state and national parks and monuments, and national forests. As director of Sierra Club, 1945–46 and 1947–49, organized its first Conservation Committee; was also member of Conservation Committee of the American Alpine Club. As consultant on national parks and monuments to secretary of the Interior from 1961 until his death, he made

field inspections and reports for National Park Service; did same for Forest Service on wilderness and recreational areas as part of his assignments. Represented National Parks Association at congressional hearings and conferences as trustee of that group. Donated Laura G. Heald Grove in Prairie Creek Redwoods State Park in California to State Park Commission. Established Great Basin National Park Association in 1955, when Lehman Caves National Monument in Nevada was threatened with deletion from National Park System. During World War II served in U.S. Army as climatologist. Was famed for his snowfall predictions in Sierra, based on his knowledge of glaciers. Was member of advisory boards of Desert Protective Council, Trailfinders, and Friends of the Three Sisters Wilderness. Was staff reporter for *National Wildlife News*. Among publications in which his work appeared are *Sierra Club Bulletin, National Parks Magazine, Western Outdoor Quarterly*, and *Westways*. Died July 28, 1967.

MICHAEL McCLOSKEY

HEINTZLEMAN, B. FRANK
(1888–1965)
Born December 3 in Fayetteville, Pennsylvania. Pennsylvania State Forest Academy, B.F. 1907; Yale Forestry School, M.F. 1910. Entered U.S. Forest Service at Portland, Oregon, as forest assistant in 1910; transferred in 1918 to Tongass National Forest in Alaska; and later became assistant regional forester. From 1934 to 1936 was assigned to cooperative forestry work with timber industry in Washington, D.C. For one year was deputy administrator in charge of forest conservation, Lumber Division, National Industrial Recovery Administration. Was appointed regional forester for Alaska Region of the Forest Service, with headquarters in Juneau, in 1937. Negotiated establishment of two large pulp mills at Ketchikan and Sitka. Served as commissioner for U.S. Department of Agriculture in the territory, as representative of Federal Power Commission, and as chairman of Alaska Planning Council. During World War II directed Alaska spruce log program, cooperatively with War Production Board. In 1953, following his retirement from Forest Sevice, was appointed governor of Territory of Alaska by President Eisenhower; served four years, resigning in 1957, in anticipation of passage of Statehood Enabling Act of 1958. In recognition of his contributions to advancement of forestry, was elected a fellow of Society of American Foresters in

1951; and was awarded Sir William Schlich Memorial Medal for distinguished service to forestry in 1958; had been member of Society for fifty years. Died June 24, 1965.

SOCIETY OF AMERICAN FORESTERS

Journal of Forestry. Obituary, vol. 63:654, 1965.

Who's Who in America, 1956–57.

HENDEE, JOHN CLARE
(born 1938)
Born November 12 in Duluth, Minnesota. Michigan State University, B.S. (forestry) 1960; Oregon State University, M.F. (forest management) 1962; University of Washington, Ph.D. 1967. Worked for three years in timber management on Siuslaw National Forest in Oregon, and one year in fire research at Pacific Southwest Experiment Station in Berkeley, California. Led U.S. Forest Service research team studying recreation and people problems in resource management, 1968–76. Was congressional fellow on staffs of Senator Frank Church of Idaho and Congressman Jim Weaver of Oregon, Chairman of the House Subcommittee on Forests, 1976–77. Has been assistant station director, U.S. Forest Service, Southeastern Forest Experiment Station, from 1978 to present. His research team received award from Keep America Beautiful in 1972 for research on litter control. Received American Motors Conservation Award in 1974 for his work "applying social research to people problems of resource management." Is author or coauthor of more than eighty publications based on studies of wilderness, car camping and wildlife recreation, public involvement, technology transfer, and other human dimensions of resource management. Coedited (with Clarence A. Schoenfeld) *Human Dimensions in Wildlife Programs,* 1974; is coauthor of *Wildlife Management in Wilderness,* 1978; and senior coauthor of *Wilderness Management,* 1978.

ELDON W. ROSS

HEPTING, GEORGE HENRY
(born 1907)
Born September 1 in Brooklyn, New York. Cornell University, B.S. (for-

estry) 1929, Ph.D. (plant pathology) 1933. He began his career in forest disease research in 1931 with Bureau of Plant Industry, U.S. Department of Agriculture, and since 1933 has been associated with Southeastern Forest Experiment Station at Asheville, North Carolina. In 1934 was assigned responsibility for all forest pathology studies of Forest Service in Southeastern U.S. Named chief of Division of Forest Disease Research at Southeastern Station in 1953, was made principal scientist in forest disease research for entire Forest Service in 1962 and served in that capacity until 1971. Since 1967 has been adjunct professor of plant pathology and forestry at North Carolina State University. Was associate editor of *Phytopathology*, 1937–39, of *Journal of Forestry*, 1950–52, and of *Forest Science*, 1959–65. In 1963 received Barrington Moore Award from Society of American Foresters for achievement in biological research, and was elected a fellow in 1965. Is also a fellow of American Phytopathological Society. In 1954 received U.S. Department of Agriculture superior service award, and in 1969 was elected to National Academy of Sciences. In 1977 was named to Hall of Fame of Plant Pathology. Is author of more than 190 scientific and professional publications on tree diseases and on effect of air pollution on tree growth, a field of research in which he pioneered. In 1974 received Author's Citation Award of the International Shade Tree Conference for his publication *Diseases of Forest and Shade Trees of the United States*, 1971.

HENRY CLEPPER

American Men and Women of Science (Physical and Biological Sciences), 15th ed., 1982.

Journal of Forestry, 67(7):510, July 1969.

Who's Who in America, 41st ed., 1980–81.

HERBERT, HENRY WILLIAM [FRANK FORESTER]
(1807–1858)
Born April 7 in London, England. Cambridge University (Caius College), B.A. 1830. Immigrating to United States in 1831, taught classical languages for eight years at private school for boys in New York City. In 1833 founded magazine *American Monthly*, but retired as editor two years later. An ardent hunter and fisherman, he began writing about sports of forest and stream and gave up teaching for literary career in which he became successful. A prolific writer, as well as artist skillful at drawing with pen, he wrote historical novels, poetry, and articles and

books about sports. His novels and poetry were published under his own name; his sports writings, which he considered of less literary merit, appeared under pseudonym Frank Forester. Valuation he put on his works has been reversed by time; those about sporting scene have been of more lasting worth than his romantic fiction. Among his outdoor books that had considerable vogue during mid-1800s were *The Warwick Woodlands*, 1845; *My Shooting Box*, 1846; *The Deerstalkers*, 1849; *Frank Forester's Field Sports*, 2 vols., 1849; *Frank Forester's Fish and Fishing of the United States and British Provinces of North America*, 1850; and *The Complete Manual for Young Sportsmen*, 1856. Although wordy according to contemporary fashion, they were well written, with accurate descriptions of forest and field. His books were important because they extolled code of gentleman in sports, and significance of sportsmanship. As pioneer American writer in this genre, he influenced development of American authorship about outdoor themes. Died May 17, 1858.

HENRY CLEPPER

Dictionary of American Biography, 1932.

Dictionary of National Biography, 1949–50.

Who Was Who in American History (Historical Volume), 1607–1896, 1967.

HERBERT, PAUL ANTHONY
(born 1899)
Born August 21 in Brooklyn, New York. Cornell University, B.S. 1921, M.F. 1922; University of Michigan, Ph.D. (land use planning) 1941. Following teaching position as assistant professor of forestry at Michigan State University, 1922–26, was senior forest economist in U.S. Forest Service, 1926–30, and lecturer at Yale University School of Forestry, 1920–31. Was appointed professor of forestry and head of Department of Forestry at Michigan State University in 1931, and was director of University's Division of Conservation, 1950–56. After serving as chief of research for Michigan Department of Economic Development, 1957–67, is now consultant to Michigan United Conservation Clubs. Served in U.S. Army, 1918–19 and 1942–44. Was elected vice-president of National Wildlife Federation, 1952–60, and was president, 1961–62; magazine *National Wildlife* was initiated during his tenure. From 1931 to 1935 was associate editor (forest economics and policy) of *Journal of Forestry*, published by Society of American Foresters; and was editor of *Michigan Out-of-Doors*, 1947–53. Is former member of board of gov-

ernors of The Nature Conservancy, and is active in The American Forestry Association, National Parks and Conservation Association, Soil Conservation Society of America, and The Wildlife Society. Is author of numerous papers on forest economics, land use planning, and general conservation.

NATIONAL WILDLIFE FEDERATION

American Men of Science (Physical and Biological Sciences), 11th ed., 1967.

Who's Who in America, 39th ed., 1976–77.

HERBST, ROBERT LEROY
(born 1935)
Born October 5 in Minneapolis, Minnesota. University of Minnesota, B.S. (forest and wildlife management) 1957. He worked in various capacities in forest industry, U.S. Forest Service, and University of Minnesota from 1953 to 1957. From 1957 to 1963 served as forester for Minnesota Conservation Department and prepared more than two thousand forest wildlife management plans and supervised planting of more than ten million trees. Was executive director of Keep Minnesota Green, 1963–66; and deputy commissioner and acting commissioner, Minnesota Conservation Department, 1966–69. Was national executive director, Izaak Walton League of America, 1969–71, and led efforts to stop mining in Boundary Waters Canoe Area and coordinated National Citizens Crusade for Clean Water. During 1971–79 was Minnesota's first Commissioner of Natural Resources and led efforts for passage of some of most innovative state conservation laws in country. From 1977 to 1981 was assistant secretary of the Interior for Fish and Wildlife and Parks, and for short time served as secretary. During his administration, size of National Parks were doubled, the wildlife refuge system and national trail system were tripled, and he played major role in passage of Alaska Lands legislation. In 1981 was appointed national executive director of Trout Unlimited, where he continues to serve. Is author of *Careers in Environment*, 1973, and many magazine articles. Has received numerous awards for conservation achievement. Has served as chairman of Great Lakes Fishery Commission, of Appalachian Trail Council, and of Migratory Bird Commission, and as commissioner of UNESCO.

ROBERT L. HERBST

Who's Who in America, 42d ed., 1982–83.

HEWITT, OLIVER HAROLD
(born 1916)
Born May 21 at Blind River, Ontario, Canada; naturalized U.S. citizen in 1954. McMaster University, B.A. (biology and chemistry) 1939; Cornell University, M.S. 1941, Ph.D. 1944. Was instructor in wildlife management and ornithology at Cornell, 1942–44. Was appointed wildlife management officer with Canadian Wildlife Service in 1944; promoted to chief federal migratory bird officer and held this position until 1949, when he returned to Cornell as assistant professor of wildlife management; associate professor, 1952–57; and professor since 1957. Served as associate editor of *Journal of Wildlife Management*, 1951–53, and editor-in-chief, 1953–56; also served on committee that prepared The Wildlife Society's *Manual of Wildlife Investigational Techniques*; and was editor of the society's *The Wild Turkey and Its Management*. Is author of more than fifty publications and scientific journals on ornithology and wildlife management; his research interests have included development of techniques, waterfowl ecology, population estimation and control, and marsh and marine ecology. Taught wildlife management at University of Pretoria, Republic of South Africa, for academic year 1967–68. In addition to serving on several Wildlife Society committees, also served as secretary-general of International Union for Applied Ornithology. Retiring from Cornell in 1971, joined Mote Marine Laboratory at Placida, Florida. In 1976 retired to Charlotte Harbor, Florida, where he continues his lifelong interest in ornithology.

DANIEL Q. THOMPSON

American Men and Women of Science (Physical and Biological Sciences), 12th ed. (vol. 3), 1972.

HICKEY, JOSEPH JAMES
(born 1907)
Born April 16 in New York City. New York University, B.S. (history) 1930; University of Wisconsin, M.S. (wildlife management) 1943; University of Michigan, Ph.D. (zoology) 1949. Served as research assistant for Wisconsin Soil Conservation Committee 1941–43, and was Guggenheim fellow, 1946–47. Taught wildlife ecology and game management at University of Wisconsin starting in 1948; was professor of its Department of Wildlife Ecology, 1958–77; and represented the university at conservation conferences in France, West Germany, and England. As edi-

tor of *The Journal of Wildlife Management,* 1956–59, was also associate editor of *Proceedings of the Thirteenth International Ornithological Congress.* Organized international conference on peregrine falcon, and edited results of symposium published as *Peregrine Falcon Populations: Their Biology and Decline,* 1969. Served as officer of several ornithological societies and as collaborator, U.S. Fish and Wildlife Service. Was elected a fellow of American Ornithologists' Union in 1954, and has served on its council and its Bird Protection Committee, and was president, 1972–73. Received Aldo Leopold Medal of The Wildlife Society in 1972; Arthur A. Allen Award of the Cornell Laboratory of Ornithology in 1976; and Special Conservation Award of the National Wildlife Federation in 1982. Is a honorary life member of Linnaean Society of New York and of Wisconsin Society of Ornithology, and is former member of board of governors and first treasurer of The Nature Conservancy. Was director of National Audubon Society, 1974–83. Is author of many publications on ecology of birds, on pesticide-wildlife relationships, and on population dynamics and conservation of waterfowl. Notable are his ecological studies of songbird mortality caused by DDT in control of Dutch elm disease in Wisconsin, and of pesticidal residues in gulls, fish, and aquatic invertebrates. His book *A Guide to Bird Watching,* 1943, rev. 1975, is noteworthy contribution to avian ecology.

JOSEPH J. HICKEY
JAMES O. STEVENSON

American Men and Women of Science (Physical and Biological Sciences), 15th
    ed., 1982.
Who's Who in America, 40th ed., 1978–79.

HILE, RALPH OSCAR
(1904–1982)
Born March 18 in Plaineville, Indiana. Indiana Central College, B.A. 1924, LL.D. 1961; Indiana University, Ph.D. (zoology) 1930. Taught in Indiana public schools, 1924–26, and at Indiana University, 1926–30. Joining U.S. Department of the Interior Bureau of Fisheries in 1930, advanced successively from assistant aquatic biologist through position of assistant laboratory director, 1958–61, to senior scientist with Bureau of Commercial Fisheries, and to technical editor, Division of Biological Research, 1965–82. Received U.S. Department of the Interior's Distinguished Service Award in 1962, and served on Council of the Great

Lakes Research Institute, and as associate for Institute of Human Biology; also was research associate, Department of Fisheries and Zoology, University of Michigan. Later served as counselor for analysis, interpretation, and reporting of fishery research findings for U.S. Department of the Interior. Was active in many professional societies, including American Fisheries Society, American Institute of Fishery Research Biologists, Biometrics Society, American Society of Limnology and Oceanography, and International Limnological Society. Was associate editor of *Transactions of the American Fisheries Society*, 1939–44, and editor, 1945–48. Was president of American Fisheries Society in 1952–53, and was awarded an honorary membership in 1962. Authored or coauthored fifty publications. Best known for his work as biometrician, he was primarily interested in study of environmental effects on fish morphology and population dynamics. Was early leader in study of factors of age, growth, abundance, and distribution of fishes of Great Lakes. Died March 28, 1982.

JACK D. LARMOYEUX
ROBERT G. MARTIN

American Men and Women of Science (Physical and Biological Sciences), 14th ed., 1979.

HILL, ROBERT R.
(1885–1973)
Born March 18 in Bruning, Nebraska. Graduated from University of Nebraska in forestry in 1910. During that year was appointed to Forest Service, U.S. Department of Agriculture, and was assigned to Fort Valley Forest Experiment Station in Arizona to investigate effect of livestock grazing on ponderosa pine reproduction. This was relatively new field of study, and techniques for measuring soil and plant conditions and responses were worked out. The data showed extent of damage to range and pine reproduction and need for reduced livestock use. In 1911 was placed in charge of first party to do range survey work, wherein forage types were mapped and carrying capacity calculated. Some of first range-management plans on federal land evolved from these surveys. Was appointed director in 1918 of Santa Rita Range Experiment Station in Arizona, where original work established means of determining best grazing use and management to maintain and improve range conditions. To cut down on time consumed in detailed mapping of vegetation in small plots,

field pantograph was developed. He served as range inspector for California Region of the Forest Service, 1921–26. Was transferred to Washington, D.C., office in 1927 as inspector of grazing; drafted plan for study of range economic conditions and distribution problems on western national forests, which eventually led to studies of grazing use and stability of permits and to policy changes. His last assignment in Forest Service was as director of Division of Recreation, Wildlife and Range Management, in regional office at Milwaukee, a position from which he retired in 1945. Advocated throughout his career conservative use of rangelands, and was ahead of most of his contemporaries in recognizing, and urging correction of, damage being done to watersheds through overuse by livestock. Counseled against the department's program of attempting to increase meat production through heavier stocking on rangelands during World War I. In 1936 declared authors of *The Western Range* were unrealistic in their recommendation that national forest rangelands needed only 6.3–percent reduction in stocking to reach safe capacity and start range conditions on upward trend. In testimony to soundness of his declaration, stocking was later reduced by more than fifty percent. Died October 13, 1973.

LLOYD W. SWIFT

HOCKENSMITH, ROY DOUGLAS
(1905–1981)
Born February 27 in Gallatin, Missouri. University of Missouri, B.S. (agriculture) 1927, M.S. (soils) 1928. Was assistant professor of agronomy, 1929–30, and associate professor of agronomy in charge of soils, 1930–34, at Colorado State University; then became soils specialist with Federal Land Bank, 1934–37. Was appointed regional soil scientist for Soil Conservation Service in Amarillo, Texas, in 1937; became assistant chief, Soil Conservation Surveys Division, Washington, D.C., 1939–46; division chief, 1946–52; and, since 1952, director of Soil Conservation Service Soil Survey Operations. Was a fellow of Soil Conservation Society of America (president in 1962); also a fellow of American Society of Agronomy and of American Association for the Advancement of Science. Was member of International Society of Soil Science, chairman of Soil Technology Commission, 1950–54; and member of Soil Science Society of America and of American Society of Range Management. Participated in many international conferences, including United Nations Scientific

Conference on Conservation and Utilization of Resources in 1949, and Food and Agriculture Organization Conference on Land and Water Utilization and Conservation in 1950. Was U.S. advisor on agriculture to Caribbean Commission in 1950, U.S. delegate to Fourth International Congress of Soil Science in 1950, and participant in Fifth International Congress in 1954. Was U.S. delegate to First Pan-American Soil Conservation Congress in 1966, and participated in soil studies to locate new areas of settlement in Brazil during special assignments in 1963–66 and 1968. Received Superior Service Award of U.S. Department of Agriculture in 1959 and the department's Certificate of Merit in 1967. Died January 19, 1981.

F. GLENNON LLOYD

American Men of Science (Physical and Biological Sciences), 11th ed., 1966.

Who's Who in America, 39th ed., 1976–77.

HODGDON, HARRY EDWARD
(born 1946)
Born September 4 in Brattleboro, Vermont. University of Maine, B.S. (wildlife biology) 1968; University of Massachusetts, M.S. 1971, Ph.D. (wildlife biology) 1978. Conducted research on population dynamics and behavior of unexploited beaver population in central Massachusetts. Became manager of conservation activities, National Rifle Association of America, Washington, D.C., 1975; and assistant director and director, Hunting and Conservation Division, 1976–77. Was appointed field director of The Wildlife Society, 1977, and executive director, 1982. Served as editor of *The Wildlifer* and member of executive committee and board of directors of Renewable Natural Resources Foundation since 1981. Has served as chairperson or member of numerous national and international committees and advisory boards for professional organizations and legislative and executive branches of government. His professional affiliations include American Society of Mammalogists, Animal Behavior Society, Society for Range Management, and International Association of Fish and Wildlife Agencies. Has authored more than forty technical and popular articles and reports.

THOMAS M. FRANKLIN

HOLBROOK, STEWART HALL
(1893–1964)

Born August 22 in Newport, Vermont. Colebrook New Hampshire Academy; Pacific University, D.H.L. 1957; Willamette University, Litt.D. (honorary) 1959. Served in U.S. Army, 1917–19. Was associate editor, *The Lumber News*, Portland, Oregon, 1923–25, and editor, 1926–34. His first book, *Holy Old Mackinaw*, a natural history of American lumberjack, was published in 1938. A year later, was appointed director of "Keep Washington Green" program to promote forest-fire prevention and reforestation. His 1943 book *Burning an Empire*, the story of American forest fires, became classic in its field. During next two decades, wrote series of books on historical themes and conservation subjects, including, for children, *Tall Timber*, and several histories of forest products companies, including *Green Commonwealth*, a history of Simpson Logging Company, and *Yankee Loggers*, an account of International Paper Company. In all, wrote forty books and hundreds of newspaper and magazine articles, many of which treated of natural resource protection and management. Was effective interpreter of conservation needs and progress whose writings received wide public acceptance. Although best known as popularizer of national and regional history, his contributions to literature of forest conservation were valuable in advancing movement because they reached class of readers not generally interested in technical and scientific works. Received Distinguished Service Award from American Forest Products Industries in 1963. Died September 3, 1964.

JAMES B. CRAIG

HOLMES, JOSEPH AUSTIN
(1859–1915)

Born November 23 in Laurens, South Carolina. Cornell University, B.S. 1881; University of Pittsburgh, D.Sc.; University of North Carolina, LL.D. Beginning in 1881 was professor of geology and natural history at University of North Carolina until 1891, when he was appointed state geologist, first in nation, on establishment of North Carolina Geological Survey. Directed also to investigate state's timber resources, in 1892 employed W. W. Ashe (q.v.), who was thus one of country's first state forestry employees, and who made one of earliest state forest surveys ever published. In 1899 Holmes was a founder of Appalachian National Forest Reserve Association, and was one of first persons to propose federal acquisition of woodland in southern Appalachians for forest and park purposes a proposal consummated with passage of Weeks Law of 1911, genesis of which may be credited to him, and subsequent acquisition of 1.5 million acres of national forests and parks in North Carolina. Went with U.S. Geological Survey in 1904, was appointed chief of technological branch investigating mine accidents in 1907, and in 1910 became director of newly created Bureau of Mines. Worked with Gifford Pinchot and others to bring about transfer, in 1905, of forest reserves from U.S. Department of the Interior to U.S. Department of Agriculture, where they have become present 188-million-acre national forest system. As secretary of Section on Minerals of the National Conservation Commission, helped compile first inventory of the nation's natural resources. Died July 12, 1915.

HENRY CLEPPER
Dictionary of American Biography, 1932.
Who Was Who in America, 1897–1942.

HORNADAY, FRED EUGENE

(born 1900)

Born June 28 in Indianapolis, Indiana. Wharton School of Finance and Commerce, University of Pennsylvania, B.S. (journalism) 1924. Was field secretary with Chamber of Commerce of the United States, 1924–26; and was with advertising department, *United States Daily* (later *U.S. News and World Report*), 1926–28. For The American Forestry Association was business manager, 1928–45; inaugurated promotional and advertising programs for the association's magazine *American Forests*; and served as secretary, 1945–56, executive vice-president, 1956–66, and special consultant, 1967–68. Retired December 31, 1968, having served the association for forty years, the longest service of any Association employee. Is staunch defender of national forests and parks, and enthusiastic outdoorsman and participant in the association's Trail Riders of the Wilderness program. Conducted pioneer trip in Bob Marshall Wilderness Area in 1933, and conducted twelve other trips in western wilderness areas. Was acquainted with more members of The American Forestry Association than any other staff member, having planned its annual meetings from 1929 to 1966. Is member of Society of American Foresters and of Conservation Committee, and member-at-large of National Council, Boy Scouts of America. Served as chairman, National Advisory Council Steering Committee, Keep America Beautiful, Inc., 1967, receiving its plaque for meritorious service. Was chairman, Natural Resources Council of America, 1966–67; was member of Tree Committee of D.C. Commissioners' Planning and Urban Renewal Advisory Council; served on President Eisenhower's Council for Youth Fitness; and participated in Sixth World Forestry Congress, Madrid, Spain, 1966.

KENNETH B. POMEROY

Who's Who in America, 39th ed., 1976–77.

HORNADAY, WILLIAM TEMPLE
(1854–1937)

Born December 1 near Plainfield, Indiana. Educated at Oskaloosa College, and Iowa State Agricultural College; University of Pittsburgh, Sc.D. 1906; Yale University, 1917; Iowa State College, Ph.M. 1923. At Ward's Natural Science Establishment in Rochester, New York, which supplied mounted specimens for museums, became scientific taxidermist, collected vertebrate animals in different parts of world, and on one early trip established definitely the previously disputed existence of Florida crocodile. In 1882 became chief taxidermist of U.S. National Museum in Washington, D.C. Instrumental in starting National Zoological Park in Washington, D.C., he served as its superintendent for two years until resigning from government service in 1890 after dispute with superiors over plans for the park's future. Subsequently engaged in private business in Buffalo, New York, until called upon in 1896 to become first director and builder of New York Zoological Park. World renowned as zookeeper, became equally famous as champion of wildlife protection, a cause in which he remained active and articulate after retiring from zoo administration in 1926. With caustic tongue and pen, denounced hunting for sport and inveighed against what he regarded as malevolent influence of manufacturers of sporting arms and ammunition. Worked for laws against sale of wild game and importation of wild bird plumage, and for hunting-bag limits. His efforts were credited with helping to save American bison, pronghorn antelope, and Alaskan fur seal from threatened extinction. Established Permanent Wild Life Fund in 1913, and served as its trustee and chief administrator until his death. Of some twenty books, two of his better-known volumes are *Our Vanishing Wild Life*, 1913, and *Thirty Years' War for Wildlife*, 1913. Died March 6, 1937.

CHARLES H. CALLISON

Dictionary of American Biography, supp. 2, 1958.

National Cyclopaedia of American Biography, 1897.

New York Herald Tribune. Obituary, March 8, 1937.

New York Times. Obituary, March 7, 1937.

Who Was Who in America, 1897–1942.

HOSMER, RALPH SHELDON
(1874–1963)

Born March 4 in Deerfield, Massachusetts. Harvard University, B.S. (agriculture) 1894; Yale University, M.F. 1902, member of first graduating class in School of Forestry. Entered government service in Division of Soils, U.S. Department of Agriculture, in 1896; after two years transferred to Division of Forestry, recently reorganized under Gifford Pinchot. Became first superintendent of Division of Forestry of the Territory of Hawaii in 1904. As territorial forester, obtained establishment of system of forest reserves and put Division of Forestry on sound operating basis. Was advisor at The White House Conference of Governors in 1908 and chairman of Territorial Conservation Commission of Hawaii, 1908–14. In 1914 became professor of forestry and head of Department of Forestry at New York State College of Agriculture at Cornell University. Retired from this position in July 1942 as emeritus professor of forestry. Was member of Research Council of Northeastern Forest Experiment Station, 1926–42; and secretary of Forestry Section. Was member of International Congress of Plant Sciences, 1926; New York State Conservation Advisory Council, 1932–41; The American Forestry Association; and honorary life member of Empire State Forest Products Association, 1924. Was a fellow of American Association for the Advancement of Science and of Forest History Society. Was charter member of Society of American Foresters and served as president in 1923, councilman in 1930–33, and held many other offices and committee assignments. Was elected a fellow in 1932 and was awarded Sir William Schlich Memorial Medal in 1950. Was author of many articles, bulletins, and books; especially noteworthy are *Impressions of European Forestry*, 1921; *The Cornell Plantations—A History*, 1947; *The Society of American Foresters—An Historical Summary*, 1940 and 1950; and *Forestry at Cornell*, 1950. Died July 19, 1963.

SOCIETY OF AMERICAN FORESTERS

American Men of Science (Physical and Biological Sciences), 10th ed., 1960.

Journal of Forestry, 61(9):686, September 1963.

HOUGH, FRANKLIN BENJAMIN
(1822–1885)
Born July 22 in Martinsburg, New York. Union College, graduated 1843; Western Reserve Medical College, M.D. 1848. While practicing medicine in New York State, was also director of state census of 1854. During Civil War was surgeon in Union Army. Resuming his medical practice in Lowville, New York, was superintendent of state census of 1865, and of U.S. census of 1870. His findings as census administrator alerted him to extent of depletion of the country's timberlands. At 1873 meeting of American Association for the Advancement of Science in Portland, Maine, presented paper *On the Duty of Governments in the Preservation of Forests*. Association appointed committee, of which he was chairman, to memorialize Congress on importance of promoting cultivation of timber and preservation of forests. In August 1876 Congress appropriated two thousand dollars to commissioner of Agriculture to employ agent to investigate consumption of timber and other forest products and best means for renewal of forests. Hough was given assignment on August 30, 1876; thus began first action by federal government toward forest policy. His modest office became Division of Forestry in 1881, Bureau of Forestry in 1901, and present U.S. Forest Service in 1905. Was fluent writer of papers and speeches, publishing his first *Report upon Forestry* in 1877 and his second in 1880. In his third report of 1882, he described European systems of forestry that he had studied in person. Was superseded but not dismissed as head of Division of Forestry in 1883; remained on duty to write fourth official report of 1885. In 1882 published book *Elements of Forestry*, and started *American Journal of Forestry*, which was discontinued after one year for lack of support. One of his last contributions to advancement of forestry was his drafting of legislation in 1885 for forestry commission in New York State. Died June 11, 1885.

HENRY CLEPPER

Dictionary of American Biography, 1933.

Who's Who in American History (Historical Volume), 1607–1896.

Jacobsen, Edna L. "Franklin B. Hough, a Pioneer in Scientific Forestry in America," *New York History XV*. New York State Library, Albany, July 1934, pp. 317–21.

HOWARD, WILLIAM GIBBS
(1887–1948)
Born February 17 in Medford, Massachusetts. Harvard University, B.A. 1907, M.F. 1908. Entered U.S. Forest Service in 1908 as forest assistant, and in 1909 joined New York State Forest Fish and Game Commission as forester. He became assistant head of Division of Lands and Forests in the successor New York Conservation Commission in 1910, and director of that division in the succeeding New York Conservation Department in 1927, a position he held until his death. Organized in New York one of first effective state forest-fire control organizations, which became a model for numerous other states, and directly supervised it until he became head of Division of Lands and Forests. In addition, carried on an expanding program of development of New York's forest preserve in Adirondack and Catskill regions for public recreation, and fathered many policies for administration of preserve. Was leading spirit in program of acquiring and reforesting abandoned agricultural lands and in enactment of New York Forest Practice Act, which provides technical forestry assistance to woodland owners. Was active from 1911 until his death in Society of American Foresters and served that organization as vice-president, member of its council, and chairman of New York Section; was elected a fellow of the society in 1942. Was one of founders of National Association of State Foresters in 1920, and president 1933. Died October 30, 1948.

W. D. MULHOLLAND

HOWE, SYDNEY
(born 1928)
Born May 12 in Waterbury, Connecticut. Graduated from Loomis School, Windsor, Connecticut, in 1945; was exchange student at Radley College, England, 1946; Yale University, B.A. (sociology) 1949; University of Michigan School of Natural Resources, M.S. (conservation) 1954. Served in U.S. Army, 1950–52, and was with Aluminum Limited in Canada, 1954–57. Then for seven years was executive director of Farmington River Watershed Association, a citizens' organization in Connecticut.

In April 1965 joined Conservation Foundation, Washington, D.C., and in June 1969 was elected as its president. Served as executive director of Center for Growth Alternatives, 1973–75. In 1976 became executive director of Human Environment Center (formerly Urban Environment Foundation), a Washington, D.C., organization convening urban, minority, and environmental conservation interests in common efforts. Is a fellow of Roosevelt Centennial Youth Project, and also serves as member of board of directors of Environmental Law Institute and as vice-president of Rockywold-Deephaven Camps, Inc., a family business in New Hampshire.

RAYMOND F. DASMANN
SYDNEY HOWE

HUBACHEK, FRANK BROOKES
(born 1894)
Born August 10 in Minneapolis, Minnesota. University of Minnesota, B.A. 1915, LL.B. 1922; Harvard Law School, 1915–17; Cornell College, L.H.D. (honorary) 1962; Beloit College, LL.D. 1970. Engaged in practice of law beginning in 1922 as partner of Hubachek, Kelly, Rauch and Kirby, Chicago. In World War I was U.S. Navy Air Corps pilot, and served in Office of Price Administration during World War II. Since 1926 has been active in protection and management of wilderness areas, particularly Quetico-Superior region along Minnesota-Ontario border. In 1948 established Quetico-Superior Wilderness Research Center, dedicated to investigations concerned with maintenance of wilderness areas and their utilization for benefit of science and humanity. In 1957 created and endowed Wilderness Research Foundation, a nonprofit Illinois corporation of which he is trustee and president emeritus, to sponsor scientific research in wilderness ecology. Located on Fall Lake, north of Ely and Duluth, Minnesota, the center provides research facilities for visiting scientists and permanent staff. It is operated under advisory guidance of university scientists, U.S. Forest Service, and other agencies concerned with wilderness ecology. Received The American Forestry Association's Conservation Award in 1957; later served as association director. Was elected honorary member of Society of American Foresters in 1953. In recognition of his leadership in advancing scientific knowledge of wilderness ecology, in 1968 received American Motors Conservation Award.

HENRY CLEPPER

HUBBS, CARL LEAVITT
(1894–1979)

Born October 18 in Williams, Arizona. Stanford University, A.B. 1916, A.M. 1917; University of Michigan, Ph.D. (zoology) 1927. After four years as assistant curator of ichthyology and herpetology at Field Museum of Natural History, Chicago, joined staff of Museum of Zoology, University of Michigan, in 1920, and rose from instructor to professor of zoology and curator of fishes. In 1944 joined Scripps Institution of Oceanography (University of California at San Diego), as research biologist and emeritus professor. As founder of Michigan Department of Conservation's Institute for Fisheries Research in 1930, was active in conservation work for more than fifty years. In 1939–40 was field representative for U.S. Department of the Interior in Alaska and in same year was vice-president of The Wildlife Society. Was instrumental in getting unique habitat of Devils Hole pupfish (*Cyprinodon diabolis*) added to Death Valley National Monument in 1952 and in having refuge area developed for native fishes of Owens Valley, California, in 1967. Similar efforts to conserve Torrey Pines and Mission Bay, near San Diego, were successfully concluded. In 1963 was invited by Japan Fisheries Resource Conservation Association to lecture in Japan. In 1964 received Leidy Award and Medal of the Academy of Natural Sciences of Philadelphia; in 1966 received Fellows Medal of the California Academy of Sciences; and 1965 was elected foreign member of Linnaen Society of London. From 1964 through 1967 served as vice-president for conservation and chairman of Committee on Conservation of American Society of Ichthyologists and Herpetologists. His achievements were recognized by his election to National Academy of Sciences in 1952. Was member of American Fisheries Society beginning in 1920, was elected honorary life member, and in 1973 received the society's Award of Excellence. Hubbs Sea World Research Institute, San Diego, was named for and dedicated to him in 1977. Was author of more than six hundred scientific publications and reviews, and senior author of *Fishes of the Great Lakes Region*, 1941–64. Died June 30, 1979.

C. GORDON FREDINE
ROBERT RUSH MILLER

American Men and Women of Science (Physical and Biological Sciences), 14th ed., 1979.

Fisheries. Obituary, vol. 4, no. 5:28, 1979 (American Fisheries Society).

Who's Who in America, 40th ed., 1978–79.

HUTTON, ROBERT FRANKLIN
(born 1921)
Born July 18 in Red Lion, Pennsylvania. University of Miami, B.S. (biological sciences) 1949, M.S. 1951; University of London, Ph.D. 1954. During 1954–55 headed research program on Florida red tide for University of Miami. In 1955 joined staff of University of Florida as assistant professor and served as director of the university's field station at Saint Petersburg. Later (1955–62) was biologist-in-charge and parasitologist for Florida State Board of Conservation Marine Laboratory at Saint Petersburg. From 1962 to 1965 was chief marine biologist and assistant director of Division of Marine Fisheries, Department of Natural Resources, Boston, Massachusetts. From 1965 to 1972 served as first executive secretary of American Fisheries Society. In 1972 joined National Marine Fisheries Service as Associate Director for Resource Management; and in 1975 became state coordinator for marine resources in National Oceanic and Atmospheric Administration. In 1965 received Massachusetts Governor's Award as state conservationist of year. Since 1965 has served as member of National Conservation Committee of Boy Scouts of America. Was treasurer of Natural Resources Council of America, 1966–69. Was elected president of American Fisheries Society for 1976–77. During 1980–81 chaired Marine Resources Study Committee for South Carolina Wildlife and Marine Resources Department. In 1981 was appointed as first chairman of Common and Scientific Names of Aquatic Invertebrates Committee of the American Fisheries Society, and in 1981 was elected to honorary life membership in that society. Has served as chairman of Statistical Needs Committee of the Atlantic States Marine Fisheries Commission, and on both Biological Committee and Estuarine Committee of the Commission. Directed research on problems such as parasite and disease investigations, fish taxonomy and ecology, shrimp and oyster investigations, red tide, seagrass ecology, algae taxonomy, dredge-and-fill studies, bulkhead investigations, artificial reef studies, shellfish depuration, lobster culture and ecology, and estuarine fisheries studies. Also directed management programs involving enforcement of fisheries regulations, fisheries extension, water resources related to environmental protection, state-federal fisheries coordination, marine mammals, and endangered species. New larval trematode *Giganobilhar-*

zia hutoni, and new trematode *Neostictodora hutoni,* were named in his honor. Is author of more than fifty scientific papers. Holds professional certification as fisheries scientist in American Fisheries Society, and is a fellow of American Association for the Advancement of Science.

ROBERT F. HUTTON
ELWOOD A. SEAMAN

American Men and Women of Science (Physical and Biological Sciences), 12th ed. (vol. 3), 1972.
Leaders in American Science, 7th ed., 1966–67.
Who's Who in America, 42d ed., 1982–83.

ILLICK, JOSEPH SIMON
(1884–1967)

Born September 16 near Easton, Pennsylvania. Lafayette College, B.A. (biology) 1907, D.Sc. (Honorary) 1925; Biltmore Forest School, North Carolina, B.F. (forestry) 1911, F.E. (forest engineering) 1913; Juniata College, Sc.M. (honorary) 1925; Syracuse University, LL.D. 1952. Began his teaching career at Pennsylvania State Forest Academy at Mont Alto in 1907, advanced to professor of silviculture, and left in 1919 to become chief of Bureau of Silviculture and later director of research for Pennsylvania Department of Forests and Waters. Was state forester of Pennsylvania, 1927–31. In latter year went to New York State College of Forestry at Syracuse University as head of Department of Forest Engineering and Management, and was appointed dean of the college in 1945. Retired in 1952 as dean emeritus. Was former chairman of Division of Education in Society of American Foresters, served on the society's council, 1954–57, and was elected a fellow in 1957. Was first chairman of Council of Forestry School Executives organized in 1948, and was member of board of trustees of Charles Lathrop Pack Forestry Foundation. Was a fellow of American Association for the Advancement of Science. Was author of twelve books, ten major bulletins, and many articles on forestry and education; wrote *Pennsylvania Trees,* 1913 (four later editions); *Tree Habits: How to Know the Hardwoods,* 1924; and *Outline of General Forestry,* 3d edition, 1939. Was one of America's outstanding forestry educators and leader in development of education in related fields of natural resources. Died August 31, 1967.

HENRY CLEPPER

Journal of Forestry. Obituary, 65(11):848–49, November 1967.

JAHN, LAURENCE ROY
(born 1926)

Born June 24 in Jefferson, Wisconsin. University of Wisconsin-Madison, B.S. (zoology) 1949, M.S. (wildlife management) 1958, Ph.D. (wildlife ecology/zoology) 1965. Carried out research and management of migratory bird populations and aquatic habitats as wildlife biologist with Wisconsin Department of Natural Resources, 1949–59. Served as northcentral field representative of Wildlife Management Institute from 1959 until joining institute staff in Washington, D.C., as director of conservation in 1970, then as secretary 1971–75, and vice-president 1971 to present. Served as secretary-treasurer of North American Wildlife Foundation since 1974, president of The Wildlife Society 1979–80, chairman of National Watershed Congress, executive committee member of National Research Council's Board on Agriculture, council representative of American Association for the Advancement of Science, chairman of Natural Resources Council of America, board member of Citizens Committee on Natural Resources and of National Institute for Urban Wildlife, chairman of U.S. Army Corps of Engineers Environmental Advisory Board, program committee chairman of annual North American Wildlife and Natural Resources Conference, 1972 to present, among other positions. Also has served in advisory capacity to Congressional Office of Technology Assessment, Delta Waterfowl Research Station, National Marine Fisheries Service, International Association of Fish and Wildlife Agencies, Soil Conservation Society of America, National Coordinating Committee on Fish and Wildlife in Federal Water Resources Projects, U.S. departments of Defense and State, and for nearly all natural resource agencies within departments of Agriculture and Interior, state of Wisconsin, and others. Was elected a fellow of American Association for the Advancement of Science in 1971. His contributions in area of waterfowl and wetland management have received several awards, as have a number of his many authored, coauthored, and edited publications on land, water, and wildlife management and conservation at both scientific and popular levels.

RICHARD E. McCABE

American Men and Women of Science (Physical and Biological Sciences), 15th ed., 1982.

Who's Who In America, 42d ed., 1982–83.

JAMES, HARLEAN
(1877–1969)
Born July 18 in Mattoon, Illinois. Stanford University, B.A. (history) 1898; graduate studies at University of Chicago and Columbia University. Following secretarial work in Hawaii, became executive secretary of Women's Civic League in Baltimore during 1911–16, then was with National Defense Council and U.S. Department of Labor during World War I. Was executive secretary of American Civic Association, 1921–35, and of American Planning and Civic Association, 1935–58. Served also as executive secretary of National Conference on State Parks, 1935–57, and on her retirement was made member of board of directors; Conference is now unit of National Recreation and Parks Association. At various times was collaborator with National Park Service on recreational planning, and was on advisory committee of U.S. Department of the Interior. American Scenic and Historic Preservation Society presented her with bronze medal in 1943 and gold medal in 1953. Was honorary vice-president of The American Forestry Association, and honorary corresponding member of American Association of Landscape Architects. Was author of several books, including *Land Planning in the United States for the City, State and Nation*, 1926, and *Romance of the National Parks*, 1939. Was editor of American Planning and Civic Association *Annuals* during 1927–57, and of *Yearbook of Park and Recreation Progress*, 1942. Died November 15, 1969.

HENRY CLEPPER

Evening Star, Washington, D.C. Obituary, November 19, 1969.

Who's Who of American Women, 1961–62.

JARDINE, JAMES TERTIUS
(1881–1954)
Born November 28 in Cherry Creek, Oneida County, Idaho. Utah Agricultural College, B.S. 1905; studied at University of Chicago summers of 1905 and 1906. Taught English at Utah two years; then was employed by Forest Service, U.S. Department of Agriculture until 1920. During this period became first chief of studies for this bureau of grazing use and management on western rangelands resulting in several publications, of which classic bulletin *Range Management on the National Forests*, 1919, was issued with Mark Anderson as junior author. Contribution of the bulletin was method devised by Jardine for estimating forage supply and

grazing capacity of rangelands. It summarized basic principles of range management on numbers of livestock, grazing seasons, and other matters, and this publication is regarded as foundation statement of science and art of range management. Was director of Oregon Agricultural Experiment Station, 1920–31. Returning to U.S. Department of Agriculture, Washington, D.C., was chief officer of experiment stations beginning in 1931, and director of research for the department, 1936–41. Pioneered field of range and livestock management, and through his keen analytical mind and command of English made major contribution to principles of grazing use of western public lands. Was awarded honorary D.Sc. degrees from three American colleges. Perhaps more than any other individual, he initiated science of range management. As chief of grazing studies in Forest Service, exercised strong leadership, organizing work into projects, and proceeding with establishment of field stations, of which Great Basin Experiment Station in Utah (where studies on plant succession were conducted) is example. Died October 24, 1954.

LLOYD W. SWIFT

American Men of Science, 7th ed., 1944.

Talbot, M. W., and Cronemiller, F. P. "Some of the Beginnings of Range Management," *Journal of Range Management*, vol. 14, March 1961.

JEMISON, GEORGE MEREDITH
(born 1908)
Born July 11 in Spokane, Washington. University of Idaho, B.S. 1931; Yale University, M.F. 1935; Duke University, Ph.D. (tree physiology) 1942; D.Sc. (honorary) University of Idaho, 1967. Entered U.S. Forest Service in 1931 as junior forester assigned to fire danger measurement studies at Northern Rocky Mountain Forest and Range Experiment Station, Missoula, Montana; continued in research and was transferred in 1937 to Southeastern Forest Experiment Station at Asheville, North Carolina, where he engaged in forest-fire and forest-management research. Was made director of Northern Rocky Mountain Station in 1950; from 1954 to 1957 was director of Pacific Southwest Forest and Range Experiment Station at Berkeley, California. In 1957 was assigned to Washington, D.C., office of Forest Service as assistant chief of Branch of Research, and in 1966 was appointed deputy chief in charge of research. Retiring from government service in 1969, became professor of forest management at Oregon State University, retiring as professor emeritus in

1974. Was member of council of Society of American Foresters, 1962–66, having been elected a fellow in 1961. Served as president from 1968 to 1971 of International Union of Forest Research Organizations. His research publications include seventy papers on forest-fire behavior, fire control techniques, and silviculture of pines and hardwoods. In 1959 was leader of group of foresters sent by United States to observe forest conditions and forestry practices in Russia. His honors include Distinguished Service Award of U.S. Department of Agriculture, 1967; Barrington Moore Award, 1971; and Bernhard Fernow Award, 1979.

HENRY CLEPPER
GEORGE M. JEMISON

American Men of Science (Physical and Biological Sciences), 11th ed., 1966.

"Jemison Joins Oregon Faculty," *Journal of Forestry*, 67(6):424, June 1969.

JENKINS, ROBERT ELLSWORTH, JR.

(born 1942)

Born September 30 in Lewistown, Pennsylvania. Rutgers University, B.A. 1964; Harvard University, Ph.D. 1971. Joined staff of The Nature Conservancy in 1970 and became that organization's vice-president for science programs in 1972, a position he continues to hold. Was cofounder of Center for Applied Research in Environmental Sciences, 1971, and founded and served as director of State Natural Heritage Programs from 1974 to present. Was member, conservation section of U.S. Commission for International Biological Program, 1970–75; Federal Commission for Research on Natural Areas, 1970 to present; and U.S. National Commission for UNESCO, 1974–76. Was research associate, Smithsonian Institution, 1971–73; member of board of directors of Rare Animal Relief Effort (RARE), 1974–76; Parks and Preserves Commission U.S./Soviet Environmental Protection Agreements, Advisory Council for the Kai Moka Foundation, 1976–80; Natural Areas Commission U.S. Man and the Biosphere Program, 1978 to present; Advisory Council to Center for Plant Conservation, 1983 to present; board of directors of Massachusetts Planned Parenthood League, 1970–73; and Advisory Council to Conservation Biology Institute, 1983 to present. As member of several ecological and environmental organizations, received American Motors Conservation Award in 1978. Was Henry Rutgers scholar in 1963–64; Richmond fellow in 1965–69; research fellow for Organization of Tropical Studies in 1966; demographic fellow with Population Council, 1969–71; and a fellow of American Association for the Advancement of Science and member of its council, 1972–73.

THE NATURE CONSERVANCY

American Men and Women of Science (Physical and Biological Sciences), 15th ed., 1982.

Who's Who in America, 42d ed., 1982–83.

JENKINS, ROBERT MERLE
(born 1923)
Born June 18 in Kansas City, Missouri. University of Oklahoma, B.S. 1948, M.S. (fisheries biology) 1949. Began his professional career with Oklahoma Game and Fish Department in 1949, managing selected ponds and small lakes in northeastern Oklahoma for improved sport fishing; and also conducted field investigations of sport fishery of forty-six-thousand-acre Grand Lake. In 1952 joined staff of Oklahoma Fishery Research Laboratory, a joint venture of University of Oklahoma and Oklahoma Game and Fish Department (later Oklahoma Department of Wildlife Conservation), and in 1953 was appointed director. From 1958 to 1963 was assistant executive vice-president for Sport Fishing Institute and coeditor of the institute's monthly *SFI Bulletin* and of its former biennial review series *Fish Conservation Highlights*. His studies of research needs for better understanding of ecology of large reservoirs contributed to development within U.S. Bureau of Sport Fisheries and Wildlife (later U.S. Fish and Wildlife Service) of national reservoir research program; was designated as program's first (and only) director in 1963. Continued to serve in that post until termination of program in 1983, when he retired from government service. Then helped organize consulting firm of Aquatic Ecosystems Analysts, Fayetteville, Arkansas, holding rank of senior scientist, from 1983 to present. As chairman of Reservoir Committee, Southern Division, American Fisheries Society, was principal organizer of first Reservoir Fishery Resources Symposium, at University of Georgia in 1967. Has published more than sixty scientific papers on fisheries resource subjects, as well as numerous popular articles, including *Bibliography on Reservoir Fishery Biology in North America*, 1965. Was president of American Fisheries Society in 1970–71, and is certified fisheries scientist (American Fisheries Society). Received Meritorious Ser-

vice Award of U.S. Department of the Interior in 1980. As one of original trustees of Sport Fishery Research Foundation, was its first secretary, 1962–63, and has continued to serve as trustee since then.

RICHARD H. STROUD

American Men and Women of Science (Physical and Biological Sciences), 15th ed., 1982.

Who's Who in America, 38th ed., 1974–75.

Who's Who in Government, 2d ed., 1975–76.

JESKE, WALTER EMIL
(1929–1983)
Born August 26 in Leola, South Dakota. Iowa State University, B.S. 1951; Harvard University, M.P.A. 1970. Taught vocational agriculture in Waverly, Iowa, 1951–60, and was editor of *Journal of Soil and Water Conservation* and assistant executive secretary of Soil Conservation Society of America, 1960–65. Was education and publications staff leader in information and public affairs for U.S. Soil Conservation Service and had been selected as executive vice-president of Soil Conservation Society of America, to assume duties in September 1981. Was a fellow of American Association for the Advancement of Science and of Soil Conservation Society of America, and received three president's citations from that society. Was founder and member of executive committee of Alliance for Environmental Education, 1973–81, and chairman of Federal Interagency Committee on Education, Subcommittee on Environmental Education, 1977–81. Was delegate to UNESCO-United Nations Environmental Program Intergovernmental Conference on Environmental Education in Tbilisi, Soviet Union, in 1977. Professional organization memberships included Society for Technical Communication; National Association of Government Communicators; Society for International Development; American Nature Study Society; National Association for Environmental Education; Conservation Education Association; and International Association for Ecology. In 1982 National Association for Environmental Education named its distinguished service award in his honor. Died August 16, 1983, in Arlington, Virginia.

JOHN F. DISINGER

JOHNSON, CARL SAND
(born 1915)
Born October 10 in Pine River, Minnesota. Pine River Normal School, teaching certificate 1934; Saint Cloud State Teachers College, B.ED. 1939; The Ohio State University, M.S. (education) 1947, Ph.D. (conservation) 1951. Was elementary and secondary school teacher, and secondary school principal in rural schools in Minnesota, Ohio, and Kentucky, 1934–36 and 1939–42. Was conservation education specialist for Ohio Department of Education 1946–47, and taught biology at Capital University, 1949–51. Was named director of Ohio Conservation Laboratory in 1957. From 1959 to 1979 taught conservation, conservation policy, and environmental education courses at The Ohio State University, where he was member of faculty of School of Natural Resources from its inception in 1969; chairman of its Division of Environmental Education, 1969–73; director of its Barnebey Center for Environmental Studies, 1970–79; and headed workshop for teachers at Antioch College's Outdoor Education Center, 1962–65. Is a fellow of Ohio Academy of Science, and founding member and past chairman of its conservation section. Has been instructor at University of Chicago, Montana State University, and Saint Cloud State Teachers College during summer sessions. His Ph.D. dissertation was instrumental in establishing school forest program through Ohio Division of Forestry in 1951. Among more than forty publications he authored or coauthored was a study of quality and use of materials in classrooms and other educational settings, *A Survey of Printed Materials for Conservation Teachers*, 1966.

JOHN F. DISINGER

American Men and Women of Science (Physical and Biological Sciences), 12th
    ed., 1972.

JOHNSON, RAYMOND EARL
(born 1914)
Born October 26 in Peru, Nebraska. Doane College, B.A. (biology) 1936; University of Nebraska, M.A. (limnology and botany) 1938; University of Michigan, Sc.D. (ichthyology and geology) 1942. Was in military service, 1942–45. Worked for Minnesota Department of Conservation, 1945–51, and as assistant federal-aid supervisor, 1951–55. Joined U.S. Fish and Wildlife Service as assistant regional director, 1955–58. Went to Washington, D.C., as chief, Branch of Federal Aid, 1958–60;

became chief, Division of Sport Fisheries, 1960–65; and assistant director for servicewide research, 1965–70, responsible for identifying contaminants causing widespread mortality in fish and wildlife, and stressing importance of water quality. Was sent to advise other countries—including Japan, Germany, Kenya, and Mexico—in these matters. When Environmental Protection Agency was created in 1970, served on loan as acting commissioner, Office of Pesticides, setting up new pesticides registration system and beginning its research program. Returning to Fish and Wildlife Service, headed new Office of Environmental Quality, 1971–73. In 1973 became deputy director, Division of Environmental Systems and Resources, National Science Foundation, and in 1974 became director, Division of Advanced Environmental Research and Technology. Since retiring from federal government in 1975, has been consultant to National Wildlife Federation. Served as federal commissioner, Ohio River Valley Water and Sanitation Commission, 1963–72; president of American Fisheries Society, 1973–74; and U.S. observer to International Union for Conservation of Nature and Natural Resources Conference on African Wildlife, Tanzania, 1961. Was member of U.S. delegation to OECD Conference on pesticides in environment, Paris, 1966; National Research Council Committee on chlorofluoromethane emissions, 1979; and International Advisory Council on Acid Rain, 1982. Received Civil Engineering Achievement Award of the American Society of Civil Engineers, 1963; Special Service Award of the Fish and Wildlife Service, 1965; and U.S. Department of the Interior's Citation for Distinguished Service, 1968. Publications include numerous technical papers, and chapters in books of Fish and Wildlife Service's Council of Environmental Quality and American Fisheries Society. His comprehensive knowledge of scientific basis for conservation has been of inestimable value in guiding federal agencies and private organizations with which he has been associated.

SHIRLEY A. BRIGGS

American Men and Women of Science (Physical and Biological Sciences), 15th ed., 1982.

Who's Who in America, 40th ed., 1978–79.

JONES, DALE ALLAN
(born 1925)
Born March 8 in San Jose, California. Utah State University, B.S. (wild-

life management) 1950. In 1950 joined Utah Department of Fish and Game as biologist; later became regional manager, assistant chief of game management, and chief of game management. Joined U.S. Forest Service in 1958 as wildlife biologist with successive assignments in Shoshone National Forest, regional office at Denver, Colorado, and San Juan National Forest. Then became director of wildlife and fish in regional office at Albuquerque, New Mexico, and in 1977 director of wildlife management, U.S. Forest Service. Has been active in The Wildlife Society, serving as president of two chapters, as Southwest region council representative, vice-president, and president. Was also active in International Association of Fish and Wildlife Agencies and several other professional societies. In 1977 received American Motors Conservation Award; Western Association of Fish and Wildlife Agencies Conservationist of the Year Award; and New Mexico Game and Fish Department Conservation Award. Has authored or coauthored several important publications on mule deer ecology and management, including *The Oak Creek Mule Deer Herd in Utah*, which received The Wildlife Society's Monograph of Year award in 1978.

THOMAS M. FRANKLIN

JONES, GOMER EDWARD, JR.
(born 1927)
Born March 8 in Wilkes-Barre, Pennsylvania. Wilkes College, B.S. (chemical engineering) 1948. Joined professional staff of Boy Scouts of America, first as program and camping specialist and later as chief executive officer of local councils, 1948–76. In those capacities, directed several camps and, in addition to other responsibilities, developed three historical trails. In 1976 was appointed vice-president for wildlife heritage with National Wildlife Federation; established the federation's Wildlife Heritage and Land Heritage Programs, 1976–80. Then became senior vice-president for administration and resources with National Audubon Society, 1980–81. Returned to National Wildlife Federation to serve as senior vice-president of wildlife heritage and corporate relations, 1981–83. Then became president and chief executive officer of National Institute for Urban Wildlife, 1983 to present. Has raised millions of dollars for organizations he has served and has expertise in development and management of natural areas, wildlife sanctuaries, and reserves. Caused more than three hundred thousand acres of private lands to be

donated to, or purchased for, wildlife purposes. Received 1978 Professional Fund Raiser of the Year Award from the National Society of Fund Raising Executives.

NATIONAL INSTITUTE FOR URBAN WILDLIFE

Who's Who in America, 42d ed., 1982–83.

JORDAN, DAVID STARR
(1851–1931)
Born January 19 in Gainesville, New York. Cornell University, M.S. 1972; Indiana Medical College, M.D. 1875; Butler University, Ph.D. 1878. Awarded LL.D by Cornell University 1886; Johns Hopkins University 1902; Illinois College 1903; Indiana University 1909; University of California 1913; and Western Reserve University 1915. Taught at various schools, including Cornell University, Butler University, and Indiana University, 1887–95. Was in charge of fishery investigations of U.S. Fish Commission for the Pacific Coast in 1880; of fur seals in Bering Sea, 1896–97; Japan 1900; Hawaii 1901; Samoa 1902; and Alaska 1903. Was president of Indiana University, 1885–91, and of Stanford University, 1891–1913, and chancellor of Stanford University, 1913–16. Was elected president of California Academy of Sciences, serving 1896–1904 and 1908–12. Was dominant ichthyologist of his time by virtue of his work and influence on associates and students, writing more than six hundred ichthyological papers; was author and coauthor of many books, including *A Manual of Vertebrate Animals of Northern U.S.*, 1876–1929; *Synopsis of Fishes of North America*, 1883; *Fishes of North and Middle America*, 1896–1900; *American Food and Game Fishes*, 1902; *A Guide to the Study of Fishes*, 1905; *The Genera of Fishes*, 1917–20; *Classification of Fishes*, 1923; and *Checklist of the Fishes and Fishlike Vertebrates of North and Middle America North of Venezuela and Columbia*, 1930. Died September 19, 1931.

WILLIAM R. GOULD

American Men of Science, 4th ed.

Copeia, no. 1, 1964.

Dictionary of American Biography, 1933.

Who Was Who in America, 1897–1942.

World Who's Who in Science, 1968.

JUDAY, CHANCEY
(1871–1944)

Born May 5 near Milersburg, Indiana. University of Indiana, B.A. 1896, A.M. 1897, LL.D. (honorary) 1933. Was biologist, Wisconsin Geological and Natural History Survey, 1900–1901 and 1905–31. At University of Wisconsin, 1908–31, served as lecturer in limnology and plankton organisms; directed training of graduate students specializing in limnology; and was professor of limnology, 1931–42. Although he retired from teaching in 1942, the university retained him as research associate to prepare comprehensive review of Wisconsin limnology. Held many high positions in scientific organizations: president, American Microscopical Society, 1923; president, Ecological Society of America, 1927; and president, Wisconsin Academy of Sciences, Arts and Letters for two years and secretary for nine years. As major motivating force in formation of Limnological Society of America, was elected as first president in 1935 and reelected in 1936. Was a fellow of American Association for the Advancement of Science, and belonged also to American Society of Zoologists, American Society of Naturalists, and International Limnological Society. In 1943 was awarded Leidy Medal of Honor by Academy of Natural Sciences of Philadelphia. His publications number more than one hundred and include papers on smaller crustaceans, the diurnal movements of plankton, anaerobic organisms of lake bottoms, chemistry of lake waters, growth of freshwater fish, photosynthesis, and many other aspects of limnology. Among his best-known and larger works are *Hydrography and Morphometry of the Lakes* in the series "Inland Lakes in Wisconsin," and two extensive reports (published jointly with E. A. Birge) on dissolved gases and plankton of Wisconsin lakes. Attracted many collaborators, and his advice and cooperation were sought by state and federal conservation agencies. Died March 29, 1944.

EDWARD SCHNEBERGER

American Men of Science, 7th ed., 1944.

Frey, David G. *Limnology in North America*. Madison: University of Wisconsin Press, 1963.

Noland, Lowell E. *Chancey Juday*, Limnological Society of America. Special Publication No. 16, pp. 1–3.

JUDD, BENJAMIN IRA

(born 1904)

Born December 8 in Granite, Utah. Utah State University, B.S. 1928, M.Sc. 1929; University of Nebraska, Ph.D. (agronomy) 1936. Was appointed assistant scientist in Resettlement Administration in 1936; following year was named assistant soil conservationist in Soil Conservation Service, U.S. Department of Agriculture. Has been professor of agronomy at Arizona State University, Tempe, since 1937; and head of Department of Agronomy from 1937 to 1950. Has studied conservation and served as consultant in Central America, Jamaica, Mexico, and Virgin Islands. Was visiting professor in Puerto Rico, 1963–64. Sponsored Arizona Conservation Club and was named Arizona Conservation Educator of the Year, 1965. Has written widely on agronomy, tropical agriculture, conservation, soil science, and range management. Has been active member of American Association for the Advancement of Science, Conservation Education Association (board of directors), Ecological Society of America, American Society of Agronomy, American Society of Range Management, and Soil Conservation Society of America. Has been leading influence in conservation education for youth and adults alike.

WAYNE KESSLER

American Men and Women of Science (Physical and Biological Sciences), 14th ed., 1979.

KALMBACH, EDWIN RICHARD

(1884–1972)

Born April 29 in Grand Rapids, Michigan. Was self-educated in higher biological sciences of ornithology, mammalogy, entomology, botany, and ecology. Honorary doctorate was awarded to him by University of Colorado, 1955. His career in wildlife economics and conservation began as assistant director of Kent Scientific Museum in 1903. In 1910 joined U.S. Bureau of Biological Survey in Washington, D.C., as assistant biologist, and advanced to biologist in 1924, senior biologist in 1928, and director of Wildlife Research Laboratory in Denver, Colorado, under U.S. Fish and Wildlife Service in 1934. Retired from that position in 1954. Represented government's interest in wildlife conservation and management at numerous scientific conferences. Was active in affairs of many societies of biological sciences, such as American Ornithologists' Union, Society of Mammalogists, Wildlife Society, and Cooper and Wilson ornithological societies. Was instrumental in founding and developing government's series of duck stamps and United States postage stamps displaying wildlife species. Designed 1941–42 duck stamp (ruddy duck). Among many conservation honors he received are U.S. Department of the Interior's Distinguished Service Award, 1955; Aldo Leopold Award from The Wildlife Society, 1958; and Founders Day Award, Izaak Walton League of America, 1958. Is widely recognized for his research on economic ornithology and mammalogy, botulism, and as wildlife artist. Was author of numerous publications and reports that helped guide government's policies and practices relating to conservation and management of nation's wildlife resources, for example: *The Armadillo*; *Botulism—A Recurring Hazard*; and *Wildlife in a Developing Hemisphere*. Died August 26, 1972.

CECIL S. WILLIAMS

American Men of Science (Physical and Biological Sciences), 10th ed., 1960.

KAUFERT, FRANK HENRY
(born 1905)
Born December 2 in Princeton, Minnesota. University of Minnesota, B.S. (forestry) 1928, M.S. 1930, Ph.D. (forest pathology) 1935. After year of teaching in University of Minnesota School of Forestry, in 1936 joined firm of E. I. du Pont de Nemours as research technologist in forest pest control. Returning to University of Minnesota in 1940 as associate professor of forestry, went on leave during World War II to serve as senior wood technologist in Forest Products Laboratory, operated by U.S. Forest Service in Madison, Wisconsin. In 1946 was advanced to professor and in 1947 to director of School of Forestry, University of Minnesota, and later to dean of College of Forestry and now dean emeritus. In 1954 was director of Society of American Foresters forestry research project, and was senior author of project's report, *Forestry and Related Research in North America*, 1955. A member of council of Society of American Foresters, 1950–53, was elected a fellow in 1955, and was chairman of Committee for the Advancement of Forestry Education, 1959–63. Was president of Forest History Society, 1956–57 and 1963–64, and was also president of Forest Products Research Society, 1957–58, and of Association of State College and University Research Organizations, 1966–68. For sixteen years was president of Keep Minnesota Green, Inc. Was as-

sistant administrator of U.S. Department of Agriculture Cooperative State Research Service, 1963–64, and since then has served on the department's Cooperative Research Advisory Committee. Was director of American Forestry Association and trustee of Wilderness Research Foundation.

HENRY CLEPPER

American Men and Women of Science (Physical and Biological Sciences), 15th ed., 1982.

Who's Who in America, 1974–75.

KEEN, FREDERICK PAUL
(1890–1980)

Born November 20 in San Diego, California. University of California, Berkeley, B.S. (agricultural sciences) 1914. Was subsequently appointed entomological ranger, Bureau of Entomology, U.S. Department of Agriculture, Ashland, Oregon. Advanced successively to more responsible positions, including senior entomologist in charge, Forest Insect Laboratories, Portland, Oregon, and Berkeley, California. Was appointed special assistant to chief, Division of Forest Insect Investigations, Bureau of Entomology and Plant Quarantine, 1952–55. Retired January 1, 1956. Intensively studied climatic cycles as evidenced by tree rings and their interrelationship to outbreaks of western pine beetle. From these and related studies, developed relative susceptibility classification of ponderosa pines to bark-beetle attack. This led to use of tree-classification system in managing interior-type pine stands. Supervised bark-beetle survey and control operations in Arizona, California, and Oregon, and performed research in many phases of forest insects in western United States. Is author of more than fifty scientific publications on forest insects and their control, including Insect Enemies of Western Forests, U.S. Department of Agriculture Miscellaneous Publication 273, revised, 1952; Biology and Control of the Western Pine Beetle, U.S. Department of Agriculture Miscellaneous Publication 800; and Cone and Seed Insects of Western Forest Trees, Technical Bulletin No. 1169, U.S. Department of Agriculture, 1958. In addition, contributed substantially to textbook Forest Insects. Received award for superior service, U.S. Department of Agriculture, in 1947, and first award for distinguished service in forestry from Western Forestry and Conservation Association in 1953. Also received Conservation Award, American Forestry Association in 1954.

Served on national council of Society of American Foresters during 1942–45, and was elected a fellow in 1955. Was president, Pacific Coast Entomological Society, in 1946. Died February 27, 1980, in Walnut Creek, California.

J. W. BONBERG
JAMES R. LYONS

American Men of Science (Physical and Biological Sciences), 11th ed., 1965.

KELLEY, CLAUDE DONAHUE
(born 1907)

Born September 22 in Pine Hill, Alabama. Educated in public schools in Alabama, began career in accounting, banking, and finance. In addition to his business interests, spent much of his time in conservation endeavors starting in 1940 when he was elected president of local wildlife federation in Alabama. Served as regional director of Alabama Wildlife Federation and later as its president, and is now permanent member of advisory committee. In 1948 was elected to his first term as director and in 1950 became president of National Wildlife Federation, continuing in office until 1961. During his administration, the federation expanded to fifty affiliates from thirty-one state affiliates with all operations consolidated in Washington, D.C. Organized National Wildlife Federation Endowment to provide solid financial structure for organization, serving as president, 1957–69; a building for its permanent headquarters was constructed in District of Columbia. In addition, the federation initiated annual Conservation Conference and new publication *National Wildlife*, and organized youth education programs. In 1962 was appointed director of Alabama Department of Conservation and continued as administrator of this agency until 1968. Then was appointed southeastern field representative of National Wildlife Federation in 1969. Thereafter was appointed and served as Conservation Commissioner for state of Alabama until his retirement in 1976.

NATIONAL WILDLIFE FEDERATION
CLAUDE D. KELLEY

KELLEY, EVAN WILLIAM
(1882–1966)

Born October 19 in Sierra City, California. Had no formal education beyond elementary school; received honorary masters degree in forest engineering from Montana State University in 1940. Entered U.S. Forest Service in California as guard on Yuba Forest Reserve in 1906; in 1919 became first forest supervisor of Eldorado National Forest. His outstanding work running sawmill in France for U.S. Army won him decorations and promotion to rank of major. After war, served as fire control inspector in Washington, D.C., office of Forest Service, 1920–25; in 1925 was named regional forester for Eastern Region and in 1929 was named regional forester for Northern Region (Montana, northern Idaho, and northeastern Washington), where he gained wide recognition for his work in reorganizing and developing fire control methods. Innovations during his administration included construction of intensive system of motor truck trails by means of then-new crawler tractors and bulldozers; greatly intensified detection of fires; faster initial attack; a highly organized system for rapid build-up and supply of forces on large fires; active part in development and use of portable two-way radios; and development of "smokejumping" by specially trained and equipped parachutists. During World War II was in charge of emergency rubber project in California. Became member of Society of American Foresters in 1920 and was elected a fellow 1949. Died October 3, 1966.

SOCIETY OF AMERICAN FORESTERS

"We Present Evan W. Kelley." *Journal of Forestry*, vol. 48:499–500, 1950.

Journal of Forestry. Obituary, vol. 65:72 1967.

KEMP, ROBERT JAMES
(born 1926)
Born March 30 in Dallas, Texas. University of Texas, B.S. (biology) 1949, M.S. (zoology) 1950. Entered Texas Parks and Wildlife Department in 1950, and served as regional director in both coastal and inland fisheries branches until 1972; as director for Fish and Wildlife, 1972–74; and as director of Fisheries Division, 1974 to present. Has pioneered in use of innovative approaches to reservoir management in Texas. Originated multiple-predator stocking concept that has resulted in large increases in recreational fishing opportunity for Texas sport fishermen. Such species as Florida largemouth bass, smallmouth bass, striped bass, and walleye are now well established throughout state. Is responsible for building of Gulf Coast's first marine fish hatchery to raise marine fishes to enhance fish populations in Texas bays. Spearheaded difficult battle

that resulted in conservation measures for overharvested populations of red drum and spotted seatrout. Also instituted standardized sampling procedures for all division programs. Has explored use of marine game fishes in freshwater power plant impoundments. Is current chairman of Gulf States Marine Fisheries Commission and is state representative for Gulf of Mexico Fishery Management Council. Is member of American Fisheries Society, International Association of Fish and Wildlife Agencies, and Southeastern Association of Fish and Wildlife Agencies. In 1980 was honored as Texas Conservationist of the Year and in 1982 received Heddon Hall of Honor award for his contributions in fisheries management.

WILLIAM P. RUTLEDGE

KIMBALL, THOMAS LLOYD
(born 1918)
Born February 21 in Los Angeles, California. Attended Phoenix Junior College; Brigham Young University, B.S. (soil conservation) 1939; Colorado State University, Ph.D. (honorary) 1975. Except for four years in U.S. Air Force during World War II, was employed by Arizona Game and Fish Department from 1939 to 1952. During this tenure, served as wildlife project leader, federal aid coordinator, chief of game, and director during his last five years with agency. Was director of Colorado Game and Fish Department, 1952–60; executive vice-president of National Wildlife Federation, 1960–81 (retired); and honorary president, 1981 to present. While in state work, served for two terms as president of Western Association of Game and Fish Commissioners and for one term as president of Midwest Game and Fish Commissioners. Relinquished position of first vice-president of International Association of Game, Fish and Conservation Commissioners when he left state work. Had several special assignments, serving as member of advisory board for Wildlife and Game Management and National Advisory Board for Sport Fisheries and Wildlife, U.S. Department of the Interior; advisory board on Wildlife, Department of Agriculture; and advisory board on Water Quality Criteria, Department of Health, Education, and Welfare. Also served on advisory groups to departments of Commerce, Energy, State, and Transportation, and was member of U.S. National Commission for UNESCO and Man and the Biosphere Program. Is past chairman of Natural Resources Council of America, and was member of board of gov-

ernors for National Shooting Sports Foundation; board of trustees for
J. N. "Ding" Darling foundation; advisory board of Keep America Beautiful; and National Conservation Committee of the Boy Scouts of America. Has served as consultant to wildlife agencies in four states. Is author
of numerous articles and technical bulletins on wildlife conservation and
management, and has contributed frequently to *National Wildlife* and
International Wildlife magazines and *Conservation News.* Has received
several awards: Nash Motors Certificate of Merit, 1953; Colorado Wildlife Federation, 1962; Colorado Division, Izaak Walton League of America, 1960; Colorado Game and Fish Commission, 1960; Northeast Outdoor Writers Association, 1963; U.S. Department of the Interior,
Conservation Service Award, 1964; University of Arizona's Distinguished Citizen Award, 1964; Winchester-Western's Outdoorsman's Citation, 1964; National Shooting Sports Foundation Certificate of Merit,
1964; Eugene Baker Award of the Association of Conservation Engineers, 1965; SOAR Award of the Boy Scouts of America, 1972; Passenger Pigeon Award of the Michigan United Conservation Clubs, 1972;
Distinguished Service Award of the American Forestry Association,
1974; Audubon Medal of the National Audubon Society, 1979; and
Whooping Crane Award of the National Wildlife Federation, 1981. Has
been member of The Wildlife Society, The American Forestry Association, International Union for the Protection of Nature and Natural Resources, and Society of American Foresters, and was elected a fellow of
American Association for the Advancement of Science in 1963.

Louis S. Clapper

Who's Who in America, 42d ed., 1982–83.

King, Ralph Terence
(1900–1977)
Born June 30 in Saint Paul, Kansas. Utah State Agricultural College, B.S.
1924, M.A. (zoology) 1925. Remained there for one year as instructor
in zoology, and then did special work at University of Minnesota, and
also served as head of Department of Biology at College of Saint Thomas
at Saint Paul, 1925–29. Held position of research fellow, 1929–32, and
from 1932 to 1937 was on faculty of Department of Economic Zoology
of University of Minnesota. During same years was also state biologist
for Minnesota Conservation Department. It was during his association
with University of Minnesota that he became well known for his research

on ruffed grouse. As one of organizers of professional group that formed Society of Wildlife Specialists in 1936, he was first and only president of that organization; in 1937, when it became The Wildlife Society, he was one of its founders. In 1937 became chairman of Department of Forest Zoology at State University College of Forestry at Syracuse University in New York. Also became director of Roosevelt Wildlife Forest Experiment Station located at same institution. Was awarded two Fulbright lectureships in 1959 and 1960 in Denmark and Israel. Was senior member of Society of American Foresters, member of Ecological Society of America, and a fellow of American Association for the Advancement of Science. Was elected honorary member of The Wildlife Society in 1964. Authored numerous scientific papers and resource articles. Retired from College of Forestry in 1965. Died April 9, 1977, in Sun City, Arizona.

MAURICE M. ALEXANDER

American Men of Science (Physical and Biological Sciences), 11th ed., 1966.
Who Knows—and What, 1954.
Wildlife Society Bulletin, Obituary, Vol. 5, no. 4:212, 1977.

KING, WILLIS
(born 1908)
Born May 24 in Fayette County, Ohio. Wilmington College, Ohio, B.Sc. (education) 1929; Haverford College, M.A. (biology) 1930; University of Cincinnati, Ph.D. (zoology) 1939; North Carolina State University, D.Sc. (honorary) 1968. Became first wildlife technician for Great Smoky Mountains National Park, 1934–40, where he carried out original field studies culminating in report *A Survey of the Amphibians and Reptiles of Great Smoky Mountains National Park*, and also initiated the park's fishery program. Was first fishery biologist employed by state of North Carolina, 1949–44; was acting director of Wildlife Resources Commission, 1947–48, and chief of fish management, Tennessee, 1949–50. In 1951 joined U.S. Bureau of Sport Fisheries and Wildlife, Branch of Federal Aid, where he helped implement Dingell-Johnson program policies and procedures. Served as assistant regional director, U.S. Fish and Wildlife Service, Atlanta, 1956–57, for both sport and commercial fisheries. Returned to Washington in 1957 to head new branch of fishery management services, Division of Fishery Services, where he developed cooperative programs with Indian tribes, national parks, U.S. Department of Defense, and other federal entities throughout United States, thereby

helping to open many waters to recreational fishing. A highlight was establishment of Cooperative Fishery Unit program, a joint endeavor with states, twenty-five universities, and Fish and Wildlife Service, emphasizing training and research. His last position was assistant director for Cooperative Services, 1970–73. Was awarded U.S. Department of the Interior's Distinguished Service Award in 1971. Authored more than thirty publications dealing with fishery management, herpetology, and environmental subjects; was principal author of special report of Outdoor Recreation Resources Review Commission, *Sport Fishing, Today and Tomorrow*, 1962; edited *Wild Trout Management*, 1975 (Symposium I), 1980 (Symposium II). Was active in the American Fisheries Society throughout his career.

WILLIS KING

American Men and Women of Science, 12th ed., 1972.

KINNEY, JAY P.
(1875–1975)
Born September 18 in Snowdon (town of Otsego) New York. Cornell University, B.A. 1902, M.F. 1913; National University, LL.B. 1908. After several years as high-school principal, was appointed assistant examiner, U.S. Patent Office, 1906. In 1910 was appointed assistant forester, U.S. Indian Service, U.S. Department of the Interior, with instructions to organize forestry unit. As head of unit for twenty-three years under various titles, he developed strong and effective organization to manage Indians' forest- and rangelands, under principles of sustained yield, for benefit of Indian owners. In 1933 became general production supervisor in charge of Civilian Conservation Corps activities on Indian reservations. In 1942 was appointed assistant director of Soil Conservation, Office of Land Utilization, U.S. Department of the Interior. In 1945, under special exception to mandatory requirement of retirement at age seventy, was appointed advisor in forestry in U.S. Department of Justice. In 1954 retired from full-time duty, but during next thirteen years continued as consultant in the same department. Retired permanently in 1967, after distinguished service with federal government over span of sixty-one years. While with U.S. Department of Justice, his training in law and forestry, his long experience as head of Indian forestry organization, and his lifelong reputation as man of integrity and moral courage, made him valuable contributor in preparation of cases, and as witness, in claims

brought before U.S. Court of Claims and Indian Claims Commission. Was a fellow of Society of American Foresters, and active in Forest History Society. In addition to many magazine articles, authored four authoritative books of recognized merit in their fields: *The Essentials of American Timber Law*, 1917; *The Development of Forest Law in the United States*, 1917; *A Continent Lost—A Civilization Won*, 1937; and *Indian Forest and Range*, 1950. In retirement, authored *Facing Indian Facts*, 1973; and *Like Other Man, The American Indian Resented Restraint*, 1974. Died December 2, 1975.

GEORGE S. KEPHART

Who's Who Among American Authors, 1933–35 and 1936–39.

Who's Who in Government, 1933.

Who's Who in the Nation's Capital, 1934–35.

KNEIPP, LEON FREDERICK

(1880–1966)

Born November 30 in Chicago, Illinois. Educated in public schools of Chicago. Began his forestry career in 1900 as ranger on forest reserve in Territory of Arizona, with General Land Office. When forest reserves were placed under U.S. Department of Agriculture and Forest Service was established in that department in 1905, was one of eight men from various parts of the West brought into Washington, D.C., to draft new rules and procedures for administration of these reserves, later to be known as national forests. As assistant chief in charge of lands, 1920–46, was instrumental in adding to national forest system about twenty million acres east of Mississippi River, and about five million acres in the West. As recognized authority on outdoor recreation, in 1924 served as executive secretary of advisory council of the National Conference of Outdoor Recreation. Pioneered in movement for preservation of wilderness tracts and in development of Forest Service program for maintenance of designated wilderness areas. Wrote widely on forestry subjects and was author of important sections of *A National Plan for American Forestry and The Western Range*. Retired from Forest Service in 1946 after nearly forty-seven years of continuous service. Died October 29, 1966.

SOCIETY OF AMERICAN FORESTERS

Journal of Forestry. Obituary, 65:72–73, January 1967.

KOZICKY, EDWARD LOUIS
(born 1918)

Born February 1918 in Long Branch, New Jersey. University of Maine, B.S. (wildlife) 1941; Pennsylvania State University, M.S. 1943, Ph.D. 1948. Served in U.S. Army, 1943–46. Was leader of Iowa Cooperative Wildlife Research Unit, 1948–56. Conducted research on eastern wild turkey, bobwhite quail, ringnecked pheasant, clapper rail, and other species. Refined census techniques for upland gamebird populations. Was director of conservation, Winchester Group, Olin Corporation, 1956–83. Published more than one hundred articles and booklets on wildlife management and hunter education, and coauthored *Shooting Preserve Management: The Nilo System*, 1966. Received Meritorious Service Award from U.S. Department of the Interior, and Outstanding Achievement Award from Pennsylvania State University, 1982; also was elected to Iowa Conservation Hall of Fame and Hall of Fame of the North America Association of Hunter Safety Coordinators. Received awards from National Rifle Association of America, Illinois Federation of Sportsmen's Clubs, Migratory Waterfowl Hunters, Quebec Federation of Hunters and Anglers, North American Gamebird Association, and Missouri Department of Conservation. Served on boards of directors of The American Forestry Association, Wildlife Management Institute, World Wildlife Fund, North American Gamebird Association, Orthopedic Foundation for Animals, and Wildlife Legislative Fund of America. Was member of advisory board of Illinois Department of Conservation and is past-president of The Wildlife Society and of Illinois Association of Hunting Preserves. Is currently executive vice-president of North American Association of Hunter Safety Coordinators, and distinguished visiting scientist at Caesar Kleberg Wildlife Research Institute, Texas A&I University.

LAURENCE R. JAHN
EDWARD L. KOZICKY

American Men and Women of Science, 14th ed., 1979.

LACEY, JOHN FLETCHER
(1841–1913)

Born May 30 in Martinsville, Virginia (now West Virginia). Was educated in public and private schools in Virginia and Iowa. Entered Union Army in 1861 and was discharged with brevet rank of major in 1865.

Was elected to Congress in 1889 and served through 1907. As chairman of House Committee on Public Lands, was author of much of early legislation affecting national parks, wildlife, and forests. Among measures he fought through Congress were Yellowstone Park Protection Act of 1894, which established foundation for National Park Service; Lacey Act of 1900, which ended market hunting and interstate shipment of wildlife or wildlife products taken in violation of state law; and Transfer Act for Forest Reserves of 1905, which established U.S. Forest Service. Died September 29, 1913.

JAMES B. TREFETHEN

Biographical Directory of the American Congress, 1961.

Who Was Who in America, 1897–1942.

Who's Who in America, 1912–13.

LAGLER, KARL FRANK
(born 1912)
Born November 15 in Rochester, New York. Rochester University, B.A. 1934; Cornell University, M.S. 1936; University of Michigan, Ph.D. (zoology) 1940. Was investigator in fishery management at University of Michigan, 1937–39, and instructor in zoology, 1939–44. Successively became assistant professor, associate professor, and in 1955 professor in fisheries and zoology; was chairman of Department of Fisheries, 1950–65. Served as research associate for Institute for Fisheries Research, Michigan Department of Conservation, and as advisor to U.S. Operations Mission Kasetsart at University of Hawaii. Was technical consultant to Associated Fishing Tackle Manufacturers, 1948–50, and was intermittently member of Great Lakes Research Institute, 1948–60. Participated in expeditions to Upper Great Lakes, Western Europe, Alaska, and Southeast Asia; served as fisheries advisor in Thailand in 1964–65; and coordinated African lake projects under Food and Agricultural Organization of the United Nations in 1966–67. In 1961 received gold medal and diploma from French Academy of Agriculture. Holds memberships in American Academy of Arts and Sciences, Society of Ichthyologists and Herpetologists, Society of Limnologists and Oceanographers, and American Fisheries Society; and is a fellow in Academy of Zoology and in Institute of Fisheries Research Biologists (president, 1964–65). His published works include *Guide to the Fishes of the Great*

Lakes and Tributary Waters (junior author with Hubbs), 1941, revised as *Fishes of the Great Lakes Region,* 1964; *Freshwater Fishery Biology,* 1952; *Peches Continentales* (coauthor with Vibert), 1961; *Ichthyology,* 2d ed. (senior author and editor with Bardach, Miller, and Passino), 1977; and *Growth Policy, Population, Environment, and Beyond* (with Chen et al.), 1974. Has been active in educational television since 1968, producing several TV films on acquatic resources. Was elected president of International Academy of Fisheries Scientists of Rome, Italy, in 1968.

PHILIP A. DOUGLAS
RICHARD H. STROUD

American Men and Women of Science (Physical and Biological Sciences), 15th ed., 1982.

Who's Who in America, 42d ed., 1982–83.

LANGLOIS, THOMAS HUXLEY
(1898–1968)
Born February 19 in Detroit, Michigan. University of Michigan, B.S. 1924, M.S. 1925; Ohio State University, Ph.D. 1935. Was fisheries biologist, Michigan Department of Conservation, 1924–27, and state fish pathologist, 1927–29. As chief of fish propagation and management, Ohio Division of Conservation and Natural Resources, 1930–46, expanded fish cultural program, organized fish management section with staff of trained biologists, and led movement for liberalized fishing. Served as professor of zoology at Ohio State University, and as director of Franz Theodore Stone Institute of Hydrobiology, 1938–56. As director, initiated programs of instruction in limnology and fisheries, emphasizing ecological approach to aquatic problems; resulting research yielded valuable information on Lake Erie. Was president, American Fisheries Society, 1940; and was active in American Society of Limnology and Oceanography. Was author of many scientific reports, including *Ecology and Sociology of Fish and People, Ice on Lake Erie,* and *The Western End of Lake Erie and Its Ecology.* Died December 5, 1968.

DONALD J. LEEDY

American Men of Science (Physical and Biological Sciences), 11th ed., 1965.

LATHAM, ROGER MARION
(1914–1979)

Born January 12 in Sandy Lake, Pennsylvania. Pennsylvania State University, B.S. (entomology, zoology) 1950, M.S. (wildlife management) 1951, Ph.D. (zoology) 1957. Graduated in first class to complete Pennsylvania Game Commission's Leffler School of Conservation in 1937, and was assigned as game protector, 1937–38, then as research technician, 1938–44. During World War II was detailed to medical research project on arctic subjects at Cornell University. Returned to Pennsylvania Game Commission as chief, Division of Research, 1951–57. Was appointed outdoor editor of *Pittsburgh Press* in 1957 and worked in this position until his death. Served as regional representative for The Wildlife Society for six years; director of Trout Unlimited; director of Hawk Mountain Sanctuary Association; director of Pennsylvania Roadside Council; president of Pennsylvania Outdoor Writers Association; and president of Outdoor Writers Association of America. Was active as member of Governor's Advisory Committee of Conservation (Pennsylvania) Northeast Forest Resources Committee; Pennsylvania Wildlife Resources Committee; Citizens' Advisory Committee to Outdoor Recreation Resources Review Commission; founder, Conservation Committee, Allegheny Trails Council, Boy Scouts of America; and as associate director, Allegheny County Soil and Water Conservation District. Was author of *Pennsylvania's Deer Problem*, 1950; *Food of Predaceous Animals in Northeastern United States*, 1950; *The Ecology and Economics of Predator Management*, 1951; *The Pennsylvania Bounty System*, 1951; *The Bobwhite Quail in Pennsylvania*, 1952; and *The Complete Book of the Wild Turkey*, 1956. Received Nash Conservation Award, 1954; Jade of Chiefs, Outdoor Writers Association of America, 1961; Conservation Award, Pennsylvania Forestry Association, 1963; Outstanding Conservationist Award, Keystone Chapter, Soil Conservation Society of America, 1965; and International Outdoorman of the Year, 1968, Winchester-Western. Died May 15, 1979, in climbing accident in Swiss Alps.

RALPH W. ABELE

LAWRENCE, WILLIAM MASON
(born 1918)

Born October 2 in Brooktondale, New York. Cornell University, B.S. 1938, Ph.D. 1941. Served in U.S. Navy in World War II. Before graduation worked as fish hatchery helper for State of New York Conservation Department and, subsequently, as game research investigator in 1941, senior aquatic biologist in 1946, chief of Bureau of Fish in 1952, assistant director of Division of Fish and Game in 1955, and its director in 1957. Became assistant commissioner in 1958 and deputy commissioner of Conservation Department in 1964. Was appointed deputy commissioner for environmental management in 1970 in newly created State of New York Department of Environmental Conservation, from which he retired in 1974. Since retirement, has worked as consultant on natural resources projects for several state and federal government agencies. These projects included *The National Plan for Marine Fisheries, Initial Joint National Marine Fisheries Services/Coast Guard Program For Enforcement of Fishery Regulations Under Extended Jurisdiction for the National Marine Fisheries Service; Effective State Marine Fisheries Management* for Council of State Governments; *Eastland Fisheries Survey of the Great Lakes, and A Report to the Congress; Eastland Fisheries Survey for the Atlantic States Marine Fisheries Commission.* Is member of American Fisheries Society (president, 1959); Atlantic Fishery Biologists (president, 1952); The Wildlife Society; International Association of Fish and Wildlife Agencies (president, 1969); New York Academy of Sciences; American Association for the Advancement of Science; and Professional Fisheries Association of New York. Is member of Sigma Xi and Phi Kappa Phi honorary fraternities. Continues to serve as U.S. Commissioner of Great Lakes Fishery Commission (chairman of Commission, 1973 and 1974). Was chairman of Nuclear Power Siting Committee, which advised State of New York Atomic and Space Development Authority on selection of sites for future use in nuclear electric power generation. Also represented New York as commissioner on Atlantic States Marine Fisheries Commission (chairman, 1971–73), alternate commissioner on Great Lakes Commission, alternate to commissioner from New York on Delaware River Basin Commission, and commissioner on Great Lakes River Basin Commission. In 1976 received Seth Gordon Award of the International Association of Fish and Wildlife Agencies for "outstanding contributions to fish and wildlife management." The American Fisheries Society elected him to honorary life membership in 1977.

ROBERT F. HUTTON

American Men and Women of Science (Physical and Biological Sciences), 15th ed., 1982.

LEEDY, DANIEL LONEY
(born 1912)
Born February 17 in Butler, Ohio. Miami University, Oxford, Ohio, B.A. 1934, B.Sc. 1935; Ohio State University, M.Sc. 1938, Ph.D. (wildlife ecology) 1940. Was instructor in wildlife management at Ohio State University, 1940–42. Became leader, Ohio cooperative wildlife research unit, U.S. Fish and Wildlife Service, 1945–48; coordinator of national cooperative wildlife research unit program in Washington, D.C., 1949–57; chief, Branch of Wildlife Research, 1957–63; chief, Division of Research and Education, Bureau of Outdoor Recreation, 1963–65; and research scientist, Office of Water Resources Research, U.S. Department of the Interior, 1965–74, after which he retired. Subsequently has served as research director/senior scientist and consultant for National Institute for Urban Wildlife. Was a charter member of The Wildlife Society, president in 1952, and executive secretary in 1953–57. Has served on many committees and was representative of the society in American Institute of Biological Sciences, 1964–72. Was elected a fellow of American Association for the Advancement of Science in 1956. Received American Motors Conservation Award in 1958, U.S. Department of the Interior's Distinguished Service Award in 1975, Distinguished Alumni Award of Ohio State University in 1975, and The Wildlife Society's Aldo Leopold Award in 1983. Is author or coauthor of nearly one hundred articles in biological and other scientific publications.

LEE E. YEAGER

American Men and Women of Science (Physical and Biological Sciences), 15th ed., 1982.

Who's Who in America, 42d ed., 1982–83.

LEFFLER, ROSS LILLIE
(1886–1964)
Born August 7 in Butte, Montana. Attended University of Michigan School of Engineering. In 1910 began work as timekeeper in Carnegie Steel Corporation, Duquesne, Pennsylvania; on his retirement in 1957 was assistant to executive vice-president for operations of U.S. Steel Corporation. Was appointed by President Eisenhower in 1957 as first assistant secretary for fish and wildlife in U.S. Department of the Interior; was instrumental in establishing Arctic Wildlife Range in northeastern Alaska and Key Largo Coral Reef Preserve off coast of Florida. Had

served previously (1927–57) as member of Pennsylvania Game Commission and as its president, 1928–44. Claimed as his proudest achievement the establishment of the commission's training school near Brockway, Pennsylvania, later named in his honor. Helped organize first Pennsylvania chapter of Izaak Walton League of America, serving as president and later as director of national organization. Was one of founders of Pennsylvania Federation of Sportsmen's Clubs and served as its first secretary. In 1961 was elected to board of directors of National Wildlife Federation; was elected president in 1963 and served one year before ill health necessitated retirement. As member of numerous other conservation organizations, was former president of International Association of Game, Fish and Conservation Commissioners; vice-president of Boone and Crockett Club; director of World Wildlife Fund; and honorary director of International Wild Waterfowl Association. Devoted many years service to Boy Scouts of America, was life member of its executive board, and received Scouting's three highest awards. Died December 14, 1964.

NATIONAL WILDLIFE FEDERATION

Who Was Who in America, 1961–68.

LEONARD, JUSTIN WILKINSON
(1909–1975)
Born October 28 in Moulton, Iowa. Grinnell College (Iowa), B.A. 1931; University of Michigan, A.M. 1932, Ph.D. 1937. Was employed in Michigan Department of Conservation, 1934–64, serving successively as fisheries investigator and associate aquatic biologist, 1934–39. Was director of Hunt Creek Experiment Station, 1939–42; associate fisheries biologist, 1946–48; fisheries biologist, 1949–50; and assistant deputy director for research, 1951–64. As U.S. Army medical entomologist, worked in malaria control with Sanitary Corps in South Pacific, 1943–36. Became professor of natural resources and zoology at University of Michigan, School of Natural Resources, in 1964, and was chairman of Department of Wildlife and Fisheries until 1967, when he became chairman of Department of Resource Planning and Conservation. His activity in scientific societies included service to American Fisheries Society (honorary member) as associate editor, 1940–55; The Wildlife Society as president, 1956; American Society of Limnology and Oceanography as vice-president, 1951; and Michigan Academy of Science, Arts, and Letters as president, 1962. Was author of more than seventy bulletins and

journal articles; coauthored with his wife *Mayflies of Michigan Trout Streams*, 1962; with S. W. Allen of *Conserving Natural Resources*, 3d ed., 1966; and with S. H. Spurr, et al.) *Rampart Dam and the Economic Development of Alaska*, vol. 1, summary report, 1966. Served three-year term on board of directors of Michigan Rural Rehabilitation Corporation, was governor's designee for McIntyre-Stennis Fund, and served on Governor's Committee on Control of Botulism. Later served on National Academy of Sciences study group concerned with biology and renewable resources. Was eloquent teacher of ecological concepts and issues. Made fifteen-unit videotape series, *Ecology: Man and Environment*, for University of Michigan Television Center, which won national acclaim. A final tribute, to have been presented in autumn of 1975, was Outstanding Teacher Award from University of Michigan, announced posthumously. Died May 26, 1975.

REEVE M. BAILEY
C. GORDON FREDINE

American Men and Women of Science (Physical and Biological Sciences), 12th ed., (vol. 4), 1972.

LEONARD, RICHARD MANNING
(born 1908)
Born October 22 in Elyria, Ohio. University of California Law School, LL.D. 1932. Joined Sierra Club in 1930; has been member of board of directors since 1938; president, 1953–55; and honorary president since 1979. Was founder of Conservation Law Society in 1963, an organization established to use law to aid conservation and wilderness projects; for this accomplishment received American Motors Conservation Award in 1964. In addition, has been a founder of Trustees for Conservation; founder-secretary of American Conservation Films, vice-chairman of Committee on Legislation for International Union for the Conservation of Nature; member of board of directors of The Wilderness Society, 1948–82; president, now chairman, of Save-the-Redwoods League, 1975–80; and was founder and national director of California Chapter of Izaak Walton League of America. Helped create Conservation Associates as nonprofit counseling service to help conservation organizations acquire parks, open spaces, and reserves. Is author of *Belaying the Leader*, 1946, and contributor to *Manual of Ski Mountaineering*, 1942; *Going Light with Backpack and Burro*, 1951; and *A Climbers' Guide to*

the High Sierra, 1954. Is honorary member, American Alpine Club. Received Albright Award in 1972 and John Muir Award in 1973.

LUELLA K. SAWYER

Sierra Club Handbook, 1967.

Who's Who in the West, 11th ed., 1968.

Who's Who in America, 42d ed., 1982–83.

LEOPOLD, ALDO
(1886–1948)
Born January 11 in Burlington, Iowa. Yale University, Ph.B. 1908, M.F. 1909. Entered U.S. Forest Service in 1909 as forest assistant in Arizona; was promoted in 1911 to deputy forest supervisor, and in 1912 to supervisor of Carson National Forest in New Mexico. In 1917 became assistant district forester for operations of Southwestern District. Was a pioneer in wilderness preservation who interested other forest officers in wilderness ecology, and was mainly responsible for establishment of Gila Wilderness Area in New Mexico, first in national-forest wilderness system. From 1925 to 1927 was associate director of Forest Products Laboratory at Madison, Wisconsin. Leaving government service in 1928, became game consultant for Sporting Arms and Ammunition Manufacturers' Institute. Game surveys he made during this time were published in 1931 as *Report on a Game Survey of the North Central States*. This report was one of first intensive studies of game populations ever undertaken in America and won for him *Outdoor Life* medal. During year of private practice as consulting forester, completed his book *Game Management*, 1933, and was appointed professor of game management at University of Wisconsin. This chair, created especially for him, he held with distinction until his death. Was active in many conservation movements outside his official duties. Served on council of Society of American Foresters, 1927–31, and was associate editor of *Journal of Forestry*, 1936–47. At various times was director of National Audubon Society and vice-president of The American Forestry Association. As one of organizers of The Wilderness Society in 1935, served on its council thereafter and was vice-president in 1945. Was organizer of The Wildlife Society in 1937, and served as its president in 1939. Was active also in Ecological Society of America, and was its president in 1947. Was appointed by President Franklin D. Roosevelt to Special Committee on

Wild Life Restoration in 1934. From 1943 until his death, was member of Wisconsin Conservation Commission. His best-known book, *A Sand County Almanac,* was published posthumously in 1949. The Aldo Leopold Award, established in his honor by The Wildlife Society, has been awarded annually since 1950. Died April 21, 1948.

HENRY CLEPPER

American Forests. Biography. August and December 1954.

Dictionary of American Biography, 1941–50. 1970.

Journal of Forestry. Obituary, August 1948.

Journal of Wildlife Management. Obituary, October 1948.

National Wildlife. Biography. April-May 1965.

Who Was Who in America, 1950.

LEOPOLD, ALDO STARKER

(1913–1983)

Born October 22 in Burlington, Iowa. University of Wisconsin, B.S. (agriculture) 1936; Yale University School of Forestry, 1936–37; University of California, Ph.D. (zoology) 1944. In 1934 began his career as junior biologist for Soil Erosion Service of U.S. Department of Agriculture, in Wisconsin. Then served five years as field biologist for Missouri State Conservation Commission, 1939–44. Became director of field research for conservation section of Pan-American Union in Mexico in 1944. In 1946 became instructor at University of California at Berkeley and by 1957 had advanced to professor; then for eleven years was associate director of University Museum of Vertebrate Zoology; and in 1968 joined School of Forestry and Conservation. Became professor emeritus at University of California at Berkeley in 1978. Was Guggenheim fellow, 1947–48; and president of The Wildlife Society, 1957–58. Also served as president of California Academy of Sciences, 1959–71, and as advisor on conservation and fauna for National Park Service and U.S. Fish and Wildlife Service. Received Audubon Medal from National Audubon Society in 1966; Aldo Leopold Award from The Wildlife Society in 1965; and Distinguished Service Award from American Institute of Biological Sciences in 1980. Was member of many conservation and wildlife organizations. Was author of numerous publications, including *Game Birds and Mammals of California,* 1951; was coauthor of *Wildlife in Alaska,*

1953; *Wildlife of Mexico,* 1959; (with editors of *Life*) *The Desert,* 1961; and *The California Quail,* 1977. Died August 23, 1983.

THE CONSERVATION FOUNDATION

American Men and Women of Science (Physical and Biological Sciences), 15th ed., 1982.

Who's Who in America, 42d ed., 1982–83.

LEOPOLD, LUNA BERGERE
(born 1915)

Born October 8 in Albuquerque, New Mexico. University of Wisconsin, B.S. (zoology) 1936, D.Sc. (honorary) 1980; University of California at Los Angeles, M.A.; Harvard University, Ph.D. (geology) 1950. From 1936 to 1938 advanced from junior engineer to associate engineer with Soil Conservation Service, U.S. Department of Agriculture, in New Mexico. Was in U.S. Engineers office in Los Angeles, 1941–42, and during World War II was captain in U.S. Air Force's air weather service for three years. In 1946 was with Bureau of Reclamation, U.S. Department of the Interior, then was engaged in 1947 as head meteorologist for Pineapple Research Institute in Hawaii. From 1950 to 1971 was hydraulic engineer for U.S. Geological Survey, and since 1966 has been senior research hydrologist. Since 1973 has been professor of geology at University of California at Berkeley. In 1958 U.S. Department of the Interior presented him with Distinguished Service Award, and Geological Society of America gave him Kirk Bryan Award. In 1963 received Royal Netherlands Geographical Society Veth Medal, and in 1971 received Rockefeller Public Service Award. Long active in Sierra Club, he became member of its board of directors in 1968. Was member of American Society of Civil Engineers, American Meteorological Society, American Geological Society American Geophysical Union, and National Academy of Sciences. Coauthored *The Flood Control Controversy,* 1954; *Fluvial Processes in Geomorphology,* 1964; *Water,* 1966; and *Water in Environmental Planning,* 1978.

THE CONSERVATION FOUNDATION

American Men and Women of Science (Physical and Biological Sciences), 15th ed., 1982.

Who's Who in America, 42d ed., 1982–83.

LIEBER, RICHARD
(1869–1944)
Born September 5 in Germany. Educated at the Royal Lyceum, Duessel-
dorf; Wabash College, D.Sc. (honorary) 1938. Immigrated to the United
States in 1891; became naturalized citizen in 1901. From 1892 to 1900
was employed by newspapers in Indianapolis, Indiana, then was associated with firm of importers in Indianapolis, 1905–18. Early developed
interest in conservation and parks. Was chairman of board of governors
of Fourth National Conservation Congress in 1912, and of Indiana State
Park Commission, 1915–19. In 1919, when all conservation agencies of
state government of Indiana were combined in Department of Conservation, he was elected to office of director of the department, and served
until his resignation in 1933. In addition to his work in Indiana, was
active in National Conference on State Parks, formed in 1921; was president from 1930 to 1939, and chairman of its board thereafter. Was also
vice-president and director of American Planning and Civic Association,
and was member of advisory board and consultant for National Park
Service. Wrote *America's Natural Wealth: A Story of the Use and Abuse
of Our Natural Resources*, 1942, and contributed to *American Planning
and Civic Annual*, 1935–43. Among honors accorded him was Pugsley
gold medal awarded in 1933 by American Scenic and Historic Preservation Society. During previous year, monument was dedicated in his honor
at Turkey Run State Park, Indiana. Died April 15, 1944.

BARRY S. TINDALL

Lieber, Emma, *Richard Lieber*. Indianapolis, Ind.: Privately printed, 1947.

Parks (National Conference on State Parks). Washington, D.C., 6 (10): 1–5, October 1966.

Planning and Civic Comment, April 1944, pp. 45–46.

Who Was Who in America, 1943–50.

LINCOLN, FREDERICK CHARLES
(1892–1960)
Born May 5 in Denver, Colorado. University of Colorado, Sc.D. (hon-
orary), 1956. After serving as curator of birds at Colorado Museum of
Natural History in Denver, joined U.S. Biological Survey in March 1920.
In this and its successor agency, Bureau of Sport Fisheries and Wildlife of
U.S. Department of the Interior, he worked until his death. As chief of

Section of Distribution and Migration of Birds, organized and directed bird-banding program to study movements and population dynamics of migratory birds. Headed continental investigation of status of migratory waterfowl; developed concept of four continental flyways, now the basis for formulating hunting regulations for migratory birds; and devised Lincoln Index, a formula for estimating total populations of waterfowl from recoveries of banded birds. In his last years of government service, served as special assistant to director of Bureau of Sport Fisheries and Wildlife. Received highest honor of U.S. Department of the Interior, its Distinguished Service Award, in 1956, and was elected a fellow of American Ornithologists' Union in 1934 and served as its treasurer, 1945–47. Was author of three hundred scientific and popular articles, including *Bird Migration*, 1939, and was coauthor (with John C. Phillips) of *American Waterfowl*, 1930, and (with Ira N. Gabrielson) of *Birds of Alaska*, 1959. Died September 16, 1960.

JOHN W. ALDRICH

American Men of Science, 9th ed., 1955.

Auk. Obituary, vol. 79 (3), 1962.

LINDUSKA, JOSEPH PAUL
(born 1913)
Born July 25 in Butte, Montana. University of Montana, B.A. (zoology) 1936, M.A. 1939; Michigan State University, Ph.D. 1950. Carried out research on ecology and land-use relationships of small mammals on southern Michigan farmland. Served as fishery biologist in Yellowstone National Park; as research entomologist on war-associated projects at Orlando laboratory of U.S. Department of Agriculture; and as game biologist with Michigan Department of Conservation. In 1947 became project leader and carried out pioneering studies on effects of pesticides on wildlife at Patuxent Research Refuge of U.S. Fish and Wildlife Service. Was appointed assistant chief of the service's Branch of Game Management in 1951. In 1956 joined Remington Arms Company as director of wildlife management and four years later was promoted to director of public relations and wildlife management. Returning to government service in 1966, was appointed associate director of Bureau of Sport Fisheries and Wildlife and in 1973 was designated senior scientist. From 1974 until his retirement in 1978, was vice-president for science, National Audubon Society. Served as executive secretary of Outdoor Writers

Association of America and chairman of that organization's conservation council; was also member of board of directors of The Wildlife Society for three years, and president, 1967–68. Was member of board of directors of Wildlife Management Institute. Was presented The Wildlife Society Conservation Education Award in 1963, and also in that year received Jade of Chiefs award of Outdoor Writers Association of America for service to conservation. Received Conservation Service Award of U.S. Department of the Interior in 1964, and The Wildlife Society's Aldo Leopold Award in 1984. Well known for technical and popular writings in wildlife biology and conservation, he was editor of *Waterfowl Tomorrow*, published by Bureau of Sport Fisheries and Wildlife in 1964.

DURWARD L. ALLEN
JOSEPH P. LINDUSKA

American Men and women of Science (Physical and Biological Sciences), 15th ed., 1982.

Who's Who in American, 41st ed., 1980–81.

LORENZ, JACK
(born 1939)
Born March 14 in Saint Louis, Missouri. University of Tulsa, B.A. (journalism) 1961. Executive director of the Building Owners and Managers Association, Saint Louis, 1961–65; financial public-relations specialist for several large corporations, 1965–67; director of environmental affairs for Falstaff Brewing Corporation, 1969–72; editor of *Outdoor America* magazine of Izaak Walton League of America, 1973–74; executive director of the league, 1974 to present. Under his direction, Izaak Walton League of America was named Conservation Organization of the Year in 1980 by National Wildlife Federation. Is author of many magazine and newspaper articles ranging from impact of sport fishing on United States economy to examination of environmental impacts of dredging activities in Atlantic Coast salt marshes. Has served as chairman of board of American League of Anglers since 1981; and as member of advisory boards of Everglades Protection Association since 1979, National Arbor Foundation since 1974, and Hunter Education Council since 1981. Also has been advisor to North American Association of Hunter Safety Coordinators since 1982. Is member of Outdoor Writers Association of America; board of advisory governors of National Freshwater Fishing Hall of Fame; steering committee for National Hunting

and Fishing Day; Dingell-Johnson Fund Expansion steering committee; and board of directors of Global Tomorrow Coalition.

IZAAK WALTON LEAGUE OF AMERICA

LOVEJOY, PARRISH STORRS
(1884–1942)
Born January 23 in Princeton, Illinois. University of Michigan Department of Forestry, 1903–5. Entered U.S. Forest Service in 1905; became supervisor of Cheyenne (now Medicine Bow) National Forest in Wyoming in 1909, and of Olympic National Forest in Washington in 1910. Leaving federal service in 1912, returned to University of Michigan as assistant professor of forestry. In 1920 was employed as staff writer by Curtis Publishing Company; his articles in *Country Gentleman* promoted improved land use, restoration of cutover forests, and farm forestry. Because these writings, together with his articles published in other periodicals, were given national circulation, he was one of most influential contemporary spokesman for rational land-use policy. Was commissioned in 1923 to organize Michigan Land Economic Survey, which was first of its kind in United States and forerunner of land-planning studies by other states. This work for Michigan Department of Conservation led to creation of state game refuge system of which he took charge in 1925 as first chief of Game and Fur Division. Because of ill health, retired from active work in 1930, but continued as advisor on land policy to the department. Was early proponent of utilization and management of wildlands for wildlife, applying forestry practices for this purpose. In June 1942, bronze tablet in commemoration of his service to conservation was dedicated in Pigeon River State Forest of Michigan. Defined conservation as reason applied to environment. Died January 20, 1942.

HENRY CLEPPER

Journal of Wildlife Management. Obituary 7 (1): 125–28, January 1943.

Journal of Forestry. Obituary, 40 (4): 337, April 1942.

LOVEJOY, THOMAS EUGENE
(born 1941)
Born August 22 in New York City. Yale College, B.S. 1964; Yale University, Ph.D. (biology) 1971. Wildely recognized for his work on tropical

forests, he joined staff of World Wildlife Fund in 1973 and currently serves as organization's vice-president for science. Pursued field work on population ecology of rain forest birds and epidemiology of eighteen associated arboviruses in Brazil, 1966–71; conducted research on then-declining osprey population at mouth of Connecticut River, 1966–67; was research associate in biology at University of Pennsylvania, 1971–74; and has been research associate in ornithology at Academy of Natural Sciences of Philadelphia since 1971. In recent years, has participated in work of many natural resource organizations, scientific bodies, and awards committees, and has lectured on biological/environmental topics. Among his activities are: director (1973) and chairman since 1974 of Wildlife Preservation Trust International; treasurer since 1973 of International Council for Bird Preservation, Pan-American Section; coordinator since 1974 of J. Paul Getty Wildlife Conservation Prize; and member since 1975 of Species Survival Commission, International Union for the Conservation of Nature and Natural Resources. Is member of several national and international scientific societies and is widely published writer and commentator on natural resource subjects.

LOUIS S. CLAPPER

LOWDERMILK, WALTER CLAY

(1888–1974)

Born July 1 in Liberty, North Carolina. Oxford University, B.A. (Rhodes scholar) 1915; University of California, Ph.D. 1929; Israel Institute of Technology, Dr. Tech. Sci. (honorary) 1952. Was employed by U.S. Forest Service, 1915–17 and 1919–22, then was research professor of forestry at University of Nanking, China, 1922–27. Was project leader for erosion streamflow research for Forest Service's California Forest and Range Experiment Station, 1927–33, and designed and supervised establishment of San Diemas Hydrological Station. From 1933 to 1947, was with Soil Conservation Service, U.S. Department of Agriculture (initially, Soil Erosion Service, U.S. Department of the Interior), as assistant chief, associate chief, and chief of research. Representing U.S. Department of Agriculture, made soil and water conservation surveys in Europe, North Africa, and Mid-East. From 1947 to 1957 served as consultant to French colonial governments in Algeria, Morocco, and Tunisia, and British Colonial Office in eleven African colonies; and was advisor on flood control in Japan. For United Nations Food and Agriculture Organization, developed soil and water conservation program in Israel and curriculum in agricultural engineering (The Lowdermilk School of Agricultural Engineering) at Technion University; from Israel, received Medallion of Valor Award in 1961 and Macabee Award in 1964. Was president of American Geophysical Union of Earth Sciences, 1941–44. Was elected a fellow of Soil Conservation Society of America (was president, 1941–43), and a fellow of Society of American Foresters. Was author of many publications, including *Conquest of the Land Through 7,000 Years*, 1939, and *Palestine, Land of Promise*, 1940. Died May 6, 1974.

JOHN S. BARNES

American Men of Science (Physical and Biological Sciences), 10th ed., 1961.

Bancroft Library, University of California at Berkeley, has a two-volume oral history of his lifetime activities.

International Who's Who, London, 1968–69.

World Who's Who in Science, 1968.

MCARDLE, RICHARD EDWIN
(1899–1983)
Born February 25 in Lexington, Kentucky. University of Michigan, B.S. (forestry) 1923, M.S. 1924, Ph.D. 1930, Sc.D. (honorary) 1953; Syracuse University, LL.D. 1961; University of Maine, Sc.D. (honorary) 1962. Was junior forester to silviculturist, Pacific Northwest Forest and Range Experiment Station, 1924–34; dean, University of Idaho School of Forestry, 1934–35; and director, Rocky Mountain Forest and Range Experiment Station, 1935–38, and Appalachian Forest Experiment Station, 1938–44. Was appointed assistant chief of U.S. Forest Service in charge of cooperative programs (state and private), 1944–52; and was chief, 1952–62. Received U.S. Department of Agriculture's Distinguished Service Award, 1957; Rockefeller Public Service Award, 1960; President's Gold Medal for Distinguished Federal Civilian Service, 1961; Sir William Schlich Memorial Medal of the Society of American Foresters, 1962; Knight Commander Order of Merit, Germany, 1962; and The American Forestry Association's John Aston Warder Medal, 1978. Was president of Fifth World Forestry Congress in Seattle in 1960, and member of U.S. Delegation to Sixth World Forestry Congress in Madrid in 1966. Is a fellow of Society of American Foresters and three-term member of its council. Since 1958 has been director of The American Forestry

Association. Was a founder of North American Forestry Commission of the Food and Agriculture Organization of the United Nations. Died October 4, 1983.

HENRY CLEPPER

American Men and Women of Science (Physical and Biological Sciences), 14th ed., 1979.

Who's Who in America, 1974–75.

MCATEE, WALDO LEE
(1883–1962)
Born January 21 in Japala, Indiana. University of Indiana, A.M. (biology) 1904, Sc.D. (honorary) 1961. His entire professional career (1904–47) was with Biological Survey of U.S. Department of Agriculture and its successor agency, Fish and Wildlife Service of U.S. Department of the Interior. Contributed much to research in food of birds and mammals, and developed and became director of Biological Survey's Division of Food Habits Research. Served for many years as treasurer of American Ornithologists' Union, and was instrumental in creation of The Wildlife Society and in establishment of its *Journal of Wildlife Management*, of which he was initial editor. A versatile and proficient entomologist, for twenty-seven years he held position of acting curator of Hemiptera in U.S. National Museum. Late in his career, served as technical advisor to chief of Biological Survey and to director of Fish and Wildlife Service. His extensive knowledge of food of birds led to his publishing critiques of protective coloration and certain Darwinian theories. A monumental typescript that is the work of a lifelong project—the compilation of *American Bird Names, Their Histories and Meanings*—remains unpublished in Fuertes Library at Cornell University. His writings exceed twelve hundred items, exclusive of abstracts and similar notes. A member of many scientific societies, he was a fellow of American Association for the Advancement of Science. Received Distinguished Service Award with gold medal from U.S. Department of the Interior. Was one of outstanding biologists and leading conservationists of his times. Died January 7, 1962.

E. R. KALMBACH

Kalmbach, E. R. "In Memoriam: W. L. McAtee." *Auk*, 80(4):474–85, October 1963.

Terres, John K. "McAtee, Food Analyst of the Birds." *Audubon*. November-December, 1946; 362–68.

———. "W. L. McAtee, 1883–1962." *Journal of Wildlife Management*, 27(3):494–99, July 1963.

MCCABE, RICHARD EDWARD
(born 1946)
Born August 1 in Madison, Wisconsin. Wartburg College, Waverly, Iowa. B.A. (English) 1969; University of Wisconsin–Madison, M.S. (journalism/wildlife ecology/ag journalism) 1971, doctoral studies in mass communications, 1973–76. Coordinated aquatic and open space management program as faculty member at University of Wisconsin–Madison, 1972–76. Has served as director of publications for Wildlife Management Institute in Washington, D.C., since 1977. Served on board of directors and executive committee of Environment Wisconsin, 1972–73. Is member of Wisconsin Academy of Sciences, Arts and Letters; Outdoor Writers Association of America; Mason-Dixon Outdoor Writers Association; The Wildlife Society; and National Capital Chapter of The Wildlife Society. Has served as consultant on public relations, mass communication, technical and feature writing, and natural history for such organizations as Smithsonian Institution, National Geographic, and Time/Life. Has written more than ninety popular and technical articles on such topics as wildlife conservation, land-use management, and ethnozoology. Received recognition for wetland and open space preservation efforts, and has been cited for his historical and conservation writings, and for editorial and design work on award-winning books produced for Wildlife Management Institute.

LAURENCE R. JAHN

MCCABE, ROBERT ALBERT
(born 1914)
Born January 11 in Milwaukee, Wisconsin. Carroll College (Waukesha, Wisconsin), B.A. 1939; University of Wisconsin, M.A. 1943, Ph.D. (wildlife management) 1949. As student manager on Faville Grove Wildlife Area, conducted field research on upland gamebirds and on wildlife management on southern Wisconsin farms, 1940–43. Joined staff of University of Wisconsin as Arboretum and wildlife refuge biologist,

1943–45; as instructor in Department of Wildlife Management (later Wildlife Ecology) in 1945; professor in 1956; and department chairman, 1952–79. Was secretary of board for Wisconsin Exposition Department, 1960–68; secretary of advisory board for Wisconsin Department of Resource Development, 1961–62; member of Research Advisory Committee for Wisconsin Department of Natural Resources, 1952 to present, and chairman, 1955–56 and 1970–71; and as chairman of National Academy of Sciences Subcommittee on Vertebrate Pest Problems, 1966–67, U.S. Department of the Interior Policy Committee on lead/iron shot evaluation, 1973–74. In foreign service, with Rockefeller Foundation support, conducted surveys of wildlife training in Uganda, Tanzania, Kenya, Rhodesia, and South Africa in 1965, and worked on research program on impala in Northern Frontier District of Kenya in 1967. Was Fulbright professor in ecology in Zoology Department, University College, Dublin, 1969–70; and advisor to Irish Office of Public Works (National Parks), Dublin, 1970–80, and to Ethiopian Department of Wildlife Management in 1972. Is life member of The Wildlife Society, and was president, 1976–77. Is a fellow of American Ornithologists' Union; was president of Wisconsin Society for Ornithology, 1971–72, and vice-president for science in 1977; and was president of Wisconsin Academy of Science, Arts and Letters in 1979. Received Carroll College Distinguished Alumnus Award in 1977, and Wisconsin Award of Wisconsin Chapter of The Wildlife Society in 1981. Is member of nine professional societies, including British Ornithological Union and British Ecological Society. Is author of numerous scientific articles on wildlife ecology and management, including classic work on Hungarian partridge. Has earned national and international acclaim for academic and research program administration.

ORRIN J. RONGSTAD

American Men and Women of Science, 14th ed., 1979.

McCloskey, John Michael
(born 1934)
Born April 26 in Eugene, Oregon. Harvard College, B.A. magna cum laude (American government) 1956; University of Oregon, J.D. 1961. Served in U.S. Army, 1956–58. Represented Sierra Club and Federation of Western Outdoor Clubs on conservation matters in Pacific Northwest, 1961–65; was assistant to president of Sierra Club in 1965, conservation

director in 1966–68, and executive director since 1969. Was principal legislative advocate for establishment of Redwood National Park in 1968. Also initiated idea of Executive Order to protect roadless areas in National Forests, which in turn led to roadless area review studies. Also was a principal author of United Nation's Charter for Nature. Is author of numerous articles in professional and legal journals on environmental subjects. Received California Conservation Council Professional Award in 1969, and Sierra Club's John Muir Award in 1979. Is vice-chairman of International Union for Conservation of Nature and Natural Resources's Commission on Environmental Law, Policy, and Administration, and co-chairman of OSHA/Environmental Conference. Was cofounder of Western Forest Environment Discussion Group, co-chairman of Mining Committee of the National Coal Policy Project, chairman of Environmental Subcommittee of the Committee on Surface Mining and Reclamation of the National Research Council, and member of board of the Ford Foundation's Energy Policy Project and President's Commission for an Agenda for 1980s. Is member of board of directors of League of Conservation Voters.

SIERRA CLUB

Who's Who in America, 41st ed., 1980–81.

McCOMB, JOHN ANDREW
(born 1938)
Born February 20 in Ames, Iowa. Iowa State University, University of Arizona, B.S. (electrical engineering) 1962. From 1970 to 1977 was field representative for Sierra Club in Arizona, Colorado, New Mexico, and Utah, where issues focused heavily on management of federal lands and energy development. During this time, played major role in passage of Federal Land Policy and Management Act. Moved to Sierra Club's Washington, D.C., office in 1977, where he continued to work on public land-related matters, including numerous wilderness bills, Forest Service RARE II program, and Alaska National Interest Lands Conservation Act. In 1980 assumed management of Washington Office, and in 1983 became conservation director, his present position. His current responsibilities include overall direction of Sierra Club Conservation Department staff and programs, located in San Francisco, Washington, D.C., and eleven field offices.

JOHN A. McCOMB

McGee, William John
(1853–1912)
Born April 17 near Farley, Iowa. Largely self-educated in anthropology, geology, and hydrology; honorary doctorate awarded by Cornell College, Iowa, 1901. Joined U.S. Geological Survey in July 1883, but resigned in 1893 to become ethnololgist in Bureau of American Ethnology. Served as first director of Saint Louis Public Museum, 1905–7. Following creation by President Theodore Roosevelt of Inland Waterways Commission in March 1907, was elected vice-chairman and secretary. In March 1907 was appointed as expert on soil waters in U.S. Department of Agriculture Bureau of Soils. Served on committee with Gifford Pinchot that arranged Governors Conference on the Conservation of Natural Resources, held in The White House in May 1908. As secretary of Section of Waters for the National Conservation Commission, helped compile first inventory of nation's natural resources in 1908, and was recording secretary of Joint Conservation Conference, Washington, D.C., December 1908. Was president of American Association for the Advancement of Science, 1897, and was a founder of Geological Society of America, and as editor established its *Bulletin*. Was author of more than one hundred scientific publications; wrote monograph *Soil Erosion*, 1911, one of early treatises on this subject. Was one of principal founders of conservation movement at turn of century. Died September 4, 1912.

HENRY CLEPPER

McGee, Emma R. *Life of W. J. McGee*. Farley, Iowa: Privately printed, 1915.

Who Was Who in America, 1897–1942.

McGuire, John Richard
(born 1916)
Born April 20 in Milwaukee, Wisconsin. University of Minnesota, B.S. 1939; Yale University, M.F. 1941; University of Pennsylvania, M.A. (economics). Spent his entire forty-year career with U.S. Department of Agriculture Forest Service, starting as junior field assistant in North Central states in 1939 and retiring as agency's chief. Following number of years as forest economist at Northeastern Forest Experiment Station in Upper Darby, Pennsylvania, became chief of the station's division of forest economics research. In 1962 was assigned to national headquarters office in Washington, D.C., as staff assistant in research. Became deputy chief for program planning and legislation in 1967, associate chief in 1971, and

in 1972 was made chief. Was instrumental in passage of 1974 Forest and Rangeland Renewable Resources Planning Act and of 1976 National Forest Management Act. Developed program of international forestry cooperation with his counterparts in Canada and Mexico, and later led forestry delegation to Soviet Union to negotiate agreement for scientific and technological exchange with U.S. In 1977 developed Canada-United States Spruce Budworm Program in which the two countries combined research and development to control the insect. In 1979 received President's Award for Distinguished Civil Service. Has also received National Civil Service League Award, U.S. Department of Agriculture's Distinguished Service Award, and University of Minnesota's Outstanding Achievement Award. Since retirement in 1979 has been active as university lecturer and teacher and as consultant on policy matters. Is a fellow of Society of American Foresters.

JOHN C. BARBER

American Men and Women of Science (Physical and Biological Sciences), 14th ed., 1979.

Who's Who in America, 40th ed., 1978–79.

MACKAYE, BENTON
(1879–1976)
Born March 6 in Stamford, Connecticut. Harvard University, B.A. 1900; A.M. (forestry) 1905. Was research forester in U.S. Forest Service from 1905–18, making field examinations of timberlands. Made watershed investigations of areas for acquisition as national forests under Weeks Law of 1910, particularly in White Mountains of New Hampshire. In 1918–19 was specialist in land colonization for U.S. Department of Labor. For several years was instructor in forestry at Harvard Forest in Massachusetts. Was active in promoting 2,050-mile footpath stretching from Maine to Georgia, and in 1921 wrote article on subject for *Journal of the American Institute of Architects*, which earned him sobriquet of father of Appalachian Trail. In 1928 made regional survey of Massachusetts for Governor's Committee on Open Spaces. In 1930 article in *New Republic*, he proposed what called "the townless highway," an idea that developed into familiar beltways around municipalities of today. In 1933 was consultant to Indian Service in planning study for reservations in South Dakota, New Mexico, and Arizona. Was on regional planning staff of Tennessee Valley Authority, 1934–36. In 1937 made plan known

as Bay Circuit Project for developing series of state parks encircling Boston, Massachusetts. Was consultant of U.S. Department of Agriculture from 1938 to 1941 on flood-control policies of Forest Service, and on staff of Rural Electrification Administration in 1942–43. In 1944–45 made study of possible development under proposed Missouri Valley Authority. Was one of key organizers of The Wilderness Society in 1935, a member of its governing council, president 1945–50, and honorary life president from 1950. After World War I wrote publication *Employment and Natural Resources* for U.S. Department of Labor, and in 1928 a book, *The New Exploration: A Philosophy of Regional Planning*, reprinted in 1962. His published works include *From Geography to Geotechnics*, 1968, and *Expedition Nine: A Return to a Region*, 1969. The latter work is a selection of his essays published by The Wilderness Society and presented to him on his ninetieth birthday. In 1966 received Conservation Service Award of U.S. Department of the Interior. Died December 11, 1976.

MICHAEL NADEL
PAUL H. OEHSER

Congressional Record, H4867–4877, June 11, 1968.

Journal of Forestry, 45:295–96, April 1947.

Living Wilderness, vol. 39, no. 132:6–34, Jan.–Mar., 1976.

Who's Who in America, 1946–47.

McNARY, CHARLES LINZA
(1874–1944)
Born June 12 near Salem, Oregon. Attended Leland Stanford Junior University; studied law; was admitted to Oregon bar in 1898, and began practice in Salem. Was deputy district attorney of third judicial district, 1906–13; dean of law department of Willamette University, 1908–13; and associate justice of Oregon State Supreme Court, 1913–15. Was appointed U.S. senator to fill unexpired term in May 1917, was elected in his own right in 1918, and served continuously until his death. His chief senatorial interests were agriculture, reforestation, irrigation, reclamation, and waterpower development. Was influential in construction of Bonneville Dam on Columbia River in Oregon. As chairman of Senate's Select Committee on Reforestation, 1923, conducted series of hearings across nation to acquire information on problems of public and private

forestry. The hearings were major factor in enactment of Clarke-McNary Act of 1924, which established tradition of federal-state-private cooperation in forest protection and provided substantial financial assistance to state forestry agencies. The McNary-Woodruff Act of 1928 provided additional funds for public purchase of private forestland, and McSweeney-McNary Act of 1928 established broad program of federal forest research and provided for forest inventories. Was made chairman of Senate Committee on Agriculture and Forestry in 1926. Died February 25, 1944.

ELWOOD R. MAUNDER

Biographical Directory of the American Congress, 1774–1961, Washington, D.C., 1961.

National Cyclopaedia of American Biography, 1945.

Who Was Who in America, 1943–50.

MCNULTY, HESTER PURDY
(born 1923)

Born February 20 in Pittsburgh, Pennsylvania. University of Colorado, B.S. 1947, M.S. (nutrition and biochemistry) 1949. Joined League of Women Voters of the United States in 1955, and has been active in its environmental projects in Virginia and Colorado; served as water chair of League of Women Voters of Fairfax County, Virginia, 1959–61, and for Virginia State League, 1961–63. Was chair of Potomac River Basin Inter-League Committee, 1965–72, and also participated in several other groups dedicated to cleaning up Potomac River, including Fairfax County Potomac Advisory Committee and Citizens Council for a Clean Potomac, of which she served on steering committee. Managed environmental projects for League of Women Voters of Colorado, 1971–77, and currently serves as water and oil-shale coordinator. From 1973 to 1978 was on board of directors of Colorado Open Space Council, and for several years was member of Colorado Citizen's Committee for U.S. Army Corps of Engineers. Also served on Boulder Colorado Board of Health 1976–81, as vice-president 1979–80, and president 1980–81. Was chairman of State of Colorado 208 Policy Advisory Group and member of Colorado Groundwater Policy Task Force. Was elected to board of directors of League of Women Voters of the United States in 1978 and served two years as its Natural Resources Coordinator. Participated in 1980 Environmental Protection Agency's groundwater and

waste-water strategy workshops. Was appointed to the agency's Municipal Advisory Group to Construction Grants Division, 1980–82.

LEAGUE OF WOMEN VOTERS OF THE UNITED STATES

MADSON, JOHN BENJAMIN
(born 1923)
Born November 24 near Ames, Iowa. Served in U.S. Army Air Force,
1942–46. Iowa State University, B.S. (wildlife biology) 1951, plus additional year in fisheries biology (graduate studies). Was information officer
and editor of *Iowa Conservationist,* Iowa Conservation Commission,
1952–55; staff writer specializing in natural history features, *Des
Moines Register,* 1956–58; assistant director of conservation for Winchester-Western Division of Olin Corporation at East Alton, Illinois,
1958–79 (retired). Since then has been full-time free-lance writer specializing in outdoor magazine articles, books, and motion-picture scripts,
and has written hundreds of articles for newspapers and magazines.
While with Winchester-Western, wrote widely distributed series of publications on major American big and small game species, hunter ethics,
history of game management, and conservation careers. His books include *Stories from under the Sky,* 1961; *Out Home,* 1980; and *Where
the Sky Began,* 1982. Is past-president of Association of Great Lakes
Outdoor Writers, has served on boards of National Wildlife Federation
and Outdoor Writers' Association of America, and has been chairman of
the latter's Conservation Council. His awards include Conservation Education Award of The Wildlife Society, 1966, and Jade of Chiefs award of
Outdoor Writers' Association of America, 1967. Was inducted into Iowa
Conservation Hall of Fame in 1977.

LAURENCE R. JAHN

MALSBERGER, HENRY JAMES
(1902–1980)
Born October 15 in Pottstown, Pennsylvania. Pennsylvania State University, B.S. (forestry) 1925. Began his forestry career with lumber company
in Florida, then in 1928 joined newly organized Florida Forest Service.
Was advanced to district forester in 1931, to assistant state forester in
1934, and to director of forests and parks in 1937, a position later
changed to state forester and park executive. During his period with

Florida Forest Sevice, helped train camp superintendents for Civilian Conservation Corps and wrote textbook on state's forest resources for school system. In 1945 was appointed forester and manager for Southern Pulpwood Conservation Association at Atlanta, an organization founded in 1939 by pulp and paper industry in the South to stimulate improvement in forest practices and to encourage growing of trees. Built up field force of professional foresters who conducted field demonstrations of tree planting, conservative harvesting, and proper forest management. Association sponsored popular forestry education, and established training camps for boys with joint sponsorship by industry and public agencies. Under his direction much forestry literature and many documentary films on fire prevention and forest conservation were distributed for public information. Was vice-president of Society of American Foresters, 1958–61, and was elected a fellow in the latter year. In 1965 received American Motors conservation award. Retired in 1968. Died May 18, 1980.

HENRY CLEPPER

Journal of Forestry. Biography, 48:423–33, June 1950; 66(5):427, May 1968.

MARSH, GEORGE PERKINS
(1801–1882)
Born March 15 in Woodstock, Vermont, Dartmouth College, graduated 1829, LL.D. (honorary) 1886; Harvard University, LL.D. 1856. Held public office during most of his life. Was on Vermont Governor's Council in 1835; was member of U.S. House of Representatives, 1843–49; and was minister to Turkey, 1849–53. Was fish commissioner of Vermont, 1857–59, then reentered diplomatic service as minister to Italy, 1861–82. Throughout his career, was student of science, particularly of natural history. Wrote several books on grammar and linguistics, and an early one, *The Camel*, 1856, on a zoological topic. Among natural scientists, was best known for his monumental *Man and Nature*, 1864, which was later titled *The Earth as Modified by Human Action* in its 1874 edition. One of most significant books on natural resources by an American published during nineteenth century, it delineated for first time the basic principles of conservation, principles that have endured for more than a century. A scholar with wide-ranging interests, he painstakingly explained relationship of soil, water, and vegetative cover, and demonstrated by hundreds of references to European scientific knowledge that destruction

of grass and forest cover causes alteration in soil and water, and that man himself was changing physical condition of the earth. Assembled impressive body of data showing how fire, overgrazing, and cutting of forests contributed to decline of agriculture, water supplies, cities, and indeed whole civilizations; pointed for proof to extensive areas of once-productive land that had become desert in China, Europe, and North Africa. Presented case for forest preservation as support of American civilization. Died July 23, 1882.

HENRY CLEPPER

Biographical Directory of the American Congress. Washington, D.C. United States Government Printing Office, 1961.

Dictionary of American Biography, 1933.

Hart, James D., ed. *The Oxford Companion to American Literature*, 4th ed. New York: Oxford University Press, 1965.

Lowenthal, David. *George Perkins Marsh, Versatile Vermonter.* New York: Columbia University Press, 1958.

Who Was Who in America (Historical Volume), 1607–1896.

MARSHALL, GEORGE
(born 1904)

Born February 11 in New York City. Columbia University, B.A. 1926, M.A. 1927; Robert Brookings Graduate School of Economics and Government, Ph.D. 1930. Was assistant editor from 1921 to 1931 of *Encyclopedia of the Social Sciences.* Was economist in National Recovery Administration, Washington, D.C., 1934–37. Instrumental in formation of The Wilderness Society, he has served on its council since 1936, and was managing editor from 1957 to 1961 of *Living Wilderness.* Edited *Arctic Wilderness,* writings by his brother, the late Robert Marshall (1956, 1970). Joining Sierra Club in 1950, was elected to its board of directors in 1959, and was its president in 1966–67. A strong supporter of Wilderness Preservation Act of 1964, he has written widely for conservation magazines on wilderness and related subjects. Is director of Trustees for Conservation, Sierra Club Foundation, and California Conservation Council; was charter member of Adirondack Mountain Club, and is active in Federation of Western Outdoor Clubs.

SIERRA CLUB

Sierra Club Handbook, 1967.
Who's Who in America, 39th ed., 1976–77.

MARSHALL, ROBERT
(1901–1939)

Born January 2 in New York City. New York State College of Forestry, B.S. 1924; Harvard Forest School, M.F. 1925; Johns Hopkins University, Ph.D. (plant physiology) 1930. From 1925 to 1928 was research silviculturist with U.S. Forest Service's Northern Rocky Mountain Forest and Range Experiment Station in Montana. Then spent two years studying tree growth, climate, geography, and social conditions in arctic Alaska. In 1933 was appointed director of forestry in Office (now Bureau) of Indian Affairs, U.S. Department of the Interior, and was effective in stimulating higher degree of participation by Indians in management of their forest and range resources. In 1927 returned to Forest Service as chief of Division of Recreation and Lands, and was influential in advancing the service's policies on recreation and preservation of wilderness areas. In addition to his official duties, he helped found The Wilderness Society in 1935, and served on its council and executive committee. One of leaders of group of foresters and fellow conservationists who advocated socialization (public ownership) of nation's commercial timberlands, he delineated his views in pamphlet *The Social Management of American Forests*, 1930, and in book *The People's Forests*, 1933. Also wrote *Arctic Village*, 1933; *Doonerak or Bust*, 1938; and *North to Doonerak, Amawk and Apoon*, 1939. In addition, was author of articles on silviculture, forest recreation, and social management of woodland, and contributed section on recreation to *A National Plan for American Forestry* (Senate Document No. 12), 1933. Died November 30, 1939.

HENRY CLEPPER

Journal of Forestry. Obituary, 38(1):61–62, January 1940.

MARTIN, CLYDE SAYERS
(1884–1963)

Born September 19 in Waynesburg, Pennsylvania. DePauw University, B.Sc. 1905; Yale University, M.F. 1907. During 1907–20, was employed by Weyerhaeuser Timber Company as timber cruiser and forest engineer. Was appointed consulting forest engineer for government of India, and served in that capacity, and later as chief forest engineer for government of Madras, from 1920 to 1930. Returning to U.S., engaged in sawmilling for three years in western Oregon, became chief forester for Western Pine Association in 1934, and five years later returned to Weyerhaeuser Timber Company as chief forester. Under his direction, Weyerhaeuser company established Clemons Tree Farm in 1941; it marked start of national tree-farm movement. Pioneered numerous other developments for advancement of industrial forestry. As trustee of American Forest Products Industries, helped to expand the industry's program for improved forest protection and practices. As member of Society of American Foresters since 1918, participated actively in its affairs: was chairman of Columbia River Section, 1935–46, and of Puget Sound Section, 1943–44; was member of Committee on Private Forestry, elected vice-president for term 1946–47, elected a fellow in 1947, and was president in 1948–49. Died February 10, 1963.

SOCIETY OF AMERICAN FORESTERS

Journal of Forestry. Obituary, vol. 61:320, 1963.

MASON, DAVID TOWNSEND
(1883–1973)
Born March 11 in Newark, New Jersey. Rutgers University, B.S. (civil engineering) 1905; Yale University, M.F. 1907, M.S. 1908. From 1907 to 1915 worked for U.S. Forest Service; after U.S. Army service in World War I taught until 1919 at University of California School of Forestry. During 1919 prepared regulations for Timber Valuation Section, Bureau of Internal Revenue. Began work as consulting forester in 1921 in Portland, Oregon, and continued thereafter, except from 1931 to 1935, when he was manager of Western Pine Association. During his professional life, was persistent advocate of sustained-yield management in American forestry and in so doing influenced or actually wrote much of legislation that brought sustained yield into widespread practice. Was member of Timber Conservation Board in 1931, and executive officer of Lumber Code Authority under National Recovery Act in 1934. Since 1938 had served as chairman of advisory committee to Bureau of Land Management for Oregon and California Revested Lands, and also as member of Research Advisory Committee of the Pacific Northwest Forest and Range Experiment Station. Was elected a fellow of Society of American Foresters in 1948 and of Forest History Society in 1966. Received Conservation Award from The American Forestry Association in 1957; Forestry Award from Western Forestry and Conservation Association in 1961; Conservation Service Award from U.S. Department of the Interior in 1954, and its Appreciation Award in 1963; and Distinguished Service

Award from Oregon State University in 1966. In 1966, David T. Mason Professorship of Forest Land Use was endowed in his honor at Yale University School of Forestry by Louis W. and Maud Hill Family Foundation. Died September 3, 1973.

CARL A. NEWPORT

Loehr, Rodney C. *Forests for the Future, the Diaries of David T. Mason*. St. Paul, Minn.: The Forest Products History Foundation, 1952.

Richardson, Elmo. *David T. Mason: Forestry Advocate*, Santa Cruz, Ca.: Forest History Society, 1983.

MATHER, STEPHEN TYNG
(1867–1930)

Born July 4 in San Francisco, California. University of California, Bachelor of Letters 1887, LL.D. 1924; George Washington University, LL.D. 1921. From 1887 to 1893 was reporter for *New York Sun*. Then engaged in production and marketing of borax until his partial retirement in 1913. Publicly critical of early management of national parks for their lack of central administration, adequate appropriations, accommodations, roads, and personnel, he was challenged by Franklin K. Lane, secretary of the Interior, to come to Washington and "run them yourself." On January 21, 1915, was appointed assistant to the secretary. When National Park Service was created, he became its first director in May 1917, and served in this office until forced to retire by illness in November 1928. During his administration of Park Service, seven national parks (Acadia, Bryce Canyon, Grand Canyon, Hawaii, Lassen Volcanic, Mount McKinley, Zion) and fourteen national monuments were established. Studies initiated under his direction resulted in later creation of Great Smoky Mountains, Shenandoah, and Mammoth Cave National Parks. In January 1921 was leader in organization of National Conference on State Parks, which was largely responsible for creation of state parks and recreation areas in nearly all states. Was member of National Capital Park and Planning Commission from its creation in 1924 until his retirement from government service. In 1927 received Pugsley Gold Medal of American Scenic and Historic Preservation Society. Memorials to him are numerous. A ranger district in Yosemite National Park bears his name. A high pass in Sierra Nevadas, traversed by John Muir Trail, is Mather Pass. A peak in Alaskan Range is Mount Mather. Across Cascades and through Mount Rainier National Park runs Mather Memorial

Highway. The canyon of Potomac River below Great Falls has been named and dedicated as Mather Gorge. Died January 22, 1930.

HORACE M. ALBRIGHT
HOLT BODINSON

Shankland, Robert. *Steve Mather of the National Parks*. New York: Alfred A. Knopf, 1951.

Who Was Who in America, 1897–1942.

MAUNDER, ELWOOD RONDEAU
(born 1917)
Born April 11 in Bottineau, North Dakota. University of Minnesota, B.A. 1939; Washington University at Saint Louis, M.A. (modern European history), 1947; London School of Economics and Political Science, 1948. Was reporter and feature writer for Minneapolis newspapers, 1939–41, then served as combat correspondent in Coast Guard during World War II, and did public relations work for Methodist church, 1948–52. Since 1952 was secretary and executive director of Forest History Society, Inc., with headquarters in Santa Cruz, California, and since 1957 editor of quarterly journal *Forest History*. Retired from the society in 1978. From 1964 to 1969 was curator of forest history at Yale University Library. Under his leadership, Forest History Society had been internationally effective in stimulating scholarly research and writing in annals of forestry and natural resource conservation generally; forty-six repositories and archival centers have been established in U.S. and Canada at universities and libraries for collecting and preserving of documents relating to forest history. As writer and editor, has made significant contributions to this hitherto neglected aspect of history, and in recognition of his services Society of American Foresters elected him honorary member in 1968. Is also a founding director of International Oral History Society, and is active member of Agricultural History Society, American Academy of Political and Social Science, American Historical Association, Organization of American Historians, Oral History Association, Society of American Archivists, and The American Forestry Association.

HENRY CLEPPER

Directory of American Scholars, vol. 1, *History*, 5th ed., 1969.

Who's Who in the East, 10th ed., 1965.

MAXWELL, GEORGE HEBARD
(1860–1946)

Born June 3 in Sonoma, California. Educated at St. Matthew's Hall, San Mateo, California. Began his law career as court stenographer in 1879. In that year, organized National Irrigation Association and as executive secretary led movement for national irrigation policy. It culminated in passage of Reclamation Act in 1902. In 1903 organized nation's first water-users association in Arizona. Thereafter was foremost exponent of governmental policy on river regulation and flood control, and was active in National Flood Prevention and River Regulation Commission. At first Conservation Congress held in Washington, D.C., in 1905, launched public attack against land grabbers and antiquated laws that permitted them to despoil public domain. His last great achievement was starting in 1930 of Muskingum Conservancy District in Ohio, precursor of the Tennessee Valley Authority type of land and water administration. Was also pioneer advocate of contour plowing, later effectively promoted by Soil Conservation Service. Author of several books now out of print, he is to be remembered for *Golden Rivers and Treasure Valleys*. During era of conservation development, was recognized as leader and father of irrigation movement. Died December 1, 1946.

HENRY CLEPPER

Journal of Forestry. Obituary, 45(4):286–87, April 1947.

Who Was Who in America, vol. 2, 1943–50.

MERRIAM, CLINTON HART
(1855–1942)

Born December 15 in New York City. Yale University Sheffield Scientific School, 1874–77; Columbia University College of Physicians and Surgeons, M.D. 1879. Practiced medicine until 1885, when he was appointed first head of Division of Economic Ornithology and Mammalogy, which in 1905 became Bureau of Biological Survey, in U.S. Department of Agriculture. One of earliest advocates of laws for bird protection, helped prepare model legislation for states. Upon his retirement from Biological Survey in 1910, became affiliated as research associate with Smithsonian Institution, and for three decades conducted investigations in botany, zoology, and ethnology. During and subsequent to his association with Smithsonian, devoted himself to study of fauna and flora and Indian tribes of the West, particularly in California and

Nevada. Made exploring trips through all states and Bermuda. His long list of contributions to natural history and conservation includes service as president of American Ornithologists' Union, 1900–02; president of Biological Section of Washington Academy of Sciences, 1891–92; chairman of U.S. Geographic Board, 1917–25; president of American Society of Mammalogists, 1919–21; and president of American Society of Naturalists, 1924–25. Was member of National Academy of Sciences, and was associate editor of *National Geographic Magazine* and zoological editor of *Science*. Author of more than four hundred papers on biological and ethnological subjects, he wrote twenty-nine books and book-length reports, including *Birds of Connecticut*, 1877; *Mammals of the Adirondacks*, 1882–84; and *Life Zones and Crop Zones of the United States*, 1898. Died March 19, 1942.

Eve Herbst

National Cyclopaedia of American Biography, 1906.

New York Times. Obituary, March 20, 1942.

Who Was Who in America, 1943–50.

Merriman, Daniel
(born 1908)
Born September 17 in Cambridge, Massachusetts. Groton School 1921–27. Harvard University, B.S. 1930; University of Washington, M.S. 1934; Yale University, Ph.D. (zoology) 1939. Rose from assistant professor at Yale in 1942 to professor in 1976 and professor emeritus in 1977. During his academic career, also served as aquatic biologist in charge of striped-bass investigations for Connecticut State Board of Fish and Game, 1936–38; master of Davenport College, 1942–66; president of Yale Chapter of Sigma Xi, 1943–44; chairman of Commission of Food Resources of Coastal Waters of National Research Council, 1943–46; director of Bingham Oceanographic Laboratory, 1942–66; member of board of editors of *Journal of Marine Research*, 1943–60; trustee of Bermuda Biological Station of Woods Hole Oceanographic Institute, 1944–46; a fellow of New York Zoological Society since 1944; and research associate in Department of Fishes and Aquatic Biology of the American Museum of Natural History, 1945–62. Served as member of advisory committee on Biology of the Office of Naval Research, 1949–52; consultant to National Science Foundation, 1951–54; commissioner of Connecticut State Board of Fish and Game, 1953–56; member of advisory

committee for Susquehanna Fishery Study, 1957–60; consultant to President's Scientific Advisory Commission, 1960–61; director of Connecticut River Ecological Study for Connecticut Yankee Atomic Power Company, 1964–74; director of Sears Foundation for Marine Research, 1966–77; consultant to various electric power companies from Maine to New York since 1971. In 1979 became chairman of Third International Congress on History of Oceanography, held at Woods Hole in 1980. Also served on board of editors for multivolume series "Fishes of Western North Atlantic," on honorary editorial advisory board for *Deep-Sea Research*, and editorial board of *Limnology and Oceanography*. His memberships include American Association for the Advancement of Science, Sigma Xi, American Fisheries Society, and Society of Ichthyologists and Herpetologists, History of Science Society, and Connecticut and New York academies of science. Retired in 1977 but continues to provide useful consulting and advisory services.

C. GORDON FREDINE

American Men and Women of Science (Physical and Biological Sciences), 15th ed., 1982.

Who's Who in America, 40th 3d., 1978–79.

MICHAUD, HOWARD HENRY
(born 1902)

Born October 12 in Berne, Indiana. Bluffton College, B.A. (biological science) 1925; Indiana University, (zoology) 1930. For twenty years was teacher in public schools of Fort Wayne, Indiana, serving in summers as chief naturalist, Indiana State Parks. From 1945 until retiring in 1971, was professor of conservation at Purdue University, Department of Forestry and Natural Resources. Was delegate to United Nations Conference on World Resources, 1948 and 1966. Active in local, state, and national conservation organizations, he served as president of Conservation Education Association, 1956–57; of Indiana Division, Izaak Walton League of America, 1953; and of National Association of Biology Teachers, 1948. His work with Soil Conservation Society of America led to honorary membership in 1961. Received Charles S. Osborn award for conservation from Purdue University in 1959, and Merit Award of National Wildlife Federation in 1961. Has contributed numerous articles to *School Science and Mathematics, American Biology Teacher, Indiana Academy of Science Proceedings*, and numerous conference reports, and is author of section of 1966 *World Topics Yearbook*, Indiana state publications on state parks, and several bibliographies. Helped prepare series of five booklets on conservation and outline for teaching conservation in Indiana schools for state's department of public instruction. In retirement, has served as editor of newsletter of Environmental Education Association of Indiana since 1972. Has been engaged in erosion-control work associated with city park system as member of West Lafayette Board of Parks and Recreation. Perhaps his most important contribution, however, is the instruction and guidance he gave to his many students during his professional teaching career.

WILSON F. CLARK
JUNE McSWAIN

American Men and Women of Science (Physical and Biological Sciences), 15th ed., 1982.

MILLER, ALDEN HOLMES
(1906–1965)
Born February 4 in Los Angeles, California. University of California at Los Angeles, B.A. 1927; University of California, Berkeley, M.A. 1928, Ph.D. 1930. From instructor in zoology at University of California in 1931, advanced to professor in 1945. Became curator of birds at the university's Museum of Vertebrate Zoology in 1939 and was named director in 1940. In 1960 was also appointed curator of birds in Museum of Paleontology. During his career, made field studies of vertebrates in western U.S., Central America, South America, and Australia. Was awarded William Brewster memorial medal of American Ornithologists' Union in 1943, and served as the union's president, 1953–56. Was member of National Academy of Sciences and a fellow of American Association for the Advancement of Science. For many years, served on Committee on Classification and Nomenclature of North American Birds and on International Committee on Zoological Nomenclature. Was editor of *Condor* from 1939 until his death. Author of numerous scientific papers and other writings on birds, animal ecology, and evolution, he published his last book, *Lives of Desert Animals*, in 1964. Died October 9, 1965.

NATIONAL AUDUBON SOCIETY

Who Was Who in America, 1961–68.

MOFFETT, JAMES WILLIAM
(1908–1967)

Born August 3 in American Fork, Utah. University of Utah, B.A. 1933, M.A. 1935; University of Michigan, Ph.D. (zoology and limnology) 1939. Served Michigan Department of Conservation as aquatic biologist in Institute for Fishery Research, 1939–41. Joining U.S. Fish and Wildlife Service in 1941, was assigned to California for work on lakes of Sierras and later became chief of Central Valley Investigations. In 1950 became chief of Great Lake Fishery Investigations, Bureau of Commercial Fisheries, in Ann Arbor, Michigan, where he was nationally and internationally known for planning and supervision of research for control of sea lamprey, which had ruined commercial and sport fishing for lake trout and other valuable species in Great Lakes. In 1959 was recognized for accomplishment of sea-lamprey control by U.S. Department of the Interior Unit Award. Was member of U.S. delegation in negotiations with Canada on Great Lakes fishery treaty, 1952–55; and acting executive secretary of Great Lakes Fishery Commission, 1956–57. Became laboratory director Bureau of Commercial Fisheries Great Lakes Research Laboratory in 1959, and in this capacity reorganized fishery and limnological research programs for greater effectiveness. Was president of American Fisheries Society, 1959–60, and a founder of American Institute of Fishery Research Biologists. Was author of numerous scientific articles and papers. Posthumously received U.S. Department of the Interior Distinguished Service Award in 1968. Died June 6, 1967.

DONALD J. LEEDY

American Men of Science (Physical and Biological Sciences), 11th ed., 1966.

MOORE, EMMELINE
(1872–1963)

Born April 29 in Batavia, New York. Wellesley College, A.M. 1906; Cornell University, Ph.D. (aquatic botany) 1914; Hobart College, Sc.D. (honorary) 1939. Taught in public schools and two-year colleges; was substitute professor in botany at Huguenot University, and teacher at Wellington College, Cape Colony, South Africa; then was instructor and assistant professor at Vassar College. Starting as research biologist, was promoted to chief aquatic biologist and director of New York Conservation Department State Biological Survey. Was New York's first investigator-biologist in field of fish culture; in 1958 she christened a New York state marine research vessel that was named The Emmeline M., after her. Her leadership of New York biological survey of aquatic resources in the state can be viewed as classic accomplishment, possibly best early state survey carried out. In retirement, served as honorary fellow at University of Wisconsin and as research assistant at Yale University Laboratory of Oceanography. Was elected in 1928 as first woman president of American Fisheries Society. Author of numerous scientific papers and monographs, she will be remembered for her contributions in fish disease studies and pollution surveys. Died September 12, 1963.

ELWOOD A. SEAMAN

American Men and Women of Science (Physical and Biological Sciences), 10th ed., 1961.

MORTON, JULIUS STERLING

(1832–1902)

Born April 22 in Adams, New York. University of Michigan, B.A. 1854; Union College, New York, A.B. 1856. Then became farmer and newspaper editor in Nebraska. From 1858 to 1961 was secretary of Territory of Nebraska, and later a member of Territorial legislature and of Board of Agriculture. Tree planting was his hobby, and in 1872 he offered resolution to Board of Agriculture that it set aside April 10 as tree-planting day. It was so proclaimed by governor, and in 1885 legislature designated April 22 (Morton's birthday) as Arbor Day, a legal holiday. Other states followed Nebraska's example, and Arbor Day is now observed in all states and in many nations throughout world. Was influential in inducing Congress to pass Timber Culture Act of 1873; this law offered free land to settlers who would plant trees on their claims. Act helped stimulate tree planting, but was not generally successful, and was repealed in 1891. Served as secretary of Agriculture, 1893–97, and during part of this period was also president of The American Forestry Association. Creation of Arbor Day was conservation achievement of his life and career. Died April 27, 1902.

HENRY CLEPPER

Dictionary of American Biography, 1934.

Who Was Who in America, 1897–1942.

MOTT, WILLIAM PENN, JR.

(born 1909)

Born October 19 in New York City. Michigan State University, B.S. (landscape architecture) 1931; University of California, Berkeley, M.S. (landscape architecture and city planning) 1933. Was landscape architect and planner for National Park Service, 1933–40; planning and housing advisor for Contra Costa County, California Housing Authority, 1940–43; private landscape architect in park and recreation master planning and design, 1943–46; superintendent of parks in Oakland, California, 1946–62; general manager of East Bay Regional Park District, California, 1962–67; director of California Department of Parks and Recreation, 1967–75; and consultant to director of Moranga Park and Recreation Authority, Moranga, California, 1975–77. Has served as president and executive officer of California State Park Foundation since 1975, and general manager of East Bay Zoological Society, Oakland, California since 1977. Was director, 1949–54, and president, 1951–52, of American Institute of Park Executives, which awarded him honorary life fellowship. Was consultant to U.S. Department of State on national and local park interests in Costa Rica in 1960, and was consultant on parks to Commonwealth of Australia in 1965. Was director of National Association of State Outdoor Recreation Liaison Officers, 1967–75; panelist at The White House Conference on Natural Beauty, 1965; on board of trustees for National Parks and Conservation Association, 1980 to present; and is professional fellow of American Association of Zoological Parks and Aquariums. Has served as trustee and vice-president of National Recreation and Park Association, and received its Distinguished Fellow Award in 1971. Has held leadership positions in numerous civic groups, including California Roadside Council, California Conservation Council, Save San Francisco Bay Association, and Save-the-Redwoods League. Received award for outstanding professional contributions from American Institute of Landscape Architects in 1968, and Cornelius Amory Pugsley Silver Medal from American Scenic and Historic Preservation Society in 1973 and 1983.

NATIONAL RECREATION AND PARK ASSOCIATION

MUIR, JOHN

(1838–1914)

Born April 21 in Dunbar, Scotland; immigrated to United States in 1849.

Majored in chemistry and geology at University of Wisconsin, (no degree) 1863, LL.D. (honorary) 1897; Harvard University, A.M. (honorary) 1896; Yale University, Litt.D. 1911; University of California LL.D. 1913. At age of twenty-nine walked one thousand miles from Indiana to Gulf of Mexico, then took ship to California, arriving in 1868. Made geological studies in Yosemite Valley and Sierra Nevada, and during 1871–72 his first writings on Yosemite were published in *Overland Monthly* and in *New York Daily Tribune*. Turned from geologist to conservationist as he observed results of land and water despoilation by business monopoly. His concern for forests and mountains resulted in his helping to start magazine *Picturesque California*. After Yosemite trip in 1889, wrote series of articles for *San Francisco Bulletin*, describing destruction of forests and urging federal management for watershed protection. An act of 1891 created Sierra Forest Reserve of four million acres; Yosemite Park became reality in 1906. Meanwhile, in 1892, was a founder and first president, 1892–1914, of Sierra Club. His plans for national park system were submitted to President Taft in 1911, but he did not live to see National Park Service established in 1916. Was a fellow of American Association for the Advancement of Science and president of American Alpine Club. Was author of a dozen books; among his most influential were *The Mountains of California*, 1894; *The Yosemite*, 1912; *Our National Parks*, 1901; and *Travels in Alaska*, 1915. Died December 24, 1914.

MICHAEL McCLOSKEY

Dictionary of American Biography, 1934.

National Cyclopaedia of American Biography, 1907.

Who Was Who in America, 1897–1942.

MULFORD, WALTER

(1877–1955)

Born September 16 in Millville, New Jersey. Cornell University, B.S. (agriculture) 1899, F.E. (forest engineer) 1901; University of Michigan, Sc.D. (honorary) 1938. Established state forestry program in Connecticut in 1901; was first man in America to hold title of state forester. During 1904–5 held brief assignments with U.S. Bureau of Forestry and served as assistant in Yale School of Forestry. From 1905 to 1911 taught silviculture at University of Michigan; then returned to Cornell in 1911 to rebuild instruction in forestry there and supervise construction of Fernow Hall. In 1914 became head of Division of Forestry, University of California at Berkeley, where he directed its development into a department in 1939, and then into School of Forestry in 1946, retiring as dean in 1947. Planned and supervised construction of forestry building in 1948, now designated Mulford Hall. Was inspiring teacher and effective writer on silviculture and forest management. Made notable contributions to development of strong forest policies in California as member of State Board of Forestry and of State Chamber of Commerce. A dedicated member of Society of American Foresters, served as president in 1924, and contributed many articles to *Journal of Forestry*. Was elected as a fellow of American Association for the Advancement of Science. From 1933 to 1950 was consulting editor of American Forestry Series (McGraw-Hill Book Company), which under his leadership grew to twenty-three volumes of technical forestry subject matter. Was vice-president of First World Forestry Congress at Rome in 1926; president of trustees of Institute of Forest Genetics, 1932–33; and in 1942 was appointed as advisor to National Bureau of Forestry Research of China. Died September 7, 1955.

WOODBRIDGE METCALF

Journal of Forestry. Obituary, 53:852, 1955.

Who's Who in America, 1952–53.

MURIE, OLAUS JOHANN
(1889–1963)
Born March 1 in Moorhead, Minnesota. Pacific University, Oregon, B.A. 1912, D.Sc. (honorary) 1949; University of Michigan, M.S. 1927. Was conservation officer with Oregon State Game Commission, 1912–14, and field naturalist and curator of mammals at Carnegie Museum of Natural History, Carnegie Institute, in Pittsburgh, 1914–17. From 1920 to 1926 conducted field research in Alaska for Biological Survey, U.S. Department of Agriculture, and in 1927 started study of elk of North America. As field naturalist for Biological Survey, conducted research expeditions to British Columbia and made special inspections of national forests, Indian reservations, and other public lands as basis for land-management recommendations. Conducted biological survey of Aleutian Islands, 1936–37, and led scientific expedition to New Zealand during 1948–49, on invitation of New Zealand government to make recom-

mendations on problems of introduced wapiti. In 1956 led expedition to Brooks Range in Alaska under sponsorship of The Wilderness Society, New York Zoological Society, and Conservation Foundation; Arctic Wildlife Range was established in this area in 1960. Was awarded Aldo Leopold Award in 1952 by The Wildlife Society in recognition of his contribution to cause of wildlife conservation; Cornelius Amory Pugsley Bronze Medal of the American Scenic and Historic Preservation Society in 1954; and in same year, Conservation Award of The American Forestry Association. In 1959 was awarded Audubon Medal by the National Audubon Society, and John Muir Award of the Sierra Club in 1963. Was elected to council of The Wilderness Society when it was incorporated in 1937, and remained on the council until his death. Became director of The Wilderness Society in 1945, and was president from 1950 to 1957. Was one of five trustees of Robert Marshall Wilderness Fund set up by late Robert Marshall to promote wilderness preservation. A member of many scientific and conservation organizations, he was also president of The Wildlife Society; national director of Izaak Walton League of America; and member of American Committee for International Wildlife Protection. Contributed many articles to technical and general periodicals, including *The Elk of North America*, published in 1951. Considered the definitive work on this subject, the book received The Wildlife Society's 1961 award for outstanding ecological publication. Also wrote *A Field Guide to Animal Tracks*, 1954; *Alaska-Yukon Caribou*; *Food Habits of the Coyote in Jackson Hole, Wyoming*; *Fauna of the Aleutian Islands and Alaska Peninsula*; and *Jackson Hole with a Naturalist*, 1963. *Wapiti Wilderness* was published posthumously in 1966 with Margaret Murie as coauthor. Died October 21, 1963.

MICHAEL NADEL

Living Wilderness, Summer-Fall 1963 (no. 84).

Who Was Who in America, 1961–68.

MURPHY, ROBERT CUSHMAN
(1887–1973)
Born April 29 in Brooklyn, New York. Brown University, Ph.B. 1911, Sc.D. (honorary) 1941; Columbia University, A.M. 1918; San Marcos University (Lima, Peru), honorary doctorate 1925; Long Island University, Sc.D. (honorary) 1964. In 1911 became curator of mammals and birds at The Brooklyn Museum, and in 1917 was named head of its

Department of Natural Science. Joining staff of American Museum of Natural History in 1921 as associate curator of birds, served as assistant director, 1924–26, as curator of oceanic birds, 1924–42, as chairman of Department of Birds, 1942–54, as Lamont curator, 1949–55, and as curator emeritus and research associate thereafter. From 1940 to 1952 was president of Biological Laboratory at Cold Spring Harbor, Long Island, New York. Over period of three decades, led ornithological expeditions to foreign regions, particularly to tropical and subantarctic America. A pioneer in ecology of oceanic birds, he was consultant to several South American governments on conservation and economic aspects of bird populations. Was member of numerous scientific commissions, including Pacific Science Board and National Research Council. Awards and medals were conferred on him for his scientific contributions. Received bronze medal of John Burroughs Association in 1938; Cullum medal of American Geographical Society in 1940; Frances K. Hutchinson Medal of the Garden Club of America in 1941; and Elliott Medal of National Academy of Sciences in 1943. Was president of American Ornithologists' Union, 1948–50, having received its William Brewster memorial medal in 1937, and is honorary president of National Audubon Society. His writings are extensive, and include books *Oceanic Birds of South America*, 2 vol., 1936; *Land Birds of America* (coauthor), 1953; and *Rare and Exotic Birds*, 1964. His career has been notable for his influence on advancement of ecological knowledge about birds, especially oceanic birds, and for his investigations of economic importance of certain species. Died March 19, 1973.

National Audubon Society

American Men of Science (Physical and Biological Sciences), 11th ed., 1966.

World's Who's Who in Science, 1968.

NADEL, MICHAEL
(born 1901)
Born February 20 in Glasgow, Scotland. At College of the City of New York, he majored in literature and writing. Served for four years as member of New York State Conservation Commissioner's Advisory Committee on Fish and Game; was vice-president and board member of New York State Conservation Council and editor of its *Bulletin*; and was first vice-president of Sportsmen's Council of the Marine District of New York. For two years was contributing editor of *Game Breeder and*

Sportsman, conducting a monthly department on wildlife restortation. For ten years conducted conservation activities for urban children in voluntary program that he initiated in 1944. His major conservation activities from 1944 to 1954 were centered in preservation of wilderness of New York State's Forest Preserve. His long concern with wilderness led to his appointment in 1955 as assistant executive secretary, later assistant executive director, of The Wilderness Society in Washington, D.C.; in 1964 became editor of *The Living Wilderness* and was elected secretary of the society. Became editor emeritus in 1971, and was special consultant, 1971–79. Prepared original distribution of materials that alerted country to proposal for national wilderness preservation system, and contributed to development of Wilderness Act of 1964. In addition to his writings for various publications on conservation subjects, he contributed chapter "Scenic, Historic, and Natural Sites" for *Origins of American Conservation*, 1966, and revised chapter "Parks and Wilderness" for *America's Natural Resources*, 1967, and eight biographies to *Leader's of American Conservation*, 1971, by Natural Resources Council of America. Additional affiliations, past and present, include The Wildlife Society, American Fisheries Society, Outdoor Writers Association of America, Audubon Naturalist Society of the Central Atlantic States, The Nature Conservancy, and Thoreau Society. Received Nash Conservation Awards Program Exceptional Merit Award in 1958.

THE WILDERNESS SOCIETY
MICHAEL NADEL

NEEDHAM, JAMES GEORGE
(1868–1957)
Born March 16 in Virginia, Illinois. Knox College, B.S. and M.S.; Cornell University, Ph.D., 1898; Lake Forest University, Litt.D. (honorary) 1921, D.Sc. 1929. Awarded King Memorial Gold Medal by Peking Society of Natural History, 1930. In 1907 was appointed assistant professor of limnology (became full professor in 1911), formally establishing for first time in American university the subject of limnology as field for instruction and research. Previously had conducted investigations for State of New York on aquatic life in Adirondack mountains, the purpose of which was to develop methods for maintaining and increasing food supply of native fishes. His lifelong interest was in ecology of freshwater environment, and he made significant contribution to knowledge in three

major groups of aquatic insects: Ephemeroptera, Plecoptera, and Odonata. Three comprehensive books resulted from this special interest: *A Monograph of the Plecoptera or Stone-flies of America, North of Mexico*, 1925; *The Biology of Mayflies*, 1935; and *A Manual of the Dragonflies of North America*, 1954. Was author or coauthor of more than a dozen books and numerous popular and scientific papers. *The Life of Inland Waters*, 1915, and companion laboratory manual *A Guide to the Study of Freshwater Biology*, 1927, were indispensible texts for many early students of limnology. Two additional titles give some notion of breadth of his understanding and interest in biology and ecology of total environment: *About Ourselves*, a survey of human nature from zoological standpoint, 1941; and *The Natural History of the Farm*, a guide to practical living in wild nature, 1913. Was president of Entomological Society, 1923; a founder of Limnological Society and its second president in 1937; and vice-president of Ecological Society, 1936. Died July 24, 1957.

DWIGHT A. WEBSTER

American Men of Science, 9th ed., 1955.

NELSON, DEWITT
(born 1901)
Born January 13 in Madrid, Iowa. Iowa State College, B.S. (forestry) 1925. Joined U.S. Forest Service in California and during next nine years served as ranger on Tahoe National Forest, then assistant supervisor and supervisor of both Trinity and Shasta national forests. In 1934 became supervisor of San Bernardino National Forest, and subsequently was Forest Service liaison officer with Civilian Conservation Corps for U.S. Army's Ninth Corps Area. Between 1936 and 1944 was supervisor of Tahoe and San Bernardino forests. In 1944 was appointed California's state forester, and in 1953 director of Department of Natural Resources. In 1961 was named director of newly formed Department of Conservation, where he supervised five thousand employees and had annual budget of forty million dollars until his retirement in 1966. During 1966–67 was visiting professor of forestry at Iowa State University, and in 1968 was Regents' professor at University of California and visiting professor of forestry at Oregon State University. From 1972 to 1983 was associated with Natural Resources Management Corporation of Eureka, California. At various times was president of Society of American For-

esters (1956–57) and of National Association of State Foresters (1951); director and honorary vice-president of The American Forestry Association; member of the Secretary of Agriculture's Advisory Committee on Soil and Water Conservation; member of advisory committee to the President's Commission on Outdoor Recreation Resources Review; and chairman of Western Governors' Mining Advisory Council. Swedish Royal Academy of Science awarded him the Greater Linneaus Medal in 1954. Is a fellow of Society of American Foresters and received Sir William Schlich Memorial Medal Award in 1973.

PAUL CASAMAJOR
JAMES R. LYONS

Who's Who in America, 34th ed., 1976–77.

Who's Who in the West, 11th ed., 1968.

NELSON, GAYLORD ANTON
(born 1916)

Born June 4 in Clear Lake, Wisconsin. San Jose State College, B.S. 1939; University of Wisconsin Law School, LL.B. 1942. Was in U.S. Army wartime service for forty-six months. Practiced law in Madison, Wisconsin, 1946–48. Was elected to U.S. Senate in 1962 after serving as state senator for ten years and as governor of Wisconsin for four years. In his eighteen years in Senate (1962–80), earned reputation as staunch environmentalist. Founded Earth Day, Operation Mainstream, and Green Thumb to employ the elderly in conservation projects. Was sponsor of 1964 Wilderness Act, and coauthor of National Hiking Trails System Act, and of legislation establishing Apostle Islands National Lakeshore, the Upper Great Lakes Regional Commission, and Saint Croix Wild and Scenic River. Introduced legislation in Congress to control strip-mining; protect and complete acquisition of Appalachian Trail; and ban use of DDT, of 2–4–5T (agent orange), and of phosphates in detergents. Has been chairman of The Wilderness Society since 1981, and has received many awards and honors.

THE WILDERNESS SOCIETY

Who's Who in America, 42d ed., 1982–83.

NELSON, JESSE W.
(1874–1958)
Born April 28 in rural Indiana. After three years of business college, his first employment was on Colonel William F. Cody's horse ranch in Wyoming and as participant in Cody's Wild West Show. Appointed ranger of Yellowstone Park Timber Reserve, U.S. Department of the Interior, in 1901, was thus one of first men to join in protection and administration of public lands that were forerunner of national forests. Occupied successively positions of ranger and forest supervisor in Wyoming; chief of grazing, Rocky Mountain Region in Denver; inspector of grazing, Washington, D.C. office; and for fourteen years, chief of Division of Range and Wildlife Management in California Region. His final assignment was as superintendent of newly established San Joaquin Experimental Range in California, from which he retired in 1941 after forty-one years of government service. One of early leaders in administration of public lands, he was a man of integrity with sense of fairness and desire to work for welfare of both resources and local people. His personal characteristics made it possible for him to deal with grazing and other users of public land who had history of opposition to regulation and management of their activities on timber reserves and national forests. That few of his many decisions were appealed to higher authority was proof of his ability to gain confidence of users in his lifelong objective of sound wildland administration. Although not technically trained, he had appreciation of scientific methods. As keen judge of people, he sought out promising young professionals and helped advance their careers. Died April 15, 1958.

LLOYD W. SWIFT.

Talbot, M. W. "Buffalo Bill's Top Hand." *American Forests Magazine*, vol. 66, May 1960.

NEWELL, FREDERICK HAYNES
(1862–1932)
Born March 5 in Bradford, Pennsylvania. Massachusetts Institute of Technology, B.Sc. (mining engineering) 1885. Joined Geological Survey, U.S. Department of the Interior, in 1888 as hydraulic engineer; became hydrographer in 1890 and for next decade made surveys for irrigation projects in arid West. On passage of Reclamation Act in 1902, was made chief (reclamation) engineer in Geological Survey, and when Reclamation

Service (now Bureau of Reclamation) became independent bureau in 1907, was named its director, serving until 1964. After being head of Department of Civil Engineering at University of Illinois, 1915–19, was founding president of Research Service, an organization of engineering consultants. Helped organize American Society of Civil Engineers (president in 1919), and was secretary of National Geographic Society. Was influential in conservation affairs; appointed to U.S. Public Land Commission in 1903, participated in report to President Theodore Roosevelt that helped bring about transfer of forest reserves from U.S. Department of the Interior to U.S. Department of Agriculture, making possible their subsequent administration as national forests by Forest Service. As member of Inland Waterways Commission, proposed that President Roosevelt call nationwide meeting on natural resources that resulted in historic White House Conference of Governors in May 1908. Among his books were *Hydrography of Arid Regions*, 1891; *Agriculture by Irrigation*, 1894; *The Public Lands of the United States and Their Water Supply*, 1895; *Irrigation in the United States*, 1902; and *Water Resources, Present and Future Uses*, 1919. For his contributions he was awarded Cullum Gold Medal by American Geographical Society. Died July 5, 1932.

HENRY CLEPPER

Dictionary of American Biography, 1934.

Who Was Who in America, 1897–1942.

NOONAN, PATRICK FRANCIS
(born 1942)
Born December 2 in Saint Petersburg, Florida. Gettysburg College, B.A., 1965; Catholic University, M.A. (city and regional planning) 1967; American University, M.A. (business administration) 1971. His career in land conservation began in 1965 when he was hired as park planner by Maryland-National Capital Park and Planning Commission. In 1969 joined The Nature Conservancy as vice-president and director of operations, and directed initiation, negotiation, and purchase of all conservancy's land acquisitions, doubling level of activity from one hundred acquisitions a year in 1969 to two hundred a year in 1973, when he was appointed president. During his eight-year tenure through 1981, the conservancy established 25 state Natural Heritage Programs, acquired more than 2,000 parcels of land, valued in excess of $500 million, and established largest private sanctuary system in the world, encompassing some

700 nature preserves. A balanced development program was established, including new 30-member corporate advisory committee, with more than 300 corporate supporters by 1980, and successful direction of $20 million Land Conservation Revolving Fund campaign, which exceeded its goal by raising more than $40 million. Received American Motors Award for his distinguished contributions to conservation, 1974; Horace Albright Medal for his services to field of land conservation, 1977; and special award from the secretary of the Interior, for his professional work in land conservation, 1980. Is member of board of advisors of School of Forestry and Environmental Studies at Duke University; trustee of Student Conservation Association; and member of Appalachian Trail Advisory Committee to U.S. Department of the Interior. In 1980 founded American Farmland Trust, an expanding nonprofit organization focusing on preservation of farmland and plight of family farm in America, and serves as chairman of the trust's National Advisory Board. In 1983 received Conservation Award of Natural Resources Council of America for his service to land conservation in America.

PATRICK F. NOONAN

Who's Who in America, 42d ed., 1981–83

NORINE, JAMES MELVIN
(born 1939)
Born December 31 in Cokato, Minnesota. St. Cloud State University, B.S. (biology and physical education) 1963. Taught biology and physical and outdoor education, 1963–76. Also coached basketball, football, and golf, and was actively involved as volunteer instructor of hunter safety and shooting sports, in which he is still active. Served in U.S. Marine Corps Reserve for six years. Next joined staff of National Rifle Association's Competitions Division, and became Manager of their Hunter Education Department, 1976–78; has been director of Hunter Services Division since 1978. Is life member of National Rifle Association and holds memberships in several other hunting and wildlife organizations. Is secretary of National Rifle Association's Hunting and Wildlife Conservation Committee and chairman of Shooting Sports Safety Committee for National Safety Council. Is active hunter who has hunted throughout most of United States and the Canadian provinces.

NATIONAL RIFLE ASSOCIATION OF AMERICA

OBERHOLTZER, ERNEST C.
(1884–1977)
Born 1884 in Davenport, Iowa. Harvard College, B.A. 1907, graduate studies in landscape architecture; Northern Michigan University of Marquette, L.H.D. (honorary). Beginning in 1908 has made many canoe explorations in Canadian wilderness, from Rainy Lake watershed of Minnesota and Ontario to Barren Lands of Northwest Canada. His studies of geography, wildlife, and Indians were presented in numerous lectures and articles. In 1926 fought proposal for series of dams that would have damaged water level of lakes along international boundary from Rainy Lake to Pigeon River, thus destroying beauty of canoe country. Battle resulted in formation of Quetico-Superior Council of which he became president in 1927 and which, supported by conservation groups, was dedicated to conservation of forests, wildlife, and related natural resources of Minnesota-Ontario border lakeland. In 1934 President Franklin D. Roosevelt appointed President's Quetico-Superior Committee of five members; Oberholtzer became executive secretary. Helped bring about passage of Shipstead-Newton-Nolan Act as well as air-space reservation over roadless area of Superior National Forest, now the well-known Boundary Waters Canoe Area. Authored many articles on scientific and recreational aspects of the area. As one of founders of Wilderness Society, was member of its governing council from its inception in 1935 to 1968, and since then has been honorary vice-president. Among his honors was U.S. Department of the Interior's Conservation Award in 1967. Died June 6, 1977.

MICHAEL NADEL

Minneapolis Tribune, April 28, 1967.

Wilderness Society, biographical files.

ODUM, EUGENE PLEASANTS
(born 1913)
Born September 17 in Newport, New Hampshire. University of North Carolina, B.A. 1934, A.M. 1936; University of Illinois, Ph.D. 1939. Began his professional career as instructor at Western Reserve University in Cleveland, 1936–37, and following doctoral studies, became first resident biologist at Edmund Niles Huyck Preserve (subsequently Institute of Man and Science) at Rennselaerville, New York, 1939–40. In 1940 went to University of Georgia as instructor in zoology. Currently is di-

rector of University of Georgia's Institute of Ecology. Played major role in establishment in 1954 of University of Georgia's Marine Institute at Sapelo Island. A pioneer in the field of radiation ecology, he was selected in 1955 as delegate to first Atoms-for-Peace Conference in Geneva. Was appointed University of Georgia Alumni Foundation distinguished professor in zoology in 1957, and Callaway Foundation professor of ecology in 1972. In 1957–58 was awarded National Science Foundation senior postdoctoral fellowship for year's study and research in western United States and at Oxford, England. In 1962 was appointed chief scientist, Special Training Division, Oak Ridge Associated Universities. Serves or has served in advisory capacity to National Science Foundation, Oak Ridge National Health Laboratory, U.S. Fish and Wildlife Service, National Academy of Sciences, U.S. Office of Technology Assessment, governing board of the American Institute of Biological Sciences, boards of trustees of The Nature Conservancy and The Conservation Foundation, and on U.S. Department of Energy's Environmental Advisory Committee. Among his numerous awards are Georgia Scientist of the Year, 1968; Mercer Award, 1956; "Eminent Ecologist" award from Ecological Society of America, 1974; (jointly with his brother Howard T. Odum) French L'Institut de La Vie, 1975; Tyler Ecology Award, 1977; Distinguished Service Award from American Institute of Biological Sciences, 1978; and Meritorious Teaching Award from Association of Southeastern Biologists, 1978. Has been elected to National Academy of Sciences, American Academy of Arts and Sciences (fellow), American Association for the Advancement of Science, American Ornithologists' Union, and Wilson Ornithologists' Union. In addition to numerous scholarly papers, authored *Fundamentals of Ecology*, 1953, and *Ecology*, 1962, both of which have undergone subsequent editions and remain landmark texts. Has been visiting lecturer at numerous major universities in United States and abroad and, as one of country's foremost ecologists, is in great demand as advisor, speaker, and author.

Sydney Johnson
Richard E. McCabe

American Men and Women of Science (Physical and Biological Sciences), 15th ed., 1982.

Who's Who in America, 40th ed., 1978–79.

OLMSTED, FREDERICK ERSKINE
(1872–1925)
Born November 8 in Hartford, Connecticut. Graduated from Sheffield
Scientific School of Yale University in 1894 and entered U.S. Geological
Survey. While on field work with Survey, met Gifford Pinchot, who inspired him to seek further training in field of forestry. Following this
advice, studied under Sir Dietrich Brandeis in Germany and India during
1899 and 1900, returning to join Pinchot as agent in U.S. Division of
Forestry on July 1, 1900. Between 1902 and 1905 directed important
work of locating boundaries of vast areas of public forestlands, which
became present system of national forests, and was made assistant forester in 1903. After Transfer Act of 1905, his first work in newly created
Forest Service was to develop effective inspection system, of which he
became chief inspector in 1906. There began fight for decentralized administration, and when western inspection districts were created he became chief inspector of the California District in 1907. The following
year, was made first district forester in California, and during following
three years he brought new district to high state of efficiency. Wishing to
be closer to woods and in position to promote good forest management
by private timber owners, resigned from Forest Service in June 1911 and
joined Fisher and Bryant in firm of consulting foresters in Boston, Massachusetts. In 1914 opened office as consulting forester in San Francisco,
where he organized and became directing head of Tamalpais Fir Protective Association in Marin County, one of first of such districts for watershed protection. Was also employed as forester by Diamond Match Company to introduce conservative cutting and good management of its
forest areas in California. Was dedicated member of Society of American
Foresters, serving as president in 1919. During his later years wrote
many articles promoting effective fire protection and good forest management on all forestlands in United Sates.

WOODBRIDGE METCALF

Journal of Forestry. Obituary, 23:337–39, April 1925.

OLMSTED, FREDERICK LAW, SR.
(1822–1903)
Born April 26 in Hartford, Connecticut. Yale University, honorary member class of 1847, LL.D. 1893; Amherst College, A.M. 1867; Harvard
University, LL.D. 1893. Is considered principal founder of landscape ar-

chitecture in United States; spent his early years in farming, a nursery business, and active participation promoting creation of parks as playgrounds for nation. Was driving force behind establishment and layout of Central Park in New York City, and was appointed superintendent of the park in 1857. Was secretary of U.S. Sanitary Commission, 1861–63, and upon his resignation founded Urban League Club to carry out his work. After Civil War, traveled to California, where he became first Commissioner of Yosemite State Park. There formulated enduring conservation and park-use policies. Engaged in landscape planning for University of California, Johns Hopkins, Stanford, Amherst, Trinity, West Point, Yale, Smith, and Harvard. Helped plan Arnold Arboretum and worked on George W. Vanderbilt's Biltmore estate near Asheville, North Carolina. Designed public parks for New York City, Brooklyn, Boston, Trenton, and other cities, including Capitol grounds and terraces and World's Fair in Chicago (1893). Created nation's first planned garden suburb in Riverside, Chicago. Was authoritative writer on landscaping and park planning, and had editorial interest in magazine *Garden and Forest*. As most notable landscape designer of his era, had national influence on development of parks and beautification of urban environment. Died August 28, 1903.

Mary DiGiulian

Dictionary of American Biography, 1934.

Milde, Gordon T., and Wenmayr, V. Michael. *Frederick Law Olmsted, Sr.* Amherst, Mass.: University of Massachusetts Press, 1968.

Who Was Who in America, 1897–1942.

Olson, Sigurd Ferdinand

(1899–1982)

Born April 4 in Chicago, Illinois. Served in U.S. Army, 1918. University of Wisconsin, B.S. 1923; University of Illinois, M.S. (biology) 1931; Hamline University, LHD (honorary) 1961; Northland College, D.Sc. (honorary) 1961; Macalester College, D.Sc. (honorary) 1963; University of Minnesota, LHD (honorary) 1979; Beloit College, D.Sc. (honorary) 1979. Was head of biology department, 1922–35, and dean, 1935–45, at Ely (Minnesota) Junior College; and instructor in zoology at U.S. Army University, England, 1945. Was lecturer for U.S. Army in Germany, Italy, France, and Austria, 1946; consultant to Izaak Walton League of America, 1947–82; and lecturer and free-lance writer urging wilderness preservation in United States, 1947–82. Also was consultant to President's Quetico-Superior Committee, 1947; member of National Advisory Board of Parks, Monuments, and Historic Sites, 1950; and president of National Parks Association, 1953–58. Served The Wilderness Society as member of its council in 1956, as vice-president in 1963–68, and as president in 1967–71; was member of secretary of U.S. Department of the Interior's Advisory Committee on Conservation, 1960–66; and consultant to director of National Park Service, 1962. Authored *The Singing Wilderness*, 1956; *Listening Point*, 1958; *The Lonely Land*, 1961; *Runes of the North*, 1963; *The Hidden Forest* (with L. Blacklock), 1969; *Open Horizons*, 1969; *Wilderness Days*, 1972; *Reflections from the North Country*, 1976; and *Of Time and Place*, 1982. Was elected to Izaak Walton League Hall of Fame in 1963. Sigurd Olson Environmental Institute was founded at Northland College in 1972, and the building was dedicated to him in 1981. Received Medal of The John Burroughs Memorial Association in 1974; Robert Marshall Award of The Wilderness Society in 1981; and numerous additional honors, including Frances K. Hutchinson Medal of The Garden Club of America; Horace Marden Albright Scenic Preservation Medal of the American Scenic and Historic Preservation Society; John Muir Award of the Sierra Club; and was elected fellow of Association of Interpretive Naturalists. Died January 13, 1982, in Ely, Minnesota.

STEVEN SORENSEN

American Men and Women of Science (Physical and Biological Sciences), 12th ed. (vol. 4), 1972.

Who's Who in America, 40th ed., 1978–79.

ORDWAY, SAMUEL HANSON, JR.
(1900–1971)
Born January 20 in New York City. Harvard University B.A. 1921, LL.B. 1924. Was admitted to New York State bar in 1925. From 1937 to 1939 was member of U.S. Civil Service Commission, and during 1940–41 was president of National Roster of Scientific and Professional Personnel. Has served as trustee for Association for Protection of the Adirondacks since 1935 and as treasurer for two years. Became vice-president of The Conservative Foundation in 1949, also serving as executive vice-president, 1948–61; president, 1961–65; trustee beginning in 1962; and chairman of board of trustees from 1969 until his death. Was trustee of

Open Space Action Committee, and of American Conservation Association. Was chairman of Natural Resources Council of America in 1954. In 1964 became co-chairman of board of governors of Pinchot Institute for Conservation Studies. For two terms, was member of Secretary of the Interior's Advisory Committee on Conservation. Was author of numerous reports and articles, including Alaska Program Analysis for U.S. Department of the Interior; also wrote books *A Conservation Handbook, Resources and the American Dream,* and *Prosperity Beyond Tomorrow.* Died December 29, 1971.

THE CONSERVATION FOUNDATION

Who's Who in America, vol. 35, 1968–69.

ORELL, BERNARD LEO
(1914–1983)
Born January 26 in Portland, Oregon. Oregon State University, B.S. (forestry) 1939, B.S. (education) and M.F. 1941; Dakota Wesleyan University, Doc. Bus. Admin. (honorary) 1963. Was training officer, 1941–42, and protection inspector, 1946–47, for Oregon State Forestry Department. Served in U.S. Army, 1942–46. Was assistant professor of forestry at University of Washington College of Forestry, 1947–49, and state forester of Washington, 1949–53. Joined Weyerhaeuser Company in Saint Paul, Minnesota, in 1953 as vice-president, handling public and industry relations. Transferred to Tacoma, Washington, in 1958 to direct and coordinate resource relations and public-affairs activities of Weyerhaeuser Company and its subsidiaries. In 1959 was elected a fellow of Society of American Foresters. Was president of Forest History Society, director of National Recreation Association and of American Forestry Association, and member of executive committee of National Association of Manufacturers. During his presidency of American Forest Products Industries, Inc., 1964–67, initiated its transition to American Forest Institute, and served on that organization's board of directors and executive committee. Was member of President's Outdoor Recreation Resources Review Commission, 1959–64, and of advisory council to Public Land Law Review Commission. Was chairman of Forest Industries Council; member of Forestry Affairs Committee; and chairman of Forest Management Committee of the National Forest Products Association. Received 1968

Industry Statesmanship Award from that organization. Died May 5, 1983.

WILSON B. SAYERS

Who's Who in America, 42d ed., 1982–83.

OSBORN, FAIRFIELD
(1887–1969)
Born January 15 in Princeton, New Jersey. Princeton University, A.B. 1909–10; New York University, D.Sc. 1955, Kenyon College, LL.D. 1959; University of Buffalo, D.Sc. 1962; Hofstra University, LL.D. 1966. Became member of board of trustees and of executive committee of New York Zoological Society in 1923, served as secretary for four years, and in 1940 became president and chairman of board. After World War II, took lead in organizing The Conservation Foundation and in 1948 became its first president, serving until 1962, when he became chairman of board. Was awarded Medal of Honor from Theodore Roosevelt Memorial Association in 1949, and Frances K. Hutchinson Medal of The Garden Club of America in 1952. The Institute Océanographique of France presented him Prix Manley Bendall in 1957. Three years later, received Medal of Honor of the City of New York. Awards were followed by Louis Bromfield Memorial Medal in 1963 from Friends of the Land; and Gold Medal of the New York Zoological Society and First Conservation Medal of San Diego Zoological Society, both in 1966. Was chosen honorary vice-president of Fauna Preservation Society in London and of The American Forestry Association. In 1952 was member of Secretary of the Interior's Advisory Committee on Conservation. Was a foreign fellow of Zoological Society of London and a fellow of New York Academy of Sciences. Also was member of American Committee of International Council of Museums, Council of Save-the-Redwoods League, and International Committee for Bird Preservation. Was author of *Our Plundered Planet*, 1948, for which he received the Gutenberg Award and National Award; is known also for his book *Limits of the Earth*, 1953. Was editor of *The Pacific World*, 1944, and of *Our Crowded Planet*, 1962. Died September 16, 1969.

THE CONSERVATION FOUNDATION

Who's Who in America, 1968–69.

OWINGS, MARGARET WENTWORTH
(born 1913)

Born March 29 in Berkeley, California. Mills College, B.A. 1934; Radcliffe College, postgraduate work, 1935. Solo exhibitions of her paintings have been held at Santa Barbara Museum of Art; Sanford University Museum and Art Gallery; The Fine Arts Museums of San Francisco; and Museum of International Folk Art, Museum of New Mexico, in Santa Fe. From 1963 to 1969 was commissioner of California State Parks Commission, and from 1964 to 1967 led successful opposition by California State Parks Commission to construction of freeway through Pacific Creek Redwoods State Park, site of the world's tallest trees. Was first woman to be board member of African Wildlife Leadership Foundation from 1969 to 1980; board member of Defenders of Wildlife from 1969 to 1974; regional trustee of Mills College from 1962 to 1968; and has been trustee of Environmental Defense Fund since 1972. In 1964 received citation from National Audubon Society for her work toward getting bounty removed from California mountain lion. Conceived, organized, and launched in 1967 the Rachel Carson Memorial Fund of National Audubon Society (now administered by Environmental Defense Fund). In 1969 founded and currently is president of four-thousand-member organization, Friends of the Sea Otter. Contributed to Sierra Club book in 1965, and wrote article "They're Still Shooting the Tule Elk" for September 1965 issue of *Audubon* magazine; "Perils of the Southern Sea Otter" for Spring 1981 issue of *Humane Society News*; and "The Southern Sea Otter" for November 1980 issue of *Monterey Life*. Received Conservation Service Award of U.S. Department of the Interior, 1979; Directors Conservation Award of California Academy of Sciences, 1979; American Motors Conservation Award for Nonprofessionals, 1980; Joseph Wood Krutch Gold Medal of the Humane Society, 1980; and Audubon Medal, 1983.

Who's Who in America, 42d ed., 1982–83.

PACK, CHARLES LATHROP
(1857–1937)

Born May 7 in Lexington, Michigan. Brooks School, Cleveland; Trinity College, LL.D. 1918; Syracuse University, Dr. Bus. Adm. 1925; Oberlin College, LL.D. 1926; Rutgers University, Sc.D. 1930. Attended The White House Conference of Governors in 1908 as forester advisor. President Theodore Roosevelt appointed him member of National Conservation Commission, 1908. Was president of The American Forestry Association, 1916–20; of National Conservation Congress, 1913; and of American Nature Association, 1922. Was awarded *Ordre Merite Agricole* in France, 1919. After World War I, was active in reforestation of England, France, and Italy. With his son, Arthur Newton Pack, organized American Tree Association in 1922, serving as its president until 1937. Founded Charles Lathrop Pack Forestry Foundation in 1930, then the only privately endowed foundation dedicated to forestry; its purpose was to promote scientific and professional management of forests through scientific publications, granting of individual fellowships for advanced training, and program of specific large-scale projects. Created demonstration forests at Yale, Cornell, Washington, and Michigan universities and New York State College of Forestry at Syracuse to show possibilities of forest management. Endowed professional chairs of forestry at four colleges. Provided numerous scholarships in forestry and endowed twelve colleges with funds to award annual prizes for essays and articles on forestry. As pioneer in forestry education, established, within his forestry foundation, the Pack Education Board, which granted awards for specific studies in conservation in United States and abroad. In 1908, with Gifford Pinchot, helped form National Conservation Foundation, which emphasized concept of conservation through judicious use of timberlands. Established foundations at Yale and at University of Michigan. In 1923 founded and published *Forestry News Digest*. Was author of *Schoolbook of Forestry*, 1922; *Trees as Good Citizens*, 1923; *Forestry Primer*, 1926; and, both with Tom Gill, *Forestry and Mankind*, 1929, and *Forest Facts for Schools*, 1931. Died June 14, 1937.

TOM GILL

Butler, Ovid. "Foundation for the Forest." *American Forests*, 1948.

Dictionary of American Biography, vol. 22, supp. 2.,

Evans, Mary, comp. *Biological References*. University of Illinois Library School.

Gill, Tom. "Charles Lathrop Pack." *Journal of Forestry*, 35:622–23, 1937.

Who Was Who in America, 1897–1942.

PACK, RANDOLPH GREENE
(1890–1956)
Born June 8 in Cleveland, Ohio. Williams College, 1909–11; attended

Pennsylvania State College as special forestry student; University of Michigan, D.Sc. (honorary) 1953. His positions have been director, Friends of the Land and New England Forest Foundation; member of American Citizens Committee and Utilization of Resources; honorary member, Society of American Foresters; vice-president, American Nature Association and The American Forestry Association; and director and member of executive board of The Conservation Foundation. Became president of Charles Lathrop Pack Forestry Foundation in 1937, a position he held until his death. During that time, initiated a number of important studies and concentrated efforts of the foundation on specific fields of forestry. At his direction, the foundation published a number of research findings which, through lack of federal appropriations, might otherwise have been delayed for years. Authorized publication and wide distribution of report of Forestry Committee of U.N. Food and Agriculture Organization. Extended activities of Pack foundation beyond United States through studies of tropical timber resources of Caribbean. Under his authorization, the foundation created and for a number of years supported Mexican Institute of Renewable Natural Resources. In recognition of his international contributions, U.S. government invited him to take part in three international conferences. In 1950, initiated project to provide scholarships in School of Public Administration at Harvard, to enable federal and state government conservation workers to study lag between knowledge and performance in entire field of conservation. Died December 25, 1956.

TOM GILL

Butler, Ovid. "A Foundation for the Forest." *American Forests*, 1948.

Gill, Tom. *Ten Years of Fact-Finding*. Charles Lathrop Pack Forestry Foundation.

Pack Foundation. Charles Lathrop Pack Forestry Foundation.

Who Was Who in America, 1951–60.

PALMER, EPHRAIM LAURENCE
(1888–1970)
Born July 8 in McGraw, New York. Cornell University, M.A. 1911, Ph.D. 1917. Taught botany and natural sciences at Iowa State Teachers College, 1913–19. Joined faculty of Cornell University in 1919, and until his retirement in 1952 was involved heavily in nature and conservation education, directed many graduate students, and had profound influence

on science education. A prolific writer, he wrote quarterly *Cornell Rural School Leaflets*, 1919–52; wrote six articles a year and served as nature editor for *Nature* magazine, 1925–59; was contributing editor to *Natural History* magazine, 1960–62; and wrote many other articles for numerous journals and publications. His *Fieldbook of Natural History* is considered a classic. Was consultant in nature education to National Wildlife Federation, 1950–57, and contributed in many ways to other national organizations, including Boy Scouts of America; American Nature Study Society (president, 1936–37); Ecological Society of America; National Council of Nature Study Supervisors of Department of Science Education of the National Education Association; National Association of Biology Teachers (president, 1947); National Audubon Society (director, 1943–49); International Union for the Conservation of Nature and Natural Resources (received its Hornaday Gold Medal, 1961); and National Committee on Policies in Conservation Education. Received Nash Conversation Award, 1954. Throughout his long and productive professional career, he was instrumental in education of many present-day conservation educators, and in this his influence on conservation education in United States will be felt for many years to come. Died December 18, 1970.

WILSON F. CLARK

PARENTEAU, PATRICK ALOYSIUS
(born 1947)
Born May 7 in Omaha, Nebraska. Regis College, B.S. 1969; Creighton University School of Law, J.D. 1972; George Washington University, National Law Center, L.L.M. (environmental law) 1975. As staff attorney and intern coordinator at Legal Aid Society of Omaha, Nebraska, 1972–74, conducted trial and appellate practice before state and federal courts, and specialized in civil, consumer, and welfare rights, and housing law. In 1975–76 was Natural Resources Law Institute teaching fellow at Northwestern School of Law, Lewis and Clark College, specializing in water resources law. In 1976 joined staff of National Wildlife Federation as counsel (in trial and appellate practice) in environmental issues, drafting testimony and legislation, preparing rule-making petitions and comments, and policy analysis. In 1978–80 taught classes in natural resources law at American University, George Washington University, and Georgetown University. Conducted wildlife law seminar (summer ses-

sions) at Vermont Law School in 1981 and at Northwestern School of Law and Lewis and Clark College in 1982. Became director of Resources Defense Division for National Wildlife Federation in 1979, consolidating that organization's legal, legislative, and research functions into coordinated advocacy program. In 1981 became vice-president for resources conservation for the federation, managing the federation's interdisciplinary teams of scientists, attorneys, lobbyists, and resource specialists working on wide range of domestic and international environmental issues. Also develops and implements national conservation policy through congressional initiatives, law-reform litigation, federal administrative rule-makings, and public participation projects, and administers a network of five regional natural resource centers.

Louis S. Clapper

PARKER, LANSING ARTHUR
(1912–1965)
Born June 17 in Minneapolis, Minnesota. University of Minnesota School of Forestry, B.S. 1935. Began career in 1935 as project forester in U.S. Soil Conservation Service in Minnesota, and from 1938 to 1944 was area biologist. In 1945 joined U.S. Fish and Wildlife Service, and served first in Division of Federal Aid—the unit that administers federal funds made available to states for cooperative programs in restoration of wildlife resources—and in 1948 was advanced to assistant chief of the division. In 1957 was appointed assistant director in charge of all cooperative services, and in 1963 was made associate director. From 1960 to 1965 was associate editor for forest wildlife management and recreation of *Journal of Forestry*. Was charter member of The Wildlife Society and honorary member of International Wild Waterfowl Association. In 1966 U.S. Department of the Interior posthumously conferred on him its highest honor, the Distinguished Service Award, "in recognition of an admirable and public-spirited career." Died October 25, 1965.

Henry Clepper

PARTAIN, LLOYD ELMER
(born 1906)
Born February 3 in Waldron, Arkansas. Oklahoma A&M College, School of Agriculture, B.S. (agricultural education) 1931. From 1928 to

1935 was high-school teacher and instructor at Oklahoma State University. Joined U.S. Soil Conservation Service in 1935 as information officer and assistant state coordinator in Oklahoma; became extension soil conservationist in States Relations Division, Washington, D.C., 1937–42. Then transferred to War Savings Division of the Treasury Department, and in 1943 joined Curtis Publishing Company in Philadelphia, where he served variously during next two decades in editorial, sales, marketing, and research assignments. In 1962 returned to Soil Conservation Service, where he was assistant to administrator for environmental development. Is past president (1949–50), and a fellow of Soil Conservation Society of America, and past-president (1956–62) of Pennsylvania Forestry Association. Was director and vice-president of The American Forestry Association; and member of board of directors of National Audubon Society. From 1958 to 1962 was member of advisory council for the Outdoor Recreation Resources Review Commission, and served on Commission on Education in Agriculture and Natural Resources for the National Research Council–National Academy of Sciences. Since 1953 has been member of National Council and Conservation Committee for Boy Scouts of America. Long prominent as conservation lecturer and writer, he has been interpreter of relationships of business, industry, and natural resources, and exponent of outdoor recreation, natural beauty, and quality of environment.

HENRY CLEPPER

PEARSON, GUSTAF ADOLPH
(1880–1949)
Born November 14 in Holdredge, Nebraska. University of Nebraska, M.A. (botany and forestry) 1907. Became forest assistant, U.S. Forest Service, 1907, and was in charge of Fort Valley Forest Experiment Station, Flagstaff, Arizona, 1909–29. Was director of the service's Southwestern Forest and Range Experiment Station, 1930–35, then relinquished directorship in 1935 and, as senior silviculturist, took over management and development of Fort Valley Experimental Forest. Retired in 1944, but continued as Forest Service collaborator. His research in reforestation, forest meteorology, forest ecology, and silviculture brought about development and adoption of procedures used in management of *Pinus ponderosa* that are materially increasing productivity of this valuable species. Was trustee of Northern Arizona Society of Science

and Art; and a fellow of American Association for the Advancement of Science and of Society of American Foresters. Was author of *Natural Reproduction of Western Yellow Pine*, 1923; *Forest Types in the Southwest as Determined by Climate and Soil*, 1931; *Timber Growing and Logging Practice* (with R. E. Marsh), 1935; and *Forest Land Use*, 1940; also was author of government bulletins and contributions to technical journals. Received 1944 award of Society of American Foresters for best article on forestry. Died January 31, 1949.

J. H. Allison

Who Was Who in America, 1943–50.

PEARSON, THOMAS GILBERT
(1873–1943)

Born November 10 in Tuscola, Illinois. Guilford College, B.S. 1897; University of North Carolina, B.S. 1899, LL.D. 1924; graduate study at Harvard University. While teaching biology at Guilford College, 1899–1901, and at North Carolina State Normal and Industrial College for Women, 1901–4, became alarmed at widespread slaughter of birds and game animals, which were then without legal protection. In 1902 organized and incorporated Audubon Society of North Carolina, which was granted authority of state law-enforcement agency, and as secretary of the society functioned as state game commissioner, 1903–10. Became secretary of National Association of Audubon Societies (later renamed National Audubon Society) when it was organized in 1905. Was appointed its executive officer in 1910, was president from 1922 to 1934, and was president emeritus thereafter, retiring officially in 1942. Is credited with development of National Audubon Society into one of nation's largest and most influential bodies devoted to conservation of wildlife and all resources. For years, was author of much of educational material distributed by the society. In 1922 founded International Committee for Bird Preservation and was its chairman until 1938. Was also founder and chairman of National Committee on Wildlife Legislation; member of advisory board on Migratory Bird Treaty Act for twenty years; national director of Izaak Walton League of America; and official collaborator of U.S. National Park Service and U.S. Fish and Wildlife Service. Received decorations for his international activities in bird conservation from Luxembourg in 1925 and from France in 1937; and was awarded John

Burroughs medal in 1939 for his contributions to American conservation. Wrote numerous articles on ornithological and conservation subjects for scientific and popular magazines, and was author of several books, including *Stories of Bird Life*, 1901; *The Bird Study Book*, 1917; and *Adventures in Bird Protection*, an autobiography, 1937. In addition, was editor-in-chief of *Birds of America*, 3 vols. 1917, and was coeditor of *The Book of Birds*, 1937. Died September 3, 1943.

NATIONAL AUDUBON SOCIETY

Audubon, 45:26–29 and 45:370–71, 1943.

National Cyclopaedia of American Biography, 1947.

Who Was Who in America, 1943–50.

PECHANEC, JOSEPH FRANK
(born 1910)
Born March 10 in Nampa, Idaho. University of Idaho, B.S. (forestry) 1932, D.Sci. (honorary) 1969. Was employed in U.S. Forest Service from 1933 until retiring in 1971. Was in Forest Service from 1933 until retiring in 1971. Was in charge of spring-fall range research program of Intermountain Forest and Range Experiment Station at U.S. Sheep Experiment Station, Dubois, Idaho, 1933–45. Directed livestock range and big-game habitat research for Forest Service in Washington and Oregon, 1945–53, and was chief, Division of Range Management Research, Washington, D.C., 1953–56. Was director of Southeastern Forest Experiment Station, Asheville, North Carolina, 1956–62, and of Intermountain Forest and Range Experiment Station, Ogden, Utah, 1962–71. Served as member of U.N. team in Somalia, East Africa, to investigate industrial and agricultural resources of the country and outline program to help prepare Somalia for its independence in 1951. Was member of four-person team evaluating range forage technical assistance programs in Middle and Near East for Foreign Operations Administration (FAO) for four months in 1954. In that same year, served as chairman of FAO Technical Meeting on Forest Grazing in Rome. Spent three months in Iran with International Executive Service Corporation to review organization and programs of Iran's Institute of Forest and Range Research in 1973. Has authored more than sixty publications resulting from his research in ecology and range management. Was a founder and first president of Society for Range Management in which he is a fellow and life

member. Received Superior Service award from U.S. Department of Agriculture in 1967.

WILLIAM D. HURST

PEECHATKA, WALTER NORMAN
(born 1939)

Born September 3 in East Stroudsburg, Pennsylvania. Pennsylvania State University, B.S. (forestry) 1961. Began his career in October 1961 with Pennsylvania Department of Forests and Waters as service forester; also provided technical forestry assistance in two different four-county areas through 1966 (except for two years' interim military service). In 1967 was named assistant supervisor of the department's cooperative forest-management program overseeing work of thirty-five service foresters and land-treatment programs carried out as part of P.L. 566 and P.L. 534 projects. In 1969 joined Pennsylvania Department of Agriculture's Soil and Water Conservation Commission as program specialist for watershed development, and worked closely with U.S. Geological Survey in research program on water pollution resulting from soil erosion on highway construction sites. In 1971 was named acting director of Pennsylvania Soil and Water Conservation Commission, then director of Bureau of Soil and Water Conservation within reorganized Pennsylvania Department of Environmental Resources. In this capacity, helped to create innovative cost-sharing program that supported hiring of district staff for soil and water conservation. Was also charged with administering the state's pioneering legislation in soil erosion and sediment control. In 1982 became executive vice-president of Soil Conservation Society of America, and received the society's Presidential Citation in 1983. Was president of National Association of State Soil Conservation Administrative Officers and of Pennsylvania Forestry Association. Currently serves as member of executive committee for National Conservation Tillage Information Center and of advisory committee for American Farmland Trust's Soil Conservation Project.

MAXWELL SCHNEPF

PENFOLD, JOSEPH WELLER
(1907–1973)

Born November 18 in Marinette, Wisconsin. Yale University, 1926–30;

University of Denver, 1942–45. Was variously employed from 1930 to 1933 in farming, logging, and the merchant marine; in 1933 was appointed supervisor of federal relief programs in Tennessee; and in 1935 became conservation director of National Youth Administration in Ohio. During World War II was executive officer for Office of Price Administration at Denver, Colorado, and during 1945–48 was field representative for U.N. Relief and Rehabilitation Administration in China. His professional career in conservation began in 1949, when he was named western representative of Izaak Walton League of America in Denver. From 1957 until his death, was the league's conservation director in Washington, D.C. Among his outstanding services to conservation, one is especially significant because of its multiple effects: he conceived and drafted the legislation, enacted by Congress in 1958, that created Outdoor Recreation Resources Review Commission, and served on the commission by presidential appointment. The commission's report in 1962 led to establishment of Bureau of Outdoor Recreation in U.S. Department of the Interior and the Land and Water Conservation Fund. It also influenced creation of Recreation Advisory Council, and President's Advisory Committee on Recreation and Natural Beauty. Long an officer of Natural Resources Council of America, he was its secretary, 1957–65, vice-chairman in 1966, and chairman, 1967–69. Was advisor to U.S. Department of the Interior in development of National Fisheries Center and Aquarium, and member of master-plan team for Yellowstone and Teton national parks. For two decades was one of America's most respected and influential conservation leaders. Died May 25, 1973.

HENRY CLEPPER

PETERSON, RALPH MAX
(born 1927)
Born July 25 in Doniphan, Missouri. University of Missouri, B.S. (civil engineering) 1949; Harvard University, M.S. (public administration) 1959, as result of winning Rockefeller Foundation Fellowship. Began his U.S. Forest Service career as engineer, with assignments for nine years in three national forests in California, 1949–58, then in Northern Regional Office of Forest Service, Missoula, Montana, 1959. Held administrative and engineering assignments, U.S. Forest Service, Washington, D.C., 1961–66; and was regional engineer, U.S. Forest Service, California, where he developed innovative engineering approaches for building

roads, bridges, and recreation areas, 1966–71. Was selected as deputy regional forester for Southern Region, Atlanta, 1971, and year later became regional forester for National Forest programs in thirteen southern states. Became deputy chief of U.S. Forest Service for Programs and Legislation, Washington, D.C., 1974, and received Special Achievement Award of U.S. Department of Agriculture for his efforts to achieve passage of National Forest Management Act, 1976. Was appointed chief of U.S. Forest Service (first engineer to head that agency) in 1979, and achieved agreements with Mexico and Canada to facilitate improved North American cooperation in fire-control, insect, and disease management, and other forestry programs. Is member of The American Forestry Association, Society of American Foresters, Society of Tropical Foresters, Soil Conservation Society of America, The Wildlife Society, and American Society of Civil Engineers.

REXFORD RESLER

PETERSON, ROGER TORY
(born 1908)
Born August 28 in Jamestown, New York. Art Students' League, 1927; National Academy of Design, 1928–31; Franklin and Marshall College, D.Sc. 1952, Ohio State University, D.Sc. 1962; Allegheny College, D.Sc. 1967; Fairfield University, D.Sc. 1967. From 1931 to 1934 was art teacher; then in 1934 became affiliated with National Audubon Society as education specialist and art editor of *Audubon* magazine. Following military service during World War II, in 1946 again became associated with National Audubon Society as lecturer with its wildlife film series. Since then, has served the society as artist, officer, and writer; was director, 1958–60; secretary, 1960–64; and has again served as director since 1965. In addition, has been officer and committee member of other organizations of conservationists and artists. Was president of American Nature Study Society, 1948–49, has been on board of directors of World Wildlife Fund since 1962, and is a fellow of American Association for the Advancement of Science. For his notable contributions to art and literature, he has received many honors, including William Brewster memorial medal of American Ornithologists' Union in 1944; John Burroughs medal in 1950; Geoffrey St.-Hilaire gold medal of National History Society of France in 1957; gold medal of New York Zoological Society in 1961; Arthur A. Allen medal of Laboratory of Ornithology at

Cornell University in 1967; Paul Bartsch award of Audubon Naturalists Society in 1969; Frances K. Hutchinson Medal of The Garden Club of America; gold medal of World Wildlife Fund in 1972; Joseph Wood Krutch Gold Medal of the Humane Society in 1973; Explorers Club medal in 1974; Linné gold medal of Royal Swedish Academy of Sciences in 1976; and Medal of Freedom in 1980. Since 1946 has been editor of Houghton Mifflin Field Guide Series of books; and since 1951 has been art director for National Wildlife Federation. A prolific and authoritative writer as well as artist, he is best known for *A Field Guide to the Birds*, a popular work first published in 1934. A fourth edition, extensively revised, was published in 1980. Its companion volume *A Field Guide To Western Birds*, 1941, was followed by five other bird books. In addition, is illustrator of five additional bird guides and is coauthor of six more. His influence on the spread of popular education about birds and wildlife conservation is international in scope, and he is one of America's best-known exponents of nature preservation.

NATIONAL AUDUBON SOCIETY
RICHARD H. STROUD

International Who's Who, 32d ed., 1968–69.

Twentieth Century Authors, 1st supp. New York: H. W. Wilson Co., 1955.

Who's Who in America, 42d ed.; 1982–83.

PETERSON, RUSSELL WILBUR
(born 1916)
Born October 3 in Portage, Wisconsin. University of Wisconsin, Ph.D. (chemistry) 1942. From 1969 to 1973 was governor of Delaware, initiating passage of Delaware Coastal Zone Act banning industry from two-mile strip of the state's 115-mile coastline; this was first law of its kind, which has served as model for other coastal states. Was chairman of President's Council on Environmental Quality, 1973–76; founding president of New Directors, a citizens' lobbying organization for global issues, 1976–77; and director of Congressional Office of Technology Assessment, 1978–79. Has been president of National Audubon Society since 1979. In 1979 was appointed by President Carter to twelve-member commission to investigate nuclear power plant accident at Three-Mile Island, Pennsylvania. Is chairman of Global Tomorrow Coalition; president of International Council for Bird Preservation; and

North American councilor to International Union for Conservation of Nature and Natural Resources. His awards include National Wildlife Federation's 1971 Conservationist-of-the Year Award; World Wildlife Fund's Gold Medal; National Audubon Society's 1977 Annual Medal; Frances K. Hutchinson Medal of the Garden Club of America; Fairfield Osborn Environment Science Award; and 1982 Swedish-American-of-the-Year Award.

RUSSELL W. PETERSON

Who's Who in America, 42d ed., 1982–83.

PETOSKEY, MERRILL LOUYS
(born 1923)

Born June 29 in Ortonville, Michigan. Michigan State University, B.S. 1943, M.F. 1947. Was in U.S. Army, 1943–46 and 1951–52. At Wildlife Division of Michigan Department of Natural Resources, 1947–75, served as wildlife ecologist, wildlife biologist, wildlife district biologist supervisor, federal-aid coordinator, state waterfowl biologist, superintendent of conservation school, supervisor of education and training, assistant regional manager, and chief. Was director of wildlife management, U.S. Forest Service, 1975–77, and assistant chief, Bureau of Renewable Resource Management, Executive Division, Michigan Department of Natural Resources, 1977–79. Since 1979 has been deputy administrator for natural resources and rural development, Extension Service, U.S. Department of Agriculture. Holds various positions in many other organizations: chairman, Conservation Affairs Committee, Washington Section, The Wildlife Society; past-president, Michigan Association of Conservation Ecologists; past-president, Michigan State University Forestry Alumni Association; general chairman, Second International Waterfowl Symposium, Ducks Unlimited, 1976; committee member, North American Wildlife Policy, 1973; secretary, National Flyway Council, 1970–75; member of board of directors and executive committee, National Rifle Association of America; member, Grants-in-Aid Committee, and chairman, Hunting and Wildlife Conservation Committee. Also is member of Society of American Foresters; Society for Range Management; International Association of Fish and Wildlife Agencies; Association of Midwest Fish and Wildlife Commissioners; Mississippi Flyway Council Technical Section; Michigan United Conservation Clubs; National Wildlife Federation; National Audubon Society;

Michigan Audubon Society; and American Forestry Association. Was chairman of Citizen's Advisory Committee on Educational Opportunity for Lansing, 1971–72, and was president and board member of Canada Creek Ranch Association. Was visiting lecturer, Indiana University, 1966–72. His honors and awards include: Xi Sigma Pi, 1947; MUCC Passenger Pigeon Award, 1974; and MSU-USDA Experiment Station award, 1975; Outstanding Conservation Achievement Award, Association of Midwest Fish and Wildlife Agencies, 1979; and USDA Senior Executive Bonus Award, 1982. Has written numerous technical and popular articles and talks published on natural-resources management and environmental concerns in the public interest.

C. R. GUTERMUTH

Who's Who in the Midwest, 1976.

PETTIT, TED S.
(born 1914)
Born June 3 in Far Rockaway, New York. Bard College, B.A. (economics) 1937; Columbia University, graduate work in biology and science education, 1938–42. From 1937 to 1941 was employed by National Audubon Society. In 1942 went to Boy Scouts of America as assistant director of editorial service; from 1954 was director of conservation until retiring in 1978. Authored column in *Pennsylvania Game News*, 1954–64. Was frequent contributor to *Boy's Life* and to *Scouting* magazines. Currently writes weekly column on conservation and nature topics for Somerset County, New Jersey, *Messenger-Gazette*. Is author of the following books: *Book of Nature Hobbies*, 1947; *Birds of Your Backyard*, 1949; *Book of Small Mammals*, 1958; *Web of Nature*, 1959; *Animal Signs and Signals*, 1960; *Guide to Nature Projects*, 1966; *Boy's Life Book of Conservation*, 1970; and *Wildlife at Night*, 1976, which received citation from National Science Teachers Association. Received The Wildlife Society education award in 1955; American Motors award for conservation in 1966; Keep America Beautiful citation in 1967; citation from New Jersey Department of Conservation and Economic Development in 1968; first William T. Hornaday gold medal award from Boy Scouts of America in 1979; and special awards from National Wildlife Federation and from New Jersey Association of Natural Resource Districts in 1979.

HENRY CLEPPER
TED S. PETTIT

PHILLIPS, ARTHUR MORTON, JR.
(born 1914)
Born June 18 in Rochester, New York. Cornell University, B.S. 1936, Ph.D. (fisheries) 1939. Initially employed in 1939 as laboratory assistant for fish nutrition and biochemistry, New York Conservation Department, in 1941 became assistant aquatic biologist, U.S. Fish and Wildlife Service, leading to associate to chief of Fish Nutrition Investigations, Cortland, New York, laboratory. Taught fish nutrition at Cortland Hatchery for in-service biologists, hatchery men, and students of fisheries from Cornell University. His special studies centered around vitamin requirements, metabolism, blood analysis, and physiology of fishes. Published numerous papers on nutrition, metabolism, and basic physiology of fishes; outstanding and well known among them are his studies of wild trout versus hatchery trout physiology. His *Cortland No. 6* trout food diet has been accepted throughout world as basis of hatchery fish production. Retired in 1971. Was active member of American Association for the Advancement of Science, American Fisheries Society, Ecological Society of America, and currently is member of Explorers Club. Received distinguished service award of U.S. Department of the Interior.

C. GORDON FREDINE
ELWOOD A. SEAMAN

American Men of Science (Physical and Biological Sciences), 11th ed., 1967.

PINCHOT, GIFFORD
(1865–1946)
Born August 11 in Simsbury, Connecticut. Yale University, B.A. 1889; A.M. 1901, LL.D. 1925; Princeton University, A.M. 1904; Michigan Agricultural College, Sc.D. 1907; McGill University, LL.D. 1909; Pennsylvania Military College, LL.D. 1923; Temple University, LL.D. 1931. The first native American to receive formal instruction in forestry, he studied at National School of Waters and Forests, Nancy, France, in 1900; no academic institution in U.S. offered forestry courses. In January 1892 began first systematic forest management on Biltmore forest in North Carolina. Was in private consulting practice for several years thereafter, and in 1896 was member of Forest Commission appointed by National Academy of Sciences that recommended creation of forest reserve (now national forests) from public domain, and that was responsible for Forest Reserve Act of 1897 that provided for their administration and protec-

tion. In 1898 was appointed chief of Division of Forestry, U.S. Department of Agriculture; it became Bureau of Forestry in 1901 and present Forest Service in 1905. Also in 1905 forest reserves were transferred from U.S. Department of the Interior to U.S. Department of Agriculture, and in 1907 were renamed national forests. During his administration of national forests they were increased from fifty-one million acres in area in 1901 to 175 million acres by 1910. Was organizer of The White House Governors' Conference on Natural Resources of May 1908, and was chairman of subsequent National Conservation Commission that compiled first inventory of country's natural resources. Dismissed as chief of Forest Service by President Taft in 1910, organized and became president of National Conservation Association, formed to continue fight for his conservation ideas. From 1920 to 1922 was commissioner of Department of Forestry, later secretary of Department of Forests and Waters, in Pennsylvania; and governor of Pennsylvania, 1923–27 and 1931–35. In 1900 founded School of Forestry at Yale University and also Society of American Foresters of which he was first president. Was author of numerous papers and reports on conservation topics, including books *A Primer of Forestry*, 1899; *The Fight for Conservation*, 1909; *The Training of a Forester*, 1914; and *Breaking New Ground*, his autobiography, 1947. Was largely responsible for conservation's becoming widely known and supported by public and an established in policy by both federal and state governments. Died October 4, 1946.

HENRY CLEPPER

Journal of Forestry 9 (Gifford Pinchot Commemorative Issue) vol. 63, no. 8, August 1965.

McGreary, M. Nelson. *Gifford Pinchot, Forester-Politician*. Princeton, N.J.: Princeton University Press, 1960.

Pinchot, Gifford. *Breaking New Ground*. New York: Harcourt, Brace and Co., 1957.

Who Was Who in America, 1943–50.

PINKETT, HAROLD THOMAS
(born 1914)

Born April 7 in Salisbury, Maryland. Morgan College, B.A. 1935; University of Pennsylvania, A.M. 1938; American University, Ph.D. 1953. Began as junior archivist at National Archives in 1942; successively became supervisory archivist, 1946–59; chief of Agricultural Records

Branch, 1959–62; senior appraisal archivist, 1962–68; deputy director of Records Appraisal Division, 1968–71; chief of Natural Resources Records Branch, 1971–78; and chief of Legislative and Natural Resources Records Branch, from 1978 until his retirement in 1979. Was elected to board of directors of Forest History Society in 1971, served as president, 1976–78, and was elected a fellow in 1975. Was editor of *American Archivist*, 1968–71, and was elected a fellow of Society of American Archivists in 1962. Was president of Agricultural History Society, 1982–83. Was author of many articles in conservation history; his most important publication was *Gifford Pinchot, Private and Public Forester* (1970), which in manuscript form won 1968 Book Award of Agricultural History Society.

HAROLD K. STEEN

POMEROY, KENNETH BROWNRIDGE
(1907–1975)
Born May 17 near Valley Center, Michigan. Michigan State University, B.S. 1928; Duke University, M.F. 1948. Following private employment, began twenty-three-year U.S. Forest Service career in 1933 as clerk on Nicolet National Forest in Wisconsin, advancing through line and staff positions in administration, state and private forestry, and research to chief of naval-stores research, Lake City, Florida, and finally of timber-management research, Northeastern Forest Experiment Station, Philadelphia, Pennsylvania. His research achievements included stimulation of seed production and regeneration of loblolly pine. Became chief forester of The American Forestry Association in 1956 with responsibility for legislative liaison, technical assistance to association members, Trail Riders of the Wilderness program, and general conservation activities. Until his death, was member of Secretary of Agriculture's Forest Research Advisory Committee since 1962; Secretary of Defense Conservation Award Committee since 1968; Forest Fire Prevention Committee, Society of American Foresters since 1966; and Recreation Committee, Soil Conservation Society of America since 1969. Was chairman, National Task Force–Trees for People, 1969. Was official U.S. Delegate to Fifth World Forestry Congress in Seattle, 1960, and to Sixth World Forestry Congress in Madrid, Spain, 1966. Served as secretary, Fifth American Forest Congress, 1963. Was senior author (with J. G. Yoho) of *North Carolina Lands*, 1964; senior author (with R. W. Cooper) of *Growing Slash Pine*,

1956; contributor to *American Forestry, Six Decades of Growth*, 1960, and *Forestry Handbook*, 1955; and author of 180 articles for scientific and popular magazines. Died July 31, 1975.

HENRY CLEPPER

American Men of Science (Physical and Biological Sciences), 12th ed., 1971.

Who Knows—and What, 1954.

Who's Who in the South and Southwest, 11th ed.

POOLE, DANIEL ARNOLD
(born 1922)
Born April 11 in New York City. Kent State University in 1944 (military service program); University of Montana, B.S. 1950, and M.S. (wildlife management) 1952; Drew University, L.H.D. 1974. Worked as field assistant with the Montana Fish and Game Department in 1949; became junior biologist in 1952. Was biological aide with U.S. Fish and Wildlife Service in California, 1950, and in Utah, 1951. Joined Wildlife Management Institute in Washington, D.C. 1952; edited the institute's biweekly *Outdoor News Bulletin*, 1952–69; was elected secretary in 1963, and was president from 1970 to present. Was member of board of directors of Outdoor Writers Association of America, 1956–58, and editor of *Executive News Service* of Natural Resources Council of America, 1960–65; secretary, 1966–70, vice-chairman, 1971–73, and chairman 1973–75. Was chairman of publicity committee, National Watershed Congress, 1954–62. Was elected to board of directors of Citizens Committee on Natural Resources in 1962. Serving as chairman, 1972–79. Was member of National Mosquito Control, Fish and Wildlife Coordination Committee, 1962–70; of Department of the Navy Conservation Awards Committee, 1963–68; Secretary of Defense Conservation Awards Panel, 1971; and U.S. Air Force Environmental Awards Committee in 1977. His articles on wildlife and natural resources have been published in many newspapers and periodicals. Edited monthly column on wildlife topics for *American Rifleman*, 1960–70. Was special consultant to the secretary of U.S. Department of Agriculture on resources management plan for Magruder Corridor, Bitterroot National Forest, Montana, 1966–67. Collaborated with National Park Service serving on master planning team for Yellowstone and Grand Teton national parks, 1967–70. Received Jade of Chiefs award of Outdoor Writers Association of

America in 1969 for service to conservation. Directed staff studies of organization and operation of wildlife agencies in thirteen states and one Canadian province and of fish and wildlife programs of U.S. Forest Service and Bureau of Land Management. Was trustee of the North American Wildlife Foundation, 1966–83, and of Stronghold, Inc. (Sugarloaf Mountain, Maryland), 1974 to present. Was appointed member of National Conservation Committee, Boy Scouts of America, in 1971, and chairman from 1979 to present. Was member of committee of judges, American Motors Conservation Awards Program, 1973–80, and Gulf Corporation Conservation Awards Program, 1981 to present. Is member of Secretary of Interior's Protect Our Wetland and Duck Resources (POWDR) task force; and chairman of federal activities subcommittee. Was appointed to advisory council, Electric Power Research Institute, 1983.

JAMES B. TREFETHEN
LONNIE L. WILLIAMSON

Who's Who in America, 42d ed., 1982–83.

POTTER, ALBERT F.
(1859–1944)
Born November 14 in Lone, California. Educated in San Francisco Bay area, moved to Arizona for his health. There acquired practical knowledge of livestock and range matters, and bought into sheep business, which he operated profitably and sold in 1900. Through his leadership in Arizona Woolgrowers Association was sent to Washington, D.C., to obtain acceptance of proposal that sheep should be permitted to graze on forest reserve lands. Guided Gifford Pinchot, head of U.S. Division of Forestry, on field inspection and convinced him that properly managed livestock grazing would not damage the reserves. Thus, over opposition of most forest officers of that era, official recognition of grazing as legitimate use of forested lands was established. On Pinchot's recommendation, Potter went to Washington, D.C., in 1901 to work on grazing matters. Made field examinations in Arizona, Utah, and California that led to enlargement or establishment of forest reserves by President Theodore Roosevelt. When forest reserves were transferred from U.S. Department of the Interior in 1905 and set up as national forests in U.S. Department of Agriculture, he was made chief of grazing. Was promoted to associate forester in 1910, and resigned in 1920. More than any other person, he

was architect of grazing policy of Forest Service; basic philosophy he established has largely been continued. Through his practical knowledge of sheep and cattle industry associated with use of public lands in the West, he recognized signs of overuse and understood complexities of working out proper stocking with cattle and sheep growers. Control of grazing use advanced rapidly under his direction; first regulation was issued July 1, 1905, and grazing fees became effective January 1, 1906. Certain basic principles were followed: previous users had priority; small homestead-type owners dependent on forest for forage had preferential status; adjustments in numbers were made without discontinuing use; and stockmen had voice in matters affecting their interests. Authority of secretary of Agriculture, through Forest Service, to regulate grazing use and collect fees was challenged by livestock interests, which claimed that federal authority could not override state law. Potter believed in rule of federal power to protect public land, regulate its occupancy, and charge for its use. These questions were settled in government's favor in the Fred Light case by Supreme Court ruling in 1911, thus confirming Potter's judgment. Died January 1, 1944.

LLOYD W. SWIFT

Barnes, W. C. "Retirement of Albert F. Potter." *Journal of Forestry*, vol. 18:211–13, March 1920.

Roberts, Paul H. *Hoof Prints on Forest Ranges*. San Antonio, Texas: Naylor Co., 1963.

POUGH, RICHARD HOOPER
(born 1904)
Born April 19 in Brooklyn, New York. Massachusetts Institute of Technology, B.S. 1926; Harvard Graduate School 1926–27; LL.D., Haverford College 1970. From 1927 to 1936 held various engineering positions in business and industry. Was member of research staff of National Audubon Society from 1936 to 1948. From 1948 to 1956 was chairman of Department of Conservation and General Ecology of American Museum of Natural History. Since 1957 has been president of Natural Area Council. Is active and has held office in numerous national and international conservation organizations, including position as chairman of U.S. section of International Council for Bird Preservation; director of World Wildlife Fund–U.S.; president of Linnaean Society; honorary trustee of National Parks and Conservation Association; president and director of

Defenders of Wildlife; chairman of Conservation Committee of American Ornithologists' Union; president and honorary trustee of Association for the Protection of the Adirondacks; and president of Goodhill Foundation. Received silver medal of Federation of Garden Clubs of New York State; conservation award of American Motors Corporation; Horace Marden Albright Scenic Preservation Medal of the American Scenic and Historic Preservation Society; Frances K. Hutchinson Medal of The Garden Club of America; and 1981 National Audubon Society medal. Is author of numerous scientific papers and magazine articles and the three-volume *Audubon Bird Guides*, 1946–57.

Who's Who in America, 42d ed., 1982–83.

POWELL, JOHN WESLEY
(1834–1902)
Born March 24 in Mount Morris, New York. Oberlin College and Wheaton College; Harvard University, LL.D. 1886; University of Heidelberg, Ph.D. 1886; Illinois College, LL.D. 1889; Illinois Wesleyan University, A.M. and Ph.D. After teaching school, enlisted in Union Army during Civil War, and rose to rank of major. On his return to civil life, was professor of geology at Illinois Wesleyan College, then later was curator of museum of Illinois Normal University. In 1867–68 made natural history studies in western plains and Rocky Mountains. In 1869 led his famous nine-hundred-mile boat expedition down Grand Canyon of Colorado River under sponsorship of Smithsonian Institution. Made additional western explorations in 1871, 1874, and 1875. In 1875 was made director of U.S. geological and geographical surveys in Rocky Mountain region. When western surveys were consolidated in 1879 under U.S. Geological Survey, he became director of U.S. Bureau of Ethnology, but returned to the survey in 1880 as director. Held both positions until 1894, when he was forced out of directorship of Geological Survey because of congressional opposition to his strong advocacy of extensive irrigation projects in arid West and of forest preservation of public lands. Continued as director of Bureau of Ethnology. Results of his early work were published as *Explorations of the Colorado River of the West and Its Tributaries*, 1875; also published monograph *Report on the Lands of the Arid Region of the United States*, 1878. In later years wrote numerous papers and books on scientific subjects. Died September 23, 1902.

HENRY CLEPPER

Darrah, William C. *Powell of the Colorado*. Princeton, N.J.: Princeton University Press, 1951.

Dictionary of American Biography, 1934.

International Encyclopedia of the Social Sciences, 1968.

Stegner, Wallace. *Beyond the Hundredth Meridian: John Wesley Powell*. Boston: Houghton Mifflin, 1951.

Terreli, John Upton. *The Man Who Rediscovered America: A Biography of John Wesley Powell*. New York: Weybright & Talley, 1969.

Who's Who in America, 1897–42.

PRESTON, JOHN FREDERICK
(1883–1967)

Born February 26 in Higginsville, Missouri. University of Michigan, B.A. 1907, M.Sc. (forestry) 1915. Began his professional career as timber cruiser for U.S. Forest Service in the Ozarks in 1907. Subsequent assignments took him to national forests of Montana, where he became forest supervisor. In 1920 transferred to Washington, D.C., headquarters of Forest Service as forest inspector of timber sales. In 1925 joined Hammermill Paper Company at Erie, Pennsylvania, as technical advisor in timberland acquisition, harvesting, and reforestation. Returned to U.S. Department of Agriculture in Washington, D.C., in 1936 as chief, Forestry Division, Soil Conservation Service. In this position, supervised nationwide program to induce farmers to include forestry in integrated farm conservation programs. Upon retirement in 1946 because of ill health, became free-lance writer; and as instructor in U.S. Department of Agriculture, prepared correspondence course in farm forestry. Was author of books *Developing Farm Woodlands* and *Farm Wood Crops*; bulletin *Woodlands in the Farm Plan*; and many technical and popular articles for magazines. Promoted principle that growing wood as farm crop was distinctly different type of forestry than that practiced in industrial forests and public forests. The Society of American Foresters recognized his contributions to profession by electing him a fellow in 1948. Also was member of Sigma Xi, The American Forestry Association, and Friends of the Land. Died August 24, 1967.

KENNETH B. POMEROY

Cosmos Club, Washington, D.C.

Division of Personnel, Soil Conservation Service, Washington, D.C.

PRICE, OVERTON WESTFELDT
(1873–1914)

Born January 27 in Liverpool, England. Biltmore Forest School, North Carolina, 1895–96. Studied forestry at University of Munich for two years, followed by year of practical experience in European forests. In June 1899 entered Division of Forestry of U.S. Department of Agriculture as agent; was promoted a year later to superintendent of working plans. When the division became Bureau of Forestry in 1901, was advanced to associate forester and continued in this position when the bureau was named Forest Service in 1905. Much of work of establishing national forestry on sound and permanent basis is credited to his remarkable organizing and executive ability. In 1900 was one of seven charter members of Society of American Foresters, first chairman of its executive committee, vice-president for five years, and member of editorial board of its *Proceedings*. In 1904 lectured at Yale University on practice of forestry in Bureau of Forestry. In 1905 participated in American Forest Congress organized by The American Forestry Association. In 1910 was discharged by President Taft for alleged complicity in Ballinger-Pinchot controversy. Shortly afterward, became treasurer and vice-president of National Conservation Association, organized by Gifford Pinchot to assist in fight for conservation. Later was consultant in organizing Forest Branch of Province of British Columbia, and served as forester for Letchwork Park Arboretum and forestry advisor for George W. Vanderbilt estate. Wrote *The Land We Live In*, a popular work on conservation for boys, and reports and articles on forestry. Died July 11, 1914.

KENNETH B. POMEROY

American Forestry 20(7):536, July 1914.
Forestry Quarterly 12(3):508–10, September 1914.
Journal of Forestry 38(11):838, November 1940.

PRITCHARD, HAROLD WAYNE
(born 1916)

Born March 3 near Estevan, Saskatchewan, Canada; became U.S. citizen in 1929. Iowa State University, B.S. (agricultural education) 1939. Taught vocational agriculture in Greene, Iowa, 1939–40, and in Early, Iowa, 1940–43. Served in U.S. Army Air Force, 1943–45. Taught vocational agriculture at Sac City, Iowa, 1945–49, then was appointed executive secretary of Iowa State Soil Conservation Committee, 1949–52. Was commended for service to the commitee by Iowa Association of Soil Conservation District Commissioners in 1951. From 1952 to 1966 served as executive secretary of Soil Conservation Society of America, during which period he was elected a fellow, 1959, received the society's President's Citation, and was named executive director of twelve-thousand-member professional organization. His tenure included service as editorial director of *Journal of Soil and Water Conservation*, the society's official publication. From 1860 to 1967 was member of Forest Service Central States Advisory Council, and of steering committee for U.S. Department of Health, Education and Welfare's National Conference on Water Pollution in 1960. During 1966–67 was chairman of National Farm Institute. Was elected secretary of Pan-American Soil Conservation Commission in 1966, the only member of the commission from North America. Is coauthor of book *Origins of American Conservation*, 1966.

MAXWELL SCHNEPF

Who's Who in America, 41st ed., 1980–81.

PRITCHARD, PAUL CLEMENT
(born 1944)
Born August 27 in Huntington, West Virginia. University of Missouri, B.A. 1966; University of Tennessee, M.S.P. (planning—natural resources and economics) 1970; Harvard University, certificate in business management 1973. Served as member of Georgia Governor's Task Force for State Government Reorganization, 1971–72; chief of planning in Georgia Department of Natural Resources, 1972–74; Pacific Region coordinator for coastal zone management, National Oceanic and Atmospheric Administration, 1974–75; executive director of Appalachian Trail Conference, 1975–77; deputy director, Bureau of Outdoor Recreation/Heritage Conservation and Recreation Service, U.S. Department of the Interior, 1977–80; president of National Parks and Conservation Association, 1980 to present. His professional career has been noteworthy for his role in directing Presidential National Heritage Trust Task Force; helping to create nation's Coastal Zone Management Act; fathering State Heritage Inventory; generating Washington State coastal zone management program (nation's first); and creating South Slough Estuarine Sanctuary in Oregon (also nation's first). In recognition of his accomplishments, was designated by U.S. Department of Housing and Urban

Development as a special fellow in 1973; and received Outstanding Service Award of National Oceanic and Atmospheric Administration, U.S. Department of Commerce, in 1975; Meritorious Service Award of U.S. Department of the Interior in 1980; and Gulf Oil Conservation Award in 1982.

PAUL C. PRITCHARD
RICHARD H. STROUD

PUMFREY, WILLIAM ROSS
(born 1946)
Born August 16 in Winnepeg, Canada. Occidental College, B.S. (political science) 1967; University of California at Berkeley, M.A. (energy and resources) 1984. Has lived in California most of his life, working in variety of public interest organizations as community organizer, political manager, legislative aide, and energy policy analyst. In early 1970s directed community center in Isla Vista, California, oveseeing confederation of service groups and consulting on development of number of social service projects. Managed a number of political campaigns, including one dealing with population growth and planning in Santa Barbara, and most recently a statewide initiative campaign for deposits on beverage containers—the bottle bill. Chaired statewide group called Californians Against Waste. For five years helped draft legislation, prepare testimony, and manage three offices for member of California State Senate. In energy policy area, worked on grant from National Science Foundation, studying social and institutional impacts of energy technologies, and as assistant to California energy commissioner. Appointed executive director of Zero Population Growth, heading staff located in Washington, D.C., from 1983 to present.

ZERO POPULATION GROWTH

PUTZ, ROBERT EDWARD
(born 1935)
Born April 22 in Clarksburg, West Virginia. University of Iowa, B.S. 1960, M.S. 1961; Fordham University, Ph.D. 1970. Served in U.S. Air Force, 1954–57. Entered U.S. Fish and Wildlife Service in 1962 as research parasitologist with Eastern Fish Disease Laboratory at Leetown, West Virginia. In 1972 was appointed branch chief and then chief of

Fisheries Research in Washington, D.C., and in 1974 became deputy associate director of research. In 1977 was named director of newly established National Fisheries Center at Leetown, West Virginia, supervising scientific facilities and activities in seven states. In 1982 was appointed associate director of wildlife resources in Washington, D.C., and became director of Alaska Region in 1983. Is author or coauthor of more than twenty scientific publications, most dealing with fish parasitology, and contributor to two scientific books. Represented U.S. in fisheries and natural resources exchanges with Pan American countries, Israel, Soviet Union, and People's Republic of China. Was advisor to U.S. Congress on toxic substance control and coauthor of Ashe-Putz Report, which detailed organizational recommendations for Fish and Wildlife Service. Was actively involved in development of National Aquaculture Act of 1980. Is member of six national and international professional scientific societies and holds U.S. Department of the Interior's Meritorious Service Award and other commendations.

DAVID MCDANIEL

American Men and Women of Science (Physical and Biological Sciences), 12th ed. (vol. 5), 1972.

RADONSKI, GILBERT CLEMENCE
(born 1936)
Born February in Milwaukee, Wisconsin. University of Minnesota, B.S. (fish and wildlife management) 1960. Was associated with U.S. Fish and Wildlife Service hatchery system, 1960–62; and worked as area fishery biologist with Ayerst Laboratories, Veterinary Medical Division, 1962–68, where he pioneered development of successful and broadly utilized techniques involving use of antimycin as selective fish toxicant by fisheries managers throughout United States. Was selected to serve as fisheries consultant to Wisconsin Alumni Foundation in 1975. In October 1975 joined Sport Fishing Institute as executive secretary, and was appointed executive vice-president in June 1981 and president in November 1983. Has been appointed by the secretary of Commerce to three-year term as member of Marine Fisheries Committee; is member of advisory committee to U.S. Commissioners to the International Convention for the Conservation of Atlantic Tunas; has chaired or served on numerous committees of American Fisheries Society and of International Association of Fish and Wildlife Agencies. Is certified fisheries scientist; vice-

president of Sport Fishery Research Foundation; vice-chairman of Natural Resources Council of America; and member of American Institute of Fishery Research Biologists.

SPORT FISHING INSTITUTE

RASMUSSEN, BOYD LESTER
(born 1913)
Born April 19 in Glenns Ferry, Idaho. Oregon State University, B.S. (forestry) 1935. Soon thereafter he started his career with U.S. Forest Service at Pacific Northwest Forest and Range Experiment Station in Portland, Oregon. From 1938 to 1942 was forest ranger on national forests in Oregon and Washington, then was timber staff officer until 1950, when he became supervisor of Siuslaw National Forest at Corvallis, Oregon. In 1952 was assigned to Forest Service's Division of Fire Control in Washington, D.C.; was reassigned to Intermountain Region at Ogden, Utah, in 1954 as assistant regional forester; and returned to Washington, D.C., in 1959 as assistant to deputy chief in charge of national forest resource management. Two years later was named regional forester of Northern (Rocky Mountain) Region, at Missoula, Montana. Again returned to Washington, D.C., in 1964 as deputy chief in charge of Forest Service's cooperative forestry programs and its insect- and disease-control projects. In July 1966 was appointed director of U.S. Department of the Interior's Bureau of Land Management (sixth director since formation of Bureau in 1946). Was granted U.S. Department of the Interior's Honor Award for Distinguished Service in 1968, and served on President's Quetico-Superior Committee established in 1934. Was permanent member of Forestry Panel of United States–Japan cooperative program on natural resources development, and member of task force established by the secretary of the Interior in 1969 for strengthening of regulations covering oil drilling and production on Alaska's Arctic North Slope. Thereafter, was member of Arctic Environmental Council in monitoring environmental impact of construction and operation of trans-Alaska pipeline system, until his retirement. From 1975 to 1982 served as Washington representative of National Association of State Foresters.

HENRY CLEPPER
BOYD L. RASMUSSEN

Who's Who in America, 38th ed., 1974–75.

REDFIELD, ALFRED CLARENCE
(1890–1983)
Born November 15 in Philadelphia, Pennsylvania. Haverford College and Harvard University, B.S. (biology) 1913, Ph.D. (zoology) 1917; Cambridge 1920–21; Munich, 1930–31; University of Oslo, Ph.D. (honorary) 1956; Lehigh University, Sc.D. 1965; Memorial University of Newfoundland, Sc.D. 1967. After serving as instructor of physiology at Harvard, 1918–19, was assistant professor of physiology at University of Toronto, 1919–20. Taught again at Harvard, 1921–30, was associate professor, 1930–31, professor of physiology, 1931–57, and emeritus professor since 1957. Was also director, biological laboratories, at Harvard, 1934–35, and chairman of Department of Biology, 1934–38. At Woods Hole Oceanographic Institution, was senior biologist, 1930–36 and 1942–53; trustee from 1936; research associate, 1938–40; associate marine biologist, 1940–42; associate director, 1942–56; senior oceanographer, 1953–56; and emeritus senior oceanographer from 1957. Was managing editor of *Biological Bulletin*, 1930–42. Was trustee of Marine Biological Laboratory, 1930–53; trustee of Bermuda Biological Station from 1944, and president, 1962–66. As first chairman of Natural Resources Council of America, 1946–48, was made honorary life member in 1948. Was member, National Academy of Sciences, Agassiz Medal, 1956; Physiological Society (secretary, 1929–30); Ecological Society of America (vice-president, 1944, president 1945, received eminent ecologist award, 1966); and American Society of Limnology and Oceanography (president, 1956). Received Walker Prize in Natural History, Boston Museum of Science, 1973. A prolific writer on wide range of subjects, one of his significant contributions was paper "The Biological Control of Chemical Factors in the Environment" in *American Scientist* (46:205–22). Conservation was one of many areas in which he demonstrated remarkable understanding and breadth of interest. He considered the ocean as vast organism in which biological, physical, and chemical changes are clearly and intimately interrelated. On his seventy-fifth birthday, a special volume of *Deep-Sea Research* (1965) was dedicated to him by American Society of Limnology and Oceanography. Later turned his attention to ecology of salt marsh; on his ninetieth birthday, Woods Hole Oceanographic Institution published his last book, *The Tides of the Waters of New England and New York* (1981). Died March 17, 1983.

C. GORDON FREDINE
GEORGE SPRUGEL, JR.

American Men and Women of Science (Physical and Biological Sciences), 15th ed., 1982.

Bulletin of the Ecological Society of America, vol. 47: no. 4, 1966; vol. 48: no. 4.

Who's Who in America, 41st ed., 1980–81.

REED, FRANKLIN WELD

(1877–1949)

Born May 11 in Massachusetts. After two years at Harvard University, entered Biltmore Forest School in North Carolina and then studied forestry in Europe. Entering Bureau of Forestry (now Forest Service), U.S. Department of Agriculture, in 1902, was assigned to making forest management working plans. In July 1910 was appointed associate district (now regional) forester at Ogden, Utah, and in 1911 returned to Washington, D.C., office as forest inspector. Resigned in 1913 to become forester for Indian Service (now Bureau of Indian Affairs), U.S. Department of the Interior, but re-entered Forest Service a year later and in 1919 was made district forester of new district embracing entire eastern United States. Leaving Forest Service in 1924, engaged in private consulting practice. In 1926 was with National Conference on Outdoor Recreation and two years later became forester for National Lumber Manufacturers Association. In 1931 was appointed executive secretary of Society of American Foresters and managing editor of *Journal of Forestry*, the society's official organ. Following his retirement in 1936, was made life member of the society. During 1931–32 was also active in work of U.S. Timber Conservation Board, compiling information on nation's timber supply and condition of forest industries. His various assignments in public and private forestry made him one of well-known foresters in America. Died November 26, 1949.

HENRY CLEPPER

Journal of Forestry. Obituary, 48(1):69, January 1950.

REED, NATHANIEL PRYOR

(born 1933)

Born July 22 in New York City. Trinity College, B.A. 1955. Served in U.S. Air Force, 1955–59. Began his civilian career in 1960 as manager of family real estate and hotel business, centering around Jupiter Island in Hobe Sound, Florida. His active concern with environmental matters steered him into public life and led to his serving three Florida governors as environmental consultant and in executive positions of successively greater responsibility. Became deeply involved in problems of Everglades National Park, estuaries, and other interrelated systems. Was appointed to membership on Florida Pollution Control Commission, 1968–69, then as first chairman of newly formed Department of Air and Water Pollution Control, 1969–71. His personal role as liaison between state and federal authorities was vital factor in two nationally significant reversals of environmental deterioration—signing in January 1970 of Florida Jetport Pack, and abandonment later that same year of Cross-Florida Barge Canal project. Helped select twenty-two new state parks and wilderness areas, and chaired hearings to establish air quality regions. Served as assistant secretary for Fish and Wildlife and Parks, U.S. Department of the Interior, under two presidents, 1971–77. Was appointed to State of Florida's Constitutional Revision Commission, Reclaimed Land Committee, and as chairman of Coastal Zone Committee in 1978. Currently serves as trustee of Deerfield Academy and of National Audubon Society, and is former board member of The Nature Conservancy. Was appointed as board member of South Florida Water Management District and served term on Treasure Coast Regional Planning Council. Is now serving on Florida Governor's ELMS committee; is member of Speaker of the House of Representatives Task Force on Water Issues; and is chairman of Crystal River Manatee Sanctuary committee and of Natural Resources Defense Council, Inc.

ROBERT L. HERBST

REEVES, MERILYN BRONSON
(born 1931)
Born June 22 in Burley, Idaho. Utah State University, B.S. (English) 1954; Northern State College, South Dakota, M.S. (education) 1961. Chaired Patuxent River Quality Public Advisory Council, has served on Citizens Steering Committee for the Environmental Protection Agency's Chesapeake Bay Programs since 1974; chaired Maryland's Hazardous Substances and Low Level Nuclear Waste Council, 1976–82; served on U.S. Department of Energy's Advisory Council, 1977–80; appointed to Maryland and Virginia Chesapeake Bay Legislative Advisory Commis-

sion, 1978–80 (featured in film *Chesapeake's Horizons*); appointed to Environmental Protection Agency's National Safe Drinking Water Advisory Council, 1983 to present; and was member of Maryland Task Force on Permits Simplification, 1979–83. Has served as member of board of directors of American Lung Association (1980–83) and of the association's National Air Conservation Commission, and on board of directors of National Clean Air Coalition. Has served as second vice-president and natural resources coordinator of League of Women Voters of the United States since 1980. Received 1982 Award of Achievement of Natural Resources Council of America for her work on behalf of Clean Air Act. Has received awards from Department of Health and Mental Hygiene and State Senate of Maryland in recognition of her sixteen years' work on state environmental issues. In addition, was commissioned *Admiral of the Chesapeake Bay* by Maryland Governor Harry Hughes in 1983.

LEAGUE OF WOMEN VOTERS OF THE UNITED STATES

REID, KENNETH ALEXANDER
(1885–1956)
Born April 14 in Connellsville, Pennsylvania. Yale University, Ph.B. 1917. Was appointed to Pennsylvania Fish Commission in 1932, and was instrumental in establishment of trout stream improvement demonstration area on Spring Creek in 1935, which, ironically, had to be closed in 1962 because of pollution. Resources conservation, with emphasis on water pollution abatement and control, and on fish and fishing, was his avocation until 1938, when he became executive director of Izaak Walton League of America, Chicago. His leadership rebuilt the organization into strong conservation instrument long before illness caused his retirement in winter of 1948–49. Was moving force in bringing about enactment of first federal water pollution control law, P.L. 845 of Eightieth Congress. Was cofounder of Izaak Walton League Endowment in 1945, the chief purpose of which is acquiring private interior holdings in what was then designated Roadless Area (now Boundary Waters Canoe Area) of Superior National Forest, Minnesota, to be turned over to Forest Service in fee. Defended creation of Jackson Hole National Monument, now part of Grand Teton National Park, Wyoming; later, a peak in Grand Teton Range was named Mount Reid in his honor. Long an advocate of improved communication between groups in conservation movement, he was cofounder of Natural Resources Council of America. Had leading

role, for Izaak Walton League of America, in opposition to attempt to secure ownership of vast areas of public lands in the West by consortium of livestock organization leaders and members of Congress, 1945–48. Was author of many articles and editorials, mostly in *Outdoor America*, the magazine of Izaak Walton League of America, of which he was editorial director. Organizations in which he held memberships include Society of American Foresters, American Fisheries Society, and The Wildlife Society. Died May 21, 1956.

WILLIAM VOIGT, JR.

Who Was Who in America, 1951–56.

REIDEL, CARL HUBERT
(born 1937)
Born March 5 in Chicago, Illinois. University of Minnesota, B.S. (forest management) 1958; Harvard University, master's degree (public administration) 1964; University of Minnesota, Ph.D. (forest policy and administration) 1969. Began his career with U.S. Department of Agriculture Forest Service as an assistant ranger in Toiyabe National Forest in 1958. Became district ranger in the forest in 1961. In 1964 was made chief, current information branch, information and education, in the department's intermountain region. In 1965 switched to teaching, becoming instructor in forestry and conservation at University of Minnesota. Became assistant director, Center for Environmental Studies, Williams College, in 1969; and Bullard Forest research fellow, Harvard University, in 1971. Since 1972 has been director of environmental program and of Water Resources Center at University of Vermont. Received U.S. Department of Agriculture Outstanding Performance Award in 1959; and has served on boards of directors of National Parks and Conservation Association, Conservation Law Foundation of New England, and The American Forestry Association, of which he was president in 1978. Is author of *Careers and Jobs in Forestry*, 1968, and numerous other articles on forestry and conservation.

JOHN C. BARBER

American Men of Science (Social and Behavioral Sciences), 11th ed. (suppl. 1), 1968.

REILLY, WILLIAM KANE
(born 1940)

Born January 26 in Decatur, Illinois. Yale University, B.A. (history) 1962; Harvard University, J.D. 1965; Columbia University, M.S. (urban planning) 1971. Was attorney for law firm of Ross, Hardies, O'Keefe, Babcock and Parsons, Chicago, 1965; served in U.S. Army, 1966–67. In 1969 became associate director of Urban Policy Center for Urban America, Washington, D.C., and later worked for National Urban Coalition. From 1970 to 1972 was senior staff member of President's Council on Environmental Quality. As executive director of Rockefeller Brothers Fund Task Force on Land Use and Urban Growth, was principal author of its report *The Use of Land: A Citizens' Guide to Urban Growth*, 1973. Since 1973 has been president of The Conservation Foundation, Washington, D.C. Was chairman of Natural Resources Council of America, 1981–83, and is member of board of directors of Winrock International Center for Livestock Research and Training; Sol Feinstone Environmental Awards program; and Piedmont Environmental Council. Also is trustee of American Farmland Trust and chairman of board of Partners for Livable Places. Served as delegate to 1978 White House Conference on Balanced Growth and Development and on Citizens Advisory Committee to Habitat, 1976 United Nations Conference on Human Settlements. Is author of numerous articles and addresses on conservation, including 1976 B. Y. Morrison Memorial Lecture sponsored by U.S. Department of Agriculture's Agricultural Research Service.

THE CONSERVATION FOUNDATION

Who's Who in America, 41st ed., 1981–82.

RESLER, REXFORD ADRIAN
(born 1923)

Born January 13 in Danville, Illinois. Oregon State University, B.S. (forest management) 1953, M.F. 1954. Received his first appointment with U.S. Forest Service on Siuslaw National Forest in 1953. Held positions as district ranger, deputy forest supervisor, and forest supervisor in National Forests of Pacific Northwest. Served two years in Washington, D.C., in charge of Division of Recreation and later of Division of Timber Management. In 1970 served in Pacific Northwest as deputy regional forester and regional forester. In 1972 returned as associate chief to Washington headquarters, where he served as alternate and associate to chief of U.S. Forest Service; was responsible for administration of national forests, state and private forestry programs, and research program of Forest Service. Upon retiring from Forest Service in December 1978, after thirty years of service, assumed post of executive vice-president of The American Forestry Association. Received first Saint Regis Fellowship Award and is member of Xi Sigma Pi and Phi Kappa Phi. Is widely known for his numerous articles, editorials, and speeches about forestry and natural resources.

THE AMERICAN FORESTRY ASSOCIATION

Who's Who in America, 42d ed., 1982–83.

REYNOLDS, HARRIS AQUILA
(1883–1953)
Born March 30 in West Newton, Pennsylvania. West Virginia University, Sc.B. (civil engineering) 1909; Harvard University, master of landscape architecture 1911. Soon after beginning practice of landscape architecture in Boston in 1911, became secretary of Massachusetts Forestry Association, organized in 1898. Renamed Massachusetts Forest and Park Association in 1932, it would be organization through which he would work for national programs in resource management over period of four decades. In 1913 studied communal forests in Europe, and returned to America to start movement for community forests throughout United States that resulted in creation of two thousand community forests embracing three million acres during his lifetime. As chairman of Committee on Community Forests for Society of American Foresters, was known in New England as father of town forests. In addition to this movement, helped in creation of state forests and parks, and promoted roadside beautification and elimination of billboard advertising along state highways. Was strong supporter in all of Weeks Law, which resulted in acquisition of eastern national forests. In 1913 was organizing secretary of American Plant Pest Committee, which helped obtain government appropriations for control of white-pine blister rust, Dutch elm disease, and pests of agricultural crops. Also helped to form National Conference on State Parks in 1921. Was secretary of National Forest Fire Prevention Committee, set up in 1920, which helped with enactment of Clarke-McNary Act of 1924 to provide cooperative fire control between federal government and the states. Was chairman of National Committee on Farm Forestry Extension, which succeeded in obtaining legislation by

which forestry was included in activities of Agricultural Extension Service. In 1944 organized effective New England Forestry Foundation, through which a staff of professional foresters provides complete forestry services to private owners at cost. Was one of best-known conservationists in New England and was recognized as one of America's outstanding conservation association executives. Died October 16, 1953.

HENRY CLEPPER

Journal of Forestry. Biography, 43 (5): 377, May 1945.

RICKER, PERCY LEROY
(1878–1973)
Born March 27 in Brunswick, Maine. University of Maine, B.S. 1900, M.S. 1901. Was employed as botanist in Bureau of Plant Industry of U.S. Department of Agriculture, 1901–48. In 1918 organized District of Columbia Chapter of the Wild Flower Preservation Society. Became president of Wild Flower Preservation Society when it reorganized and moved its headquarters to Washington, D.C., in 1942. Served in that position until 1964, directing and carrying out extensive program of educational work as volunteer. Was editor of the society's magazine *Wild Flower*, 1938–44. Was active in Potomac Appalachian Trail Club, and was noted photographer of wildflowers. Died January 27, 1973.

GEORGE B. FELL

RICKER, WILLIAM EDWIN
(born 1908)
Born August 11 in Waterdown, Ontario. University of Toronto, Ph.D. 1936. In 1938 was employed by International Pacific Salmon Fisheries Commission and in 1939 went to Department of Zoology, Indiana University, as director of Indiana Lake and Stream Survey. From 1950 until he retired in 1973, worked for Fisheries Research Board of Canada, successively as editor, acting chairman, and chief scientist, and has been consultant since 1973. Has done much to increase international stature of fisheries science. As result of his interest in salmon biology and salmon management, he was responsible for important advances in knowledge of quantitative relationships between food of young sockeye salmon and their growth and mortality. More recently he has brought to light evidence of excess of growth over mortality of salmon on high seas, and on

effect of selection by fishery in reducing size of salmon. For his report on new concepts of relationships between parent stock size and number of progeny, received The Wildlife Society citation for outstanding publication in fish ecology and management in 1953. In 1956 was invited to deliver Edgardo Baldi Memorial Lecture at Helsinki Congress of International Association for Theoretical and Applied Limnology. For his *Handbook of Computations for Biological Statistics of Fish Populations*, was again awarded The Wildlife Society citation in 1959. In all, has written about 150 scientific and popular articles on fisheries topics, and thirty-five on classification and distribution of stoneflies. Has also translated and made available more than one hundred publications on Russian fisheries. Additional recognition of his work includes honorary degrees from two universities; gold medals from Professional Institute of the Public Service of Canada, the Royal Society of Canada, and the Canadian Society of Zoologists; and Award of Excellence from American Fisheries Society.

K. S. KETCHEN
P. A. LARKIN

American Men and Women of Science (Physical and Biological Sciences), 14th ed., 1979.

RIPLEY, THOMAS HUNTINGTON
(born 1927)
Born November 18 in Bennington, Vermont. New York State Ranger School, 1946; Virginia Polytechnic Institute, B.S. (forestry and wildlife) 1951; University of Massachusetts, M.S. (wildlife biology) 1954; Virginia Polytechnic Institute, Ph.D. (biology) 1958. Holds Distinguished Alumnus Award, University of Massachusetts, 1981. Has held numerous research and administrative positions in forestry, wildlife biology, range, watershed, and recreation management with universities, state agencies, and U.S. Forest Service, in which he served eleven years, rising to position of chief of range and wildlife research. Joined Tennessee Valley Authority (TVA) in 1970 as director of Division of Forestry, Fisheries and Wildlife Development; was appointed manager of TVA's Office of Natural Resources, 1979. Holds adjunct appointments as professor of forestry and wildlife management, Virginia Polytechnic Institute, and professor, Department of Forestry, University of Tennessee. Is author of more than sixty papers in professional and technical journals in fields of forestry,

ecology, and wildlife biology. Was elected president, The American Forestry Association, 1981, and re-elected, 1982. Was also a fellow of Society of American Foresters, and member of The Wildlife Society, International Union of Forestry Research Organizations, The Explorers Club, Phi Kappa Phi, Xi Sigma Pi, Sigma Xi, Phi Sigma, Alpha Zeta, and Omicron Delta Kappa. A thirty-year veteran of federal government's ecology, forestry, and wildlife programs, he was named in 1983 assistant commissioner of Tennessee Department of Conservation to oversee forestry, geology, natural heritage, and land reclamation programs.

REXFORD RESLER

Who's Who in America, 42d ed., 1982–83.

ROCKEFELLER, JOHN DAVIDSON, JR.
(1874–1960)
Born January 29 in Cleveland, Ohio. Brown University, B.A. (liberal arts) 1897. M.A. (honorary) 1914, LL.D. 1937. Upon graduation, became business associate of his father's. As knowledgeable conservationist, helped preserve much of America's natural and historical heritage. His early experiences in road-building, landscaping, and resource management on his family properties left him with intense interest and appreciation for scientific and aesthetic details of conservation programming. His perspective was both historical and visionary. He understood cultural value of environmental and historical preservation and believed that timely private initiative must demonstrate that value to society and to those who govern it. Throughout his career, was concerned with problems of emerging National Park Service, and was among individuals who, through acquisition and donation of land, were responsible for establishment of Acadia National Park. In tour of western parks in 1924, recognized necessity of providing quality interpretive services to public; afterwards made anonymous gift to Park Service so that Mesa Verde Museum could be completed. Subsequently made pilot funds available to establish museums at Yellowstone, Grand Canyon, and Yosemite, and to conduct general interpretive studies of numerous park areas. During second visit to the West in 1926, undertook anonymous acquisition of thirty-three thousand acres in Jackson Hole, Wyoming, which was later given to federal government for expansion and improvement of Grand Teton National Park; also authorized acquisition, through Save-the-Redwoods League, of Bull Creek Grove, later renamed Rockefeller Red-

wood Forest in his honor. In 1928, in response to cutting of privately owned sugar and yellow pine forests within Yosemite National Park, he provided matching funds to federal government to acquire inholdings. A few years later, again came to rescue of pines and *Sequoia giganteas* by assisting California in purchase of Calaveras Groves. During same period, Great Smoky Mountain and Shenandoah national parks were authorized by Congress on condition that states in which they were located would purchase all necessary land. Funds he subsequently made available to Tennessee, North Carolina, and Virginia ensured establishment of those parks. Meanwhile, acquired and presented scenic lands along top of Palisades escarpment to states of New York and New Jersey. Also had undertaken construction of Fort Tryon Park and Cloisters Museum for New York City. Active in historic site preservation, he restored complete colonial environment of Williamsburg, Virginia; early Dutch manors of Van Cordlandt and Philipse families; and Washington Irving's home, Sunnyside. Declined most awards and other forms of public recognition for his contributions to conservation, although he did receive Conservation Service Award of U.S. Department of the Interior; the Audubon Medal for Distinguished Service to Conservation; Gold Medal of the National Council of State Garden Clubs; honorary membership in American Institute of Architects; and a fellowship in Royal Society of Science. Died May 11, 1960.

HOLT BODINSON

Fosdick, Raymond D. *John D. Rockefeller, Jr., A Portrait.* New York: Harper & Row, 1956.

Newhall, Nancy, Osborn, Fairfield, and Albright, Horace M. *A Contribution to the Heritage of Every American: The Conservation Activities of John D. Rockefeller, Jr.* New York: Alfred A. Knopf, 1957.

Who Was Who in America, 1961–68.

ROCKEFELLER, LAURANCE
(born 1944)

Born July 29 in New York City. Harvard College, B.A. (government) 1966; Columbia University, J.D. 1971. Established Americans for Alaska, a group that was instrumental in resolution in 1980 of D-2 land-distribution plan for parks, wildlife, and native and state lands in Alaska. Subsequently helped establish Barrier Islands Coalition, which supported Barrier Islands legislation passed by Congress in 1982. Also helped establish private conservation land programs in Catskill Mountain region of New York. Served as a founder or director/trustee of Environmental Planning Lobby, the Federated Conservationists of Westchester County, and Scenic Hudson, and is trustee of Rockefeller Family Fund and Rockefeller Brothers Fund. Is staff attorney with Natural Resources Defense Council, Inc., in New York City. Received Robert Marshall award from The Wilderness Society in 1983.

PAUL C. PRITCHARD

ROCKEFELLER, LAURANCE SPELMAN
(born 1910)

Born May 26 in New York City. Princeton University, B.A. (philosophy) 1932. Received honorary doctorates from State University College of Forestry at Syracuse University, 1961; George Washington University, 1964; and Texas Technological College, 1966. In 1935 began working in family offices at Rockefeller Center in New York City, where he became involved in conservation and park activities of his father, John D. Rockefeller, Jr., and developed philosophy of preservation and use that led him into active conservation career in both public and private spheres. His introduction to public service came in 1939, when governor of New York appointed him commissioner of Palisades Interstate Park Commission; was elected commission secretary in 1941 and vice-president in 1960. Also acted as the commission's representative to New York State Council of Parks and Outdoor Recreation, and in 1963 was elected chairman of the council. In 1940 was elected president of newly formed Jackson Hole Preserve, Inc., the Rockefeller-sponsored nonprofit corporation that, under his leadership, donated more than thirty-three thousand acres of land in Jackson Hole, Wyoming, to federal government in 1949 to be incorporated into Grand Teton National Park. Later, in 1956, Jackson Hole Preserve, Inc. contributed five thousand acres on island of Saint John to government in order to initiate establishment of Virgin Islands National Park. To further his conservation goals, established and became president of American Conservation Association, Inc., in 1958. In that same year President Eisenhower appointed him chairman of Outdoor Recreation Resources Review Commission. In 1965 President Johnson asked him to serve as chairman for The White House Conference on Natural Beauty. In 1966 became first president of National Recreation and Park Association, and was appointed to chairmanship of President's

Citizens' Advisory Committee on Environmental Quality, 1969–73. Throughout his career, has been associated with New York Zoological Society and now serves as its honorary chairman. Is a director of Resources for the Future, Inc. Awards for his contributions to conservation and outdoor recreation include Medal of Freedom, presented by President Johnson; Conservation Service Award of U.S. Department of the Interior; Horace Marden Albright Scenic Preservation Medal of the American Scenic and Historic Preservation Society; Fifty-Four Founders Award of Izaak Walton League of America; Distinguished Service Medal of The American Forestry Association; Audubon Medal of the National Audubon Society; Everly Gold Medal of the National Recreation and Park Association; Frances K. Hutchinson Medal of The Garden Club of America; and Gold Medal of the National Institute of the Social Sciences. Served as honorary president of Izaak Walton League of America in 1963, and is honorary member of American Society of Landscape Architects and honorary vice-president of The American Foresty Association.

HOLT BODINSON

International Who's Who, 1968–69.

Morris, Joe Alex. *The Rockefeller Brothers.* New York: Harper & Row, 1953.

Who's Who in America, 42d ed., 1982–83.

ROOSEVELT, THEODORE
(1858–1919)
Born October 17 in New York City. Graduated Phi Beta Kappa from Harvard University in 1880, and was awarded many honorary degrees in later years. Was president of New York Police Board, 1895–97, and assistant secretary of U.S. Navy, 1897–98. Served as second in command (lieutenant colonel) of First U.S. Cavalry Regiment during war with Spain. Was elected governor of New York in 1898, and vice-president of United States in November 1900. Became president on September 14, 1901, following assassination of William McKinley. Approved Newlands Reclamation Act of 1902. Used prestige of presidency to assure transfer of administration of federal forest reserves from General Land Office in U.S. Department of the Interior to Forest Service in U.S. Department of Agriculture on February 1, 1905. Gifford Pinchot, Roosevelt's friend for many years, was chief of Forest Service; they worked together to imple-

ment national program for conservation of natural resources. Roosevelt withdrew total of 234 million acres of public domain from entry as he created many national forests and mineral and coal reserves. Encouraged Inland Waterways Commission, which was prototype for regional multiple-purpose resource development projects. Sponsored first White House Governors' Conference in May 1908, which helped publicize conservation movement. Was a founding member of Boone and Crockett Club, associate member of Society of American Foresters, and an honorary fellow of The American Museum of Natural History. Was author of many books, including *Winning the West*, 1889–96. Died January 6, 1919.

ELWOOD R. MAUNDER

Concise Dictionary of American Biography, 1964.

Dictionary of American Biography, 1935.

Facts About the Presidents, 2d ed. New York: H. W. Wilson Company, 1968.

Who Was Who in America, 1897–1942.

ROTH, FILIBERT
(1858–1925)

Born April 20 in Wilhelmsdorf, Württemberg, Germany. Came to United States in 1870. University of Michigan, B.S. 1890; Marquette University, LL.D. (honorary) 1923. His microscopic studies of wood led to his appointment in 1893 as special agent and expert in timber physics in Division of Forestry in U.S. Department of Agriculture. Embarked on his career as teacher in 1898 at newly established New York State College of Forestry at Cornell University. After brief service in 1901–2 as first chief of Forestry Division in General Land Office in U.S. Department of the Interior, returned to teaching in 1903 as head of Department of Forestry at University of Michigan, the position he occupied until his retirement in 1923. Was author of numerous articles and textbooks on forest regulation and valuation. Other activities included service as Michigan's state forest warden and as member of its Conservation Commission; as organizer and later president of Michigan Forestry Association; and as representative of United States at International Forestry Congress at Brussels in 1910. Served as president of Society of American Foresters in 1917–18, and was one of first six members to be elected a fellow. A vigorous leader in many aspects of forestry, he made an outstanding contribution as respected and beloved master-teacher of hundreds of students who came under his influence. Died December 4, 1925.

Samuel T. Dana

Dana, Samuel T. "Filbert Roth—Master Teacher." *Michigan Alumnus Quarterly Review* 61 (14): 100–110, 1955.

Journal of Forestry. Memorial, 24:2–3, 1926.

"Man, Teacher, and Leader—Filbert Roth." *Journal of Forestry* 23:12–18, 1926.

Rothrock, Joseph Trimble

(1839–1922)

Born April 9 in McVeytown, Pennsylvania. Preparatory education at Freeland Seminary (now Ursinus College). In 1862 enlisted in Union Army, and advanced to captain in Twentieth Regiment of Pennsylvania Volunteer Cavalry. Harvard University, B.S. 1864; University of Pennsylvania, M.D. 1867. Taught botany at Pennsylvania State Agricultural College for two years. Became authority in forest mycology, entomology, and medical botany. In 1869 began private practice of medicine. As surgeon and botanist for Corps of Engineers' exploratory expedition west of the one-hundredth meridian, 1873–75, discovered and described numerous species of plants. In 1877 was appointed F. André Michaux lecturer in foresty methods at University of Strassburg, Germany, and returned home with conviction of need for forest conservation in United States. In 1864 helped organize Pennsylvania Forestry Association, serving as its first president. When governor of Pennsylvania appointed commission in 1893 to examine forest conditions in state, he was one of commissioners and prepared most of report. As result, legislature of 1895 established Division of Forestry in the Department of Agriculture. Became first commissioner of forestry, serving until 1904, during which period he initiated acquisition of land for state forests (authorized in 1897). Recognizing need for trained personnel to manage forests, was instrumental in 1903 in establishing Pennsylvania State Forest Academy at Mont Alto, now unit of Pennsylvania State University. During his career, was vice-president of The American Forestry Association. His long campaign for public education for forest conservation brought international recognition. Participated in American Forest Congress of 1905 and Joint Conservation Congress in December 1908, both held in Washington, D.C. Among his many writings was *Areas of Desolation in Pennsylvania*,

1915. His achievements as father of forestry in Pennsylvania were recognized in 1915 when Society of American Foresters made him honorary
member. Died June 2, 1922.

KENNETH B. POMEROY

Illick, Joseph S. "Joseph Trimble Rothrock." *The Pennsylvania German Society.*
Reprint from vol. 34, 1929.

Penn State Forestry Alumni Association. *Forestry Education in Pennsylvania.*
University Park, Pa.: 1957.

SALYER, JOHN CLARK, II

(1902–1966)

Born August 16 in Higgensville, Missouri. Central College, B.A. (biology) 1927; University of Michigan, M.S. 1931. From 1927 to 1930 was
science teacher in public schools of Parsons, Kansas; was instructor in
biology at Minot, North Dakota, 1932–33; then went to Iowa as state
biologist. In 1934 entered employ of Bureau of Biological Survey, U.S.
Department of Agriculture, which preceded Bureau of Sport Fisheries
and Wildlife, U.S. Department of the Interior. Was head of the bureau's
Division of Wildlife Refuges until 1961, when ill health forced him to
accept advisory assignment in the bureau. During years that he headed
Division of Wildlife Refuges, area dedicated to wildlife purposes rose
from 1.5 million acres to nearly 29 million acres in 279 units. Is credited
with having had major role in salvation of duck restoration program of
1934–36. Known mainly as father of National Wildlife Refuge System,
received American Motors Conservation Award in 1956 and Distinguished Service Award of U.S. Department of the Interior in 1962. Died
August 15, 1966.

DANIEL A. POOLE

U.S. Bureau of Sport Fisheries and Wildlife. News releases and personnel materials on file, Washington, D.C.

SAMPSON, ROBERT NEIL

(born 1938)

Born November 29 in Spokane, Washington. University of Idaho, B.S.
(agronomy) 1960; Harvard University, M.P.A. 1974. Spent twelve years
with U.S. Soil Conservation Service in Idaho as soil and area conserva-

tionist, and state information specialist. In 1972 served as program manager for land use in Idaho Planning and Community Affairs Agency. In 1974 transferred to Soil Conservation Service's Washington, D.C., office, where he worked with Land Use Committee and was acting director of Environmental Services Division. In 1976 and 1977 assisted Gambia, West Africa, in establishing soil and water management unit in that government's Ministry of Natural Resources. From 1978 to 1984 was executive vice-president of National Association of Conservation Districts, where he directed program of research and advocacy on soil and water conservation issues, and service to nation's 2,950 soil and water conservation districts. In 1984 became executive vice-president of The American Forestry Association. Is member of Alpha Zeta, Outdoor Writers Association of America, American Society of Association Executives, and Soil Conservation Society of America (a fellow in 1980). Was chosen 1972 Civil Servant of the Year by Boise Federal Business Association. Is charter member of board of directors of American Land Forum and is member of editorial advisory board of *The Environmentalist*. Has written widely on soil and water conservation, wildlife, outdoor subjects, and agriculture. Wrote and produced twenty-four-minute color film *Look to the Land*, 1973. His book *Farmland or Wasteland: A Time to Choose*, 1981, was named Best Book of 1982 by Natural Resources Council of America. Left the National Association of Conservation Districts in 1984.

NATIONAL ASSOCIATION OF CONSERVATION DISTRICTS

Who's Who in America, 42d ed., 1982–83.

SARGENT, CHARLES SPRAGUE
(1841–1927)
Born April 24 in Boston, Massachusetts. Harvard 1862, LL.D. 1907. After service in U.S. Army (1862–65) traveled abroad for three years furthering his knowledge of horticulture and landscape gardening. In 1873 became first director of Arnold Arboretum and developed it into world-famous center for study of trees and of plant introduction. Assembled Morris K. Jessup Collection of American Woods for The American Museum of Natural History (1881). His *Report on the Forests of North America* (1884), prepared for Tenth Census (1880), was first authoritative national survey of forest conditions. In 1884–85 served as chairman of New York Forestry Commission; its report under his aus-

pices led to establishment of Adirondack Forest Preserve and beginnings of forest conservation in the state. Founded and edited (1887–97) magazine *Garden and Forest*, a publication that combined practical and scientific information for gardeners with discussion of forestry problems. In 1896–97 was made chairman of committee appointed by National Academy of Sciences to investigate inauguration of forest policy for United States. Committee's report led to creation on February 22, 1897, of thirteen new forest reserves (twenty-one million acres) and in following year to first appropriations for protection and administration of reserves. Was a fellow of American Academy of Arts and Sciences and member or honorary member of more than twenty scientific societies around world. In 1920, Garden Club of America recognized his services to horticulture by presenting him with its first medal of honor. In 1923 received Frank N. Meyer Horticultural Medal from American Genetics Association for distinguished service in field of plant introduction. Of his many scientific publications, best known is *Silva of North America* (14 vols., 1891–1902), which laid foundation of dendrology in North America. Died March 22, 1927.

JOSEPH A. MILLER

Rehder, Alfred. "Charles Sprague Sargent." *Journal of the Arnold Arboretum*, vol. 8, April 1927.

SAWYER, ROBERT WILLIAM
(1880–1959)

Born May 12 in Bangor, Maine. Harvard University, B.A. 1902, LL.B. 1905; University of Oregon, LL.D. 1937. Admitted to Massachusetts bar and practiced until 1910. Was editor of *Bend* (Oregon) *Bulletin*, 1913–53. Was judge of County Court, Deschutes County, Oregon, 1920–27; president of Oregon Reclamation Congress, 1931–37, and of National Reclamation Association, 1946–47; and director, The American Forestry Association. As outstanding spokesman on reclamation and conservation affairs, received in 1958 The American Forestry Association's Distinguished Service Award. Was historian of note; his editorials had great impact on conservation direction of nation. Supported sustained-yield forestry and multiple-use management of natural resources. Was responsible for setting aside portion of Deschutes River as wildlife refuge, and for establishment of several state parks in Oregon. Was founder of Order of the Antelope. Was active in campaigning against littering woods, streams, and trails. Served as member of Hoover Commission Task Force on Water and Power, and of U.S. Forest Service Region Six Advisory Board, which wrote Oregon's basic forestry laws in late 1930s; and was chairman, Oregon State Highway Commission. As editor of daily newspaper, he stretched its influence far beyond boundaries of its circulation area. Died October 13, 1959.

FRED E. HORNADAY

SCHARLIN, PATRICIA JANE

Born in New York City. University of Pennsylvania, B.A. (international relations) 1950. Was a technical and staff editor at Carnegie Endowment for International Peace, 1950–55; executive editor and assistant to program officer for International Organizations Program, 1955–69, and editor-in-chief of its publications, 1969–72; director of Sierra Club International Earthcare Center, 1971; and special consultant on Law of the Sea Seminars for United Nations Institute for Training and Research, 1973. Represented public sector on variety of governmental delegations, interagency preparatory committees for conferences, and advisory committees, in positions such as observer for International Union for Conservation of Nature and Natural Resources (IUCN) at United Nations Headquarters; vice-chairman, executive committee, American Committee on International Conservation, 1981–82, and chairman, 1982; member, IUCN Commission on Environmental Policy and Law, and Commission on Education; member, US. National Committee on UNESCO Man and the Biosphere Program (MAB) and Delegation to Fifth Session of International Coordinating Committee; special information consultant to U.S. MAB Directorate on Biosphere Reserves, and to U.S. Delegation to Antarctic Treaty Power Meeting to draft Conservation Convention on Marine Living Resources, 1977; and member, Antarctic Section of Oceans Affairs Advisory Committee, U.S. Department of State, 1977. Her publications include *Non-Governmental Organizations: A Force for Change in the Law of the Sea* (with R. Stein), 1975; *The Sinai: Egypt Learns to Care for Its Historic Desert Wilderness* (with R. Eber), 1980; *The United Nations and the Environment: After Three Decades of Concern, Progress Is Still Slow, Ambio,* 1982. Also, in *Sierra Magazine:* "Letter from Nairobi," 1974; "Hope for the Great Whales," 1976; and "Editorial on Antarctica," 1979.

JAY COPELAND

SCHENCK, CARL ALWIN
(1868–1955)
Born March 25 in Darmstadt, Germany. Studied forestry at German universities, 1886–90, and entered state forest service of Hesse-Darmstadt. Granted Ph.D. by University of Giessen in 1894, and honorary degree of Doctor of Forest Science by North Carolina State College in 1952. On recommendation of Gifford Pinchot, was appointed forester of Biltmore estate, a 120,000-acre tract owned by George W. Vanderbilt in North Carolina, in 1895. Started first American school of applied forestry at Biltmore, September 1, 1898. A two-year course, it was never recognized as being of full professional standing, although some of its graduates were able foresters who served capably in government and industry. The school, disbanded in 1913, was comparable to German master school; Schenck taught most of courses himself. Wrote textbooks on forest management, mensuration, finance, silviculture, and logging and lumbering; these were used not only by Biltmore students, but at other, later schools as well. Served in German army during World War I, then returned to United States, where he lectured on forestry and taught at Montana State University. As one of first forestry educators in United States, he was dominant leader who helped pioneer new profession of forestry in America. Made his last visit to United States in 1952 at age of eighty-four. Died May 15, 1955.

HENRY CLEPPER

The Biltmore Immortals, vol. 2. Privately printed, 1957.

Schenck, Carl Alwin. *The Biltmore Story*, Ovid Butler, ed. Saint Paul, Minnesota: American Forest History Foundation, 1955.

SCHMITZ, HENRY
(1891–1965)
Born March 25 in Seattle, Washington. University of Washington, B.S. (forestry) 1915, M.S. 1919; Washington University, Saint Louis, Ph.D. 1919; University of Alaska, D.Sc. (honorary) 1955. Was appointed instructor in forestry at University of Idaho in 1919. Following service in U.S. Navy during World War I, was promoted to professor of forestry in 1923. Named director of Division of Forestry, University of Minnesota in 1925, he was advanced to deanship of College of Agriculture, Forestry, and Home Economics in 1944. In 1952 became president of University of Washington and served until retirement in 1958; then was president

emeritus. Was vice-president (1939) and a fellow of American Association for the Advancement of Science; vice-president (1942) of The American Forestry Association; and honorary vice-president and an organizer of Fifth World Forestry Congress held in Seattle in 1960. Was member of Botanical Society of America, American Phytopathological Society, and American Wood Preserves Association. Became member of Society of American Foresters in 1921; became a fellow in 1940; served as associate editor of *Journal of Forestry* for nine years and editor-in-chief for four years; was president of the society, 1942–45; and received its Sir William Schlich Memorial Medal, 1964. Contributed numerous papers to forestry, educational, and scientific journals on subjects ranging from wood-destroying fungi to higher education. At time of his death, was writing history of College of Forestry, University of Washington. Died January 20, 1965.

SOCIETY OF AMERICAN FORESTERS

American Men of Science (Physical and Biological Sciences), 10th ed., 1961.

Journal of Forestry. Obituary, vol. 63:230, March 1965.

Who Was Who in America, 1961–68.

SCHNEPF, MAX OWEN

(born 1941)

Born October 26 in Rock Rapids, Iowa. Iowa State University, B.S. (journalism and fish and wildlife management) 1964. Served as editor of publications for Iowa Conservation Commission, 1964–65. Was appointed editor of Soil Conservation Society of America's *Journal of Soil and Water Conservation* in 1965; continuing under his leadership, the *Journal* has become authoritative periodical on science and art of good land use, and has generated profound influence on land-use planning and conservation of renewable natural resources, not only in United States but throughout much of world. Among his innovative ideas have been several special issues of *Journal* devoted to a single topic, reprinted as special publications, and read throughout North America. Was editor of *Farmland, Food and the Future*, and currently serves on editorial board of *Journal of Environmental Education*. Received Soil Conservation Society of America's Presidential Citation in 1968 and 1973, and was named a fellow in 1976.

WALTER N. PEECHATKA

SCHOENFELD, CLARENCE ALBERT
(born 1918)

Born June 12 in Mineral Point, Wisconsin. University of Wisconsin, B.A. (journalism) 1941, M.S. (journalism/wildlife management) 1949. As high-school sophomore in 1933, began his environmental career editing newsletter for conservation club organized by Aldo Leopold. Wrote for *Field & Stream*, 1940–55; initiated environmental news column in *Wisconsin* (Madison) *State Journal*, 1956. Joined staff at University of Wisconsin–Madison in 1949. After joining faculty in 1953, introduced one of first interdisciplinary college courses in his field, "Environmental Management Problems, Principles and Policies," and pioneered master's-degree program in environmental communications. In 1969, became founding chair of University of Wisconsin-Madison Center for Environmental Communication and Education Studies, a consortium in fields of education, journalism, and natural-resource management. Author of six books on outdoor recreation and conservation, he was founding editor of international *Journal of Environmental Education* and its editor until 1976. Authored *The Environmental Communication Ecosystem: A Situation Report*; edited (with J. Disinger) three volumes on *Environmental Education in Action*; coauthored (with J. Hendee) award-winning monograph *Wildlife Management in Wilderness*; and compiled (with R. Gullierie) *Annotated Bibliography of Environmental Communication Research and Commentary*. Drafted working paper that became National Environmental Education Act of 1970. As president of National Association for Environmental Education (NAEE) in 1980, established National Commission on Environmental Education Research. Was elected to boards of directors of The American Forestry Association in 1976 and National Wildlife Federation in 1983. In 1982 was named Conservation Educator of the Year by National Wildlife Federation and received NAEE's first Walter E. Jeske Award for service to environmental education.

JUDITH M. SCHULTZ

SCHURZ, CARL
(1829–1906)

Born March 2 in Liblar, near Cologne, Germany. Entered University of Bonn in 1846 but was forced to flee before finishing because of his activities in 1848 revolution. Later received honorary Doctor of Laws degrees from Harvard University, University of Wisconsin, and Columbia University. Came to United States in 1852 and settled in Wisconsin. Was appointed minister to Spain in 1860 but resigned in 1861 to enter Union Army. During Civil War, commanded divisions at Fredericksburg, Gettysburg, and Chattanooga, and was discharged as major general. Was Washington correspondent of *New York Tribune*, 1865–66, and editor of *Detroit Daily Post*, 1866–67, of *Saint Louis Westliche Post*, 1867–68, and of *New York Evening Post*, 1881–83. Served as U.S. senator from Missouri, 1869–75, and secretary of U.S. Department of the Interior, 1877–81. As Interior secretary—first U.S. citizen of German birth to sit in presidential cabinet—he vigorously enforced laws protecting government timber from trespassers, and recommended policies of forest conservation, such as regulated timber sales, forest reserves, federal forest service, and national forestry commission. Ever the foe of patronage and corruption, he administered his department strictly on merit system. Was influential exponent of reform, high principles of public service, and enlightened citizenship. Was author of *Speeches* (1865) and *Henry Clay* (1887). Died May 14, 1906.

JOSEPH A. MILLER

Fuess, Claude M. *Carl Schurz, Reformer.* New York: 1932.

SCOTT, DOUGLAS WILLARD
(born 1944)
Born July 16 in Vancouver, Washington. University of Michigan, B.S. (forestry) 1966; graduate work (nondegree thesis research, *The Origins and Drafting of the Wilderness Bill: 1930–56*). In summers of 1964 and 1965, was employed as ranger at Carlsbad Caverns National Park. His interest in conservation movement began in February 1967 when he attended National Park Service hearing on wilderness proposal for Isle Royale National Park. Worked for National Audubon Society as Nature Center Planner (summer 1967) and for The Wilderness Society as intern and lobbyist (summer 1968). In summer 1969, was staff assistant to Senator Philip Hart, and worked on legislation to establish Sleeping Bear Dunes National Lakeshore. During academic year 1969–70, was full-time coordinator of "Teach-in on the Environment" at University of Michigan and served on national committee for Earth Day, 1970. Became coordinator of federal affairs for The Wilderness Society in Washington, D.C., where he worked on wilderness legislation, including East-

ern Wilderness Areas Act; helped coordinate campaign to defeat funding for supersonic transport, and coordinated conservationists lobbying for national interest lands provisions in Alaska Nature Claims Settlement Act, 1970–73. In 1973 became Northwest representative for Sierra Club and was closely involved with enactment of Hells Canyon Natural Recreation Area, Olympia National Park Expansion Act, Endangered American Wilderness Act, and Alpine Lakes Wilderness. His work in grassroots and legislative strategy concerned River of No Return Wilderness (Idaho), proposed Oregon Wilderness Act, and U.S. Forest Service roadless areas. Was coordinator of Citizens for America's Endangered Wilderness, 1975–78; lobbying coordinator of Alaska Coalition working for enactment of Alaska National Interest Lands Bill, 1978–80; and director of federal affairs for Sierra Club, 1980–83, and deputy conservation director, 1983 to present. Is member of national committee of League of Conservation Voters.

DOUGLAS W. SCOTT

SCOTT, JOHN WILLIAM
(1897–1956)

Born July 1 in Lewis County, Missouri. University of Missouri, B.A. 1894, M.A. 1897; University of Chicago, Ph.D. (zoology) 1904. After teaching biology in Kansas City high schools, joined Department of Zoology at Kansas State College in 1911. From 1913 until his retirement, was head of Department of Zoology at University of Wyoming, where he was also professor of zoology and research parasitologist from 1913 to 1945, becoming emeritus professor in 1951. Author of numerous scientific papers with early research interests in marine biology and embryology, he later became interested in parasitology, first of domestic animals (he discovered insect vector of swamp fever in horses) and then of wildlife. His studies of parasites of sage grouse led him to classic investigation of mating behavior in that species. Throughout his career, took active part in conservation work. Worked through Izaak Walton League of America, of which he was Wyoming state president; national director, 1934–46; and honorary president from 1952 until his death. An advocate of model game and fish laws, was executive secretary of Wyoming State Board of Fish and Game, 1937–39, and helped put into effect new policies of game management and conservation. Having traveled extensively in behalf of conservation, after retiring he became chairman of

National Committee on Policies in Conservation Education and helped found Conservation Education Association of which he became honorary president in 1953. Died August 15, 1956.

J. P. SCOTT

American Men of Science, 9th ed., 1955.

SCOTT, THOMAS GEORGE
(born 1912)
Born May 22 at Youngstown, Ohio. Iowa State University, Ph.D. (zoology) 1942. Was assistant to State entomologist of Iowa in 1935. Was extensive wildlife conservation specialist, 1935–37, and instructor, 1938, at Iowa State University; became leader, Iowa Cooperative Wildlife Research Unit, and biologist, U.S. Fish and Wildlife Service, 1938–48. Was game specialist and head, Section of Wildlife Research, Illinois State Natural History Survey, 1950–63; adjunct professor of zoology, Southern Illinois University, 1955–63; professor of zoology and senior staff member, Center of Zoonosis Research, University of Illinois, 1960–63. Then became head, Department of Fisheries and Wildlife, and associate director, Marine Science Center, Oregon State University, 1963–72, and was staff ecologist, National Water Commission, in 1970. Became director of Denver Wildlife Research Center, U.S. Fish and Wildlife Service, 1972; became senior scientist, 1975; and was transferred to editorial in 1978 until retiring in 1983. Received Nash Conservation Award Certificate of Merit in 1957; was elected a fellow of American Association for the Advancement of Science in 1960; received American Motors Professional Conservation Award in 1966; Meritorious Service Award from Fish and Wildlife Service in 1973; Citation of Merit from Iowa State University in 1979; Aldo Leopold Award from The Wildlife Society in 1982 (was honorary member from 1979); and Distinguished Service Award from Oregon State University in 1983. Was editor of *Journal of Wildlife Management*, 1962–65; edited its *Third Ten-Year Index for 1965–66, 1967–76*, and *Checklist of North American Plants for Wildlife Biologists*, 1980; and served as president of The Wildlife Society in 1968. His professional affiliations include American Society of Mammalogists, Ecological Society of America, American Ornithologists' Union, and American Fisheries Society. Has written more than eighty titles in ornithology, mammalogy, wildlife management, food habits, conservation, and pesticides. His special research interests are predation, especially of

red fox, and wildlife ecology. Three of his important publications are *Some Food Coactions of the Northern Plains Red Fox*, 1943; *Comparative Analysis of Red Fox Feeding Trends on Two Central Iowa Areas*, 1947; and (senior author) *Red Foxes and a Declining Prey Population*, 1955.

THE WILDLIFE SOCIETY
GLEN C. SANDERSON

American Men and Women of Science (Physical and Biological Sciences), 14th ed., 1979.

Wildlife Society News 106, October 1966.

Wildlife Society Bulletin, vol. 10, no. 2: 185–6, 1982.

SEAMAN, ELWOOD ARMSTRONG
(born 1916)
Born August 17 in Wheeling, West Virginia. College of Wooster, Ohio, B.A. 1939; University of Michigan, graduate work in fisheries biology, 1946–47; Marshall College, M.S. (aquatic biology) 1950. For three years beginning in 1939, was fisheries biologist for Ohio Department of Conservation, then field executive with Boy Scouts of America, 1941–42. During World War II served in U.S. Navy and was engaged in research on malaria and filariasis. Was chief of Division of Fisheries for West Virginia Conservation Commission, 1946–54, then was head of biological consulting firm in Pittsburgh, Pennsylvania. In 1956 became executive secretary of Sport Fishing Institute, Washington, D.C., and between 1957–69 was special assistant for natural resources in U.S. Department of the Air Force. Served as assistant to commissioner, Bureau of Reclamation, 1970–79, attaining senior scientist status, and finished his career with U.S. Fish and Wildlife Service in 1980 after completing special one-year study of fishes of Potomac River. Long active in American Fisheries Society, he was secretary-treasurer from 1957 to 1966, vice-president in 1967, and president in 1968. Originated the society's *Newsletter*, was largely responsible for its present quarterly *Journal*, and established its permanent headquarters in Washington, D.C. Is certified by the society as fisheries scientist, and was elected to honorary membership of the society in 1977. Is now operating tree farm in Shenandoah Valley of Virginia, and is doing part-time consulting work in aquatic biology. Is a fellow of American Association for the Advancement of Science. In

1967 was member of British Royal Society expedition to Aldabra Island in Indian Ocean. Is author of some forty scientific papers on fish management and related subjects.

ROBERT F. HUTTON

American Men and Women of Science (Physical and Biological Sciences), 14th ed., 1979.

Who's Who in America, 1966–67.

Who's Who in Ecology, 1973.

Who's Who in Government 1972–73.

SEARS, PAUL BIGELOW

(born 1891)

Born December 17 in Bucyrus, Ohio. Ohio Wesleyan University, B.S. 1913, B.A. 1914, D.Sc. 1937; University of Nebraska, M.A. 1915, LL.D. 1957; University of Chicago, Ph.D. (botany) 1922; Marietta College, Litt.D. 1951; University of Arkansas, LL.D. 1957; Bowling Green State College, D.Sc. 1958; Oberlin College, D.Sc. 1958; Wayne State University, LL.D. 1959. Was instructor in botany at Ohio State University, 1915–17 and 1918–19; and assistant and associate professor at University of Nebraska, 1919–28. Was professor and head of botany department at University of Oklahoma, 1928–38; served also as botanist for State Biological Survey of Oklahoma. From 1938 to 1950 was professor at Oberlin College, then in 1950 became affiliated with Yale University as professor of conservation and chairman of Conservation Program, where he established country's first graduate program in conservation of natural resources; became emeritus professor in 1960. From 1953 to 1955 also served as chairman of Yale's botany department. Was president of Ecological Society of America, 1948, and of American Association for the Advancement of Science, 1956, and of American Society of Naturalists. Was member of National Science Board, 1958–64. For two years was visiting professor in Tom Wallace Chair of Conservation at University of Louisville. Served as chairman of Yale Nature Preserve, and as chairman of board and honorary president of National Audubon Society. Received Eminent Ecologist Award, 1965, from The Ecological Society of America; Browning Award, 1972, from Smithsonian Institution; and Distinguished Service Award, 1976, from The American Institute of Biological Sciences. Is author of ten books, including Deserts on the March,

1935; *This Is Our World*, 1937; *Life and the Environment*, 1939; *The Living Landscape*, 1964; and *Lands Beyond the Forest*, 1969.

THE CONSERVATION FOUNDATION

American Men and Women of Science (Physical and Biological Sciences), 11th ed., 1965.

International Who's Who, 30th ed., 1966–67.

World Who's Who in Science, 1968.

Who's Who in America, 41st ed., 1980–81.

SETON, ERNEST THOMPSON
(1860–1946)

Born August 19 in South Shields, Durham, England. Was educated in Toronto, Canada, Collegiate Institute and Royal Academy of Arts and Sciences in London. His interest in natural sciences arose from his early life on Quebec farm. Following his art education abroad, traveled throughout Canada and United States, sketching and writing, mostly about wildlife, woodcraft, and nature lore. From 1898 onward, was popular lecturer on wildlife and natural resources. Was cofounder of Boy Scouts of America, and was organization's chief scout from 1910 to 1916. Later founded Woodcraft League of America, which, like Boy Scouts, was intended to inculcate concepts of nature instruction and knowledge about outdoors into training of American youth. A prolific and successful author, he wrote *Wild Animals I Have Known*, 1898, followed by forty additional books, one of most popular of which was *Lives of Game Animals*, 1925 (four volumes). His last book, *The Trail of an Artist Naturalist*, was published in 1940. Was awarded John Burroughs medal in 1928. Was president of Seton Institute, Santa Fe, New Mexico. Died October 23, 1946.

FRED E. HORNADAY

Twentieth Century Authors. New York: H. W. Wilson Company, 1942.

SHANKLIN, JOHN FERGUSON
(born 1903)

Born February 9 on Fishers Island, New York. New York State College of Forestry, Syracuse, B.S. 1924. Was privately employed until 1933, when he joined National Park Service. In 1942 was appointed special assistant for land utilization in office of the secretary of the Interior; in 1944 was made assistant director of forests, director in 1947, forest conservationist in 1950, and chief of land-use management in Division of Land Utilization in 1951. From 1950 to 1962 was forester in several divisions of office of the secretary. In 1962 was named assistant director for federal coordination of newly created Bureau of Outdoor Recreation. Retired from U.S. Department of the Interior in April 1968, continuing as consultant. Has been active in several conservation organizations: was chairman (1951–52) of Washington Section, Society of American Foresters and also chairman (1948–62) of the society's Committee on Natural Areas, which seeks to preserve under virgin conditions representative samples of recognized forest types. Was member of board of governors of The Nature Conservancy, 1961–66, and had long been director of Forest History Society. Also has long been active in Boy Scouts of America and has been member of National Council's Conservation Committee. Is author of several conservation publications of U.S. Department of the Interior, and coauthor of book *American Forestry: Six Decades of Growth*, 1960. Among honors accorded him are Silver Beaver and William T. Hornaday Gold Medallion in Conservation by Boy Scouts of America, 1957; merit citation by National Civil Service League, 1957; Distinguished Service Award with gold medal by the secretary of the Interior; and election to fellow in Society of American Foresters, 1961, and in Forest History Society, 1976.

HENRY CLEPPER

American Men and Women of Science (Physical and Biological Sciences), 13th ed., 1976.

Who's Who in America, 1968–69.

SHARPE, LOIS KREMER
(born 1906)
Born November 15 in Milwaukee, Wisconsin. Milwaukee-Downer College, B.A. (English and history) 1927; University of Rochester, M.S. (geology and geography) 1932; Northwestern University, Ph.D. (geology) 1942. Joined national staff of League of Women Voters of the United States as program specialist in water resources, 1960–70, and was staff coordinator for all environmental programs and projects for the league, 1970–76. While on the league's staff, was appointed to following committees: Environmental Advisory Board to the Chief, U.S. Army Corps

of Engineers, 1972–76; Environmental Advisory Committee to the Administrator of the Federal Energy Office, 1973–75; Advisory Committee for Project Independence, Federal Energy Administration, 1974–75; and National Academy of Sciences Advisory Committee on the IIASA, 1976–78. Was consultant to Conservation Foundation on its National Center for Voluntary Action project on environmental volunteers in America in 1972, and to Office of Technology Assessment's Committee, 1974–78, as well has having served on Materials Board of the National Academy of Science, 1975–77; on executive committee of Natural Resources Council of America; and on National Research Council's Committee on Gas Production, 1977–78. Also has served as federal commissioner on Interstate Commission on the Potomac River Basin, 1979–83; as consultant to National Science Foundation and on its Advisory Committee for Science and Society, 1978–79, and on Advisory Committee for Science, 1979–82; as member of Water Data for Public Use Committee of U.S. Geological Survey, 1979–80; and as member of National Science Foundation's Proposal Evaluation Committee of the Science for Citizens Project, 1977. Was recently appointed for third term to Fairfax County, Virginia, Water Authority. Received American Motors Conservation Award in professional class, 1972. Is author of *Know Your River Basin*, 1958, and *Who Pays for a Clean Stream?*, 1966.

LEAGUE OF WOMEN VOTERS OF THE UNITED STATES.

SHARPE, MAITLAND S.
(born 1945)
Born July 13 in Washington, D.C. Swarthmore College, B.A. (political science, with high honors) 1967; Stanford University, graduate degree program (political science) 1967–68. Entered conservation field as consultant to National Parks for the Future Project, conducted by Conservation Foundation, 1972. Joined staff of Izaak Walton League of America as coauthor and editor of *A Citizens Guide to Clean Water*, 1972; environmental affairs director, 1973–82; and conservation director and associate executive director, 1982. Has worked extensively on National Park policy and management, water policy, water quality, water resource development projects. National Forest management, public rangeland management, and variety of budgetary and fish and wildlife issues, while also directing lobbying, policy, and planning activities of Izaak Walton League. Has spoken and published on wide range of conservation topics,

with emphasis on privatization, rangeland management, and other public-lands issues. Has served on boards of Alliance of Environmental Education, Coalition for Water Project Review, and Council for a Sound Waterways Policy, and on executive committee of Natural Resources Council of America and National Fish and Wildlife Coordinating Committee. Is vice-president of River Country Voices and member of U.S. Man and the Biosphere Committee on Rangelands (MAB III).

IZAAK WALTON LEAGUE OF AMERICA

SHELDON, CHARLES
(1867–1928)
Born October 17 in Rutland, Vermont. Yale University, civil engineering degree, 1890. In 1898 was engaged to handle mining and railroad interests in Mexico, where he became interested in desert bighorn sheep and, by time of his retirement from active business in 1903, became leading authority on this species. Then devoted full time to exploration and study of wild sheep of North America. During 1906–8 explored northern slopes of Alaska Range and particularly Mount McKinley, where he engaged in mapping and collecting scientific specimens for National Museum and Bureau of Biological Survey. Largely as result of his activity, this area was set aside as McKinley National Park. Was author of Alaska Game Law Act of 1925, a model for laws of its kind. Was largely instrumental in calling National Conference on Outdoor Recreation by President Calvin Coolidge in 1924. Was active in organization as well as inception and conduct of the conference, which functioned until 1929. As member of Council of National Parks, Forests and Wildlife, laid groundwork for establishment of Great Smoky Mountains National Park. In his later years, was involved in strengthening legislation for protection of migratory game birds. Was chairman for many years of Conservation Committee of the Boone and Crockett Club. From 1912 to 1918 was a director of American Game Protection Association. Was member of Explorers Club, New York Zoological Society, American Ornithologists' Union, American Society of Mammologists, and Biological Society of Washington. Among his books were *The Wilderness of Denali*, *The Wilderness of the Upper Yukon*, and *The Wilderness of the North Pacific Coast Islands*. Died September 21, 1928.

JAMES B. TREFETHEN

SHELDON, WILLIAM GULLIVER

Who Was Who in America, 1897–1942.

Who's Who in America, 1927–28.

SHELDON, WILLIAM GULLIVER
(born 1912)
Born January 13 in New York City. Yale University, B.A. 1933; Cornell University, M.S. 1946, Ph.D. (vertebrate zoology) 1948. During summers 1930–32, collected mammals from British Columbia for U.S. National Museum, and conducted ecological study of northern mountain sheep. Was forest surveyor for Weyerhaeuser Timber Company in Washington State, 1933–34, and field assistant and collector for Sage Expedition in western China, collecting mammals and birds for The American Museum of Natural History, 1934–35. Served in U.S. Army during World War II. Was leader of Massachusetts Cooperative Wildlife Research Unit at University of Massachusetts, 1948–72. Was charter member of The Wildlife Society and of The Wilderness Society, and was active in conservation work on various committees for The Wildlife Society, American Society of Mammologists, Northeastern Birdbanding Association, American Ornithologists' Union, Boone and Crockett Club, and others. Received John Pearce Memorial Prize from Northeastern Section of The Wildlife Society in 1967 in recognition of his work in reintroducing wild turkeys into Massachusetts. Wrote more than seventy-five popular and scientific articles, including classic volume *The Book of the American Woodcock,* 1967; *The Wilderness Home of the Giant Panda,* 1975; and *Exploring for Wild Sheep in British Columbia in 1931 and 1932,* 1981.

LAURENCE R. JAHN
WILLIAM G. SHELDON

American Men and Women of Science, 14th ed., 1979.

SHELFORD, VICTOR ERNEST
(1877–1968)
Born September 22 in Chemung, New York. University of Chicago, B.S. (biology) 1903, Ph.D. (zoology) 1907. Was assistant in zoology at University of West Virginia, 1900–01, before teaching at University of Chicago, 1904–14. At University of Illinois, began as assistant professor, 1914–68; and became professor, 1927–46, and emeritus professor, 1946–68. Was also biologist in charge of research laboratories for Illi-

nois Natural History Survey, 1914–29; and in charge of marine ecology, Puget Sound Biological Station, in alternate years between 1914 and 1930. Was editor of *Naturalists' Guide to the Americas*, 1926; and was on editorial board of *Ecology*, 1920–28. Was member of board, Grasslands Research Foundation, and was on National Research Council's Committee on the Ecology of Grasslands, 1932–39, and on Committee on Wildlife, 1931–36. Was vice-chairman of Organizing Committee for the Ecological Society of America, 1914–15, and president in 1916; was chairman of Committee on Preservation of Natural Conditions, 1917–38; and received Eminent Ecologist Award in 1968. In 1946 promoted organization of Ecologists' Union, which later became The Nature Conservancy. Did much to establish physiological ecology and population ecology on firm basis, although his major contributions, efforts, and reputation were in community ecology. Was author of many scientific papers; his book *Animal Communities in Temperate America*, 1913, is generally recognized as furnishing impetus for getting animal ecology recognized as distinct biological science. Greatly concerned with use of experimental studies both in laboratory and in field, he summarized his ideas, equipment, and methods in book *Laboratory and Field Ecology*, 1929. In order to expound his new biome concept, he collaborated with Frederick E. Clements in producing book *Bio-Ecology*, 1939. His last major book, *The Ecology of North America*, 1963, was effort to describe all of biomes and major seral communities in North and Central America, with respect both to vegetation and to animal constituents. Is often said to have been father of animal ecology in Western Hemisphere. Died December 27, 1968.

GEORGE SPRUGEL, JR.

American Men of Science, 9th ed., 1955.

Bulletin of the Ecological Society of America; vol. 48, no. 4, 1967; vol. 49, no. 3, 1968; vol. 50, no. 1, 1969.

SHERRARD, THOMAS HERRICK
(1874–1941)
Born May 17 in Brooklyn, Michigan. Yale University, B.A., 1897; did graduate work at Harvard University and at forestry school of University of Munich, Bavaria. From 1899 to 1907 held various federal forestry assignments in Washington, D.C., and was appointed supervisor of Pike National Forest in Colorado in 1907. A year later, became supervisor of

Mount Hood National Forest in Oregon, where he served until 1933. When Civilian Conservation Corps (CCC) program was organized in 1933, was appointed CCC inspector for North Pacific Region of U.S. Forest Service, in Portland, Oregon. In 1935 was assigned to Division of Recreation and Lands, the position he held at time of his death. Was one of seven charter members of Society of American Foresters, on November 30, 1900. Division of Geographic Names, Washington, D.C., in 1947 approved naming of viewpoint on Larch Mountain on the Mount Hood National Forest in Oregon in his honor. Was prominently identified in conservation circles as public-lands administrator who emphasized use of forestlands for recreational purposes. Was also codesigner of well-known Forest Service pine tree shield badge. Died January 21, 1941.

ALBERT ARNST

Journal of Forestry. Obituary, 39:330, 1941.

SHIELDS, GEORGE OLIVER
(1846–1925)
Born August 26 in Batavia, Ohio. Attended common school in Delaware County, Iowa; beyond that, was self-educated. Founded magazine *Recreation* in 1894, continuing as editor and publisher until 1905, when it passed out of his hands; magazine was merged with *Outdoor Life* in 1927. From 1905 to 1912 published *Shields' Magazine.* Used his publications to advance conservation causes, such as Camp Fire Club, which he organized in 1897 and of which he was president from 1897 to 1902, and League of American Sportsmen, which he founded in 1898 and of which he was the only president. As his personal fortunes declined after 1908, the league also declined, and eventually died with him. Crusaded for legal bag limits of game, for banning automatic shotguns, and for other wildlife protective laws. Helped obtain passage by Congress in 1900 of Lacey Act, the first federal law regulating interstate commerce in and importation of wild birds and game. After failure of his magazine, devoted his full time to lecturing and writing on conservation. In his writings, used pseudonym Coquina. Was editor of *The Big Game of North America*, 1890, and of *American Game Fishes*, 1892, and was author of five books. Died November 10, 1925.

CHARLES H. CALLISON

Dictionary of American Biography, 9(1): 106, 1936.

Pearson, T. Gilbert. *Adventures in Bird Protection.* Chapter 19, pp. 336–45.

Who Was Who in America, 1897–1942.

SHIRLEY, HARDY LOMAX

(born 1900)

Born November 20 in Orleans, Indiana. Indiana University, B.A. (science) 1922; Yale University, Ph.D. (botany) 1928; University of Helsinki, honorary doctorate; Syracuse University, D.Sc. (honorary) 1966. After teaching mathematics at University of Nevada, 1922–25, was assistant in biochemistry at Boyce Thompson Institute of Plant Research, 1927–29. His career with U.S. Forest Service began with appointment as silviculturist at Lake States Forest Experiment at Saint Paul, Minnesota, 1929–39; then advanced to directorship of Allegheny (later named Northeastern) Forest Experiment station at Philadelphia, Pennsylvania, 1939–45. In 1945 was appointed assistant dean of State University of New York College of Forestry at Syracuse University; was promoted to deanship in 1952, and served in that position until his retirement in 1966; then was designated dean emeritus. His influence on higher education in forestry and related fields of natural resources management has been profound. For years, was chairman of Advisory Committee in Education in Forestry for the Food and Agriculture Organization of the United Nations. Was member of Committee on Forestry for the National Research Council, 1933–37, and was representative to the council's Division of Biology and Agriculture, 1944–46. Is a fellow of American Association for the Advancement of Science and of Society of American Foresters, on whose council he served during 1944–45 and for which organization he functioned as editor-in-chief of *Journal of Forestry* from 1946 to 1949. Has written widely on forestry and educational subjects for scientific and technical periodicals, and is author of book *Forestry and Its Career Opportunities,* 1973.

HENRY CLEPPER

American Men and Women of Science (Physical and Biological Sciences), 14th ed., 1979.

Journal of Forestry, 64(7): 484, July 1966.

Who's Who in America, 42d ed., 1982–83.

SHOEMAKER, CARL DAVID
(1872–1969)

Born June 20 in Napoleon, Ohio. Ohio State University, B.A. 1904, LL.B. 1907. After practicing law in Ohio, in 1912 bought *Evening News* in Roseburg, Oregon. In 1915, while publishing this newspaper, was appointed head of fish and game agency in Oregon, thus initiating lifelong interest and career in conservation. After ten years as state game warden, resigned to carry on private conservation work. Was commissioned by states of Oregon and Washington to go to Washington, D.C., in 1928 in effort to get appropriation for screening of irrigation ditches. In 1929 was sent back to Washington, D.C., to work on fisheries conservation problems. Then in 1930, when Special Committee of the Senate on Conservation of Wildlife Resources was established, he was first special investigator and later secretary, a position he held until subcommittee was abolished in December 1947. Was one of group of five persons who prepared original Coordination Act in 1934. Drafted original Migratory Bird Hunting Stamp (Duck Stamp), Pittman-Robertson Federal Aid in Wildlife Restoration Act (1937), and Dingell-Johnson Federal Aid to Fisheries Act (1950). Joined J. N. "Ding" Darling and others in organizing National Wildlife Federation in 1936. Long the federation's conservation director, he continued as its conservation consultant after his retirement. During his tenure, the federation initiated services such as *Conservation News* and *Conservation Report*, which he edited until 1953, and annual observance of National Wildlife Week. Was appointed member of first Federal Water Pollution Control Advisory Board. Also served as advisor to both departments of Agriculture and of the Interior, and was general counsel for International Association of Game, Fish and Conservation Commissioners from 1952 to 1960. Initiated *Legislative News Service* for Natural Resources Council of America, and edited the council's *Executive News Service* through 1960. In 1951 was awarded Aldo Leopold Award by The Wildlife Society, and in 1953 received U.S. Department of the Interior's Special Citation for outstanding service. Also was recipient of medal of honor in Hunting and Fishing Hall of Fame. Was honorary president of National Wildlife Federation and life member of The Wildlife Society. Died April 2, 1969.

LOUIS S. CLAPPER

Journal of Wildlife Management. Obituary, 33(4): 1055–56, October 1969.

SHUPP, BRUCE DANIEL
(born 1939)
Born December 5 in eastern Pennsylvania. Pennsylvania State University 1957–59. By 1969 had developed and sold prosperous horticulture/landscape business. Returned to Pennsylvania State University, B.S. (fishery biology) 1970. Commenced fisheries career at Pendells Creek National Fish Hatchery, U.S. Fish and Wildlife Service, Michigan, 1970–71; advanced to the service's Central States Fishery Management Station, Princeton, Indiana, to manage federal lands in Indiana, Illinois, and Missouri. Cooperated with Missouri Department of Conservation in developing effective Saint Louis Urban Fishing Program, 1971–72. In 1972 joined New York's Department of Environmental Conservation and progressed from regional fisheries management biologist to statewide warmwater fisheries program supervisor with special assignments: to develop New York's Urban Fishing Program; to lead in developing ten-year State Conservation Fund Fiscal Management Plan; to design and implement successful *I Love New York: Hunting and Fishing* promotional program; to encourage research for culture of walleye, muskellunge/northern pike hybrids, and bass management. In 1980 became chief of New York's Bureau of Fisheries. Since 1970 has been active member of American Fisheries Society (AFS): as chairman of Ways and Means Committee; member of Management and Administrators Sections, Certified Fisheries Scientist; past-president of New York Chapter and chairman of first Annual Workshop Committee; and arrangements chairman, Northeast Division's Acid Rain/Fisheries Symposium. Was very active in supporting Dingell-Johnson expansion legislation, chairs the AFS carp exploitation committee, and is steering-committee chairman for AFS 1984 annual meeting. Has authored several articles for *Fisheries* and other publications, presented numerous papers, and been panelist at many professional and public meetings.

WILLIAM A. PEARCE

SIMMS, DENTON HARPER
(born 1912)
Born December 21 in Alamogordo, New Mexico. University of Missouri, B.A. and B.J. 1935. Joined U.S. Soil Conservation Service (SCS) in 1935 as messenger in Albuquerque, New Mexico, regional office; became member of regional Information Division in 1938, chief in 1943,

and in 1951 was promoted to director of the service's Information Division of SCS, where he gave meritorious and imaginative leadership in conservation information and education until retirement in 1968. Directed SCS information program during period when agency's responsibility grew from main concern with erosion control to direct involvement in more than fifteen major activities. Was elected a fellow of Soil Conservation Society of America in 1958, and was awarded Presidential Citations by the society in 1959 and 1962. Received American Motors Conservation Award in 1967 and U.S. Department of Agriculture's Superior Service Award in 1959. Is author of many articles and publications in field of soil and water conservation, and writes and collects in field of Western American history. Is author of *The Soil Conservation Service*. Was leader in conceiving, developing, and publishing five conservation education cartoon booklets issued by Soil Conservation Society of America. Is member of Outdoor Writers Association of America; Conservation Education Association; The Wilderness Society; Audubon Naturalist Society; and Soil Conservation Society of America.

F. Glennon Loyd

Who's Who in the Southwest, vol. 5, 1956.

SIRI, WILLIAM EMIL
(born 1919)
Born January 2 in Philadelphia, Pennsylvania. University of Chicago, 1937–43; University of California, 1947–50 (physics). As staff physicist from 1943 to 1974 in Lawrence Berkeley Laboratory, University of California, conducted research in application of physics to medicine. As staff senior scientist, formed and headed until his retirement in 1981 the laboratory's multidisciplinary Energy Analysis Program. His principal avocational activities include environmental action and mountaineering. Conducted overseas scientific and mountaineering expeditions, including University of California Andean Expeditions, 1950, 1952 (leader); California Himalayan Expedition, 1954 (leader); International Physiological Expedition to Antarctica, 1957–58 (field leader); and American Mount Everest Expedition, 1963 (deputy leader). Has been member of Sierra Club since 1944; on its board of directors, 1955–74; was president, 1964–66, and treasurer, 1966–69; and has been honorary vice-president since 1974. Has been president since 1968 of Save San Francisco Bay Association; and is director of California League of Conser-

vation Voters. Is past-director of Sierra Club Foundation (1964–78); of Planning and Conservation League; and of American Alpine Club. Received California Conservation Council Honor Award, 1965; National Geographic Society Hubbard Medal, 1963; Geographical Society of Philadelphia Elisa Kent Kane Medal, 1963; Sol Feinstone Environmental Award, 1977; and Sierra Club's William E. Colby (1975) and Francis P. Farquhar (1979) awards. Is author of textbook on biophysics and of other scientific publications, and of articles on conservation, energy, and mountaineering.

Sierra Club Handbook, 1967.

Who's Who in America, 42d ed., 1982–83.

Who's Who in the West, 11th ed., 1968.

World Who's Who in Science, 1968.

SKOK, RICHARD ARNOLD

(born 1928)

Born June 19 in Saint Paul, Minnesota. University of Minnesota, B.S. 1950; M.F. (forestry) 1954; Ph.D. 1960. U.S. Army, 1950–52. Was assistant professor, School of Forestry, University of Montana, 1958–59. At University of Minnesota College of Forestry at Saint Paul, was assistant professor, 1960–61; associate professor, 1962–63; professor since 1965; associate dean, 1971–74; and dean since 1974. For U.S. Department of Agriculture, was chairman of McIntire-Stennis advisory board, 1977–78; and member of Joint Council on Food and Agricultural Science, 1979. Has been trustee of Wilderness Research Foundation, which operates Quetico-Superior Wilderness Research Center with headquarters in Duluth, Minnesota, since 1977. Is a fellow of Society of American Foresters; member of Forest Products Research Society; and was president of Association of State College and University Research Organizations, 1981–82.

HENRY CLEPPER

American Men and Women of Science (Physical and Biological Sciences), 15th ed., 1982.

Who's Who in America, 42d ed., 1982–83.

SMITH, ALLEN E.
(born 1941)
Born August 10 in Norwalk, Connecticut. University of New Hampshire, B.S. (engineering and business administration) 1966. Served in U.S. Marine Corps. Directed a state-commissioned research project, *The Feasibility of Particle Board Manufacture in New Hampshire*, 1965, at University of New Hampshire. Held management positions (1966–75) with Perkin-Elmer Corp., Digilab, Inc., and Dunham, Inc. Is member of Sierra Club National Wilderness Committee, and is officer of New England chapter. Is active in The Wilderness Society, Appalachian Mountain Club, Vermont Natural Resources Council, Society for the Protection of New Hampshire Forests, and U.S. Forest Service citizen planning process. Directed field inventory of wilderness-area proposals in White Mountain and Green Mountain national forests for congressional hearings that preceded passage of 1975 Eastern Wilderness Areas Act. Was production consultant for national TV special "America's Wild Places," 1974. From 1975 to 1979 was chief financial officer for Sierra Club; and reader-editor of John Hart's *Walking Softly in the Wilderness*, 1977. From 1979 to 1982 was executive assistant to assistant attorney general, Land and Natural Resources Division, U.S. Department of Justice; implemented major reorganization of the division and served on Attorney General's Task Force on Litigation Management Support. Since 1982 has been president and chief executive officer of Defenders of Wildlife. Is also member of numerous other professional and environmental organizations. In 1983 was elected to steering committee of League of Conservation Voters.

DEFENDERS OF WILDLIFE
ALLEN E. SMITH

SMITH, ANTHONY WAYNE
(born 1906)
Born February 5 in Pittsburgh, Pennsylvania. University of Pittsburgh, B.A. 1926; Yale University, LL.B. 1934. During 1932–33 was secretary to Governor Gifford Pinchot of Pennsylvania. Then was with law firm in New York City, and was admitted to practice in courts of New York State and of District of Columbia. From 1937 to 1956 held several positions, including assistant general counsel of Congress of Industrial Organizations and executive secretary of its Committee on Regional Development

and Conservation. From 1958 to 1980 was president and general counsel of National Parks and Conservation Association. Was member of executive committee of Citizen's Committee on Natural Resources, and was also on steering committee of National Watershed Congress and on executive committee of Citizen's Conference on the Potomac River Basin. In addition, has been president of South Central Pennsylvania Citizen's Association, an organization concerned with planning of Potomac River Basin. For two decades has been active in organizations and movements for improved watershed management, river-basin planning, forestry, soil conservation, and wildlife management.

PAUL C. PRITCHARD

Who's Who in America, 42d ed., 1982–83.

SMITH, GLEN ALBERT
(1880–1858)
Born September 15 near Rich Hill, Missouri. Was largely self-educated in forest, range, and wildlife management. In early adulthood worked in Kansas, Texas, and Montana on cattle drives, on cattle ranches, and in various capacities for lumber companies. Entered U.S. Forest Service in 1907 and retired in 1942, having served thirty-five years—thirty years in Northern region, two in Intermountain region, and three in Rocky Mountain region. His assignments were divided among several key administrative positions, including ranger, supervisor, and assistant regional forester in charge of range and wildlife management. It is estimated that he traveled forty thousand miles with saddle- and packhorses in course of inspecting these activities. A wise and courageous administrator, he always placed welfare of resources above other considerations in dealing with the public or his fellow workers. Understood need for research and used it in his own work, although he himself was nontechnical. Held the line against public pressure for increased grazing use of forest in his region during World War I, when damage from such use was continuing unchecked on most other western national forests. As assistant regional forester in Intermountain region, brought to light the damage that had been done there for years, and motivated program working toward better watershed protection and conservative use of range and wildlife resources. Was founder, and for ten years chairman, of Montana Sportsmen Association. Organized Dude Ranchers Association. Was member of Society of American Foresters, and served on its council. Was

also member of American Society of Range Management. Died February 14, 1958.

LLOYD W. SWIFT

SMITH, HERBERT AUGUSTINE
(1866–1944)
Born December 6 in Southampton, Massachusetts. Yale University, B.A. 1889, Ph.D. 1897. Entered Bureau of Forestry (now U.S. Forest Service) in 1901 in charge of editorial and public educational activities. Was member of early group that spearheaded forest conservation movement, and was pioneer in introducing study of conservation in public schools. A student of economic and political history, he was for more than three decades advisor to successive chiefs of Forest Service, for whom he prepared annual reports and wrote and edited other official papers. In 1908 became member of editorial board of *Proceedings* of Society of American Foresters, the publication that preceded *Journal of Forestry*, of which he was editor-in-chief from 1935 to 1937. One of best-informed individuals of his era on history of conservation movement, he assembled much material on the subject for deposit in Library of Congress. His technical papers on history of forestry and conservation set standards of literary quality for the profession. In 1939 was elected a fellow of Society of American Foresters. Following his retirement from Forest Service in 1937, aided Gifford Pinchot in writing the latter's personal memoirs of early history of Forest Service. Died July 21, 1944.

HENRY CLEPPER

"Herbert A. Smith, 1866–1944." *Journal of Foresty*. 42:625–26, December 1944.

Who Was Who in America, vol. 2, 1943–50.

SNIESZKO, STANISLAS FRANCIS
(1902–1984)
Born January 28 in Krzyz, Poland. Jagiellonian University, M.S. (bacteriology) 1924, Ph.D. 1926. Was awarded Polish government fellowship in Leipzig in 1928 and Rockefeller fellowship at University of Wisconsin, 1929–32. In 1936 became assistant in bacteriology at University of Maine, and advanced to assistant professor. After receiving U.S. natural-

ization in 1944, served in chemical corps of U.S. Army during World War II, attaining rank of captain. In 1946 became chief bacteriologist and laboratory director at U.S. Fish and Wildlife Service Microbiological Laboratory (now called National Fish Health Research Laboratory), Kearneysville, West Virginia; was director until retiring in 1972 and was senior scientist from 1972 until his death. Was chairman of Fish Disease Committee of the American Fisheries Society for many years. Was convener of major symposia on fish diseases by American Fisheries Society and by New York Academy of Science. Edited five specialized texts on fish diseases for T. F. H. Publications, Neptune, New Jersey. Also edited *Symposium on Diseases of Fishes and Shellfishes* published by American Fisheries Society in 1970. Was author of more than one hundred scientific papers on fish diseases and pathology, cellulose decomposition bacteria, and miscellaneous viral and bacterial subjects. His studies have been published in German, French, and Polish journals. Held professional certification as fisheries scientist in American Fisheries Society; was a fellow of American Association for the Advancement of Science, and was member of Society of Microbiologists, Society of Experimental Biologists, and New York Academy of Science. Among his many awards are Distinguished Service awards from U.S. Department of the Interior, American Fisheries Society, and Wildlife Disease Association; Barnett L. Cohen Award for excellence from American Society for Microbiology; and honorary doctor of science from University of West Virginia. Was internationally recognized as teacher, researcher, and innovative administrator—the American dean of fish diseases. Died January 13, 1984.

ELWOOD A. SEAMAN

American Men of Science (Physical and Biological Sciences), 11th ed., 1967.

SPURR, STEPHEN HOPKINS
(born 1918)
Born February 14 in Washington, D.C. University of Florida, B.S. (botany) 1938; Yale University, M.F. 1940, Ph.D. 1950. His research career began in 1940 at Harvard Forest, where he served as acting director and assistant professor. During 1950–52 was associate professor of forestry at University of Minnesota. From 1952 to 1971 served on faculty of University of Michigan as professor of silviculture; was dean of School of Natural Resources, 1962–65; and has been dean of Horace H. Rackham School of Graduate Studies since 1965. From 1971 to 1974 was

president of University of Texas, Austin. Currently is professor in University of Texas Lyndon B. Johnson School of Public Affairs, and member of botany department faculty. While at Harvard Forest, gained international reputation in photographic interpretation as author of *Aerial Photographs in Forestry* (1948) and its revision *Photogrammetry and Photointerpretation* (1960). From work with aerial photographs, became involved in various studies of measurement of significant characteristics of forests, and published *Forest Inventory* (1952). In addition to research in remote sensing and measurements, carried out wide range of studies in silviculture and ecology. Was Oberlaender Trust Fellow in Germany in 1950; became a National Science Foundation science fellow at University of California at Berkeley during 1957–58; and served as Fulbright Research Scholar in New Zealand and Australia in 1960. Became second American to be chosen honorary member of New Zealand Institute of Foresters. A National Science Foundation Science Faculty fellowship gave him opportunity for further study and writing, and in 1964, he published *Forest Ecology*. Has held numerous committee and executive assignments, including six years on council of Society of American Foresters; was also founder and first editor of its journal, *Forest Sciences*, and president, 1980–81. Is former governor of The Nature Conservancy. Was one of founders of Organization for Tropical Studies, and president, 1967–68. Served on President's Advisory Panel on Timber and the Environment; headed study team that analyzed Rampart Dam proposal in Alaska for Natural Resources Council of America; and has been member of National Academy of Sciences' Committee on Renewable Resources for Industrial Materials. Chaired Council of Graduate Schools in U.S., and Graduate Record Examination Board. Was trustee of Institute for International Education; Carnegie Foundation for the Advancement of Teaching; Educational Testing Service; and Carnegie Council on Policy Studies in Higher Education. Currently serves on Yale University Council. Received honorary Doctor of Science degree from University of Florida, and was awarded Wilbur L. Cross Medal by Yale University.

R. KEITH ARNOLD
JAMES R. LYONS

American Men and Women of Science (Physical and Biological Sciences), 15th ed., 1982.

Who's Who in America, 41st ed., 1980–81.

STAHR, ELVIS JACOB, JR.
(born 1916)
Born March 9 in Hichman, Kentucky. University of Kentucky, B.A.
1936; Oxford University (Rhodes scholar), B.A. 1938, B.C.L. 1939,
M.A. 1943. Received twenty-six honorary degrees during his distinguished career as public administrator and educator. Was dean of College
of Law and provost of University of Kentucky, vice-chancellor of University of Pittsburgh, president of West Virginia University, secretary of U.S.
Army, and president of Indiana University. Was president, National Audubon Society, from 1968 to 1979, and thereafter was president emeritus. Served in 1956–57 as executive director of President Eisenhower's
Committee on Education Beyond High School. Is director of Alliance to
Save Energy, World Environment Center, and Environmental and Energy
Study Institute, and is Washington partner of San Francisco law firm of
Chickering and Gregory. Is former director of Chase Manhattan Bank
and Federal Reserve Bank of Chicago, among others. As Audubon pres-
ident, was member of U.S. Delegation to the Stockholm Conference, of
National Commission for World Population Year, and of International
Whaling Commission.

CHARLES H. CALLISON
ELVIS J. STAHR, JR.

National Audubon Society. Staff biographies.

Who's Who in America, 42d ed., 1982–83.

STEEN, HAROLD KARL
(born 1935)
Born May 12 in Vashon, Washington. University of Washington, B.S.F.
1957, M.F. 1962, Ph.D. 1969. Began his career with U.S. Forest Service
in forest management in 1957, and was involved with forest-fire research
at the service's Pacific Northwest Forest and Range Experiment Station,
1962–64. In 1969 joined Forest History Society as assistant director,
edited *Journal of Forest History,* was associate director for research and
library services, and was appointed executive director in 1978. In 1970
received faculty appointment at University of California, Santa Cruz,
where he taught courses in conservation history and general forestry. Has
been active on history committees for Society of American Foresters and
for Sierra Club. In 1979, was elected deputy leader of Forest History

Group of IUFRO. His most important publication is *The U.S. Forest Service: A History*, 1976 (reprinted 1977).

RONALD J. FAHL

STEPHENS, EDWIN SYDNEY
(1881–1948)
Born September 4 in Columbia, Missouri. University of Missouri, B.A. 1903. After year at Harvard University, entered family firm, Stephens Publishing Company, and became its president in 1931. For thirty years was ardent sportsman. Led reform movement in Missouri that would reach from his state to affect wildlife management of all states. In 1935, seeing political wildlife management fail, he demanded new concepts through Conservation Federation of Missouri, which he led in campaign to amend state constitution through initiative petition. In the end, Missouri adopted constitutional amendment that gave power to four-man Conservation Commission. Its principle and legal provisions have survived unchanged since 1936 partly because he accepted chairmanship of the commission, and in ten years created strong tradition of nonpartisan policymaking that did not interfere with professional administration. Stood for long-range programs and research, technical skill, and nonpolitical decisions. Aldo Leopold wrote that Stephens "belongs to a group of conservationists . . . who might be called the statesmen of wildlife management . . . because they created the legal, political, and financial framework within which it could operate." Was honorary life member of The Wildlife Society and of Outdoor Writers Association of America, and honorary life president of Conservation Federation. Died October 17, 1948.

CHARLES H. CALLISON

Man and Wildlife in Missouri, 1950.

Missouri Conservationist, December 1948 (special edition).

STODDARD, HERBERT LEE, SR.
(1889–1970)
Born February 24 in Rockford, Illinois. Was self-educated in ornithology, ecology, and forest-wildlife management. Early in his career, worked as taxidermist in natural history museums: during 1910–13 and 1920–24

with ornithology division of Milwaukee (Wisconsin) Public Museum; and during 1913–20, with Field Museum of Natural History in Chicago. Joined Biological Survey, U.S. Department of Agriculture, in 1924 as leader of Cooperative Quail Study Investigation. On completion of this research and after year in Washington, D.C.—where he assisted with organization of first game management fellowships—resigned in 1931 to become director of Cooperative Quail Study Association at Thomasville, Georgia, a research, service, and consulting organization. When this organization disbanded in 1943, became consultant in upland game and forest management in Deep South. Was active in organization of Inland Bird Banding Association, was its first treasurer in 1922, and served for many years on National Advisory Committee on waterfowl. Was author of numerous ornithological and wildlife management papers, and his book *The Bobwhite Quail: Its Habits, Preservation and Increase*, 1931, won for him Brewster Medal awarded by American Ornithologists' Union in 1936. When Tall Timbers Research, Inc., a privately endowed institution dedicated to biological research, and particularly to ecology of fire, was established in 1959, he was elected vice-president and became president in 1963. Received the Outdoor Life Award, 1928, for wildlife conservation, Eastern Division. Was elected a life fellow of American Ornithologists' Union in 1936, and honorary member of The Wildlife Society in 1940 and of Wisconsin Society of Ornithologists, Inc. in 1940. Died November 19, 1970.

ROY KAMAREK

American Men of Science (Physical and Biological Sciences), 11th ed., 1965.

Stoddard, H. L. *Memoirs of a Naturalist*. University of Oklahoma Press, 1969.

STOEL, THOMAS BURROWES, JR.

(born 1941)

Born June 18 in Portland, Oregon. Princeton University, B.A. cum laude (mathematics) 1962; Harvard Law School, J.D. magna cum laude 1965; Rhodes Scholar, Balliol College, Oxford University, Ph.D. (law) 1968. Was law clerk to Associate Justice John M. Harlan, U.S. Supreme Court; staff attorney for Cabinet Task Force on Oil Import Control; assistant director, then deputy director, of Cabinet Committee on Education, 1970; and executive assistant, then special assistant, to director, Office of Management and Budget. Has been senior staff attorney of Natural

Resources Defense Council since cofounding the council in 1971; has been director of its International Project since 1974. Is president of Global Tomorrow Coalition; vice-chairman of American Committee on International Conservation; and member of Program Planning Advisory Group and of Commission on Environmental Policy, Law, and Administration for the International Union for Conservation of Nature and Natural Resources. Was lecturer on environmental law, Harvard Law School, in 1976 and 1977. His publications include: *Fluorocarbon Regulation* (with two coauthors), 1980; chapter, "Domestic Environmental Aspects," in *Ocean Thermal Energy Conversion*, 1977; chapter "Protection of the Environment," in *The Energy Question: An International Failure of Policy*, vol. 2, 1974; "Atoms for Peace" (coauthored with Jacob Scherr) in *Amicus Journal*, 1979; and "The National Forest Management Act" in *Environmental Law*, 1978.

JAY COPELAND

STONE, EDWARD HARRIS, II
(born 1933)
Born August 28 in Lanesboro, Pennsylvania. State University of New York, B.S. (forestry) 1955. Was engaged in private practice, 1955–56, and was landscape architect for his post in U.S. Army, 1956–57. Was landscape architect with U.S. Forest Service with assignments in Rocky Mountain and Alaska regions, 1958–65, becoming the service's first chief landscape architect, Washington, D.C., 1965–79; has been assistant director of recreation since 1979. Has been instrumental in increased professional involvement by landscape architects throughout this and other federal agencies. Served on National Advisory Council on Historic Preservation, 1975–76, and as juror for highway design awards competitions held by U.S. Department of Transportation. For many years served on board of U.S. Civil Service Examiners for profession of landscape architecture. Received Arthur S. Fleming Award of U.S. Junior Chamber of Commerce for outstanding federal government service, 1969. Was president of American Society of Landscape Architects, 1975–76, during which time he introduced programs, such as film *Legacy for Living*, that have had lasting effects on the profession. Served as his professional society's representative at American Design Bicentennial, Inc., and was its secretary-treasurer. Was awarded American Society of Landscape Architects President's Medal in 1979. Has been frequent

speaker on environmental design subjects at Smithsonian Institution, International Forestry Union of Research Organizations, Soil Conservation Society of America, International Federation of Landscape Architects, and many universities. Supervised development of publications for U.S. Forest Service, which has led to significant advancements in visual resource management and planning for highway and forestry programs.

AMERICAN SOCIETY OF LANDSCAPE ARCHITECTS

Who's Who in America, 42d ed., 1982–83.

STROUD, RICHARD HAMILTON

(born 1918)
Born April 24 in Dedham, Massachusetts. Bowdoin College, B.S. (biology) 1939; University of New Hampshire, M.S. (zoology and fisheries) 1942; Yale University, graduate studies (ecology) 1947–48; Boston University, graduate studies (education) 1948. Was fishery research specialist for Tennessee Valley Authority, 1942 and 1946–47, and was in U.S. Army, 1943–45. Was chief aquatic biologist, Massachusetts Division of Fisheries and Game, 1948–53; and assistant executive vice-president, 1953–55, and executive vice-president, 1955–81, of Sport Fishing Institute. Has been aquatic resources consultant since 1982; editor for Marine Recreational Fisheries Symposium (annual series) since 1982; and senior scientist at Aquatic Ecosystems Analysts since 1983. Has served on more than fifty major committees, commissions, task forces, study groups, and boards in advisory capacity to many federal, state, and private conservation agencies. Was fisheries expert advisor to U.S. Senate Select Committee on Government Operations, and member of World Panel of Fishery Experts of United Nations. Has also been advisor on fish conservation to authorities in Canada, France, Great Britain, Japan, Mexico, Sweden, and to Food and Agriculture Organization of the United Nations. Was member-at-large and member of Conservation, Jamboree, and Project SOAR committees of Boy Scouts of America, 1955–77, and received its SOAR Award in 1972. Was founder in 1962 and has continued to be trustee of Sport Fishery Research Foundation; was managing vice-president, 1962–81. Became honorary life member in 1981 of Natural Resources Council of America; and was treasurer, 1961–67, vice-chairman, 1968–69, and chairman, 1969–71. Has long served American Fisheries Society in diverse committee assignments; is certified by the society as fisheries scientist, was elected honorary life

member in 1975, and was president in 1979–80. Was Pentelow lecturer, University of Liverpool, England, in 1975, and was invited (with R. G. Martin) by Japan Sport Fishing Foundation to lecture in Japan in 1976. Is a fellow of American Institute of Fisheries Research Biologists, receiving organization's Outstanding Achievement Award in 1981; and has been member of board of directors, National Coalition for Marine Conservation, since 1975. Has helped plan or has initiated, organized, chaired, summarized, or edited thirty-five major scientific fisheries symposia; and has published more than 130 scientific and semitechnical papers, book chapters, and articles on fisheries subjects, several of book length. These include *Fisheries Report for Some Central, Eastern, and Western Massachusetts Lakes, Ponds, and Reservoirs, 1951–52, 1955*; fish conservation section in *The Fisherman's Encyclopedia*, 1963; (with P. A. Douglas) *A Symposium on the Biological Significance of Estuaries*, 1971; *Marine Recreational Fisheries*, vols. 1, 2, 7, and 8, 1976, 1977, 1982, and 1983; and (both with Henry Clepper) *Black Bass Biology and Management*, 1975, and *Predator-Prey Systems in Fisheries Managment*, 1979. Was author-editor of Sport Fishing Institute's monthly *SFI Bulletin*, 1955–81. Was principal architect of federal legislation to establish both inland and marine water quality research laboratories, reservoir fisheries, and marine game fish research programs. In 1966 he directly negotiated unique, private, ten-year agreement between American billfish angling interests and Japanese commercial tuna-fishing interests that stopped vandalism of Japanese long-line gear sets, in return for their transfer to waters at least fifty miles seaward of more than one hundred U.S., Mexican, and Central American sport-fishing ports serving billfish waters. Was principal early proponent of two-hundred-mile-wide coastal marine fisheries conservation zone, leading to eventual enactment of federal Fish Conservation and Management Act of 1976 (PL 94–265). In recognition of these accomplishments, received Conservation Achievement Award of National Wildlife Federation in 1976. As president of American Fisheries Society (1979–80), engineered successfully the establishment of new fisheries technical journal, *North American Journal of Fisheries Management*. Was initiator and chief architect of draft bill (1980) for federal legislation, introduced into Ninety-eighth Congress (1983) as H. R. 2965, to encourage coastal states to license their marine anglers according to uniform national standards.

PHILIP A. DOUGLAS
RICHARD H. STROUD

American Men and Women of Science (Physical and Biological Sciences), 15th ed., 1982.

Two Thousand Men of Achievement, 3rd ed., 1971.

Who's Who in America, 42d ed., 1982–83.

Who's Who in the World, 6th ed., 1982–83.

STUART, ROBERT YOUNG
(1883–1933)
Born February 13 in Cumberland County, Pennsylvania. Dickinson College, B.A. 1903, M.A. 1906, D.Sc. (honorary); Yale School of Forestry, M.F. 1906. Was appointed in 1906 as forest assistant in U.S. Forest Service and was assigned to timber sales in Montana. Two years later was promoted to inspector in district headquarters at Missoula; in 1910 was advanced to assistant district forester; and in 1912 was transferred to Washington, D.C., office as assistant to chief of Branch of Silviculture. In 1917 was commissioned captain in Tenth (Forest) Engineers, was sent to France for duty in timber acquisition for U.S. Army, and in 1919 was promoted to major in Twentieth (Forest) Engineer Regiment. Returned to Forest Service in 1919. Was selected in 1920 by Gifford Pinchot, Commissioner of Forestry in Pennsylvania, to be his deputy, and became commissioner himself in 1922. On creation of Pennsylvania Department of Forests and Waters, during Pinchot's governorship, Stuart became its first secretary, a cabinet position. Reentered Forest Service in 1927, and was advanced to chief on May 1, 1928. During early years of his administration, his leadership kept Forest Service active and efficient despite pressures for retrenchment in federal expenditures and personnel. With advent of Franklin D. Roosevelt's administration, helped prepare Forest Service for expanded role it would play under New Deal. As chairman of Forest Protection Board, notably advanced standards of protection of federal timberlands. Served for eight years on council of Society of American Foresters, was president in 1927, and was elected a fellow in 1930. Died October 23, 1933.

HENRY CLEPPER

Smith, Herbert A. "Robert Young Stuart." *Journal of Forestry,* 29:885–90, December 1933.

SUDWORTH, GEORGE BISHOP
(1864–1927)
Born August 31 in Kingston, Wisconsin. University of Michigan, B.A. 1885. After teaching botany at Michigan Agricultural College during 1885–86, became botanist in Division of Forestry, U.S. Department of Agriculture, 1886–95; was dendrologist in Bureau of Forestry, 1895–1904; and chief of dendrology in Forest Service from 1904 until his death. Explored many of early western forest reserves on foot, and discovered and named numerous new species and varieties of trees and plants. Was author of scores of publications on dendrology and forestry, and was leading authority on the subject. His *Check List of North American Forest Trees*, first published in 1898 and reissued since, is classic reference work of nomenclature and range of native trees. Among his other publications on dendrology are *Forest Flora of the Rocky Mountain Region, Forest Flora of Tennessee, Nomenclature of the Arborescent Flora of the U.S., Trees of the U.S. Important in Forestry, The Forest Nursery*, and *Forest-Trees of the Pacific Slope*. For the last fifteen of his forty-one years with Forest Service, was member of Federal Horticulture Board, which was responsible for policies relating to shipment of plants and nursery stock to prevent spread of plant diseases and insect pests. Was active member of Society of American Foresters and of other scientific and botanical organizations. Died May 10, 1927.

HENRY CLEPPER

Journal of Forestry. Obituary, 25:511–12, May 1927.
Who Was Who in America, 1897–1942.

SULLIVAN, CARL ROLLYN, JR.
(born 1926)
Born February 20 in Marietta, Ohio. West Virginia University B.S. (forestry and wildlife management), 1950; Ohio University M.S. (hydrobiology), 1953. From 1951 to 1955 was assistant chief of Fish Division of the West Virginia Conservation Commission. Was land manager and later public-relations manager for Kaiser Aluminum at Ravenwood, West Virginia, between 1956 and 1962. During this period, also served four-year appointment with West Virginia Conservation Commission Policy Board. Between 1962 and 1964, planned, organized, and directed West Virginia's highly successful centennial celebration. In 1964 journeyed to Alaska to undertake similar assignment for Alaska Purchase

Centennial. After 1967 Alaska Centennial, opened public relations/advertising business in Alaska; and in 1972 accepted position of executive secretary with Sport Fishing Institute, Washington, D.C. In 1975 became executive director of American Fisheries Society. His present responsibilities include doing legislative work on national conservation issues, editing bimonthly journal *Fisheries*, acting as liaison with federal resources agencies, monitoring marine and freshwater fisheries developments, and coordinating the society's wide-ranging activities. Since 1975, American Fisheries Society has shown constant increase in membership, plus explosive growth in conservation, technical, and publication activities. Is member of West Virginia Department of Natural Resources Commission, vice-chairman of Renewable Natural Resources Foundation, and advisory member of Mid-Atlantic Technical Working Group, which advises the secretary of U.S. Department of the Interior on outer continental shelf hydrocarbon resources development. Also serves on the secretary of the Interior's Protect Our Wetlands and Duck Resources Committee and on its offshore Rigs to Reefs Advisory Committee.

ROBERT F. HUTTON

Who's Who in America, 42d ed., 1982–83.

SWANK, WENDELL GEORGE
(born 1917)
Born September 13 in Brownsville, Pennsylvania. West Virginia University B.S. (forestry), 1941; University of Michigan, M.S. (wildlife management), 1943; Agricultural and Mechanical College of Texas, Ph.D. 1951. Began his career with West Virginia Conservation Commission as research biologist on fur-bearers and forest wildlife, 1945–48. Was instructor in wildlife management at Agricultural and Mechanical College of Texas, 1948–51; and at University of Arizona, 1951–52. After joining Arizona Game and Fish Department in 1952, led statewide wildlife research and management project until 1956. In 1956 spent year on Fulbright Award studying wildlife in Uganda and Kenya. Returning to Arizona in 1957, was named assistant director of the department in 1958, and was advanced to director in 1964. In 1968 accepted position with Food and Agricultural Organization of United Nations. Worked with that agency as head of Wildlife Division, East African Agricultural and Forestry Research Organization, 1968–70; project manager, Kenya Wildlife Management Project, 1970–74; and wildlife advisor, Govern-

ment of Dominica, 1974–75. From 1975 to present, has been professor in Department of Wildlife and Fisheries Sciences, Texas A&M University. As regional representative of The Wildlife Society, was instrumental in establishing New Mexico–Arizona Section, and served two terms as president of parent society, 1962–64. Is member of Boone and Crockett Club, Fauna Preservation Society, and Wildlife Disease Association. Also is member of International Association of Game, Fish and Conservation Commissioners, and served on its executive committee, 1966–68. Was recipient of Gulf Oil Conservation Award in 1982, and is author of book *African Antelope*; and of bulletins *Beaver Ecology and Management in West Virginia* and *Mule Deer in Arizona Chapparral*; and other publications on nutria, mourning dove, pheasant, quail, mule deer, and African wildlife.

ROBERT A. JANTZEN
WENDELL G. SWANK

American Men and Women of Science (Physical and Biological Sciences), 12 ed., (vol. 6), 1973.

Who's Who in America, vol. 35, 1968–69.

Who's Who in the West, 17th ed., 1960.

Wildlife Society News, No. 83, November 1962.

SWANSON, GUSTAV ADOLPH
(born 1910)
Born February 13 in Mamre, Minnesota. University of Minnesota, B.S. 1930, M.A. 1932, Ph.D. (zoology) 1937. Served as biologist with U.S. Soil Conservation Service in 1935, and with Minnesota Conservation Commission during 1935–36. In 1936–37 taught game management at University of Maine, then returned to University of Minnesota as professor of economic zoology from 1937 to 1944. Joined U.S. Fish and Wildlife Service as wildlife biologist in 1944; and spent 1946–48 in Washington, D.C., as chief, Division of Wildlife Research. At Cornell University, was head of Department of Conservation from 1948 to 1966, and director of Cornell Laboratory of Ornithology from 1958 to 1961. Was head of Department of Fishery and Wildlife Biology at Colorado State University, 1966–75, then became director emeritus. Studied in Denmark and other Scandinavian countries during 1954–55 and 1961–62, when he also served as consultant to United Kingdom Nature Conservancy. While

at Cornell, served as consultant to several New York State legislative committees on matters of conservation, and contributed to development of New York Fish and Wildlife Management Act and programs of conservation education for citizen leaders. In The Wildlife Society, was vice-president in 1945, president during 1954–55, and editor of its *Journal of Wildlife Management*, 1949–53; received the society's Aldo Leopold Award in 1973. Served on board of directors of National Audubon Society from 1950 to 1956. In 1968 served as Fulbright professor of conservation at University of New England, Armidale, New South Wales, Australia. Is author of many scientific publications, including (with coauthors) *The Mammals of Minnesota*, 1945; *Fish and Wildlife Resources on the Public Lands*, 1969; and *Water Law in Relation to Environmental Quality*, 1974. His activity as organizer, consultant, and advisor in field of natural resource conservation is appreciated by colleagues worldwide.

OLIVER H. HEWITT
GUSTAV A. SWANSON

American Men and Women of Science (Physical and Biological Sciences), 15th ed., 1982.

Who's Who in America, 12th ed., 1982–83.

SWIFT, ERNEST FREMONT
(1897–1968)

Born September 15 in Tracy, Minnesota. After graduating from high school, enlisted in U.S. Army in 1917. In 1926 was appointed state conservation warden in Wisconsin. Spent next twenty-eight years in service of Wisconsin Department of Conservation, in which he rose from the ranks to directorship, which he held from 1947 to 1954. Under his administration, the department employed trained biologists to get information upon which sound programs in fish and game management could be based. In 1954 he was designated assistant director of U.S. Fish and Wildlife Service, but resigned the following year to become executive director of National Wildlife Federation, from which position he retired in 1960 though continuing as consultant. Was recipient of some forty awards and citations, including Haskell Noyes Conservation Warden Efficiency Award in 1930; The Wildlife Society's Aldo Leopold Medal in 1959; and Gold Medallion for contributions to welfare of Wisconsin in 1966. Wrote numerous articles on practical conservation topics, as well as books *A History of Wisconsin Deer* and *A Conservation Saga*, the latter published in 1967. Died July 24, 1968.

Russ J. Neugebauer

Swift, Lloyd Wesley
(born 1904)
Born September 5 in Ione, California. University of California, B.S. 1927, M.S. (forestry) 1928. His career with U.S. Forest Service spanned thirty-five years, beginning with field positions in West Coast and Rocky Mountain regions. From 1943 to 1963, was director of Division of Wildlife Management in Branch of National Forest Administration, Washington, D.C. In this position, was responsible for wildlife management program on 180 million acres. Cooperative activities with state game administrations were much improved; habitat management projects were undertaken; forest officers gave increasing attention to rare and vanishing species; and fisheries scientists were employed in all regions. From 1963 to 1966, was executive director of U.S. Appeal's World Wildlife Fund, an international organization formed in 1961 to undertake worldwide programs for saving rare and endangered species. His foreign assignments on behalf of various international organizations included tours of duty in East and Central Africa, Ethiopia, Israel, Turkey, and Botswana. Was member of secretariat for Fifth World Forestry Congress in Seattle in 1960, and member of U.S. delegation to Sixth World Forestry Congress in Spain in 1966. In 1967 became special consultant for forest recreation and wildlife for National Wildlife Federation. Was first chairman of Division of Wildlife Management, Society of American Foresters. Is trustee of The Wildlife Society and former director of World Wildlife Fund. Has contributed technical papers to *Journal of Wildlife Management*, *Journal of Mammalogy*, and other publications.

James D. Davis
Lloyd W. Swift

American Men of Science (Physical and Biological Sciences), 11th ed., 1967.

Swingle, Homer Scott
(1902–1973)
Born July 29 in Columbus, Ohio. Ohio State University, B.S. 1924, M.S.

1925, D.Sc. (honorary) 1958. First worked as entomologist, but in 1934 initiated program of fisheries research at Auburn University. Under his direction it developed into largest warmwater fisheries research station in world, with two hundred experimental ponds comprising two hundred surface acres of water. An especially effective teacher, he developed curriculum in fisheries management and actively participated in training more than one hundred graduate students from U.S. and twenty foreign countries. Was appointed collaborator by U.S. Soil Conservation Service in 1937 and by U.S. Fish and Wildlife Service in 1946; received Conservation Service Award of U.S. Department of the Interior in 1951; was appointed U.S. representative on pond-fish culture to Eighth (1953) and Ninth (1957) Pacific Science conferences, and served as convener of Symposium on Recent Advances on Pondfish Cultures at Tenth (1961) Conference. Received Nash Conservation Award for research and teaching contributions to fisheries management in 1954, and was selected Man-of-the-Year in Southern Agriculture by *Progressive Farmer* magazine in 1958. Served as fisheries consultant to governments of Israel and Thailand in 1957 and to India in 1961. In 1964 participated in planning sessions in Rome for World Symposium on Warm-Water Pondfish Culture sponsored by Food and Agriculture Organization of U.N., and in 1966 served as symposium chairman. Received Aldo Leopold Award from The Wildlife Society in 1966. Was president of American Fisheries Society in 1958, and was elected to honorary membership in 1966. In 1968 Auburn University appointed him alumni research professor of fisheries, the first research chair provided under program. Later headed Department of Fisheries and Allied Aquacultures and was director of International Center for Aquacultures at Auburn University, 1970–73. Authored more than one hundred papers relating to fisheries management. Died May 10, 1973.

Donovan D. Moss

American Men and Women of Science (Physical and Biological Sciences), 12th ed., (vol. 6), 1973.

Who's Who in the South and Southwest, 1956.

Talbot, Lee Merriam
(born 1930)
Born August 2 in New Bedford, Massachusetts. University of California, Berkeley, B.A. (wildlife conservation) 1953, M.A., Ph.D. (ecology) 1963.

In 1954, after holding research positions in California and the Arctic and serving with U.S. Marine Corps, joined International Union for Conservation of Nature and Natural Resources (IUCN) conducting conservation surveys in Europe, Africa, and Asia. Starting in 1959, with his biologist/conservationist wife Marty, conducted pioneering ecosystem research in Serengeti-Mara Plains, East Africa. In 1964–65 conducted Southeast Asia conservation program of IUCN, and in 1966 became resident ecologist and field representative for international affairs with Smithsonian Institution. Was appointed senior scientist when President's Council on Environmental Quality was created in 1970, and later also became director of international activities, serving under three presidents. In 1978 became director of conservation for World Wildlife Fund International, Switzerland, and subsequently was elected director general of IUCN. In 1983 returned to Washington, D.C., as environmental consultant, writer, and fellow of East-West Environment and Policy Institute. Has worked in more than one hundred countries; served as consultant on ecology and conservation to governments, United Nations, and other organizations and industries worldwide; and organized international conservation conferences in Africa, America, Asia, and Europe. Is a fellow or member of many professional and scientific societies, and member of various National Academy of Sciences committees and panels. Has authored more than 170 scientific, technical, and conservation publications, including seven books and monographs. Has received numerous national and international scientific and conservation honors including The Outstanding Publication Award (with Marty Talbot) of The Wildlife Society; and The Albert Schweitzer Medal and Distinguished Service Award of the American Institute of Biological Sciences.

LEE M. TALBOT

American Men and Women of Science (Physical and Biological Sciences), 14th ed., 1979.
Who's Who in America; 42d ed., 1982–83.
Who's Who in the World; 6th ed., 1982–83.

TARZWELL, CLARENCE MATTHEW
(born 1907)
Born September 29 in Deckerville, Michigan. University of Michigan, B.A. 1930, M.S. 1932, Ph.D. (aquatic biology and fishery management) 1936. Was with Institute for Fisheries Research, Michigan Department

of Conservation, 1930–34, then became assistant aquatic biologist for U.S. Bureau of Fisheries and served as assistant range examiner for U.S. Forest Service, 1935–38. Was associate aquatic biologist, Tennessee Valley Authority, 1938–43; chief, biology section, U.S. Public Health Service, Savannah, Georgia, 1944–48; chief, aquatic biology section, Environmental Health Center, Robert A. Taft Sanitary Engineering Center, Cincinnati, Ohio, 1948–65; acting director, National Water Quality Laboratory, Federal Water Pollution Control Administration, Duluth, Minnesota, 1964–67; director of National Marine Water Quality Laboratory, Narragansett, Rhode Island, 1965–72; and senior research advisor, Environmental Protection Agency's National Environmental Research Center, Corvallis, Oregon, 1972–75. Has been member of numerous organizations, including Research Committee for the Water Pollution Control Federation; advisory group on waste treatment at Engineering Experimental Station of Ohio State University, 1957–59, and Committee for Standard Methods since 1968; Aquatic Life Advisory Committee for control of stream temperature for Pennsylvania Sanitary Water Board, 1959–62; advisory committee for water quality criteria of California State Water Pollution Control Board, 1961–63; and Natural Resources Council of National Academy of Sciences, 1961–63. Since 1962 has been expert advisor on Panel for Environmental Health of the World Health Organization, having been chairman, International Commission on Long-Term Effects of Toxicants on Aquatic Life, 1962–67. Was chairman, Water Pollution Control Federation's committee for development of standard methods for bioassay, 1958–75; and consultant to Kuwait Institute for Scientific Research, 1975. Was chairman of Subcommittee for Fish, Other Aquatic Life and Wildlife of important National Technical Advisory Committee on Water Quality Criteria. Received State of Ohio Conservationist of the Year Award, 1961; American Motors Professional Conservationist Award 1962; Aldo Leopold Award of The Wildlife Society, 1963; U.S. Public Health Service's Meritorious Service Medal, 1964; Distinguished Career Award of the Environmental Protection Agency, 1973; and Bronze Medal, 1974. Is honorary member of American Fisheries Society, and received the society's Award of Excellence in 1974. Is author of 120 papers in scientific journals, and was coauthor of *Methods for the Improvement of Michigan Trout Streams*, 1932.

PHILIP A. DOUGLAS
ROBERT G. MARTIN

American Men and Women of Science (Physical and Biological Sciences), 15th ed., 1982.

Who's Who in America, 42d ed., 1982–83.

TASCHER, WENDELL RUSSELL
(1898–1964)

Born August 31 in Ashkum, Illinois, University of Illinois, B.S. 1924, M.S. 1927; University of Missouri, Ph.D. (genetics) 1929. Engaged in agronomic research and teaching at universities of Illinois and Missouri until 1929; then became county agricultural agent for Osage and Clay counties, Missouri. Then followed appointment as extension soil conservationist for state of Missouri. In 1942 became extension soil conservationist for U.S. Department of Agriculture with headquarters in Washington, D.C., and served as project leader of extension soil conservation work in U.S. and territories, a position he held until his retirement in 1961. Traveled extensively throughout world making special study of plant genetics. Was active in many organizations relating to agriculture and conservation and received numerous awards for his outstanding service. Assisted in developing National Goodyear Soil Conservation District Awards Program and served as its advisor until his retirement. From its inception in Oklahoma, originated and was member of advisory committee for International Land, Pasture and Range Judging Contest. Was dedicated member of Soil Conservation Society of America, having served on many of its technical committees; in 1958 was among first to receive the society's Presidential Citation, and in 1959 was elected a fellow. As writer on conservation subjects, contributed numerous articles to *Journal of Soil and Water Conservation, Soil Conservation,* and *Extension Service Review.* Edited and issued quarterly publication entitled *Terrain,* distributed to more than seven hundred workers in conservation education. Died November 24, 1964.

RUSSELL G. HILL

TAYLOR, WALTER PENN
(1888–1972)

Born October 31 at Elkhorn, Wisconsin. University of California, B.S. 1911, Ph.D. (zoology) 1914. For seven years, until 1916, served as assistant curator or curator of mammals at University of California Museum of Vertebrate Zoology. Joined U.S. Biological Survey (later known as Fish and Wildlife Service) in 1916 and advanced from assistant to senior biologist. In cooperation with University of Arizona, served as professor of economic zoology there from 1932–35; thereafter until 1947, still with federal government, became leader of Cooperative Wildlife Research Unit at the Texas Agricultural and Mechanical College at College Station, and during most of this period also served as head of Department of Wildlife Management of the College. With the same federal connections from 1947 to 1951, served as leader of Cooperative Wildlife Research Unit and professor of zoology at Oklahoma Agricultural and Mechanical College, Stillwater. From 1954 to 1962 was professor of conservation education and biology at Claremont Graduate School, and was visiting professor of zoology at Southern Illinois University, 1957–58. From 1960 to 1966, served as lecturer at high schools and colleges under program sponsored by American Institute of Biological Sciences. Was president of Ecological Society of America, 1934. Was honorary member of American Society of Mammalogists (president 1941–42), and of Outdoor Writer's Association. From The Wildlife Society, of which he was president in 1943, received Aldo Leopold Award for distinguished service to conservation (1961); received U.S. Department of the Interior's Gold Medal Award (1951) for distinguished service; and received Honor Award from California Conservation Council (1953). Authored three hundred scientific papers, bulletins, and notes on zoology, ecology, and conservation; was coauthor of *The Birds of the State of Washington*, 1953; edited *Deer of North America*, 1956. Died March 29, 1972.

CLARENCE COTTAM

American Men of Science (Physical and Biological Sciences), 11th ed., 1967.

Journal of Wildlife Management. Obituary, Vol. 36, No. 4:1379–80, Oct., 1972.

TEER, JAMES GARTH
(born 1926)
Born March 13 in Granger, Texas. Served in U.S. Navy during World War II. Texas A&M University, B.S. (wildlife management) 1950; Iowa State University, M.S. (wildlife management) 1951; University of Wisconsin, Ph.D. (wildlife ecology-zoology) 1964. Was employed as wildlife manager, Texas Parks and Wildlife Department; instructor, Mississippi State University; research biologist, Patuxent Wildlife Research Center,

U.S. Fish and Wildlife Service; and scientist-educator and administrator, Texas A&M University, where he advanced to professor and head of Department of Wildlife and Fisheries Sciences, 1970–78, and to Caesar Kleberg Chair in Wildlife Ecology, 1968–78. Has been director of Rob and Bessie Welder Wildlife Foundation from 1979 to present. An authority on white-tailed deer in Texas, he has expressed his research interests in ecology of big and small game mammals, waterfowl, and management of private lands and rangeland habitat for wildlife. Has been active in conservation affairs and environmental protection in national and international scenes, and has published sixty-three scientific papers, numerous reports and position papers, and several monographs and chapters in books. Taught honors course as visiting professor of wildlife ecology at University of Pretoria, South Africa; held membership on research advisory council of Serengeti Research Institute, Tanzania; and served as visiting scientist-consultant to Station Biologique de la Tour du Valat, Carmague, France. Has organized and/or participated in wildlife training, research projects, conservation issues, and research evaluation projects in United States, Canada, India, Tanzania, Kenya, Botswana, Republic of South Africa, Guatemala, Argentina, Mexico, and France. Served as member or chairman of three scientific study groups of National Research Council of the National Academy of Sciences, in assignments dealing with management of wildlife and land-use on public and private rangelands in western United States. Is member of several professional societies and has been especially active in committee assignments in The Wildlife Society. Served as assistant editor of *Journal of Wildlife Management* and was responsible for starting a publication series "Kleberg Studies in Natural Resources," a monograph series issued by Texas A&M University on wildlife ecology and management. Currently is member of board of directors, National Audubon Society; member of conservation committee, Boone and Crockett Club; chairman of accreditation committee, The Wildlife Society; and member of environmental steering committee of Texas Utilities Generating Company.

ROBERT A. MCCABE

THOMAS, GERALD WAYLETT
(born 1919)
Born July 3 in Small, Idaho. Pasadena (California) Junior College, A.A. 1938; University of Idaho, B.S. (forestry) 1941; Texas A&M University,

M.S. (range science) 1951; and Ph.D. (range science) 1954. Worked for U.S. Forest Service, Targhee National Forest, Idaho, 1938–41. Served in U.S. Navy, 1942–45. Was range conservationist, U.S. Soil Conservation Service, Idaho, 1945–50; professor of range management and forestry, Texas A&M University, 1950–56; research coordinator, Texas Agricultural Experiment Station, College Station, 1956–58; dean of agriculture, Texas Technical University, 1958–70; and has been president, New Mexico State University, Las Cruces, 1970 to present. Is director of Mountain Bell and Winrock International; member of National Forests System Advisory Committee; former member of board for International Food and Agricultural Development; former member of executive board of Association of State Universities and Land Grant Colleges; and member of Association of Western Universities. During past decade or more, has served on several foreign assignments and special studies throughout world. Has authored *Progress and Change in the Agricultural Industry*, 1969, 1973; and *Food and Fiber for a Changing World*, 1976; and nearly one hundred articles on food and agriculture, agriculture and natural resources, range and wildlife management, and energy. Is a fellow in Society for Range Management and in Soil Conservation Society; and member of Sigma Xi and of Phi Kappa Phi.

CLARE W. HENDEE
WILLIAM D. HURST

American Men of Science (Physical and Biological Sciences), 11th ed., 1967.

Who's Who in America, 42d ed., 1982–83.

THOMAS, JACK WARD
(born 1934)
Born September 7 in Fort Worth, Texas. Texas A&M University, B.S. (wildlife management) 1957; West Virginia University, M.S. (wildlife biology) 1969; University of Massachusetts, Ph.D. (forestry) 1974. Served as game manager and research biologist for Texas Parks and Wildlife at Sonora and at Llano, 1957–66. Joined U.S. Forest Service in 1966 as research biologist at Morgantown, West Virginia; transferred to Amherst, Massachusetts, in 1970 to institute research on urban forestry and wildlife, and became chief research wildlife biologist at La Grande, Oregon, in 1973. Holds adjunct appointments at Oregon State University, Washington State University, University of Idaho, and Eastern Ore-

gon State College. Worked briefly in Pakistan (1979) and in India (1982), and has served frequently as consultant to provincial governments in Canada. Has written more than two hundred articles, bulletins, and book chapters, and has edited and contributed to two award-winning books: *Wildlife Habitats in Managed Forests—The Blue Mountains of Oregon and Washington* and *The Elk of North America: Ecology and Management*. Served The Wildlife Society as Texas chapter president, 1965–66; councilman, 1971–73; and president, 1977–78. Has received seven Service Awards from U.S. Department of Agriculture, in addition to Gulf Oil Conservation Award, 1983; Oregon Chapter Award of The Wildlife Society, 1979; Northeast Section's Einarsen Award, 1981; Outstanding Publication Award, 1983; and Special Recognition Service Award, 1983.

LAURENCE R. JAHN
RICHARD E. MCCABE

American Men and Women of Science (Physical and Biological Sciences), 15th ed., 1982.

THOMPSON, WILLIAM FRANCIS
(1888–1965)
Born April 3 in Saint Cloud, Minnesota. University of Washington, 1906–9; Stanford University, B.A. 1911; Ph.D. (fisheries) 1930. Served as scientific assistant to David Starr Jordan at Stanford, 1909–15. During 1911–12 was scientist for California Fish and Game Commission, and from 1912 to 1917 scientific assistant for Provincial Fisheries Department, British Columbia, Canada. From 1917 to 1924 founded research program of California Fish and Game Commission, developing pattern of investigation that was carried on for many years by California State Fisheries Laboratory. As director of International Fisheries Commission, 1924–37, and of International Pacific Salmon Fisheries Commission, 1937–43, he laid scientific foundation upon which the commissions' works are based. His early work with population dynamics, overfishing problem, and racial studies of halibut and salmon is landmark in scientific fishery management. Was professor of fisheries, University of Washington, 1930–58, and director, School of Fisheries, 1934–47; then organized and served as director of Fisheries Research Institute at university, 1947–58. Was member of Biology and Research Committee, International North Pacific Fisheries Commission, 1953–59,

and was United States member of Fifth Pacific Science Congress. Was one of original organizers and was first president of American Institute of Fishery Research Biologists. Wrote numerous scientific works, many of which were distributed as publications of halibut and salmon commissions. Died November 7, 1965.

CHARLES K. PHENICIE

American Men of Science (Physical and Biological Sciences), 10th ed., 1961.

Journal of the Fisheries Research Board of Canada. Obituary, vol. 23, no. 11, 1966.

Who Was Who in America, 1961–68.

TINDALL, BARRY SANFORD
(born 1939)
Born June 29 in Edinburg, New Jersey. Paul Smith's College of Arts and Science, A.A.S. (forestry) 1963; North Carolina State University, B.S. (recreation and park administration) 1967; The George Washington University, M.A. (government: urban and regional planning) 1973. Served in U.S. Air Force, 1957–61. Was research aide in watershed management, U.S. Forest Service, Angeles National Forest, 1963. Joined staff of National Recreation and Park Association as conservation program specialist, 1967–75; director of public affairs, 1975 to present; executive secretary of National Conference on State Parks, 1968–72; project director and editor of *State Park Statistics,* 1970; project director of *Islands of Hope: Parks and Recreation in Environmental Crisis* (William E. Brown, author), 1972; coordinated for The Nature Conservancy an analysis of public and private natural-area policies and programs, *The Preservation of Natural Diversity: A Survey and Recommendations,* 1974–75. Was consultant to National Park Service on policy and organization, 1975; on board of directors, Audubon Naturalist Society of the Central Atlantic States, 1971–74; and instructor, U.S. Department of Agriculture's Graduate School course on politics of conservation, 1973 to present. Is author of numerous articles on recreation and park issues; frequent participant in public policy forums; specialist in national recreation policy, budget, and appropriation matters. Received Special Citation from National Park Service in 1975; Distinguished Alumni Award from School of Forest Resources, North Carolina State University, in 1979; Achievement Award from Heritage Conservation and Recreation

Service in 1980; and was elected to National Association of State Outdoor Recreation Liaison Officers in 1981.

NATIONAL RECREATION AND PARK ASSOCIATION

TOUMEY, JAMES WILLIAM
(1865–1932)

Born April 17 in Lawrence, Michigan. Michigan State Agricultural College, Sc.M. 1893, D.For. (honorary) 1927; Syracuse University, Sc.D. (honorary) 1920. Taught botany at Michigan State University from 1889 to 1891 and at University of Arizona, 1891–99. Also held post of botanist in Arizona State Agricultural Experiment Station. Did special work on date palm and became recognized authority on cacti, establishing cactus garden in Tucson. In 1897 assisted in arrangement of cactus collection in Kew Garden in England. In 1899 was appointed superintendent of tree planting in Division of Forestry, U.S. Department of Agriculture. In 1900 was called to Yale University, where he became outstanding authority in dendrology and silviculture. From 1910 to 1922 served as dean of Yale School of Forestry, then retired from deanship to pursue his interest in teaching and research at that institution. Materially enlarged the university's endowments and facilities, securing gift of building Sage Hall and large accessions to library. Donated his personal collection of twenty-five hundred specimens of American trees and shrubs to forest herbarium. In 1920 was chairman of committee on forest education of Society of American Foresters, which had marked influence in shaping educational policies of forestry schools in United States. Organized Plant Science Research Club in 1928. In 1929 was member of American delegation to International Congress of Forest Experiment Stations at Stockholm, Sweden. Was elected a fellow of Society of American Foresters. Wrote *Seeding and Planting in the Practice of Forestry*, 1916 (revised 1931 with C. F. Korstian), and *Foundations in Silviculture*, 1928; and was author of eight scientific bulletins and many articles for scientific journals. Died May 6, 1932.

KENNETH B. POMEROY

American Forests 38: 366, June 1932.

Journal of Forestry. Obituary, 30: 665–69, October 1932.

TOWELL, WILLIAM EARNEST
(born 1916)

Born June 11 in Saint James, Missouri. Drury College, Springfield, Missouri, 1933–35; University of Missouri, 1935–36; University of Michigan, B.S. (forestry) 1938, M.F. (silviculture) 1938; University of Missouri, D.Sc. (honorary) 1981. Began employment at Missouri Conservation Commission in July 1938 and served there in a number of positions for almost twenty-nine years, the last ten (1957–67) as director. Served in U.S. Navy, 1943–46. Was appointed executive vice-president of The American Forestry Association in January 1967. Was elected chairman of Ozark Section, Society of American Foresters, in 1950, and elected vice-president of the society in 1981 and president in 1984. Was chairman of various committees and president in 1966 of International Association of Fish and Wildlife Agencies. Was appointed to three-year term on Federal Water Pollution Control Advisory Board by President Kennedy in 1963. Served as member of U.S. Department of Agriculture's Wildlife Advisory and Cradle of Forestry Advisory committees, and was original member of Lewis and Clark Trail Commission. Served on National Council of the Boy Scouts of America, 1968–78, was chairman of Project SOAR, and chaired National Conservation Committee of the Boy Scouts of America, 1976–78. Was chairman of Natural Resources Council of America, 1975–77. Currently serves on boards of directors of National Wildlife Federation, Forest History Society, and Forest Farmers Association, and is trustee of Land Between the Lakes Association. Awards received include Conservationist of the Year from National Wildlife Federation in 1976; Sir William Schlich Memorial Medal from Society of American Foresters in 1978; University of Michigan School of Natural Resources Alumni Society Distinguished Service Award in 1978; National Association of State Foresters Lifetime Achievement Award in 1978; and John Aston Warder Medal from The American Forestry Association in 1982. Became particularly known for his work on national forestry and conservation legislation through Areas of Agreement Committee, which he founded. Is author of numerous articles in *American Forests* magazine and other conservation publications, and speaker before many national conservation groups.

HENRY CLEPPER

Who's Who in America, 42d ed., 1982–83.

Who's Who in the World, 6th ed., 1982–83.

TRAIN, RUSSELL ERROL
(born 1920)

Born June 4 in Jamestown, Rhode Island. Princeton University, B.A. 1941; Columbia University, LL.B. 1947. U.S. Army military service 1941–46. From 1953 to 1956 served on staffs of congressional committees. In 1956 was named assistant to the secretary of the Treasury. Was appointed as judge on U.S. Tax Court, 1957. As result of his interest in African wildlife, founded African Wildlife Leadership Foundation in 1961, and became president and chairman of board of trustees. In 1964 became trustee, and in 1965 president, of The Conservation Foundation; in 1969 was appointed undersecretary of U.S. Department of the Interior. In 1970 became first chairman of President's Council on Environmental Quality and played key role in development of highly significant environmental law and policy. In 1973 became administrator of Environmental Protection Agency, serving until 1977. Became president and chief executive officer of World Wildlife Fund–U.S. in 1978, a position he currently holds. Has served as director of American Committee for International Wildlife Protection. Has been director and vice-president of World Wildlife Fund; vice-president and member of executive committee of Boone and Crockett Club; and consultant to British Fauna Preservation Society. Has served as trustee of American Conservation Association and honorary vice-president of The American Forestry Association. The Tanzania, Kenya, and Uganda national parks have each made him honorary trustee. In 1967 was awarded second annual Conservation Award of the African Safari Club of Washington. Has served as executive board member and is vice-president of International Union for the Conservation of Nature and Natural Resources, and co-chairman of The Year 2000 Committee. Also is trustee or director for several other organizations dealing with natural resources, and member of Trilateral Commission, Advisory Council on Law of the Sea, and U.S. National Commission for UNESCO. Has represented United States at variety of international environmental conferences. Has been awarded honorary degrees by number of educational institutions and has received Albert Schweitzer Medal of Animal Welfare Institute (1972), Aldo Leopold Award of The Wildlife Society (1975), Conservationist of the Year award of the National Wildlife Federation (1974), John and Alice Tyler Ecology Award (1978), Freese Award of the American Society of Civil Engineers (1978), Public Welfare Award of the National Academy of Sciences (1981), Elizabeth Haub Prize in International Environmental Law (1981), and Environmental Leadership Medal of the United Nations Environment Programme (1982). Was selected to present Marshall Lecture by Natural Resources Defense Council in 1983.

THE CONSERVATION FOUNDATION
LOUIS S. CLAPPER

Who's Who in America, 42d ed., 1982–83.

TRAUTMAN, MILTON BERNHARD
(born 1899)

Born September 7 in Columbus, Ohio. Mostly self-educated in ichthyology and ornithology; College of Wooster, D.Sc. (honorary) 1951; Ohio State University, D.Sc. (honorary) 1978. Began his career in 1930 as assistant in Bureau of Scientific Research, Ohio Division of Conservation, progressing in 1934 to assistant curator of Museum of Zoology, University of Michigan. Served in Institute for Fisheries Research, Michigan Conservation Department, as assistant director, 1935–39, and as resident associate, 1935–36. Was member of University of Michigan zoology expedition to Yucatan in 1936. Was resident biologist at Stone Institute of Hydrobiology, Ohio State University, in 1939; later became resident associate, lecturer in zoology, and curator of vertebrate collections, Department of Zoology and Entomology, Ohio State University, in 1955. Ran summer surveys on salmon in Alaska for Bureau of Commercial Fisheries, 1959–61, and served as member of Ohio State University Expeditionary Institute for polar studies in Alaska in 1965. Also has presented series of invited ornithological lectures in United States and Africa. Officially retired from Ohio State University in 1970, and was immediately appointed professor emeritus. Is author of numerous papers in fisheries biology and ornithology, and will be long remembered for his two books *Birds of Buckeye Lake*, 1940, and *Fishes of Ohio*, 1957. Discovered and described some fifteen new species and subspecies of fishes during his long productive career. Was unanimously elected, together with his wife, Mary, to Ohio Conservation Hall of Fame in 1974. In recent years, has presented guest lectures and conducted field trips for students at Ohio State University's Frany Theodore Stone Laboratory located at Put-in-Bay, Ohio.

ROBERT G. MARTIN
ELWOOD A. SEAMAN
STEVEN TAUB

American Men and Women of Science (Physical and Biological Sciences), 15th ed., 1982.

TREFETHEN, JAMES BYRON, JR.
(1916–1976)
Born June 3 in Brockton, Massachusetts. Educated at Mount Hermon School; Northeastern University, B.A. 1940; University of Massachusetts, M.S. (wildlife management) 1953. Joining staff of Wildlife Management Institute in February 1948, became editor of *Outdoor News Bulletin*, 1948–51, and served as director of publications from 1951 to 1976. Was editor of *Transactions of the North American Wildlife and Natural Resources Conference*, 1952–76, *Proceedings of the National Symposium on Wood Duck Management and Research* in 1965, and *Proceedings of the National Watershed Congress*, 1954–74. Was assistant editor, executive news service of the Natural Resources Council of America from 1968 to 1975. Was author of one hundred popular articles on conservation, nature, and outdoor recreation published in national magazines, including *American Forests, American Heritage, Audubon, National Wildlife, Outdoor Life, Sports Afield,* and *Sports Illustrated.* Was contributing editor of *Fisherman's Encyclopedia,* 1951, and of *New Fisherman's Encyclopedia,* 1964, and was senior editor of *New Hunter's Encyclopedia,* 1966. Wrote *Crusade for Wildlife: Highlights in Conservation Progress,* 1961; *Wildlife Management and Conservation,* 1964; *Americans and Their Guns: The National Rifle Association in Nearly a Century of Service to the Nation,* 1967; and *An American Crusade for Wildlife,* 1975. Was coeditor (with Clarence Cottam) of *Whitewings: The Life History, Status, and Management of the White-winged Dove,* 1968. Was recognized by Outdoor Writers Association of America with its highest honor, the Jade of Chiefs Award, for distinguished service to conservation, 1975. Received The Wildlife Society's Conservation Education Award in 1974. As editor and writer, was effective exponent of all resource conservation and expressive interpreter of art and science of wildlife management. Died December 30, 1976.

DANIEL A. POOLE
LONNIE L. WILLIAMSON

TUNISON, ABRAM VORHIS

(1909–1971)

Born April 16 in Geneva, New York. Cornell University, B.S. 1930, M.S. (biology) 1932. Was employed in 1930 as technician engaged in trout-feeding experiments for General Seafoods Corporation. Served from 1932 to 1934 as aquatic nutrition biologist with New York State Conservation Department. Joined U.S. Fish and Wildlife Service in 1944 as assistant chief of branch of game-fish hatcheries; progressed to chief in 1954, to associate director in 1957, and to deputy director in 1964. Was elected honorary member of American Fisheries Society in 1964, and served as editor of *Progressive Fish-Culturist*. His career was centered around trout nutrition, fish culture, and administrative supervision in fish and wildlife resources. Was principally responsible for dietary requirements for trout production in federal hatcheries, and was directly responsible for establishment of pellet feeding systems now widely used in state, federal, and private hatcheries. Died January 3, 1971.

ELWOOD A. SEAMAN

American Men of Science (Physical and Biological Sciences), 11th ed., 1967.

TURNER, HESTER HILL

(born 1917)

Born January 31 in San Antonio, Texas. Our Lady of the Lake College, San Antonio, B.S. 1938; Southwest Texas State College, M.A. 1940; University of Arizona, J.D. 1945; Oregon State University, Ed.D. 1956; L.H.D. (honorary) Drury College, Our Lady of the Lake College, Salem College. Was dean of students, Lewis and Clark College, Portland, Oregon, 1947–66, and national executive director, Camp Fire Girls, Inc., 1966–79. For The American Forestry Association, was director, 1973–78; vice-president, 1977–79; and president, 1980–81. Currently is director-at-large of National Wildlife Federation. Was awarded U.S. Department of Defense Medal for Distinguished Public Service.

HENRY CLEPPER

Who's Who in America, 42d ed., 1982–83.

VAN OOSTEN, JOHN
(1891–1966)
Born December 10 in Grand Rapids, Michigan. University of Michigan, B.A., M.A., and Ph.D. Served as fishery research biologist for U.S. Bureau of Fisheries from 1920 to 1927, when he was appointed chief of Great Lakes fishery investigations. His major interest was research on life histories of Great Lake fishes and factors affecting abundance and depletion of important species. Was consulted by fishery administrators of Great Lakes states, and was chairman of numerous interstate and international committees because of his knowledge of fishery regulation and management. Relinquishing administrative duties in 1949, devoted full-time to research as senior scientist until his retirement in 1961. Wrote more than ninety scientific papers during his career. The U.S. Department of the Interior conferred on him a Distinguished Service Award in 1962. Served as editor for American Fisheries Society, 1936–40; was president, 1941–46; and was elected Distinguished Service honorary member in 1952. Died January 25, 1966.

DONALD J. LEEDY

American Men of Science (Physical and Biological Sciences), 10th ed., 1961.

VAUX, HENRY JAMES
(born 1912)
Born November 6 in Bryn Mawr, Pennsylvania. Haverford College, B.S. 1933; University of California, M.S. (forestry) 1935; Ph.D. (agricultural economics) 1948. Was instructor in forestry at Oregon State University, 1937–42; and associate forest economist at Agricultural Experiment Station of Louisiana State University, 1942–43. Served in U.S. Navy, 1943–46. Entering U.S. Forest Service as forest economist in 1946, moved to University of California School of Forestry at Berkeley, where he advanced from lecturer in 1948 to dean in 1965. Was also assistant director of California Agricultural Experiment Station, 1955–65, and director of Wildlands Research Center, 1958–65. In 1965 stepped down as dean at School of Forestry, but continues teaching and research. Is a fellow of American Association for the Advancement of Science and of Society of American Foresters; from 1949 to 1955 was chairman of the society's steering committee, which conducted nationwide study of forestry education. Author of many articles on economics of natural resources use and management and on education, he has been consulting editor since

1952 of American Forestry Series of scientific and technical books for McGraw-Hill Book Company. Was director of The American Forestry Association, and is active in other scientific and resources organizations.

HENRY CLEPPER

American Men and Women of Science (Physical and Biological Sciences), 15th ed., 1982.

Who's Who in America, 42d ed., 1982–83.

VOGT, WILLIAM

(1902–1968)

Born May 15 in Mineola, New York. Bard College, B.A. (biology) 1925, Sc.D. 1953. Started his career as assistant editor for New York Academy of Sciences, 1930–32; and was curator of Jones Beach State Bird Sanctuary, 1932–35. Was with National Audubon Society as field naturalist and editor of *Bird Lore*, 1935–39. Throughout next decade, was involved in conservation work in Latin America as conservation ornithologist from Peruvian Guano Administration, 1939–42; as associate director of Division of Science and Education, Coordinator of Inter-American Affairs, 1942–43; and as chief of Conservation Section, Pan American Union, 1943–49. Was national director of Planned Parenthood Federation of America, 1951–61, and secretary of The Conservation Foundation, 1964–67. Until his death, served as representative of International Union for the Conservation of Nature and Natural Resources to the United Nations. Received field research prize of Linnaean Society in 1939; Mary Soper Pope Medal in 1949; and Lasker Foundation Award in 1951. A contributor of articles and scientific papers to natural history and general magazines, he is remembered for his books *Audubon's Birds of America*, 1937; *Road to Survival*, 1948; *El Hombre y la Tierra*, 1949; and *People*, 1960. Died July 11, 1968.

GEORGE SPRUGEL, JR.

American Men of Science (Physical and Biological Sciences), 11th ed., 1967.

Who's Who in America, 1968–69.

VOIGT, WILLIAM, JR.

(born 1902)

Born October 13 in Atlanta, Georgia. Georgia School of Technology,

1920–21. From 1925 to 1936 was reporter on newspapers in Georgia and Oklahoma; was editor-reporter for Associated Press in Missouri, New York, and Pennsylvania, 1931–36; then engaged in public-relations work in Pennsylvania until 1938. During World War II served as civilian employee of U.S. Army. After being appointed assistant executive director of Izaak Walton League of America in Chicago in 1945, opened the league's western regional office in Denver in 1947, then became national executive director in 1949, serving until 1955. From 1955 to 1960 was executive director of Pennsylvania Fish Commission. Since 1963 has been executive director of Interstate Advisory Commission on the Susquehanna River Basin, representing Maryland, New York, and Pennsylvania. Was founding secretary of National Committee on Policies in Conservation Education from 1946 to 1953, and until 1955 was treasurer of its successor organization, Conservation Education Association, which has been effective in introducing conservation as subject in public schools. Was chairman of Natural Resources Council of America, 1951–53. Was associate editor, editor, and editorial director of *Outdoor America*, the magazine of Izaak Walton League, 1945–55; and has written numerous articles about natural resources, particularly on water policy and pollution abatement, and is author of *National Fishing Guide*, 1946; *The Susquehanna Compact: Guardian of the River's Future*, 1972; and *Public Grazing Lands: Use and Misuse by Industry and Government*, 1976. Has completed manuscript on history of Izaak Walton League of America and commenced new book on controversy over Lake Alma, Georgia. Throughout his career has been forceful exponent and interpreter of legislative needs for resources, both before congressional committees and state legislatures.

HENRY CLEPPER
WILLIAM VOIGT, JR.

Who's Who in America, 1962–63.

WADSWORTH, FRANK HOWARD
(born 1915)
Born November 26 in Chicago, Illinois. University of Michigan, B.S. (forestry), M.F. 1937, Ph.D. 1938. Joined U.S. Forest Service in 1938 with assignments in silvicultural research in Arizona at Forest and Range Experiment Station, shelterbelt planting in Nebraska, and timber management research at Tropical Forest Experiment Station, Puerto Rico,

1938–56; was director of Institute of Tropical Forestry, Puerto Rico, 1956–78. Served as U.S. government consultant in American Virgin Islands for timber production; in Argentina and Peru for forestry research; in Dominican Republic for watershed management; in Brazil for nature conservation; in Paraguay for silviculture; in Guatemala for land use; in Chile for forest management; in Venezuela for research programming and forestry planning; in Mexico for biological research planning; and in Sarawak for silviculture, 1949–80. Since 1978 has been research forester, Institute of Tropical Forestry, Puerto Rico, U.S. Forest Service. From 1943 to 1980 was lecturer in tropical forestry at University of Florida, Cornell University, and Yale University; presented graduate course in tropical silviculture at University of Andes, Venezuela, 1968. Is author of eighty technical articles on tropical forestry and coauthor of two books on trees of Puerto Rico and Virgin Islands. Was chairman of Regional Forestry Research Committee of the Latin American Forestry Commission of the United Nations, and co-chairman of tropical silviculture study group of North American Forestry Commission. Was elected to board of directors of The American Forestry Association, 1979, and received the association's Fernow Award for outstanding international service to forestry, 1973.

REXFORD RESLER

American Men and Women of Science (Physical and Biological Sciences), 15th
 ed., 1982.

WALCOTT, FREDERIC COLLIN
(1869–1949)
Born February 19 in New York Mills, Oneida County, New York. Yale University, B.A. 1891, A.M. (honorary) 1917; Trinity College, D.Sc. 1928. Rose to national prominence as member of Herbert Hoover's U.S. Food Administration during World War I, receiving Legion of Honor of France and Officers Cross of Poland for his activities in European relief work. In 1911 helped found American Game Protective and Propagation Association, serving on board of directors of that organization, 1911–35. In 1935 became president of American Wildlife Institute, and was president of North American Wildlife Foundation, 1945–48. For seven years, was chairman of Connecticut Board of Fisheries and Game. Served in U.S. Senate, 1929–35, and was chairman of Special Committee for Wildlife of the Senate, 1930–35. In this capacity, was author of Walcott-

Kleberg Duck Stamp Act, which provided special funds for wildlife refuges, and assisted in drafting Forest Wildlife Refuge Act; Pittman-Robertson Federal Aid in Wildlife Restoration Act; Whaling Treaty; Coordination Act of 1934; the enabling act for Cooperative Wildlife Research Unit Program; and Migratory Bird Treaty with Mexico. Helped obtain legislation for establishment of Patuxent Wildlife Research Center of Bureau of Biological Survey, and for consolidation of Bureau of Biological Survey and Bureau of Sport Fisheries in new U.S. Fish and Wildlife Service of Department of the Interior. In 1935 was instrumental in convincing President Franklin D. Roosevelt of need for international conference on wildlife problems to be called by president of United States. This resulted in American Wildlife Conference of 1936, which was conducted under government sponsorship and which established pattern for later North American Wildlife and Natural Resources Conferences. Received Outdoor Life Award for meritorious service to wildlife conservation in 1934. Died April 27, 1949.

JAMES B. TREFETHEN

Biological Dictionary of the American Congress. Washington, D.C.: U.S. Government Printing Office, 1961.

Who's Who in America, 1948–49.

Who Was Who in America, 1951–60.

WALFORD, LIONEL ALBERT
(1905–1979)
Born May 29 in San Francisco. Stanford University, A.B. 1929; Harvard University, M.A. 1932, Ph.D. (biology) 1935. Was fishery biologist for California Department of Fish and Game, 1926–31; assistant in biology at Harvard University, 1934–35; and instructor in zoology at Santa Barbara State College, 1935–36. Joined U.S. Bureau of Fisheries (later named Fish and Wildlife Service) in 1936, and served in biological and research capacities including chief of fisheries research in Washington, D.C., 1958–60, and as director of Sandy Hook Marine Laboratory, New Jersey, from 1960 until retiring in 1971. Wrote numerous scientific papers in addition to two books, *Marine Game Fishes of the Pacific Coast from Alaska to the Equator,* 1937, and *Living Resources of the Sea,* 1958. Was editor of *Copeia,* the journal of American Society of Ichthyologists and Herpetologists, 1937–47; was for three terms chairman of Committee on Research and Statistics, International Commission for the

Northwest Atlantic Fisheries, 1955–58; and was honorary member of Atlantic Estuarine Society. Was member of Panel on Marine Productivity of the National Research Council and of Committee on the International Union of Biological Science; and was representative of U.S. Bureau of Sport Fisheries and Wildlife in the Division of Biology and Agriculture, National Research Council. Participated in numerous scientific fisheries meetings. Led United States scientific delegations to International Commission of Northwest Atlantic Fisheries and to International North Pacific Fisheries Commission, and was instrumental in interjecting modern fisheries-management procedures into international programs. At time of his death, was associate director and chief scientist of New Jersey Marine Sciences Consortium. Died April 9, 1979.

ROBERT F. HUTTON
DANIEL A. POOLE

American Men and Women of Science (Physical and Biological Sciences), 14th ed., 1979.

WALLACE, DAVID HENRY
(1916–1980)
Born February 27 in Barclay, Maryland. Washington College, B.S. 1935; University of Maryland, M.S. 1937. Was administrator of Maryland Department of Tidewater Fisheries, 1941–46, and director, 1946–49; and was chairman of Maryland Board of Natural Resources in 1949 and 1950. Was executive director of Sponge and Chamois Institute, 1951–62, and of Oyster Institute of North America, 1954–61; and deputy director for fish and game for marine region, New York State Conservation Department, and later director of Division of Marine and Coastal Resources, New York State Department of Environmental Conservation, 1962–71. Then joined National Marine Fisheries Service and its parent organization, the National Oceanic and Atmospheric Administration, where he served as associate administrator for marine resources, 1971–80. Was awarded U.S. Department of Commerce Gold Medal in 1976 for his distinguished record of international negotiations. Was honored as chief architect of management approach for North Atlantic fisheries that reduced allowable catches to levels that protected stocks and at same time increased catch for U.S. for fishermen. His other achievements included serving as commissioner on International Commission of North Atlantic Fisheries; and as chairman of U.S. delegation to the Intergovern-

mental Oceanic Commission of UNESCO, of that commission's Eighth Session in Paris in 1973, and of U.S. delegation to Intergovernmental Oceanic Commission Executive Council in Canada in 1975. Was member of Fisheries Advisory Committee to assistant secretary in U.S. Department of State, 1956–70; U.S. Fish and Wildlife advisory committee to the secretary of the Interior, 1956–60; U.S. Mission to negotiate Middle Atlantic Fisheries Agreement with Soviet Union; and was advisory member of U.S. Mission to negotiate Middle Atlantic Fisheries Agreement with Poland, 1970. Author of numerous technical and popular articles on fishes, shellfish, and ecology, he was honorary life member of National Shellfisheries Association and of Atlantic Estuarine Research Society, and was active also in American Society of Limnology and Oceanography; American Institute of Biological Sciences; Marine Technology Society; and American Fisheries Society. Was particularly active in the latter; as second vice-president of American Fisheries Society at time of his death, he was looking forward to future, and was planning, when president, to take year off to devote his full time to the society's affairs. Died January 5, 1980.

ROBERT F. HUTTON

American Men and Women of Science (Physical and Biological Sciences), 12th ed., (vol. 6), 1973.

WARD, HENRY BALDWIN
(1865–1945)
Born March 4 in Troy, New York. Williams College, B.A. 1885, Sc.D. 1921; Harvard University, A.M. and Ph.D. 1892; University of Cincinnati, Sc.D. 1920; University of Oregon, LL.D. 1932; University of Nebraska, LL.D. 1935. Went to University of Nebraska as associate professor of zoology in 1893 and had become head of Zoology Department by 1906. In 1909 was made head of Department of Zoology at University of Illinois, a position he held until his retirement in 1933 at age of sixty-eight. Was associated with biological survey of Great Lakes and with Alaska and Pacific salmon investigations. Was a fellow of American Association for the Advancement of Science, was vice-president in 1905, and was permanent secretary, 1933–37. Was president of American Fisheries Society in 1913, and member of State Conservation Commission of New York in 1918 and of State Game and Fish Commission of Oregon in 1925. An active member of Izaak Walton League of America, he con-

tributed many papers on conservation subjects to its journal *Outdoor America*, and was its national president, 1928–30. Was author of many papers on parasites and on variety of other biological subjects; was also former associate editor of *American Naturalist*. Among his well-known writings are *Freshwater Biology*, 1917, of which he was editor, and *Foundations of Conservation Education*, 1941. Founded *Journal of Parasitology* in 1914. Died November 30, 1945.

George W. Bennett

American Men of Science, 7th ed., 1944.

Who Was Who in America, 1943–50.

WARDER, JOHN ASTON
(1812–1883)
Born January 19 in Philadelphia, Pennsylvania. Jefferson Medical College, M.D. 1836. Practiced medicine in Cincinnati, Ohio, for nearly two decades, before giving up medical practice in 1855 and buying farm near North Bend, Ohio. From 1850 to 1953 edited *Western Horticultural Review* and contributed to *American Journal of Horticulture*. Fostered landscape gardening and park beautification. His writings fall into three major chronological periods. Before 1855, published two medical treatises; from 1855 to late 1860s, his publications were mostly on horticulture; and from 1870, his works were chiefly on forestry. Many papers written at request of Agricultural Division of U.S. Patent Office were published in the division's annual reports. Was first person to propose planting belt of trees on great western plains. In 1873 was U.S. commissioner to International Exhibition in Vienna, and wrote official report on forests and forestry. In 1875 founded The American Forestry Association and was its first president. In 1882 was responsible for merging the association with American Forestry Congress, of which he had been an organizer. The American Forestry Association continues as nation's oldest lay person's organization devoted to conservation. Died July 14, 1883.

Fred H. Hornaday

Dictionary of American Biography, 1936.

WATSON, CLARENCE WILFORD
(born 1894)

Born December 28 in Boston, Massachusetts. Yale University, Ph.B. 1916, M.F. 1920, Ph.D. (forest soils) 1930. After employment by U.S. Forest Service beginning in 1917, was a fellow of American Scandinavian Foundation at Royal Forestry College in Stockholm, Sweden, 1920–21, then assistant professor of forestry at University of Idaho, 1921–27. Received National Research Council Fellowship for 1930–32. Was then with Civilian Conservation Corps and was forestry supervisor of Essex County (New Jersey) Parks, 1933–35. From 1936 to 1941 was employed by More Game Birds in America Foundation and by Ducks Unlimited (Canada). From 1942 until his retirement in December 1964, was southeastern regional supervisor, Branch of Federal Aid, Bureau of Sport Fisheries and Wildlife, U.S. Department of the Interior. During those twenty-three years, made outstanding contributions to interstate and federal-state relations in fish and wildlife conservation. An honorary member of The Wildlife Society, he was a founder and first president of the society's Southeastern Section and chairman of its Forest Game Committee, 1955–64, during which time numerous cooperative state-federal forest-wildlife research and management programs were developed. Upon retirement, received U.S. Department of the Interior's Distinguished Service Award. In his honor, Southeastern Association of Game and Fish Directors, Southern Division of the American Fisheries Society, and Southeastern Section of The Wildlife Society created C. W. Watson Fund and annual award and medal for career individual making greatest contribution to wildlife conservation in southeast.

LEONARD E. FOOTE

American Men of Science (Physical and Biological Sciences), 11th ed., 1967.

WAYBURN, EDGAR
(born 1906)

Born September 17 in Macon, Georgia. University of Georgia, B.A. 1926; Harvard University, M.D. 1930. Began medical practice in 1933, served in U.S. Army Medical Corps during World War II, and for most of his professional career has been in California. Joined Sierra Club in 1939; has served on its board of directors since 1957; as vice-president 1959–61, 1964–67, and 1969–71; and as president, 1961–64 and 1967–69. Was chairman of the club's conservation committee, 1955–61;

and chairman of Eighth Biennial Wilderness Conference of the Sierra Club, 1963. Was the club's leader in successful campaigns for Redwood National Park and Golden Gate National Recreation Area. Was the key volunteer leader in decade-long campaign to preserve Alaskan national-interest lands. In addition, has served as president of Federation of Western Outdoor Clubs, 1953–55; president of Trustees for Conservation, 1958–60; and chairman, People for a Golden Gate National Recreation Area, 1970 to present. Has received awards from California Conservation Council, 1957; Marin County Conservation Council, 1965; and Marin Conservation League, 1969, for his work in behalf of California state park system. Received American Motors Conservation Award in 1964; Sierra Club's John Muir Award in 1972; and Silver Spur Award (SPUR) in 1974. In his honor, Sierra Club established in 1979 the Edgar Wayburn Award for outstanding service. Has served on the Secretary of Interior's Advisory Board on National Parks, 1979–83; on Citizen's Advisory Commission on Golden Gate National Recreation Area, 1974 to present; and as trustee of Pacific Medical Center, 1978 to present. Has contributed many articles on conservation to *Sierra Club Bulletin*, *Sierra*, and *California Medicine*, and on medical subjects to *Western Journal of Medicine*.

LUELLA K. SAWYER

Sierra Club Handbook, 1967.

Who's Who in the West, 11th ed., 1968.

Who's Who in America, vol. 35, 1968–69.

WEAVER, RICHARD LEE
(1911–1964)
Born April 6 in Howard, Pennsylvania. Pennsylvania State University, B.S. (biology); Cornell University, Ph.D. (conservation and natural history) 1938. His career in conservation progressed through positions as head of science department at Maumee Valley Country Day School in Ohio, 1933–36; naturalist at Dartmouth College, 1938–42; extension specialist in conservation at University of New Hampshire, 1942–43; director of Connecticut Audubon Nature Center, 1943–47; program director of North Carolina Resource-Use Education Commission, 1947–52; and professor of conservation at University of Michigan, 1952–64. Was Fulbright lecturer in Pakistan, 1960–61. Was key figure and office

holder in state, regional, and national professional organizations; served as president of National Association of Biology Teachers in 1950, and as president of American Nature Study Society in 1957. In 1956 received Nash Motors Award for outstanding contributions to conservation education. Author of numerous books and articles, he was best known for his writing, research, and leadership in development of conservation education philosophy, teaching techniques, and action programs. As highly effective teacher, he had strong influence on his students, many of whom became leaders in conservation and conservation education. Died 1964.

BERNARD L. CLAUSEN

American Men of Science (Physical and Biological Sciences), 10th ed., 1961.

WEBER, ISABELLE PEARSON
(born 1925)
Born January 31 in Fall River, Massachusetts. Mount Holyoke College, Phi Beta Kappa, B.S. (Latin American studies) 1946. Joined League of Women Voters' Education Fund staff as researcher and writer and subsequently as director of its energy department, 1974–81, and has been director of natural resources department since 1981. Currently serves on board of directors of Energy Conservation Coalition. Has served on several subcommittees of National Petroleum Council and on President Carter's Council for Energy Efficiency, and was appointed to advisory council of Electric Power Research Institute for 1983–87 term. Her professional experience included seven years in foreign-aid program of federal government and four years on staff of Experiment in International Living, Putney, Vermont. Among her publications are *Citizens and Energy: The National Issues, The Energy Debate—A Stand-Off*, and *Examining Energy Sources and Issues*. Also was coauthor of *Energy Dilemmas* and coeditor of *Energy Options, A Nuclear Power Primer, Blueprint for Clean Water, Tapping Our Coal Reserves*, and *Natural Gas*.

LEAGUE OF WOMEN VOTERS OF THE UNITED STATES

WELCH, PAUL SMITH
(1882–1959)
Born January 28 in Oconee, Illinois. James Millikin College, B.A. 1910; University of Illinois, A.M. 1911; University of Michigan, Ph.D. (zool-

ogy) 1913. Began his teaching career in entomology at Kansas State College, and in 1918 became assistant professor of zoology at University of Michigan where, after thirty-four years of service, he was appointed emeritus professor in 1952. His teaching of invertebrate zoology and limnology on main campus of university at Ann Arbor and at University Biological Station at Cheybogan profoundly influenced ecological philosophy of two generations of aquatic resources researchers, managers, and administrators. His scientific papers and textbooks on limnology continue to contribute to training of aquatic ecologists and fisheries scientists. Was acting director of Michigan Biological Station in 1924 and 1925, and assistant director in 1929 and 1930; was assistant curator of William Barnes Lepidoptera Collection from 1906 to 1910; and was on staff of Lake Laboratory of Ohio State University in 1917. A prominent member of several scientific societies, he was secretary-editor and president of Microscopy Society; a fellow of Entomological Society of America and second vice-president in 1925; vice-president of Ecological Society of America in 1934; and secretary-treasurer of Limnological Society from 1935 to 1945 and president in 1946. Authored textbook *Limnology*, 1935 (rev. 1952); and *Limnological Methods*, 1948. Died October 1, 1959.

PHILIP A. DOUGLAS

American Men of Science (Physical and Biological Sciences), 9th ed., 1956.

WELD, CHRISTOPHER MINOT
(born 1932)
Born July 20 in Boston, Massachusetts. Harvard College, B.A. 1954; University of Virginia, J.D. 1959. Is member of law firm of Sullivan and Worcester, Boston, Massachusetts. An avid freshwater and saltwater angler since his youth, he in time came to fish in most of world's major offshore sport-fishing grounds. During late 1960s, his extensive big-game fishing off New England coast brought him into contact with large-scale foreign fishing operations and made him aware of threat posed to America's fisheries resources. Became active leader in political effort to induce Congress to declare two-hundred-mile-wide Fishery Conservation Zone bordering U.S. ocean coastline. His interest in this and in other marine conservation issues led to his cofounding (with Frank E. Carlton) the National Coalition for Marine Conservation in 1972. Has been director and principal officer of that organization ever since, and in 1983 was

elected president. From 1972 to 1976 served on Marine Fisheries Advisory Committee of U.S. Department of Commerce. In 1976 joined steering committee of Marine Recreational Fisheries Symposium. That same year, was appointed to advisory committee to International Commission for the Conservation of Atlantic Tunas, and the following year to Law of the Seas Advisory Committee. In 1978 was selected to serve on National Sea Grant Advisory Panel. Was member of New England Fishery Management Council, 1979–82. In addition, has served as advisor to New England Council on large pelagic species (swordfish, billfish, tunas, and sharks) and on Massachusetts Fisheries Advisory Commission. Is director of numerous national and international fisheries and conservation organizations, including Atlantic Center for the Environment; Coastal Alliance; and International Atlantic Salmon Foundation. Serves on advisory boards of several other groups, and is member of several Atlantic coast and Hawaiian sport-fishing clubs. Has authored numerous articles on fisheries conservation and international fisheries law, and is editor of *Right Rigger!*, a monthly newsletter of National Coalition for Marine Conservation.

KENNETH HINMAN

WELLER, MILTON WEBSTER
(born 1929)

Born May 23 in Saint Louis, Missouri. University of Missouri, B.A. (zoology) 1951, M.A. 1954, Ph.D. 1956. Conducted research on breeding biology of prairie waterfowl, on their behavior during migration, and on wintering areas. During 1957–74 taught wildlife ecology and management at Iowa State University, where he was involved in development of coursework and curricula aimed at providing integrated background in both wildlife and fisheries resources. Conducted long-term research on wetland dynamics in relation to wildlife production to understand and utilize natural processes in management strategies. Coauthored fourth volume of Delacour's *Waterfowl of the World*. Devoted year in Argentina to studies of waterfowl and their management in Southern Hemisphere climatic regime, and problems of migratory resources in nations where national and international conservation policies were lacking. Authored *The Island Waterfowl*, 1980, which considered unique biological attributes and related conservation problems of tropical and Southern Hemisphere island waterfowl. After serving as leader of Fisheries and Wildlife

Section at Iowa State University, became head of entomology in fish and wildlife department, University of Minnesota, in 1974. Studies of waterfowl there focused on resource-use strategies over annual cycle with wetland management considerations for wintering, migrational, and breeding areas. Authored *Freshwater Marshes*, 1981, which was directed toward broadening layperson appreciation for wetlands and wetland management for wildlife. Received Gulf Oil Conservation Award, 1982, and was selected to fill Caesar Kleberg Chair in Wildlife Ecology at Texas A&M University with a focus on wetland resources, 1982 to present.

LAURENCE R. JAHN

American Men and Women of Science (Physical and Biological Sciences), 15th ed., 1982.

WENTZ, WILLIAM ALAN
(born 1946)
Born November 10 in Kenton, Ohio. The Ohio State University, B.A. (agriculture) 1969; M.S. Oregon State University (wildlife science) 1971; Ph.D. University of Michigan (wildlife management) 1976. Was assistant curator of Herbarium at Ohio State University, 1971–72, and research associate with School of Natural Resources, University of Michigan, 1974–75. Was Extension wildlife specialist, and assistant professor with South Dakota Cooperative Extension Service and with Department of Wildlife and Fisheries, South Dakota State University, 1975–80. Special assistant to secretary of South Dakota Department of Game, Fish and Parks in 1979, on leave, returned to South Dakota State University as associate professor and assistant leader of South Dakota Cooperative Wildlife Research Unit, 1980–81. Joined staff of National Wildlife Federation, Washington, D.C., as director of Fisheries and Wildlife Division in 1981, then as executive officer of Cooperative Lead Poisoning Control Information Program, from 1982 to present. Is member of American Fisheries Society, American Society of Mammalogists (life member), Sigma Xi, and The Wildlife Society. Was president of Ohio State University Student Chapter, 1968–69; South Dakota Chapter, 1980–81; and Central Mountains and Plains Section, 1980–81, of The Wildlife Society. Served The Wildlife Society as chairman of publications committee, 1980–82; chairman of conservation affairs committee, 1982–84 and 1984–86; and as editor of *Wildlife Society Bulletin*, 1978–81. Has been on boards of directors of several organizations, including South Dakota

Wildlife Federation, 1976–77; South Dakota Pheasant Congress, 1975–82; and South Dakota Committee to Protect Hunting, 1980–81. Has published numerous scientific and popular articles with emphasis on wetlands ecology and management, and taxonomy and ecology of aquatic vascular plants. Was named Wildlife Conservationist of the Year by South Dakota Wildlife Federation in 1977, and received national recognition awards from The Wildlife Society in 1981 and 1983. Currently serves on several national and regional committees that deal with resource conservation.

WILLIAM A. WENTZ

American Men and Women of Science 14th ed., 1979.

WENZEL, WALTER JOSEPH

(born 1932)

Born August 27 in Newark, New Jersey. Hobart College, B.A. (biology) 1948; University of Wyoming, M.S. (wildlife ecology and zoology) 1949. Served in U.S. Army, 1942–45. Was employed from 1950 to 1958 by New Jersey Division of Fish and Game, first as wildlife biologist, then in conservation information-education. Joined staff of Boy Scouts of America, serving as director of conservation at Philmont Scout Ranch in New Mexico, 1958–63; as associate director of conservation service at national headquarters, 1963–78; director of camping and conservation, 1978–83; and director of high-adventure and conservation service, 1983 to present. Attained rank of Eagle Scout and served in many volunteer scouting positions before becoming professional scouter. Is member of Sigma Xi honorary science society, Soil Conservation Society of America, The Wildlife Society, and National Rifle Association of America.

BOY SCOUTS OF AMERICA

WESTWOOD, RICHARD WILBUR

(1896–1961)

Born July 8 in Newton, Massachusetts. Columbia University School of Journalism, B.A. 1918. Served in U.S. Army during World War I; was wounded at Verdun and awarded *Croix de Guerre*. Beginning in 1919, worked on newspapers in New England; from 1921 to 1923, was reporter for *Christian Science Monitor*, writing frequently on conservation topics. His writings attracted attention, and he was invited to join editorial staff of *Nature Magazine*, published by American Nature Association in Washington, D.C. From assistant editor in 1923, advanced to managing editor in 1927, and in 1937 became editor, serving as such until 1960, when magazine merged with *Natural History*. Was also secretary of American Nature Association from 1927 to 1946, and was president thereafter until his death. Organized in 1922 to promote public interest in nature and out-of-doors, the association and its magazine led militant campaign for conservation of environment, particularly for protection and improvement of rural roadsides and elimination of unsightly roadside billboard advertising. Beginning in 1957 was secretary of National Roadside Commission, and as its representative before legislative committees was leader in fight for preserving natural beauty of countryside. Prominent in movement for conservation of all resources, he was notably energetic in advocating establishment of parks and recreational areas. As life member of National Parks Association, he was active in International Union for Conservation of Nature, American Nature Study Society, and other bodies dedicated to natural resources. Was especially effective in conservation education of students, as *Nature Magazine* went regularly to many schools. Died February 13, 1961.

HENRY CLEPPER

Evening Star. Washington, D.C. Obituary, February 14, 1961.

Who Was Who in America, 1961–68.

WHARTON, WILLIAM P.
(1880–1976)
Born August 12 in Beverly, Massachusetts. Harvard College, B.A. 1903; Harvard Law School. Became extensive tree planter on his lands in Massachusetts, and was manager of Groton (Massachusetts) Town Forest, which he was instrumental in establishing. Was president of Massachusetts Forest and Park Association, was active in Society for the Protection of New Hampshire Forests, and obtained endowments for promoting research in forest production. Was one of organizers of Committee for the Suppression of Pine Blister Rust in North America, and was active in organizing National Conference on the Dutch Elm Disease. To increase his knowledge of forestry, in 1913 he traveled throughout scientifically managed forests of western Europe. In recognition of his contributions to forestry, Society of American Foresters elected him to associate membership in 1924. Was a director of The American Forestry Association

from 1923 to 1950. In addition to his forestry activities, early in this century he served as secretary of American Bison Society, organization principally responsible for saving this species. After trip to western United States national parks in 1912, became influential advocate of park development and protection, and was early proponent of creation of Everglades National Park and of Olympic National Park. Helped found National Parks Association and was its president. Was early supporter of National Association of Audubon Societies, Northeastern Bird Banding Association, and numerous other conservation bodies. His interests and activities covered all phases of natural resources conservation, and for half-century he occupied positions of leadership with leading organizations in this field. Died December 13, 1976.

FRED E. HORNADAY

WHIPPLE, GEORGE CHANDLER
(1866–1924)
Born March 2 in New Boston, New Hampshire. Massachusetts Institute of Technology, S.B. (sanitary engineering) 1899. Worked as biologist in Boston Water Works, later becoming director of Mount Prospect Laboratory of New York City Department of Water Supply, Gas, and Electricity. Then became partner in sanitary engineering consulting firm of Hazen and Whipple, New York. During 1911 was professor of sanitary engineering at Harvard University, and professor of sanitary engineering at Massachusetts Institute of Technology, 1914–16. Between 1914 and 1923 was council member of Massachusetts State Department of Health. In 1917 was commissioned major, and was made member of Red Cross Mission to Russia. In 1919 became senior sanitary engineer for U.S. Public Health Association, and chief of Department of Sanitation for League of Red Cross Societies. Was a fellow of American Academy of Arts and Science. One of America's pioneers in limnology, he wrote many technical books on water, among them the classic *Microscopy of Drinking Water*, 1889; also was coauthor of one of first textbooks on limnology, *Fresh-Water Biology*, 1918. Died November 27, 1924.

PHILIP A. DOUGLAS

Who Was Who in America, 1897–1942.

WHITE, GILBERT FOWLER

(born 1911)

Born November 26 in Chicago. University of Chicago, B.S. 1932, S.M. 1934, Ph.D. (geography) 1942. Joined staff of Mississippi Valley Committee and Natural Resources Board in 1934. Was then secretary of Committees on Land and Waters Resources for the Natural Resources Planning Board, 1936–40; and was with Bureau of the Budget, 1941–42. During World War II was on overseas duty with American Friends Service Committee. In 1946 became president of Haverford College and left in 1956 to become professor of geography at University of Chicago. In 1970 moved to University of Colorado as director of Institute of Behavioral Science; retired in 1978, but continued as director of Natural Hazards Research Information Center. Was member of task force on natural resources of Hoover Commission on Reorganization of the Federal Government in 1948, and was vice-chairman of President's Water Resources Policy Commission, 1950–51. During 1954–55 was U.S. member on Advisory Committee on Arid Land Research of the United Nations Educational, Scientific and Cultural Organization, and on United Nations Panel on Integrated River Basin Development, 1956–57. Has been consultant to United Nations Development Program and to Lower Mekong Coordinating Committee. In 1960 was consultant to Senate Select Committee on Water Resources. Was chairman of task force on Federal Flood Control Policy, which drafted new national policy on flood loss reduction, and also was on Special Commission on Weather Modification of National Science Foundation, both during 1965–66. From 1972 to 1982 was president of Scientific Committee on Problems of the Environment of the International Council of Scientific Unions. Among his books are *Human Adjustment to Floods*, 1942; *Science and the Future of Arid Lands*, 1960; *Social and Economic Aspects of Natural Resources*, 1962; *Choice of Adjustment to Floods*, 1964; and *Strategies of American Water Management*, 1969. Is coauthor of *Drawers of Water: Domestic Water Use in East Africa*, 1972, and *The Environment as Hazard*, 1978; and editor of *Water, Health and Society* (writings of Abel Wolman), 1969. In 1982 edited (with M. Holdgate and M. Kassas) U.N. Environmental Programme's report *The World Environment, 1972–82*.

HENRY CLEPPER
GILBERT F. WHITE

American Men of Science (Social and Behavioral Sciences), 11th ed., 1961.

Who's Who in America, 42d ed., 1982–83.

WHITESELL, DALE EDWARD
(born 1925)
Born October 12 in Miamisburg, Ohio. Served in U.S. Army Air Force 1942–46. Ohio State University, B.S. (agriculture) 1950, M.S. (wildlife management) 1951. Entered Ohio Division of Wildlife in 1951 as wildlife district game-management supervisor. Was leader of Farmer Attitude Survey Project for the division in 1951 and 1958, and chief of Ohio Division of Wildlife, 1963–65. Has been executive vice-president of Ducks Unlimited, Inc., since 1965. As chief executive, reorganized non-profit group's fund-raising procedures and recruited staff of seasoned wildlife professionals, many of whom had served as state fish and game directors. Under his leadership, the 500,000-member organization experienced income growth rate of nearly 25 percent compounded annually, from $876,000 raised in 1965 to $34,760,000 in 1982. His strict adherence to Ducks Unlimited's policy of investing nearly eighty cents of every dollar on habitat development has enabled organization to reserve more than 3,250,000 wetland acres in Canada, where more than 70 percent of continent's wild waterfowl are produced. As result of his organizational planning, volunteer chapters increased from a few hundred in 1965 to more than three thousand nationwide in 1983. Over the years, has counseled governmental leaders from United States, Canada, and Mexico concerning management of North America's waterfowl resources. In addition, has testified before numerous state and federal commissions on behalf of waterfowl and wetland habitat conservation. Twice past-president of Ohio Wildlife Management Association, he is also twenty-year member of International Association of Fish and Wildlife Agencies.

LAURENCE R. JAHN

WHYTE, WILLIAM HOLLINGSWORTH
(born 1917)
Born October 1 in West Chester, Pennsylvania. Princeton University, B.A. cum laude 1939. Served in U.S. Marine Corps, 1941–45. Was writer for *Fortune* magazine, 1946–51, and assistant managing editor, 1951–59. Is author of a number of books, including *Is Anybody Listening?*, 1952; *The Organization Man*, 1956; *Open Space Action*, 1962; *Cluster Development*, 1964; *The Last Landscape*, 1968; and *The Social Life of Small Urban Spaces*, 1980; as well as numerous articles in popular and profes-

sional periodicals. As director of Street Life Project in New York City, also produced film *The Social Life of Small Urban Spaces*. Was member of President's Task Force on Natural Beauty, 1964–65; codirector of White House Conference on Natural Beauty, 1965; and chairman of Governor Nelson Rockefeller's Conference on Natural Beauty. Was distinguished professor of urban sociology at Hunter College, 1970–71, and member of Hudson River Valley Commission, 1964–72. Currently serves on board of New York Landmarks Conservancy, as vice-chairman of board of trustees of The Conservation Foundation, and as trustee of American Conservation Association. Received *Benjamin Franklin* magazine writing award in 1953; Liberty and Justice Book award from American Library Association in 1957; and American Institute of Architects' Institute Honor, 1983.

Who's Who in America, 42d ed., 1982–83.

WILLIAMS, DONALD ALFRED

(1905–1982)
Born July 14 in Clark, South Dakota. South Dakota State University, B.S. (civil engineering) 1928, Doctor of Agriculture (honorary) 1956. After five years in private and state engineering work, entered U.S. Soil Conservation Service in 1935 as Civilian Conservation Corps camp superintendent. From 1935 to 1947 held field and regional jobs as conservation engineer; then became assistant regional director in Pacific Coast Region, 1947–50; flood-control survey officer, office of the secretary of Agriculture, 1950–51; assistant chief of Soil Conservation Service, 1951–53; and administrator in November 1953. Retired in December 1968. During his administration, Soil Conservation Service responsibilities expanded from virtually a single program of technical assistance to soil conservation districts to an agency with major responsibilities in fifteen programs. In 1953, Soil Conservation Service was assigned responsibility for U.S. Department of Agriculture flood-prevention and river-basin investigation activities, and in 1954 for small watershed program, which carried out soil and water conservation methods in entire watershed areas. Under his leadership, resource conservation and development projects, first authorized in 1962, provided better economic opportunities for rural people through planned, integrated development of area's natural resources. Originated and directed National Inventory of Conservation Needs, carried out between 1957 and 1962, which gave nation

its first authoritative survey of land conditions, conservation needs, watershed potentials, and land-use trends on nonfederal lands of the country. Was also largely responsible for development of Great Plains Conservation Program, enacted in 1956, to provide assistance for farmers and ranchers in major area with severe land-use problems. Received Distinguished Service Award of the National Association of Soil and Water Conservation Districts in 1957; U.S. Department of Agriculture's Distinguished Service Award in 1958; and Rockefeller Public Service Award in Administration in 1967. Was international soil and water conservation consultant to Ford Foundation on its program to help India increase food production. Was a fellow of Soil Conservation Society of America and of American Association for the Advancement of Science. Died November 13, 1982.

F. GLENNON LOYD

Who's Who in America, 38th ed., 1974–75.

Who's Who in Engineering, 8th ed., 1964.

WILLIAMSON, LONNIE LEROY
(born 1939)

Born November 12 in Jackson County, Georgia. University of Georgia, A.B.J. (journalism) 1960, M.S. (wildlife management) 1969, postgraduate work in natural resource economics 1971–72. Was research associate for Southeastern Cooperative Wildlife Disease Study, University of Georgia College of Veterinary Medicine, 1966–70. Joined Wildlife Management Institute in Washington, D.C., in 1970, as editor of *Outdoor News Bulletin*. Became the institute's secretary in 1975. Is member of The Wildlife Society, The American Forestry Association, Outdoor Writers Association of America, and Mason-Dixon Outdoor Writers Association; has served the latter as president and vice-president. Is columnist for Ruffed Grouse Society's *Drummer*, and editor-at-large for *Outdoor Life*. Works extensively on conservation issues, particularly at national level, and is frequently invited to provide testimony before Congress on issues pertaining to wildlife and related resources. A respected natural resource communicator, he has authored many articles on wildlife conservation topics for national magazines and professional journals, and has received awards for outdoor writing and conservation reporting, including prestigious Jade of Chiefs Award from Outdoor Writers Association in 1983.

RICHARD E. McCABE

WIRTH, CONRAD LOUIS
(born 1899)

Born December 1 in Hartford, Connecticut. University of Massachusetts, B.S. 1923, Doctor of Landscape Architecture (honorary) 1953, New England College, Doctor of Civil Law (honorary) 1955, University of North Carolina, L.H.D. (honorary) 1958. In 1928 began work with National Capital Park and Planning Commission, and in 1931 transferred to National Park Service as assistant director in charge of land planning. In 1933 was also given supervisory responsibility for all state and county park activities of Civilian Conservation Corps; in 1935 this supervisory responsibility was extended to all bureaus of U.S. Department of the Interior. Author of Park, Parkway and Recreational Area Study Act of 1936, he directed state-by-state studies; the act was used in 1962 to establish new Bureau of Outdoor Recreation pending its basic legislation (now part of National Park Service). In 1951 became director of National Park Service and served in that capacity until his retirement in 1964. During this period initiated Mission 66, the service's protection, improvement, and extension program. Awards received for his accomplishments in conservation, planning, and park management include Distinguished Service Award of U.S. Department of the Interior; Conservation Award of American Forestry Association; Rockefeller Public Service Award; Pugsley Gold Medal and the Horace Marden Albright Scenic Preservation Medal of the American Scenic and Historic Preservation Society; and Theodore Roosevelt Medal for Conservation of Natural Resources of Theodore Roosevelt Association. Following his retirement from government, has served as executive director of Hudson River Valley Commission, 1965–66; commissioner of Palisades Interstate Park Commission, 1964–72; emeritus presidential appointee to National Capital Planning Commission, 1966–72; chairman of New York State Historic Trust, 1966–70; and consultant on conservation and park matters to Laurance S. Rockefeller and Rockefeller Brothers Fund. Is life director of National Society of Park Resources; life trustee of National Geographic Society and member of its Research and Exploration Committee; and honorary life member of Sierra Club. Is a fellow of American Society of Landscape Architects (ASLA) and of American Institute of Park Executives, and in 1972 received the former's ASLA Medal. In 1980 was founder and director of newly formed American Academy of Parks and Recreation Administration.

HOLT BODINSON
CONRAD L. WIRTH

Who's Who in America, 37th ed., 1972–73.

WOODWARD, HUGH BEISTLE
(1885–1968)
Born April 29 in Clearfield, Pennsylvania. Dickenson College, Ph.B. 1908, M.A. 1910, LL.B. 1910, LL.D. (honorary) 1959. Was admitted to Pennsylvania bar in 1911, Colorado bar in 1914, and New Mexico bar in 1915, and was licensed to practice before Supreme Court in 1923. During long legal career in New Mexico, promoted conservation as personal crusade. Was active in New Mexico Wildlife and Conservation Association, National Audubon Society, Izaak Walton League of America, The Wilderness Society, and The American Forestry Association. Served as both lieutenant governor and district attorney for Eighth Judicial District of New Mexico, and as U.S. Attorney for New Mexico, in addition to activities associated with his private law practice and work with finance and construction firms in Southwest. Made several contributions of national nature, which led to his receiving Nash Conservation Award in 1953. Was active in fighting demands by livestock interests to gain control of federal grazing lands. Was member of National Advisory Committee on Multiple Use of National Forests. Joined others in drafting early versions of Wilderness Act. Served for ten years as regional director of National Wildlife Federation and as member of board of trustees of National Wildlife Federation Endowment. During his tenure was instrumental in locating national headquarters of National Wildlife Federation in Washington, D.C. Died August 18, 1968.

NATIONAL WILDLIFE FEDERATION

WOODWELL, GEORGE MASTERS
(born 1928)
Born October 23 in Cambridge, Massachusetts. Dartmouth College,

B.A. 1950, Duke University, A.M. 1956, Ph.D. (botany) 1958, Williams College, D.Sc. (honorary) 1977. Progressed from assistant to associate professor at University of Maine, 1957–61; first served as assistant and advanced to senior ecologist at Brookhaven National Laboratory, 1961–75; director of Ecosystems Center at Marine Biological Laboratory, Woods Hole, Massachusetts, 1975 to present. Has been associate of The Conservation Foundation, 1958–61, and member of board of trustees, 1975–77; lecturer, School of Forestry, Yale University, 1969 to present; founding member of board of trustees of Environmental Defense Fund in 1967, of Natural Resources Defense Council in 1970, and of World Resources Institute in 1982. Has been long-time member of board of World Wildlife Fund and its chairman since 1981. Was chairman of the Suffolk County Council on Environmental Quality in 1972. Received New York Botanical Garden's Green World Award in 1975 and Distinguished Service Award of American Institute of Biological Sciences in 1982. Is fellow of American Association for the Advancement of Science; and is member of American Institute for Biological Sciences, of British Ecological Society, and of Ecological Society of America. Was vice-president of Ecological Society of America in 1976, and its president, 1977–78. His research studies include structure, function, and development of terrestrial and marine ecosystems; environmental cycling of nutrients, radioactive isotopes, and organic compounds, especially pesticides; ecological effects of ionizing radiation; and biotic aspects of global carbon dioxide problem.

ROBERT L. EDWARDS
ROBERT F. HUTTON

American Men and Women of Science (Physical and Biological Sciences), 15th ed., 1982.

Who's Who in America, 42d ed., 1982–83.

WRIGHT, DAVID GEORGE
(born 1931)
Born March 13 in New Philadelphia, Ohio. Served in U.S. Air Force, 1950–54. Ohio State University, B.S. (landscape architecture) 1959. Joined Muskingum Watershed Conservancy District, New Philadelphia, Ohio, as assistant manager, preparing site development plans and supervising major park construction efforts, 1959–64. Became director of education and research for American Institute of Park Executives, serving

as managing editor of *Parks and Recreation* magazine and technical specialist for park land acquisition and development projects, 1964–66; then was director of community and field services for National Recreation and Park Association, providing special assistance in comprehensive planning for recreational facilities, 1966–69. During this period was senior staff planner for study of New York City's park and recreation capital needs, a report that led to substantial improvements in park system there. Next joined staff of National Park Service, first as special assistant to associate director, 1969–73; then as associate manager in Denver Service Center with special emphasis on management of major bicentennial projects, 1973–76; as deputy director for Southeast Regional Office, managing more than fifty National Park Service facilities, 1976–78; as chief of park planning and environmental quality, Washington, D.C., 1978–79; then as associate director for planning and development, 1979 to present. In latter capacity, is responsible for all National Park planning, design, preservation, and construction projects. Was invested as a fellow in American Society of Landscape Architects in 1979. Has received distinguished service awards from both American Institute of Park Executives and American Society of Landscape Architects, and Distinguished Alumnus Award from Ohio State University's College of Engineering in 1983. Coauthored *Marinas*, 1965; *Public Beaches*, 1965; and *Coasting and Tobogganing*, 1966. Was contributing editor to *Parks and Recreation Magazine*, 1964–65.

AMERICAN SOCIETY OF LANDSCAPE ARCHITECTS

Who's Who in America, 42d ed., 1982–83.

WRIGHT, MABEL OSGOOD
(1859–1934)
Born January 26 in New York City. Promoted organization in 1898 of Audubon Society, state of Connecticut, and served as its president continuously until 1925. Was director of National Association of Audubon Societies (now National Audubon Society) from its organization in 1905 until 1928, and also served as contributing editor of *Bird Lore*, which became *Audubon* magazine. Was elected associate member of American Ornithologists' Union in 1895 and member in 1901. Birdcraft Sanctuary, near her home in Fairfield, Connecticut, was forerunner of modern outdoor educational centers; there she gathered group of children whom she called her "bird class" to teach them about nature. Author of *Birdcraft*,

1895, one of earliest successful field guides to birds, she wrote numerous other books and pamphlets that bridged gap between professional ornithologists and lay public. Among these books were *The Friendship of Nature*, 1894; *Citizen Bird*, 1897; *Four-Footed Americans and Their Kin*, 1898; *The Flowers and Ferns in Their Haunts*, 1901; and *The Garden of a Commuter's Wife*, 1902. Drawings of Louis Agassiz Fuertes, noted illustrator of birds, first appeared in her books. Died July 16, 1934.

CHARLES H. CALLISON

Auk. Obituary, 51: 564–65.

Bird Lore. Obituary, July-August 1934, p. 280.

National Cyclopaedia of American Biography, 1904.

Who Was Who in America, 1897–1942.

WRIGHT, R. MICHAEL
(born 1943)
Born July 12 in Eugene, Oregon. Stanford University, B.A. (history) 1966; Stanford University School of Law, J.D. 1970. Was appointed research associate at Stanford's Center for Research in International Studies before joining The Nature Conservancy as western regional counsel in 1972. Began International Program at The Nature Conservancy in 1974. During his five years as director, helped establish major new protected areas, including Archbold addition to Dominica's Morne Trois Pitons National Park, Corcovado National Park, and Costa Rica and Long Point National Wildlife Refuge, Canada, together with a number of smaller preserves in the Caribbean, Central America, and Canada. Received the conservancy's Certificate of Special Recognition in 1979, when he left to become vice-president and general counsel of World Wildlife Fund–U.S., where he continues to serve. Took leave of absence in 1980–81 to serve as assistant director of President Carter's Task Force on Global Resources and Environment to follow up Global 2000 Report. While directing World Wildlife Fund's park program, structured purchase of La Planada Nature Reserve in Colombian Andes. Was admitted to California bar in 1970, U.S. Supreme Court bar in 1976, and International Council of Environmental Law in 1975. Has also been elected to membership in two commissions of International Union for the Conservation of Nature: Environmental Law, Policy and Administration, and

National Parks and Protected Areas. Is founding member of boards of Costa Rica Conservation Foundation; Foundation for Educational and Social Development in the Americas (Colombia); and Asa Wright Nature Centre (Trinidad); also drafted original bylaws and serves as advisor to Falkland Islands Foundation. Was selected as one of first Rockefeller Foundation fellows in environmental affairs, 1974, and was member of U.S. Delegation to Governing Council of the United Nations Environment Programme, 1979.

R. Michael Wright

YARD, ROBERT STERLING
(1861–1945)
Born February 1 in Haverstraw, New York. Princeton University, B.A. 1883. His career in journalism began in 1887, first with *New York Sun*, then in 1891 with *New York Herald*, for which he was editor until 1900. Was with Charles Scribner's Sons as book-advertising manager, 1901–5; subsequently was editor for other companies until he became editor-in-chief of *Century Magazine*, 1913–14, and then Sunday editor for *New York Herald*. From 1915 to 1919 helped to establish National Park Service and was chief of its Educational Division. When National Parks Association was founded in 1919, he became its executive secretary, continuing until 1934. One of eight organizers of The Wilderness Society in 1935, he was its secretary-treasurer until 1937, and was president and permanent secretary until 1945; in addition, was first editor of *Living Wilderness*, the society's quarterly journal, from 1935 to 1945. Among his published works are *The National Parks Portfolio*, 1916; *Glimpses of Our National Parks*, 1916; *The Top of the Continent*, 1917; *The Book of the National Parks*, 1919; and *Our Federal Lands, A Romance of American Development*, 1928. Died May 17, 1945.

Michael Nadel

Living Wilderness, July 1945, vol. 10, no. 13; and December 1945, vol. 10, nos. 14 and 15.

Who Was Who in America, 1943–50.

YOUNG, STANLEY PAUL
(1889–1969)
Born October 30 in Astoria, Oregon. University of Oregon, B.S. 1911;

graduate work at University of Michigan where he served as assistant in geology, 1914–15. Much of his early professional life was spent in the West and Southwest, where he entered U.S. Forest Service in Arizona in 1917, then transferred to Bureau of Biological Survey as government hunter. His work on control and biology of larger mammalian predators occupied much of his long career, first in ground control work in 1919 and then in coyote control in New Mexico in 1920. Was leader of predator control in Colorado and Kansas, 1921–27; and later, in Washington, D.C., in administration and research in Bureau of Biological Survey and its successor agency, the Fish and Wildlife Service, as assistant head, Division of Economic Investigations, 1927–28. There became principal biologist in charge, Division of Predatory Animal and Rodent Control, 1928–34; chief, Division of Game Management, 1934–38; biologist, Division of Predator and Rodent Control, 1938–39; member of staff dealing with zoology, wildlife research, and North American fauna publications, 1939–57; and director of Bird and Mammal Laboratories, 1957–59. Upon his retirement in 1959, became collaborator of Bureau of Sport Fisheries and Wildlife. One of wildlife conservation's most colorful figures, he was member of wildlife expeditions to Louisiana and Mexico in 1934 and 1937. Was honorary member of The Wildlife Society, and member of American Society of Mammalogists. Received Distinguished Service Medal of U.S. Department of the Interior in 1957. A prolific writer, his best-known books include *The Wolves of North America*, 1944, and *The Puma-Mysterious American Cat*, 1946, both with Edward A. Goldman; *The Clever Coyote* (with H. H. T. Jackson), 1951; and *The Bobcat of North America*, 1958, all published by Wildlife Management Institute. Was still publishing articles on America's larger predatory animals when he was nearly eighty years old. Died May 15, 1969.

Daniel L. Leedy

American Men of Science (Physical and Biological Sciences), 11th ed., 1967.

Journal of Wildlife Management. Obituary, 33(4): 1056–57, October 1969.

Zahniser, Howard Clinton

(1906–1964)
Born February 25 in Franklin, Pennsylvania. Greenville College (Illinois), B.A. 1928, Litt. D. 1957. After graduation, taught high school for year in Greenville, then entered U.S. Department of Commerce in 1930. From 1931 to 1942 served Bureau of Biological Survey and its successor

agency, U.S. Fish and Wildlife Service, as editor, writer, and broadcaster on wildlife research, administration, and conservation, in charge of the agency's Section of Current and Visual Information. From 1935–59 was essayist and book editor of *Nature Magazine*; from 1940, was annual contributor to *Encyclopedia Britannica* on wildlife conservation and wilderness preservation. From 1942 to 1945 was principal research writer for Bureau of Plant Industry, Soils, and Agricultural Engineering in U.S. Department of Agriculture's Research Administration. As head of the bureau's Division of Information, directed its publication and research-reporting program. Was also chairman of U.S. Department of Agriculture's Special Committee on Improvement of Publications. Joined staff of The Wilderness Society in 1945 as executive secretary (later executive director) and as editor of its quarterly magazine *Living Wilderness*, for which he worked until his death. Was one of organizers in 1946 (chairman, 1948–49) of Natural Resources Council of America; president of Thoreau Society in 1957; member of Advisory Committee on Conservation to the Secretary of the Interior, 1951–54; vice-chairman of Citizens' Committee on Natural Resources in 1955; and was honorary vice-president of Sierra Club. Was free-lance writer of articles and verse, and his book contributions include chapters "Parks and Wilderness" in *America's Natural Resources*, 1957, and "Wilderness Forever" in *Wilderness: America's Living Heritage*, 1961. Was father of Wilderness Act of 1964, which he was largely instrumental in writing and seeing through to enactment. Died May 5, 1964.

MICHAEL NADEL

Living Wilderness, no. 85 Winter-Spring 1964.

Who Was Who in America, 1961–68.

ZIMMERMAN, GORDON KARL
(1910–1981)
Born November 4 in Spokane, Washington. University of Maryland, B.A. (business administration) 1932. After working as reporter for *Washington* (D.C.) *Daily News*, 1932–35, joined U.S. Department of Agriculture's newly created U.S. Soil Conservation Service in 1935, advancing through various professional public-information positions to chief of Division of Information, a position he held from 1942 to 1951. Long a close associate of H. H. Bennett, first chief of Soil Conservation Service, served as Bennett's principal public relations advisor and writer. Was

manager of public-relations department of Harry Ferguson, Inc., in Detroit, 1952–55, and then research director for National Grange in Washington, D.C., 1955–58. From 1958 to 1976 was executive vice-president of National Association of Conservation Districts, which represents more than three thousand local conservation districts in the fifty states, Puerto Rico, and Virgin Islands. Served on National Livestock and Meat Board, with the American Dairy Association, and was member of Agriculture Committee of the National Planning Association. Was chairman of Natural Resources Council of America, and served for many years as chairman of steering committee of National Watershed Congress. Was member of Citizens' Advisory Committee on Environmental Quality and of National Conservation Committee of Boy Scouts of America. Received Natural Resources Council of America's Award of Honor for 1979. Died March 15, 1981.

NATIONAL ASSOCIATION OF CONSERVATION DISTRICTS
CHARLES BOOTHBY

ZINN, DONALD JOSEPH

(born 1911)

Born April 19 in New York City. Harvard University, B.S. 1933; University of Rhode Island, M.S. 1937; Yale University, Ph.D. (marine biology) 1942. Following service, 1942–45, as aviation physiologist with U.S. Air Force, was naturalist at Marine Biological Laboratory, Woods Hole, Massachusetts, 1945–46. Joined faculty of University of Rhode Island in 1946; rose to professor in 1961 and to chairman of Department of Zoology in 1962, and is now professor emeritus of zoology. Was director of Agassiz Memorial Expedition to Penikese Island; research associate of Narragansett Marine Laboratory; and delegate to Fifteenth International Congress of Zoology. Is member of eleven professional scientific societies, and is fellow of American Association for the Advancement of Science and of Academy of Zoology. Has been member of board of directors of Rhode Island Wildlife Federation since 1947, and has served as secretary, president, and delegate to annual meetings of National Wildlife Federation. In 1960 was elected to board of directors of National Wildlife Federation; and was elected president in 1967, 1968, and 1969. His various positions include member, President's Advisory Panel on Timber and The Environment, 1968–73; member, Shoreline Erosion Advisory Panel, Army Corps of Engineers, 1976–81; president, Cape Cod Museum of Natural History, 1981–82; senior fellow since 1982 and trustee,

New England Natural Resources Center, 1975 to present; member, North Atlantic Technical Working Group Committee, Bureau of Land Management, 1978–81; and member, Falmouth Conservation Commission, 1976, and chairman, 1980–82. Author of more than one hundred research papers and articles on various aspects of animal life, he is recognized as one of nation's leading marine ecologists and has served on International Task Force for the Conservation of Aquatic Ecosystems.

WILLARD T. JOHNS
DONALD J. ZINN

American Men and Women of Science (Physical and Biological Sciences), 15th ed., 1982.

ZIVNUSKA, JOHN ARTHUR
(born 1916)

Born July 10 in San Diego, California. University of California, B.S. 1938, M.S. 1940; University of Minnesota, Ph.D. (agricultural economics) 1947. U.S. Navy 1942–45. Starting as instructor in forestry at University of Minnesota in 1946, went to University of California School of Forestry in 1948, advanced to professor in 1959, and was acting dean, 1961–62, and dean, 1965–74. Continued as professor until retiring in July 1982. Was consultant in forest economics to Stanford Research Institute, 1953–54 and 1963; to Forest Industries Council, 1955–56; to U.N. Economics Commission for Asia and the Far East in 1957; to Navajo Tribal Council in 1958; to Weyerhaeuser Timber Company in 1959; to Michigan-California Lumber Company, 1960–62; and to Forest Industries Committee on Timber Valuation and Taxation in 1963. Was member of Forestry Research Advisory Committee, U.S. Department of Agriculture. Was visiting Fulbright lecturer in forestry to Agricultural College of Norway, 1954–55, and organizer of Section of Forestry for Tenth Pacific Science Congress held in Hawaii in 1961. Has written 170 articles and publications on forest economics. Became member of Society of American Foresters, 1938; was elected a fellow in 1963; and served on the society's council, 1962–63. Was chairman of Division of Economics and Policy in 1959; member of Committee on Civil Service, 1956–61; member of advisory board for *Forest Science*, 1957–63; and was Visiting Scientists' Program lecturer, 1961–63. Served on Society of American Foresters' Forest Policy Committee, 1980–82, and was member of Task Force on 1980 Resources Planning Act Process. Is author of *U.S. Timber Resources in a World Economy*, 1967.

JAMES R. LYONS

American Men and Women of Science (Physical and Biological Sciences), 15th ed., 1982.
Journal of Forestry. Forestry News, 63:146, 1965.
Who's Who in America, 40th ed., 1978–79.

ZON, RAPHAEL
(1874–1956)
Born December 1 in Simbirsk, Russia. Immigrated to United States in 1898; became citizen in 1903. Had previously received B.A. and B.S. degrees in Russia; Cornell University, F.E. (forest engineer) 1901. Entered U.S. Forest Service in 1901 and was assigned to forest investigations; six years later was made chief of Office of Silvics and in 1920 was put in charge of special investigations in forest economics. In 1923 became director of Lake States Forest Experiment Station at Saint Paul, Minnesota, and remained there until his retirement in 1944. In 1904 became member of The Society of American Foresters and in 1918 was elected a fellow. Served on editorial board of *Forestry Quarterly* from 1905 until it merged with *Proceedings of the Society of American Foresters* in 1916 to become *Journal of Forestry*; was editor of the society's *Proceedings* during most of this time; then was managing editor of *Journal of Forestry*, 1917–23, and editor-in-chief, 1923–28. In 1952 the society awarded him Gifford Pinchot Medal. The book *Forest Resources of the World*, compiled in collaboration with William N. Sparhawk and published in 1923, was first attempt to make systematic and accurate inventory of earth's forests. A pioneer in study of relation of forests, stream-flow, and flood control, he set forth his findings in 1927 in bulletin *Forests and Water in the Light of Scientific Investigation*, which attracted widespread attention. Has published two hundred contributions to forestry literature. An enthusiast about shelterbelt planting, he helped plan Prairie States Forestry Project, which started in 1934. Died October 28, 1956.

SOCIETY OF AMERICAN FORESTERS

American Men of Science, 8th ed., 1949.
Journal of Forestry. Obituary, 54: 850, 1956.

MEMBER ORGANIZATIONS OF THE NATURAL RESOURCES COUNCIL OF AMERICA

Alliance for Environmental Education
American Committee for International Conservation
American Farmland Trust
American Fisheries Society
American Forestry Association (The)
American Institute of Biological Sciences
American Society of Landscape Architects
Appalachian Mountain Club
Appalachian Trail Conference
Association of Interpretive Naturalists
Audubon Naturalist Society (Central Atlantic States)
Boone and Crockett Club
Boy Scouts of America
Camp Fire Club of America
Conservation Foundation (The)
J. N. "Ding" Darling Foundation
Defenders of Wildlife
Environmental Defense Fund
Environmental Fund (The)
Federation of Western Outdoor Clubs
Forest History Society
Georgia Conservancy
International Association of Fish and Wildlife Agencies
Izaak Walton League of America
League of Women Voters of the United States
National Association of Conservation Districts
National Association of State Foresters
National Audubon Society
National Institute for Urban Wildlife
National Parks and Conservation Association
National Recreation and Park Association
National Rifle Association of America

National Wildlife Federation
National Wildlife Refuge Association
Natural Areas Association
Natural Resources Defense Council (includes Public Lands Institute)
Nature Conservancy (The)
North American Wildlife Foundation
Rachel Carson Council
Renewable Natural Resources Foundation
Sierra Club
Society of American Foresters
Society for Range Management
Soil Conservation Society of America
Sport Fishing Institute
Trout Unlimited
Wilderness Society (The)
Wildfowl Foundation
Wildlife Management Institute
Wildlife Society (The)
World Wildlife Fund–U.S.
Zero Population Growth

INDEX
OF
INDIVIDUAL CONTRIBUTORS
TO SECOND EDITION

Abele, Ralph W. 239
Albright, Horace M. 27, 151, 267
Aldrich, John W. 248
Alexander, Maurice M. 233
Allen, Durward L. 249
Allison, J. H. 109, 298
Arnold, R. Keith 35, 116, 362
Arnst, Albert 352

Bailey, Reeve M. 243
Barber, John C. 113, 258, 323
Barnes, John S. 252
Bennett, George W. 151, 397
Bidwell, Orville W. 92
Bodinson, Holt 23, 27, 130, 267, 329, 331, 412
Bonberg, J. W. 229
Boothby, Charles 419
Brandborg, Stewart M. 63
Briggs, Shirley A. 153, 222
Brower, David R. 68
Buchheister, Carl W. 75
Buell, Jesse H. 165, 191, 192

Callison, Charles H. 24, 39, 42, 82, 90, 96, 207, 352, 363, 364, 415
Carlander, Kenneth D. 83
Casamajor, Paul 160, 281
Clapper, Louis S. 71, 79, 88, 93, 119, 232, 251, 296, 354, 387
Clark, Sandra 45
Clark, Wilson F. 271, 295
Clausen, Bernard L. 400
Clawson, Marion 95
Clement, Roland C. 96
Clepper, Henry 26, 29, 31, 35, 38, 42, 44, 55, 59, 60, 65, 75, 82,

91–93, 95, 98, 101, 102, 116, 124, 129, 146, 150, 161, 163, 166–68, 174, 176, 177, 197, 198, 206, 209, 211, 214, 216, 218, 228, 245, 250, 253, 257, 262–64, 267, 268, 273, 283, 296, 297, 301, 305, 307, 309, 312, 318, 320, 326, 338, 347, 353, 357, 360, 369, 370, 385, 389, 391, 392, 405, 407
Cliff, Edward P. 99
Compton, Lawrence V. 138
Coolidge, Harold J. 105
Cooper, John W. 145
Copeland, Jay 54, 337, 366
Cottam, Clarence 379
Craig, James B. 205

Dana, Samuel T. 333
Dasmann, Raymond F. 119, 211
Davis, James D. 118, 374
Demmon, Elwood L. 115
Dewitt, John B. 130
Diana, James S. 40
Digiulian, Mary 288
Disinger, John F. 114, 161, 220, 221
Douglas, Philip A. 238, 368, 377, 401, 406
Dumont, Philip A. 122

Edwards, Robert L. 413
Eikleberry, Robert W. 103
Evans, Michael B. 146
Evenden, Fred G. 158

Fahl, Ronald J. 364

Fell, George B. 149, 326
Foote, Leonard E. 398
Foster, Albert B. 155
Fox, Gordon D. 175
Franklin, Thomas M. 204, 223
Fredine, C. Gordon 80, 158, 193, 212, 243, 270, 306, 319
Funk, John L. 70

Garratt, George A. 165
Gill, Tom 293, 294
Glascock, Hardin R., Jr. 169
Goodwin, Jeanne 134, 137
Gottschalk, John S. 53, 172
Gould, William R. 224
Graham, Herbert W. 41
Graham, Richard J. 120
Gregg, Frank 179
Gutermuth, C. R. 171, 305

Harper, Verne L. 188
Hartzog, George B. 189
Hendee, Clare W. 194, 381
Herbst, Eve 28, 30, 77, 269
Herbst, Robert L. 126, 173, 180, 199, 321
Hewitt, Oliver H. 373
Hickey, Joseph J. 201
Hill, Russell G. 378
Hinman, Kenneth 84, 402
Hodgdon, Harry E. 125, 156
Hornaday, Fred E. 78, 337, 346, 397, 406
Howe, Sydney 211
Hurst, William D. 300, 381
Hutchinson, D. E. 103, 131
Hutton, Robert F. 32, 48, 70, 140, 171, 214, 240, 345, 371, 395, 396, 413

Jahn, Laurence R. 60, 136, 193, 236, 254, 261, 350, 382, 403, 408
Jantzen, Robert A. 372
Jemison, George M. 218
Johns, Willard T. 420
Johnson, Sydney 286

Jones, J. Knox, Jr. 58

Kalmbach, E. R. 253
Kamarek, Roy 365
Kelley, Claude D. 229
Kephart, George S. 235
Kessler, Wayne 226
Ketchen, K. S. 327
Kimball, Thomas L. 93
King, Willis 234
Kozicky, Edward L. 236
Kutkuhn, Joseph H. 83

Larkin, P. A. 327
Larmoyeaux, Jack D. 202
Leedy, Daniel L. 51, 417
Leedy, Donald J. 238, 272, 390
Linduska, Joseph P. 249
Little, Elbert L., Jr. 123
Lorenz, Jack 62
Loyd, F. Glennon 50, 69, 175, 204, 356, 410
Lyons, James R. 133, 229, 281, 362, 421

McCabe, Richard E. 112, 113, 215, 286, 382, 411
McCabe, Robert A. 380
McCloskey, Michael 102, 195, 275
McComb, John A. 256
McDaniel, David 317
McSwain, June 94, 271
Marshall, H. T. 67
Martin, Robert G. 202, 377, 387
Maunder, Elwood R. 33, 178, 260, 332
Metcalf, Woodbridge 276, 287
Meyer, Arthur B. 98
Miller, Joseph A. 336, 341
Miller, Robert Rush 212
Mortimer, Clifford H. 56
Moss, Donovan D. 375
Mulholland, W. D. 210

Nadel, Michael 156, 259, 277, 279, 285, 416, 418
Neugebauer, Russ J. 374

Newport, Carl A. 75, 266
Noonan, Patrick F. 284

Oehser, Paul H. 259
Olson, Robert E. 193

Pardo, Richard 157
Pearce, William A. 355
Peechatka, Walter N. 339
Penfold, Joseph W. 73, 82
Peterson, Russell W. 304
Pettit, Ted S. 305
Phenicie, Charles K. 383
Phillips, Mary Lou 125
Pomeroy, Kenneth B. 25, 111, 187,
 188, 207, 313, 314, 334, 384
Poole, Daniel A. 163, 182, 334,
 388, 395
Pritchard, H. Wayne 183
Pritchard, Paul C. 79, 125, 316,
 330, 359

Rakestraw, Lawrence 25
Rasmussen, Boyd L. 318
Resler, Rexford 302, 328, 393
Rongstad, Orrin J. 255
Ross, Eldon W. 196
Roth, Charles E. 64
Rudolf, Paul O. 46
Rutledge, William P. 231

Sanderson, Glen C. 49, 344
Sawyer, Luella K. 61, 148, 244, 399
Sayers, Wilson B. 291
Schaller, Frank W. 74
Schneberger, Edward 225
Schnepf, Maxwell 300, 315
Schultz, Judith M. 340
Scott, Douglas W. 342
Scott, J. P. 343
Scott, Thomas G. 143
Seaman, Elwood A. 141, 214, 273,
 306, 361, 387, 389
Shedd, E. Warner, Jr. 38
Sheldon, William G. 350
Six, Lawrence D. 190

Smith, Allen E. 358
Smith, David C. 87
Smith, Gerald R. 40
Sorensen, Steven 289
Sprugel, George, Jr. 23, 106, 107,
 186, 319, 351, 391
Stahr, Elvis J., Jr. 363
Steen, Harold K. 109, 308
Stevenson, James O. 201
Stewart, David, Jr. 122
Stroud, Richard H. 23, 52, 98, 144,
 220, 238, 303, 316, 368
Swank, Wendell G. 372
Swanson, Gustav A. 373
Swift, Lloyd W. 89, 97, 108, 135,
 203, 217, 282, 311, 360, 374

Talbot, Lee M. 376
Taub, Steven 387
Teer, James G. 107
Thompson, Ben H. 127
Thompson, Daniel Q. 200
Thurston, Robert V. 147
Tindall, Barry S. 247
Towell, William E. 43, 99, 110, 189
Trefethen, James B. 76, 127, 128,
 181, 237, 310, 349, 394

Underhill, J. C. 136

Voigt, William, Jr. 323, 392

Walton, Grant F. 47
Webster, Dwight A. 280
Wentz, William A. 404
White, Gilbert F. 407
Williams, Cecil S. 227
Williamson, Lonnie L. 310, 388
Williamson, Robert D. 194
Wingard, Robert G. 142
Wirth, Conrad L. 412
Wright, R. Michael 416

Yeager, Lee E. 241

Zinn, Donald J. 420

Index of Biographees

Adams, Ansel 22
Adams, Charles Christopher 23
Adams, John Hamilton 24
Adams, Sherman 24
Ahern, George Patrick 25
Ahlgren, Clifford Elmer 26
Albright, Horace Marden 26
Allen, Arthur Augustus 28
Allen, Durward Leon 28
Allen, Edward Tyson 29
Allen, Robert Porter 30
Allen, Shirley Walter 31
Alperin, Irwin Mark 32
Andrews, Christopher
    Columbus 32
Andrews, Horace Justin 33
Argow, Keith Angevin 34
Arnold, Richard Keith 35
Ashe, William Willard 36
Audubon, John James 36
Avery, Carlos 37
Aylward, David Archer 38
Ayres, Richard Edward 38

Bailey, Reeve MacLaren 39
Baird, Spencer Fullerton 40
Baker, Hugh Potter 41
Baker, John Hopkinson 42
Barber, John Clark 43
Barnes, Will Croft 44
Baskett, Thomas Sebree 44
Bates, Carlos Glazier 45
Bean, Michael J. 46
Bear, Firman Edward 47
Belding, David Lawrence 48
Bellrose, Frank Clifford 48
Bennett, Hugh Hammond 49

Bennett, Logan J. 50
Benson, Arthur Ragnar 51
Berg, Norman Alf 52
Berryman, Jack Holmes 53
Bertrand, Gerard Adrian 53
Besley, Fred Wilson 54
Bethel, James Samuel 55
Birge, Edward Asahel 56
Blair, William Draper, Jr. 56
Bolen, Eric George 57
Boothby, Charles Laurence 58
Borden, Thomas Bradley 59
Bowers, Edward Augustus 59
Box, Thadis Wayne 60
Bradley, Harold Cornelius 60
Bradley, Preston 61
Brandborg, Stewart Monroe 62
Brandwein, Paul Franz 63
Brewer, George Emerson, Jr. 64
Brewer, William Henry 64
Brewster, William 65
Briggs, Shirley Ann 66
Bromfield, Louis 67
Brower, David Ross 68
Brown, Carl Barrier 69
Brown, Claudeus Jethro Daniels 69
Brown, Janet Welsh 70
Brown, Lester Russell 71
Brown, William Y. 72
Browning, Bryce Cogsil 72
Browning, George Monroe 73
Bruce, Donald 74
Buchheister, Carl William 75
Burnham, John Bird 76
Burroughs, John 76
Butler, Ovid McQuot 77
Butler, William A. 78

Cahalane, Victor Harrison 79
Cain, Stanley Adair 80
Callison, Charles Hugh 81
Carhart, Arthur Hawthorne 82
Carlander, Kenneth Dixon 82
Carlton, Frank Eberle 83
Carpenter, Forrest Almon 84
Carson, Rachel Louise 85
Cary, Austin F. 86
Chambers, Charles McKay, Jr. 87
Chapline, William Ridgely, Jr. 88
Chapman, Frank Michler 89
Chapman, Herman Haupt 90
Chepil, William Stephan 91
Clapp, Earle Hart 92
Clapper, Louis Shirley 92
Clark, Wilson Farnsworth 94
Clawson, Marion 94
Clement, Roland Charles 95
Clements, Frederic Edward 96
Clepper, Henry Edward 97
Cliff, Edward Parley 98
Clusen, Charles M. 99
Clusen, Ruth Chickering 100
Coffman, John Daniel 100
Colby, William Edward 101
Collingwood, George Harris 102
Condra, George Evert 103
Connaughton, Charles Arthur 103
Coolidge, Harold Jefferson 104
Cooper, Toby 105
Cooper, William Skinner 106
Cottam, Clarence 106
Coville, Frederick Vernon 107
Cox, Thomas Richard 108
Cox, William Thomas 109
Crafts, Edward Clayton 110
Craig, James Barkley 110
Craighead, Frank Cooper, Jr. 111
Craighead, John Johnson 112
Cutler, Malcolm Rupert 113

Dambach, Charles Arthur 114
Damtoft, Walter Julius 114
Dana, Samuel Trask 115
Darling, Frank Fraser 116
Darling, Jay Norwood 117

Dasmann, Raymond Fredric 118
Davis, Dean William 119
Davis, Herbert Spencer 120
Davis, Kenneth Pickett 120
Davis, Waters Smith, Jr. 121
Day, Albert Merrill 122
Dayton, William Adams 123
DeCoster, Lester Allen 123
Denney, Richard Nelson 124
Dickenson, Russell Errett 125
Dilg, Will H. 126
Dixon, Joseph Scattergood 126
Dodge, Marcellus Hartley 127
Doremus, Thomas Edward 127
Douglas, Marjory Stoneman 128
Drake, George Lincoln 129
Drury, Newton Bishop 129
Duley, Frank Leslie 130
Dunlap, Louise Cecil 131
Dunn, Paul Millard 132
Dutcher, William 133
Dutton, Walt Leroy 134
Dysart, Benjamin Clay 135

Eddy, Samuel 136
Edge, Mabel Rosalie 137
Edminster, Frank Custer 137
Ehrlich, Paul Ralph 138
Eicher, George John 139
Eldredge, Inman Fowler 140
Embody, George Charles 141
English, Pennoyer Francis 141
Errington, Paul Lester 142
Eschmeyer, Reuben William 143
Evans, Charles Floyd 144
Evans, Michael Brock 145
Evenden, Frederick George 146
Evermann, Barton Warren 147

Farquhar, Francis Peloubet 148
Fell, George Brady 148
Fernow, Bernhard Eduard 149
Fisher, Sherry Robert 150
Forbes, Stephen Alfred 151
Forbush, Edward Howe 152
Fosberg, Francis Raymond 152

Foster, Charles Henry
  Wheelwright 153
Fox, Adrian Casper 154
Frank, Bernard 155
Franklin, Thomas Michael 156
Frederick, Karl Telford 156
Fredine, Clarence Gordon 157
Freeman, Raymond Lee 158
Fritz, Emanuel 159
Frome, Michael 160
Frost, Sherman Lewis 161

Gabrielson, Ira Noel 162
Gannett, Henry 163
Garner, Mary Martin 164
Garratt, George Alfred 164
Gifford, John Clayton 165
Gill, Thomas Harvey 166
Gillett, Charles Alton 167
Glascock, Hardin Roads, Jr. 168
Goddard, Maurice Kimball 169
Gordon, Seth Edwin 170
Gordon, William George 171
Gottschalk, John Simison 172
Gracie, James W. 173
Graham, Edward Harrison 173
Granger, Christopher Mabley 174
Grant, Kenneth Elvard 175
Graves, Henry Solon 176
Greeley, William Buckhout 176
Green, Samuel Bowdlear 177
Gregg, Frank 178
Griffith, George Allison 179
Grinnell, George Bird 180
Gutermuth, Clinton Raymond 181

Hafenrichter, Atlee Lawrence 182
Hagenstein, William David 183
Hair, Jay Dee 184
Hall, William Logan 185
Hamilton, William John, Jr. 186
Hardtner, Henry Ernest 187
Harper, Verne Lester 187
Hartzog, George Benjamin, Jr. 189
Harville, John Patrick 189
Hawes, Austin Foster 190
Hawley, Ralph Chipman 191

Hay, Keith George 192
Hazzard, Albert Sidney 193
Heady, Harold Franklin 194
Heald, Weldon F. 194
Heintzleman, B. Frank 195
Hendee, John Clare 196
Hepting, George Henry 196
Herbert, Henry William 197
Herbert, Paul Anthony 198
Herbst, Robert Leroy 199
Hewitt, Oliver Harold 200
Hickey, Joseph James 200
Hile, Ralph Oscar 201
Hill, Robert R. 202
Hockensmith, Roy Douglas 203
Hodgdon, Harry Edward 204
Holbrook, Stewart Hall 205
Holmes, Joseph Austin 205
Hornaday, Fred Eugene 206
Hornaday, William Temple 207
Hosmer, Ralph Sheldon 208
Hough, Franklin Benjamin 209
Howard, William Gibbs 210
Howe, Sydney 210
Hubachek, Frank Brookes 211
Hubbs, Carl Leavitt 212
Hutton, Robert Franklin 213

Illick, Joseph Simon 214

Jahn, Laurence Roy 215
James, Harlean 216
Jardine, James Tertius 216
Jemison, George Meredith 217
Jenkins, Robert Ellsworth, Jr. 218
Jenkins, Robert Merle 219
Jeske, Walter Emil 220
Johnson, Carl Sand 221
Johnson, Raymond Earl 221
Jones, Dale Allan 222
Jones, Gomer Edward, Jr. 223
Jordon, David Starr 224
Juday, Chancey 225
Judd, Benjamin Ira 226

Kalmbach, Edwin Richard 226
Kaufert, Frank Henry 227

Keen, Frederick Paul 228
Kelley, Claude Donahue 229
Kelley, Evan William 229
Kemp, Robert James 230
Kimball, Thomas Lloyd 231
King, Ralph Terence 232
King, Willis 233
Kinney, Jay P. 234
Kneipp, Leon Frederick 235
Kozicky, Edward Louis 236

Lacey, John Fletcher 236
Lagler, Karl Frank 237
Langlois, Thomas Huxley 238
Latham, Roger Marion 239
Lawrence, William Mason 239
Leedy, Daniel Loney 241
Leffler, Ross Lillie 241
Leonard, Justin Wilkinson 242
Leonard, Richard Manning 243
Leopold, Aldo 244
Leopold, Aldo Starker 245
Leopold, Luna Bergere 246
Lieber, Richard 247
Lincoln, Frederick Charles 247
Linduska, Joseph Paul 248
Lorenz, Jack 249
Lovejoy, Parrish Storrs 250
Lovejoy, Thomas Eugene 250
Lowdermilk, Walter Clay 251

McArdle, Richard Edwin 252
McAtee, Waldo Lee 253
McCabe, Richard Edward 254
McCabe, Robert Albert 254
McCloskey, John Michael 255
McComb, John Andrew 256
McGee, William John 257
McGuire, John Richard 257
MacKaye, Benton 258
McNary, Charles Linza 259
McNulty, Hester Purdy 260
Madson, John Benjamin 261
Malsberger, Henry James 261
Marsh, George Perkins 262
Marshall, George 263
Marshall, Robert 264

Martin, Clyde Sayers 264
Mason, David Townsend 265
Mather, Stephen Tyng 266
Maunder, Elwood Rondeau 267
Maxwell, George Hebard 268
Merriam, Clinton Hart 268
Merriman, Daniel 269
Michaud, Howard Henry 270
Miller, Alden Holmes 271
Moffett, James William 272
Moore, Emmeline 272
Morton, Julius Sterling 273
Mott, William Penn, Jr. 274
Muir, John 274
Mulford, Walter 275
Murie, Olaus Johann 276
Murphy, Robert Cushman 277

Nadel, Michael 278
Needham, James George 279
Nelson, Dewitt 280
Nelson, Gaylord Anton 281
Nelson, Jesse W. 282
Newell, Frederick Haynes 282
Noonan, Patrick Francis 283
Norine, James Melvin 284

Oberholtzer, Ernest C. 285
Odum, Eugene Pleasants 285
Olmsted, Frederick Erskine 287
Olmsted, Frederick Law, Sr. 287
Olson, Sigurd Ferdinand 288
Ordway, Samuel Hanson, Jr. 289
Orell, Bernard Leo 290
Osborn, Fairfield 291
Owings, Margaret Wentworth 292

Pack, Charles Lathrop 292
Pack, Randolph Greene 293
Palmer, Ephraim Laurence 294
Parenteau, Patrick Aloysius 295
Parker, Lansing Arthur 296
Partain, Lloyd Elmer 296
Pearson, Gustaf Adolph 297
Pearson, Thomas Gilbert 298
Pechanec, Joseph Frank 299
Peechatka, Walter Norman 300

Penfold, Joseph Weller 300
Peterson, Ralph Max 301
Peterson, Roger Tory 302
Peterson, Russell Wilbur 303
Petoskey, Merrill Louys 304
Pettit, Ted S. 305
Phillips, Arthur Morton, Jr. 306
Pinchot, Gifford 306
Pinkett, Harold Thomas 307
Pomeroy, Kenneth Brownridge 308
Poole, Daniel Arnold 309
Potter, Albert F. 310
Pough, Richard Hooper 311
Powell, John Wesley 312
Preston, John Frederick 313
Price, Overton Westfeldt 314
Pritchard, Harold Wayne 314
Pritchard, Paul Clement 315
Pumfrey, William Ross 316
Putz, Robert Edward 316

Radonski, Gilbert Clemence 317
Rasmussen, Boyd Lester 318
Redfield, Alfred Clarence 319
Reed, Franklin Weld 320
Reed, Nathaniel Pryor 320
Reeves, Merilyn Bronson 321
Reid, Kenneth Alexander 322
Reidel, Carl Hubert 323
Reilly, William Kane 324
Resler, Rexford Adrian 324
Reynolds, Harris Aquila 325
Ricker, Percy Leroy 326
Ricker, William Edwin 326
Ripley, Thomas Huntington 327
Rockefeller, John Davidson, Jr. 328
Rockefeller, Laurance 329
Rockefeller, Laurance Spelman 330
Roosevelt, Theodore 331
Roth, Filibert 332
Rothrock, Joseph Trimble 333

Salyer, John Clark, II 334
Sampson, Robert Neil 334
Sargent, Charles Sprague 335
Sawyer, Robert William 336

Scharlin, Patricia Jane 337
Schenck, Carl Alwin 338
Schmitz, Henry 338
Schnepf, Max Owen 339
Schoenfeld, Clarence Albert 340
Schurz, Carl 340
Scott, Douglas Willard 341
Scott, John William 342
Scott, Thomas George 343
Seaman, Elwood Armstrong 344
Sears, Paul Bigelow 345
Seton, Ernest Thompson 346
Shanklin, John Ferguson 346
Sharpe, Lois Kremer 347
Sharpe, Maitland S. 348
Sheldon, Charles 349
Sheldon, William Gulliver 350
Shelford, Victor Ernest 350
Sherrard, Thomas Herrick 351
Shields, George Oliver 352
Shirley, Hardy Lomax 353
Shoemaker, Carl David 354
Shupp, Bruce Daniel 355
Simms, Denton Harper 355
Siri, William Emil 356
Skok, Richard Arnold 357
Smith, Allen E. 358
Smith, Anthony Wayne 358
Smith, Glen Albert 359
Smith, Herbert Augustine 360
Snieszko, Stanislas Francis 360
Spurr, Stephen Hopkins 361
Stahr, Elvis Jacob, Jr. 363
Steen, Harold Karl 363
Stephens, Edwin Sydney 364
Stoddard, Herbert Lee, Sr. 364
Stoel, Thomas Burrowes, Jr. 365
Stone, Edward Harris, II 366
Stroud, Richard Hamilton 367
Stuart, Robert Young 369
Sudworth, George Bishop 370
Sullivan, Carl Rollyn, Jr. 370
Swank, Wendell George 371
Swanson, Gustav Adolph 372
Swift, Ernest Fremont 373
Swift, Lloyd Wesley 374

Swingle, Homer Scott 374

Talbot, Lee Merriam 375
Tarzwell, Clarence Matthew 376
Tascher, Wendell Russell 378
Taylor, Walter Penn 378
Teer, James Garth 379
Thomas, Gerald Waylett 380
Thomas, Jack Ward 381
Thompson, William Francis 382
Tindall, Barry Sanford 383
Toumey, James William 384
Towell, William Earnest 385
Train, Russell Errol 386
Trautman, Milton Bernhard 387
Trefethen, James Byron, Jr. 388
Tunison, Abram Vorhis 389
Turner, Hester Hill 389

Van Oosten, John 390
Vaux, Henry James 390
Vogt, William 391
Voigt, William, Jr. 391

Wadsworth, Frank Howard 392
Walcott, Frederic Collin 393
Walford, Lionel Albert 394
Wallace, David Henry 395
Ward, Henry Baldwin 396
Warder, John Aston 397
Watson, Clarence Wilford 398

Wayburn, Edgar 398
Weaver, Richard Lee 399
Weber, Isabelle Pearson 400
Welch, Paul Smith 400
Weld, Christopher Minot 401
Weller, Milton Webster 402
Wentz, William Alan 403
Wenzel, Walter Joseph 404
Westwood, Richard Wilbur 404
Wharton, William P. 405
Whipple, George Chandler 406
White, Gilbert Fowler 407
Whitesell, Dale Edward 408
Whyte, William Hollingsworth 408
Williams, Donald Alfred 409
Williamson, Lonnie Leroy 410
Wirth, Conrad Louis 411
Woodward, Hugh Beistle 412
Woodwell, George Masters 412
Wright, David George 413
Wright, Mabel Osgood 414
Wright, R. Michael 415

Yard, Robert Sterling 416
Young, Stanley Paul 416

Zahniser, Howard Clinton 417
Zimmerman, Gordon Karl 418
Zinn, Donald Joseph 419
Zivnuska, John Arthur 420
Zon, Raphael 421